MW01470750

Library of Southern Civilization
Lewis P. Simpson, Editor

RECOLLECTIONS OF ALEXANDER H. STEPHENS

Alexander H Stephens

RECOLLECTIONS

OF

Alexander H. Stephens

HIS DIARY

KEPT WHEN A PRISONER AT FORT WARREN, BOSTON HARBOUR, 1865; GIVING INCIDENTS AND REFLECTIONS OF HIS PRISON LIFE AND SOME LETTERS AND REMINISCENCES

EDITED, WITH A BIOGRAPHICAL STUDY, BY

MYRTA LOCKETT AVARY

WITH A NEW INTRODUCTION BY

BEN FORKNER

LOUISIANA STATE UNIVERSITY PRESS

BATON ROUGE

Originally published in 1910 by Sunny South Publishing Company
and Doubleday, Page & Company

Manufactured in the United States of America

Louisiana Paperback Edition, 1998
07 06 05 04 03 02 01 00 99 98 5 4 3 2 1

This edition generated with the special assistance of the United States Civil War Center.

Library of Congress Cataloging-in-Publication Data

Stephens, Alexander Hamilton, 1812–1883.
Recollections of Alexander H. Stephens : his diary kept when a prisoner at Fort Warren, Boston Harbor, 1865, giving incidents and reflections of his prison life and some letters and reminiscences / edited, with a biographical study, by Myrta Lockett Avary ; with a new introduction by Ben Forkner. — Louisiana pbk. ed.
p. cm. — (Library of Southern civilization)
Originally published: New York : Doubleday, Page & Co., 1910.
Includes index.
ISBN 0-8071-2268-8 (alk. paper)
1. Stephens, Alexander Hamilton, 1812–1883—Diaries. 2. United States—History—Civil War, 1861–1865—Prisoners and prisons. 3. Fort Warren (Mass.) 4. Prisoners of war—Massachusetts—Boston—Diaries. 5. Legislators—United States—Diaries. I. Avary, Myrta Lockett. II. Title. III. Series.
E467.1.S85A3 1998
973.77'2'092—dc21
[B] 97-51139
CIP

The paper in this book meets the guidelines for permanence and durability of the Committee on Production Guidelines for Book Longevity of the Council on Library Resources. ♾

CONTENTS

CHAPTER II

CHAPTER III

CHAPTER IV

CHAPTER V

CHAPTER VI

CHAPTER VII

CHAPTER VIII

CHAPTER XII

CHAPTER XIII

CHAPTER XIV

CHAPTER XV

CHAPTER XVI

CHAPTER XVII

CHAPTER XVIII

CHAPTER XIX

CHAPTER XX

CHAPTER XXI

CHAPTER XXII

NOTE ON THE TEXT

The original manuscript of Stephens' prison journal is now held by the Special Collections in the Emory University Library. In the fall of 1994, I hired Belle Tuten—at the time a Ph.D. candidate in the Emory history department—to compare, line by line, the original manuscript with the abridged version published by Myrta Lockett Avary. Tuten subsequently sent me a full account of the differences between the two texts. In almost every instance, these differences confirm Avary's declaration at the end of her introduction that she limited herself to deleting many of the numerous references to weather and prison food, and to cutting, along with some of his commentary, several long citations Stephens copied from books he read while in prison. In a very few cases (the bedbug episode, for example), Avary has restored lines that Stephens himself had crossed out. There are no other signs that Stephens revised the journal after his release (aside from a few marginal notes). Avary also occasionally inserts in full certain letters Stephens mentions having written in prison. In general, then, even though the Avary volume does give us a substantially abridged text, there is little editorial revision of the words Stephens wrote, and the journal as published represents, all in all, a faithful shortened version of the original manuscript. As added interest, it may be worth mentioning that the Atlanta History Center holds (in box 3, folder 6) a collection of letters and papers by Myrta Avary concerning her work on the journal. I would like to thank the History Center for allowing me to read photocopies of these documents.

Acknowledgments: A number of people have helped with the preparation of this new edition—Belle Tuten, Tom Stumpf, John H. E. Paine, Nicola Mason, and especially Lewis P. Simpson (whose encouragement and support have meant more to me than I could ever express in these short lines). Thank you all.

Introduction to the 1998 Edition

BEN FORKNER

THE BOETHIUS OF CRAWFORDVILLE

For most readers today, the name of Alexander Stephens will not resonate with many definite or powerful associations. He might be remembered by a few alert students of history as the stubborn but brilliant opposition speaker and legislator who represented his district of Georgia in Congress before the Civil War, and who made a national reputation as an outspoken antisecessionist. But it is far more probable that if he were recognized at all, it would be as the somewhat unlikely, counteractive, and increasingly distant vice-president of the Confederacy. At the rare times when he is mentioned in recent histories of nineteenth-century America for a lasting accomplishment, or for a notable intellectual or literary work, it is always for the massive two-volume *A Constitutional View of the Late War Between the States,* his largely unread and, many would add, largely unreadable constitutional defense of the South published in 1867 and 1870. This was certainly the most I could claim to know about Alexander Stephens when several years ago I first opened Edmund Wilson's classic *Patriotic Gore: Studies in the Literature of the American Civil War.*

When I eventually made my way to the chapter Wilson devotes to Stephens—the longest chapter in *Patriotic Gore*, and in many respects the book's centerpiece—I was surprised that Wilson begins his discussion, not with *A Constitutional View*, but with an admiring account of the diary Stephens had kept during several months as a prisoner in Fort Warren on George's Island in Boston Harbor during the summer of 1865. The diary, under the title *Recollections of Alexander H. Stephens* (edited by Myrta Lockett Avary), had been published in 1910, almost thirty years after Stephens' death. By the time Wilson brought out *Patriotic Gore* in 1962, *Recollections* had been out of print for decades. Wilson introduces his portrait of Stephens by quoting the opening passage of the diary, and then goes on to announce emphatically that it is "one of the most remarkable personal documents of the period of the Civil War."

The diary is clearly a prime historical source, packed with insight and information from a man respected—even by his political enemies (who feared him for the same reason)—as one of the most intelligent and best-informed statesmen of his day. As the Confederate vice-president, and as a member of the U.S. Congress for many years, Stephens had moved in high places, had played key roles in every one of the great congressional midcentury debates that led to the Civil War, and had at one time befriended or battled most of the major political powers of his time. He possessed a formidable memory, and he seems to have missed nothing on his daily rounds between the official speechmaking in public places and the informal hobnobbing in boardinghouse dining rooms. The display in the diary of his insider's political recollections—wide-ranging and recklessly precise—is justification enough for Wilson's admiration. But even praise from a critic as demanding as Edmund Wilson did not fully prepare me for the abounding vitality and sheer dramatic force of the work.

One would expect in a prison diary at least a degree of the fragmentary, the routine, and the merely circular—static lists of day-to-day activities, narrative-breaking gaps where lack of energy and loss of spirit would have killed the will to write things down. In the Stephens diary, however, there is always the sense of a forward movement propelled by a restless, truth-seeking mind ready to provide its own source of interest, intrigue, and inspiration. Entries are made almost every day, and every line of thought and observation is carried through and reexamined with an urge for completeness that is never easily satisfied. Political principles are not bluntly stated and left to stand or fall on their own; they are closely and clearly argued out, to a great extent for Stephens' own peace of mind, but partly too as an exercise for the writing of letters to the high-ranking members of government who might decide his fate: President Andrew Johnson, Secretary of State William H. Seward, and General Ulysses S. Grant. And perhaps at the same time, given Stephens' great care as a lawyer in preparing his cases in advance, they show him steeling himself and storing up arguments for the public trial he half dreaded and half desired.

"Washed away in the tide of blood": these are the tolling doomsday words Mary Chesnut used in her journal to describe the final destiny of so many lives during the war. When we consider that within the familiar walls of their own homes, stronger men than Stephens had been paralyzed by the four-year panorama of death, had given up all hope of recovering meaning in the wake of such devastation, the stark potency of Stephens' effort in his cell is even more remarkable. Despite the agony of privation and uncertainty, the physical pain and suffering, the raw memories of his beloved Georgia broken and burned, the fear of never seeing his brother again, the debilitating waves of grief that caused him to hide in a corner and weep, the humiliation of being held in a half-underground cell into which holiday visitors to the fort could peer as if looking into an animal's cage at the zoo—this prison diary is not the record of a man given to submission or abject despair.

In fact, together with its historical and documentary interest, much of the fascination of the diary from the very first page lies in Stephens' conscious spirit of counterattack, of fighting fate and self-surrender with a vengeance. The purchase of the bound notebook and the daily act of writing down his thoughts and impressions are decided on with this purpose firmly in mind. On arriving at Fort Warren, Stephens almost immediately establishes for himself a reading program, ordering books from nearby Boston or borrowing them from the prison library. The list of authors he goes through is daunting, even for a man with a great deal of time on his hands: Cicero, Aristotle, Francis Bacon,

Emanuel Swedenborg, Matthew Arnold, Samuel Taylor Coleridge, William Hickling Prescott, among others. The comments and quotations he writes down are always brought to bear on his own predicament. Relevance is not simply sought, it is demanded. The Bible is a constant companion, though he reads it not so much out of duty or for hypnotic reassurance, but in the way he reads everything—critically and searchingly. Not surprisingly, Job the persecuted questioner is his favorite character in the Old Testament, and Paul, who seems to have answers to everything and is never at a loss, his favorite guide in the New. Reading the Bible in prison makes him remember and trace back the importance of religion in his life, despite his unpolitical practice of staying away from churches whenever possible. He confesses that he has always felt a deep distrust of all manifestations of public piety. He lashes out against the "cant" of preachers he has heard in his youth, and condemns them generally as a class.

Resentment, self-reflection, and a fierce resolve are not the only forces that drive the diary forward, but they are usually the ones that dominate—along with a certain practical cunning as Stephens looks for ways to improve the material conditions of imprisonment, and a surprising ability to fortify himself with humor, even when he is outraged or distressed. When Stephens hears rumors that he and several other Confederate leaders may be exiled instead of executed, he writes that he will not move anywhere except to the gallows if he cannot return to Georgia. He enjoys the news that General Ewell, a fellow prisoner who had lost a leg in the war, had decided to keep using crutches instead of buying a costly artificial leg recommended by the Fort Warren doctor. Ewell said he did not want to spend that much money until he knew if he was going to be hanged or not.

Later in his confinement, when conditions have softened, and the cook has trouble making cornbread correctly, Stephens is quick to give instructions. The cornbread improves. When the prison doctor is unable to supply straws for the nitric acid needed as medication, Stephens has the presence of mind on one of his outdoor walks to cut some stalks of green rye as a possible substitute. When tormented by bedbugs, he sets out industriously and methodically to hunt them down and kill them, one by one. Not long after moving to a more comfortable room, he is allowed to order a new mattress from Boston. When it arrives he notices at once that it has been stuffed with decayed feathers. Even after many days in a foul-smelling cell, his senses remain alive and alert enough to detect and challenge an unfamiliar rankness. He simply cannot understand how anyone could take advantage of a fellow creature in distress. He notes his dreams and tries his best to probe their origins, without much success. But he does not forget them. He worries that he cannot bring himself to abandon his half-belief in bad luck signs and old-time rural superstitions, and tries to make plans for every eventuality, including insanity, sudden death, or a lifetime in prison.

From the beginning to the end of the diary, pain and grief are never allowed to numb the will for very long. They are looked on instead as old enemies to be met and mastered one more time. And in one way or another, they always seem to be converted into new energy. It is this unfailing, steady process that gives Stephens' diary its strange and attractive sense of constant revival and progress. Here is a man who at the height of his political career described himself repeatedly in his letters as the saddest man alive, one of the most morbid-minded pessimists he could conceive of on earth—yet in prison, under no circumstance does he reveal the slightest disposition to merely lie low and endure.

Another striking feature of the diary lies in its intensity of awareness, in the needle-eye attention Stephens pays to small details and ordinary events. This is perhaps not that unusual in itself, at least not the fact that a walled-in prisoner would concentrate on the only views his reduced perspective would permit. What *is* unusual—and one more quality that raises this diary well above its considerable value as a historical document—is Stephens' astonishing desire to lift whatever happens to him into the realm of absolute importance. A mouse or a bedbug, the taste of coffee in a glass: these are all part of his existence, thus they are as worthy of contemplation as a passage in Cicero on slavery or a nightmare of Richmond smoldering in ruins. Everything can be made to stimulate the mind, to reveal perhaps greater mystery or greater meaning, and Stephens in his cell is determined that no insight be lost through inattention or contempt. This quality of the brooding intellect is clearly conveyed in his tendency to look at the world, and at himself, dramatically, in various situations of conflict or confrontation. Stephens' legal training may have helped make this a habitual mode of thought, but whatever its origins, in prison it is another way of investing even the slightest event with significance.

An amusing example of this self-dramatizing faculty, of Stephens hovering above himself, observing what he does from a distance, can be found in one of the bedbug episodes. He has just turned away from reading a bitter editorial against the South in the latest issue *Harper's Weekly,* when he suddenly recalls the scene:

> Had another row with bedbugs. I searched the coats I use as pillows, and the corners and edges of the shuck mattress; discovered a good many, though small. To none did I give quarter. Notwithstanding all my sadness of heart and lowness of spirits, the humorous did so lay hold of me while I was thus occupied, that I could hardly repress the inclination to laugh, especially when I suspected from suspension of footsteps that the guard was looking in on me engaged in this rather ungenteel work. My suspicion was but too well founded; turning toward the window, I saw him gazing upon me with intense curiosity. This did not cause me to desist.

That last sentence is characteristic Stephens, and so is the controlled but unanswerable thunderclap of accusation and moral judgment with which he concludes the incident:

> It may be a low calling and a rather mean business in the eyes of one of my guards, this of a man pursuing and slaying bed-bugs, but no one knows what he will come to. I hold nothing low or mean for a man to do which is necessary to health and comfort, when he has no one else to do it for him.

Then, too, there are the imaginary sketches that he gradually introduces into the diary. Actually, *introduce* is probably too strong a term; the sketches, like lost phantoms, seem to stray into his thoughts out of another realm of existence. Only when he finds how well they answer to his needs does he begin to summon them up at will. Most of them are invented dialogues with one of his old Georgia friends—the writer and humorist Richard M. Johnston, author in the 1870s of the extremely popular *Dukesborough Tales*. For a man used to long evening hours conversing with friends on his front porch in Crawfordville, and proud of his skills at improvised debate and verbal dueling on the fierce southern campaign circuits, lack of living discourse was a cruel cross to bear.

Stephens himself seems surprised at the odd manner in which these dialogues bloom out unpredictably in the otherwise orderly and carefully tended field of his thinking. Out of necessity, after a lifetime of faith in solid argument and pure reason, he appears to be acknowledging at last the instincts of the imagination and the solace they could bring. Certainly there is little in his many letters and political speeches—at least those that have survived—that suggests he often allowed himself such liberty with reality. When Stephens decided a couple of years later to write his *Constitutional View* in the form of dialogues, he might have been thinking back to the diary sketches. But the dialogues in *Constitutional View* are not of the same nature; they are meant to sweeten the swallow, to make a long, complicated legal argument easier to follow, and are always strictly under control. The prison sketches give the far different impression of self-healing psychodramas, necessary to Stephens' emotional balance and the direct result of a stricken but inspired mind freely casting about for a solution to solitude.

There are many other qualities and revelations in the diary worth praising. In fact, for someone who reads it for the first time—no matter what his knowledge of the Civil War or the level of his interest in its cast of vivid personalities—so many unsuspected discoveries are made that there can be no wonder Edmund Wilson felt the work should be singled out and its importance proclaimed. The real wonder is that it had remained relatively unnoticed for so long after its first appearance in 1910. Or that after the publication of *Patriotic Gore* there was no urgent demand to bring it back into print. Many extraordinary diaries, memoirs, and collections of letters have come out of the Civil War South, most of them by now reedited and easily available. All of these have their historical value, of course, and some, such as the majestic slave narrative of Frederick Douglass; or Mary Chesnut's journal of the war years, with its whirling pageantry and feverish contrasts; or Edmund Ruffin's dark, obsessive diary; or the sensitive, fine-grained letters of the Reverend Charles Colcock Jones and his family, are full of rich individual life. But it is difficult to think of any other work—certainly no other prison diary from the Civil War, or for that matter from any other time in American history—that combines political and private interest with comparable conviction and force. And even among the great personal documents of the period, for intellectual boldness, intensity, and concentration of purpose, the Stephens' diary seems to me unsurpassed. Edmund Wilson righty recognized that he had discovered a unique American autobiography, and one that deserved to be far better known.

It should be clear by now that this new edition of the diary owes a large debt to Edmund Wilson and his great revivifying survey of Civil War literature. This is not the first time, and probably not the last, that Wilson's discussions in *Patriotic Gore* will have led a reader to search out an unknown work, or reconsider a forgotten reputation. In fact, any number of new studies and recently recovered texts can be traced back in a direct line to the Wilson book. Not satisfied with his brilliant reevaluations of some of the more obvious Civil War writing (the speeches of Lincoln, the memoirs of Grant and Sherman, the novels of Harriet Beecher Stowe), Wilson turned much of his critical energy in *Patriotic Gore* to demonstrating that a great deal of the conventional wisdom concerning the lesser-read literature often fell sadly short of the whole truth. For example, Wilson (despite his oversensitive revulsion at the coarseness of the humor) did his utmost to keep that amazing American original Sut Lovingood, and his creator George Washington Harris, from sinking into the graveyard of literary history, with only an occasional academic footnote to mark their having existed. And Wilson's praise of Kate Chopin and George W. Cable definitely set in motion the critical revival that removed the stigma of provincialism from these two important writers and gave them their rightful place in early modern fiction. More to our purpose here, in *Patriotic Gore* Wilson also made his vigorous plea for a fully revised text of the Mary Chesnut journal, which had previously been available only in very incomplete versions. Fortunately for the world of letters, that plea touched a responsive chord in the person of C. Vann Woodward, who was quick to express his gratitude when he put together his definitive and widely acclaimed edition, *Mary Chesnut's Civil War,* in 1981. This new publication of Stephens' diary is a more modest enterprise, of course, but still I feel sure that the magisterial guide of *Patriotic Gore* would be pleased to see it back in print once again. And for this student, at least, there is not a little satisfaction to be garnered in that thought alone.

Given Wilson's role in bringing the diary to light, it might be worth taking a brief look at some of his reasons for esteeming, not only the diary, but the character of Alexander Stephens as well. He commends Stephens' intellectual curiosity and tenacity in general, and the candor of his self-examination, but Wilson insists chiefly on Stephens' "heroic" determination to defend his political philosophy even while a prisoner in solitary confinement under the daily threat of hanging. Early on in his presentation, Wilson claims that "the most important passages in Alexander Stephens' diary are those that are written in justification of his policy in connection with the war." I am not that sure that I could agree wholeheartedly, but those passages are beyond doubt some of the clearest and most compelling statements Stephens ever wrote concerning his fundamental doctrine. But Wilson's claim reaches much further than that. He had the keenness of vision to perceive that the doctrine Stephens took such pains to explain was as much a statement of belief in the human individual as it was an argument defending states' rights. For Stephens, the sovereignties of selfhood and statehood were based on the same power of free choice and the same primary status of independent life. Men did not agree to gather together in order to lose their freedom to act (as least not men of Stephens' stamp), but rather to strengthen it. Or to apply one of the metaphors that Stephens, a lifelong bachelor, oddly found himself unable to resist, a man and a woman agreed to the union of marriage in the same spirit, and for the same purpose. Stephens was not thinking of the Pauline injunction that it is better to marry than burn; at least it is hard to imagine he was, given his apparently radical distrust of all sexual demands and dilemmas. He was alluding to the less negative theory that marriage brings, or should bring, a greater sense of completeness to the individual, not a lesser. It was an absurd contradiction to expect an independent state—or human being—to desire an alliance that would deprive it of the very self-integrity and freedom of choice that had made it possible to enter into an alliance in the first place. This was precisely the reason Stephens placed such a high value on the Constitution, on its sanctioning of what he usually referred to as "constitutional liberty." With its eloquent and far-seeing definitions of mutual rights and responsibilities, the Constitution was in Stephens' mind founded on the central rock-bottom truth that the Union derived its very existence from the original and perennial consentment of individual states. This priority could never be denied nor reversed, and should never be forgotten.

Actually, there is little of Stephens' formal reading of the Constitution that is unique or original; many other southern statesmen and intellectuals had put forth similar arguments. What most excites Wilson's enthusiasm is the integrity of Stephens' conviction, the dedication with which he applies his principles, and the seductive thoroughness with which he imagines every conceivable objection. In the first letter he wrote from prison to President Andrew Johnson, Stephens had first anticipated and then answered anyone who might complain that "a union formed upon the principle of permitting any member to quit it at pleasure would be held together by nothing better than a rope of sand." To this complaint Stephens replies with disconcerting simplicity that the only force that can hold the government together is the "affection of the people." Expanding his marriage metaphor to include gravity and the orbiting planets, he adds the following example as evidence: "The force in the material world, which binds and holds in indissoluble union all the parts in their respective and distant spheres throughout the limitable regions of space, is the simple law of attraction."

Southern states' rights as a universal law of physics: herein lies Wilson's awe at the strange otherworldliness of Stephens' mind. Stephens was eccentric, yes, but what intrigued Wilson was the abrupt angle with which Stephens' line of life and thinking—in many respects so relentlessly southern in its origins, culture, and ambitions (farmer, slave owner, lawyer, legislator)—veered out and away from those of the other southern leaders. It was not so much the particular details of his political creed or career that Wilson found fascinating: the apparent paradox, for example, that Stephens had been one of the most unyielding antisecessionists, yet had accepted the Confederate vice-presidency the day it was offered. For Wilson, the oddity and attraction of Stephens had more to do with his intellectual absoluteness. Wilson had encountered other southern eccentrics; he was astute enough to know they were not that difficult to find in a society where some show of extravagance was not only prized, especially in public life, but often required. But here was an eccentric who made sense, who did not cultivate his differences from other men by deviating from reason, but by distilling it. According to Wilson, this was the key to Stephens' character; he made too much sense, too much at least for the fallen world inhabited by less-than-reasonable human beings.

Wilson well understood how Stephens' intellectual intransigence could only end by exasperating northern and southern apologists alike. There was too much clarity and force in what he argued to allow honest northerners undisturbed ease of conscience. And most southerners were not able or willing to follow his rigid constitutional logic down the narrow road with his same unswerving devotion. When Stephens accepted the vice-presidency, he did so in order to assert the primacy and authority of the Constitution. He believed that the legitimacy of the southern cause lay mainly in its determination to rescue the constitutional truths from northern heresies. He had made this clear immediately, but to some southern nationalists (a term Stephens could not abide) with other aims in mind, and to President Davis and his cabinet, who had a war to fight, Stephens' absolute faith in the Constitution was one conviction they would have preferred to quietly put aside from time to time, at least until the next sermon. What others considered extenuating or exceptional circumstances were of little moment to Stephens when faced with the betrayal of his ideology. As Wilson writes, "the purity and logic of his principles, the resolve to be himself and nothing but himself, will never, in the long run, allow him to be respectful to contingencies or particularly serious about results."

Stephens' strengths, according to Wilson, were fatally linked to his single greatest flaw—the fact that he actually thought that once people were made to see the truth and rightness of his position, they would have to embrace it. And if they did not, there was nothing more he could do. Wilson begins the conclusion of his chapter on Stephens by calling him an "impossibilist," an extreme idealist whose political convictions could never be made to merge with the overriding demands of practical government. Had Wilson been an ordinary historian, he might have ended his analysis here, and in doing so would have committed no injury or injustice whatsoever to Stephens' memory or cause. Whatever its degree or measure of idealism, however, lucidity of thought is never ludicrous, and Wilson is too sensitive a thinker himself to remain unswayed. He prefers instead to bypass mere impracticalities, to raise the stakes, and to argue that the ultimate value of Stephens' ideas reaches beyond politics, beyond the cruel ironies of southern slavery, beyond the Civil War, beyond even Stephens' own century. He looks past all these to raise the timeless question of each individual's inner life, and wonders if "it may not be true, as Stephens said, that the cause of the South is the cause of us all." Wilson's presenting Stephens in the guise of a modern psychological prophet may startle, but it is not meant to provoke. Nor is it that easily dismissed once the general truth of the revelation is grasped. And more than any other single statement in *Patriotic Gore,* it helps explain Wilson's attachment to the obstinate vice-president, helps explain why he could not deny the "self-sufficient citizen of Crawfordville," who had been gradually nudged into the offstage shadows during the greatest tragedy of his time, such a prominent role a hundred years later:

> There is in most of us an unreconstructed Southerner who will not accept domination as well as a benevolent despot who wants to mold others for their own good, to assemble them in such a way as to produce a comprehensive unit which will satisfy our own ambition by realizing some vision of our own; and the conflict between these two tendencies—which on larger scale gave rise to the Civil War—may also break the harmony of families and cause a fissure in the individual.

Wilson accords great significance to a single short piece of private correspondence that Stephens clearly never meant to be published: an astonishing letter he wrote from Washington to his half-brother Linton in February of 1851. It underlies almost everything that Wilson appreciates in Stephens, and is worth quoting here, exactly as it appears in *Patriotic Gore:*

> Man's life is but a dreary pilgrimage through an inhospitable clime. . . . Sometimes I have thought of all men I was most miserable—that I was particularly doomed to misfortune, to melancholy, to sorrow and grief—that my pathway of life was not only over the same mountains and heaths and deserts with others but that an evil genius was . . . following at my side and forever mocking and grinning and making those places which in the lives of others are most happy . . . most miserable. No it is useless—the misery—the deep agony of spirit and soul I have suffered no mortal on earth knows. . . . The torture of body is severe. . . . But all these are slight when compared with the pangs of an offended or wounded spirit. . . . I am tempted to tell you a secret—it is the secret of my life. . . . The secret of my life has been *revenge*. . . . Not revenge in the usual acceptation of that term—but a determination to war over against fate—to meet the world in all its forces, to master evil with good. . . . My greatest courage has been drawn from the deepest despair! . . . I have often had my whole soul instantly aroused with the fury of a lion and the ambition of a Caesar by . . . as *slight* a thing as a *look!* Oh what have I suffered from a look! What have I suffered from the tone of a remark . . . from a supposed injury? an intended injury? But each . . . such pang was the friction that brought out the latent fires.

These are jolting words—jolting in their starkness, in their despondency, and in their Job-like confoundment and hurt, but above all in the blazing faith of the letter writer in the rightness and power of his resistance, and in his unsurrenderable urge to probe his private self to the very core of what he can understand and express. They bring us back to the special qualities of the diary that go beyond political ideology and make Wilson insist on its exceptional value as a "personal" document.

What needs to be grasped here is the fact that Wilson's appreciation of the diary is a literary judgment as well, based on the same standard that he applies to all the other works discussed in *Patriotic Gore*. The principal literary accomplishments Wilson admires in the prison diary, however, are not those we associate with an imaginative style or a creative flair. He does not hesitate to praise another Civil War diary, Mary Chesnut's *Diary from Dixie* (as it was then titled), as a "work of art." But the thrilling perceptions and electric brilliances found scattered throughout Chesnut's wonderful journal are not the only proofs of literary skill, and are not perhaps among the ones that strike the deepest.

There is little, in fact, that is inventive or original in Stephens' language in his diary, but little either that needs to be excused or skipped; unlike some of his political speeches, and unlike *Constitutional View,* Stephens' style in prison is for the most part direct, clear, free of overly cautious or involved qualifications, and wholly convincing in its digressions, interruptions, and unforced choice of image. Stephens never did have much faith in the florid sentimentalism and ritual phrasemaking fashionable in political discourse. Even the fictive dialogues are more pragmatic than fanciful. The literary quality in the diary that seizes the imagination and holds it has nothing to do then with oddities or originalities of style. What impresses instead is the rarer oddity of defiant whole-mindedness, of the complete moral cohesiveness between the independence of the writing and the independence of the man. Ford Madox Ford once wrote that the highest quality of literature is the "quality that communicates, between man and men, the secret of human hearts, and the story of our vicissitudes." In this we have perhaps the most powerful attraction of the diary, the impression it gives of a solitary mind testing its freedom to disclose its own depths. Prison imposed on Stephens the conditions he seems to have needed to unlock his innermost voice, and provided him with a literary form that seems to have fit his temperament like another living skin. This is no doubt a paradox that would have afforded Stephens little relief at the time, but it is only a slight exaggeration. And it should come as no surprise that Wilson could find the same Stephens in the diary that he found in the earlier letter to Linton. After all, the diary was written as a long letter to Linton, and as Wilson so deftly phrases it, the affection between the two half-brothers was such that Linton "was almost a lobe of Alexander's brain."

Stephens' independence of mind in his public life, locally and nationally, had been conspicuous long before he became bound up with the sectional struggle and was elected to the vice-presidency. It was the one thing friends, enemies, election crowds, and newspaper editors all agreed on, and is the one thing every biographer of Stephens singles out as the lifespring of his thought and character. There is actually little distinction to be made between the private and the public Stephens. Such transparent unity of being would have been an insurmountable handicap for most politicians, with much to hide or disguise. But for Stephens even his most glaring excesses of stubbornness, intellectual pride, and thin-skinned susceptibility were excused as an overabundance of character, and were often counted in his favor, especially on his home ground.

At the time Wilson published *Patriotic Gore,* there was really no good biography of Stephens he could rely on. The nineteenth-century work by Johnston and Browne, *The Life of Alexander H. Stephens* (1878), contains a mass of interesting letters and personal anecdotes, but it was written by younger friends and admirers who could not have been objective had their lives depended on it. The only scholarly biography available to Wilson, Van Abele's *Alexander H. Stephens* (1946) is more a political chronicle than a biography, and badly disabled by a mechanical style that cranks and grinds with far more promise than purpose. In his attempt to explain the reasoning behind Stephens' behavior and ideology, Van Abele displays, inexcusably, almost no knowledge of Georgia culture and society. Even in the area he chooses to concentrate on—that of political ideology and legislative debate—his commentary is often inaccurate or confused. Stephens deserved much better. Fortunately, along with the chapter in *Patriotic Gore,* we now have the substantial, well-written, and probably definitive account by Thomas E. Schott, *Alexander H. Stephens of Georgia* (1988). This is one of the most perceptive biographies of an American statesman I have read, and the one I lean on whenever I need to locate a detail, confirm a date, or test an intuition.

As the title of Schott's biography suggests, any understanding of Stephens should begin, and probably should end as well, with his native state. Stephens' attachments to Georgia went deep and remained unshakable all his life. When he repeatedly refers to Georgia as his "country" in his letters, and in the prison diary, he seems to imply an almost mystical identity or fealty that goes well beyond the common notion of regional pride. It was of course a natural reflex in early-nineteenth-century America for a person to think in terms of his individual state instead of the abstract republic when questions of origin arose. And during the sectional crisis and the Civil War, people all over the South would ritually attest to the legitimacy of states' rights by claiming allegiance first and foremost to their own state.

Stephens' attitude toward Georgia combined natural reflex and southern doctrine, but added a personal devotion that made his home in Crawfordville more of a shrine or church than a house. There is a revealing passage in the diary in which Stephens imagines himself back in Crawfordville, pleasantly sitting on his front porch on a Sunday morning, watching the churchyard next to his garden fill with horses and carriages and crowds of people. The pleasure seems partly to derive from mutual respect and a shared sense of faith and worship; they are in their church, and he is in his. This is one of the reasons why *Georgia* has to be defined with some care whenever it appears in the diary. It can of course refer to the political entity, or to the complete geographical rhomboid bounded by its mathematical borders; but in most cases the physical image and spiritual idea of Georgia in

Stephens' mind did not go further than the precise spot where he was born and grew up—Crawfordville—and the immediate fields and forests and hamlets that surrounded it. His hometown was located in the heart of middle Georgia, a distinct region that at the beginning of the nineteenth century included elements of the settled plantation society to the south and the raw frontier world to the west, but whose dominant modes and manners were those of pioneer farmers who had made their way up largely by virtue of hard work and shrewd self-reliance, and who tended to stick by the places they had planted with an almost tribal loyalty.

Stephens was born on February 11, 1812, the third child of a couple whose trials and struggles to establish a family and provide for it were not harsher nor more hazardous than those of any number of middle-Georgia men and women setting out on their own. His father, Andrew Stephens, built the family log house on the hundred acres of farmland he had purchased near Crawfordville at the experienced age of fifteen. Having shown promise as a student when he was a young boy, Andrew had been allowed to leave home at ten to attend a nearby religious academy. He began working for himself at fourteen, as a teacher in one of the old rural field-schools. Several years later, in 1806, he married Margaret Grier, from a colonial Georgia family of northern-Irish descent, and earned for himself an enduring reputation as a frugal, self-dependent, sober-minded citizen who was as successful with his small farm as he was with his schoolchildren. Alexander remembered that his father tanned his own leather, made all the shoes for the family, and was fond of quoting the sterner couplets of Alexander Pope's verses in his classes.

Andrew's father, and Alexander's namesake, was responsible for the Stephens presence in Georgia. He had moved there with his wife and eight children late in his life, after a roving adulthood of fighting in colonial and revolutionary armies and of living on the rougher edges of the frontier that somehow seems archetypically southern even if it does strain belief to the breaking point. Still, the genuine archetypical appeal is there, and perhaps one should not be that shocked to find odd historical echoes of the old patriarch's real life in the genealogy Faulkner imagined for the Compsons in *The Sound and the Fury*. At any rate, the younger Alexander would be brought up hearing how his British-born grandfather had fought in the second Jacobite uprising for Charles Edward Stuart, the Young Pretender; had fled to America after the defeat at Culloden Moor in 1746; had lived with the Shawnee Indians in Pennsylvania; had won over the daughter of a ferryboat owner for his wife, despite the fury of her father's opposition; had fought in the French and Indian wars and the War of Independence; and finally had descended into the hills of Georgia in the early 1790s to make his fortune.

The fortune never materialized, but as the years would prove, the grandfather's strain of toughness and resilience turned out to be a more valuable inheritance than the money or land he did not have, a blessing in the blood the grandson would have to rely on often, almost from the day he was born. His mother died when Alexander was barely a month old. He was sickly and undersized as a child and would be plagued by so many diseases that he once claimed he had never known a full day's health in his life. Headaches and chronic indigestion could always be counted on when the more serious illnesses were in abeyance. The year after his mother's death, his father married Matilda Lindsay, who added three more children to her husband's household, including Linton, the half-brother who became Stephens' closest friend and confidant in later years. Apparently, there was little love lost between Alexander and his stepmother, but her death, coming as it did only a week after his father's in 1826, struck him a vicious blow when he was already half-unconscious with grief. He adored his father, and later wrote that when he first learned the news he fell on the ground and rolled back and forth in the grass. He was in such shock that he could not even weep. "My eyes were as dry as if scorched in the fire." The Stephens children were now orphans, and were divided between the families of the two mothers. Alexander, along with his brother and sister, went to stay with his uncle Aaron Grier, who lived with his sister Elizabeth (Aunt Betsey) on a farm near Raytown in Warren County.

From age fourteen on, Stephens was to be painfully aware of the world's solitude. On his uncle's farm he was not entirely without the consolation and encouragement of a family, even though he was filled with dread by his uncle's suggestion that he leave school to work on the farm. Nor did he lack for kindness of adult friends at church, who were quick to recognize his exceptional intellectual and scholarly gifts. When he expressed a desire to pursue his studies, he was helped by a series of benefactors at almost every stage of his education—first at the academy in Washington, Georgia, where he stayed at the home of Alexander Hamilton Webster, a Presbyterian minister whose middle name he adopted; and later at Franklin College in Athens (forerunner of the University of Georgia), where he was aided by a loan from the Georgia Education Society. Even so, his expenses at college exhausted the small nest egg his father had left him, and when he graduated first in his class, he was once more on his own. Most of his classmates were able to return in some semblance of style to their family's farms and plantations, where they could look ahead to law school or at the very least a paternal gift of land to help them get a start. Stephens would have been mortified to show up at his uncle's farm with a fine diploma and empty pockets. He began working immediately, the day after his graduation, as a teacher in a small school in Madison, Georgia.

Thus began another period of uncertainty that Stephens remembered as one of the most miserable of his life. He had been not only a brilliant but a popular student at college, and the contrast between his high standing there, the teachers and the friends whose society he had enjoyed, and his lowly job and meager prospects, was just one more bitter reminder that fate had fixed its eye on him as one of its permanent victims. He spent four unhappy months in Madison, lonely and in ill health, then a little over a year as a tutor for Dr. Louis LeConte's children and a few other students in Liberty County, not far from Savannah. The time in the relaxed and refined LeConte household was an interlude of relative comfort and peace of mind, but he continued to be gnawed by doubts about his future. Though he knew that Crawfordville offered little hope, Stephens preferred to be disconsolate on familiar earth. He decided to study law and returned to his hometown, where he found lodgings and began preparing for his bar examination. According to Johnston and Browne's *Life of Alexander Stephens,* once back in Crawfordville Stephens seems to have seriously contemplated suicide. He bought a notebook and began keeping a journal, pouring out his misery in one agonizing line after another.

The language in these early writings from time to time suggests that Stephens found kindred souls in certain romantic poets—not an uncommon temptation for a sensitive twenty-two-year-old, college-educated youth in the 1830s. In one overemphatic passage he sounds like a creature not to be found in nature, at once a Byronic hero and a fish out of water, superhuman and subhuman in the same desperate breath: "I must be the most restless, miserable, ambitious soul that ever lived. I can liken myself to nothing more appropriately than to a being thrown into vacant space, gasping for air, finding nothing but emptiness, but denied to die." But in other passages, self-doubt gives way to the characteristic Stephens defiance, the inner toughness that invariably saw him through every crisis. The keeping of the journal, like that of the prison diary thirty years later, was good medicine, and he used it to restore his confidence and to work his way through to a renewed pact with reality.

In July of that same year, 1834, he passed the bar examination with high praise from each of his four examiners and set up practice in Crawfordville without budging an inch. The town was still hardly more than a huddle of houses, a few stores, two churches, and a courthouse in the woods, but it was where his mother and father were buried, and years later Stephens wrote in a letter to a friend that he would have starved rather than leave. He had frequently complained in his journal that Crawfordville was a dull place for a man of his intellectual tastes and high-minded aspirations. During the first months back from the LeConte plantation, on long solitary walks in the countryside (he was too poor to buy a horse), armed with an old umbrella in case of a sudden storm, he had pipe-dreamed about a wealthy life among well-bred families in more cultivated surroundings. But he knew himself too well to pretend for long, and I think he realized along about this time that these dreams were not only futile but somehow unworthy of his middle-Georgia origins. They did not touch him in any way as close to the bone as another, more down-to-earth vision he was beginning to entertain—that of buying back his father's farm two miles outside of Crawfordville: the "old homestead," as he was fond of calling it.

The desire went deeper than nostalgia or the adult memory of a poor farm-boy banned by bad fortune from the house of his birth. To a certain extent, perhaps, Stephens may have thought of himself as the dispossessed son reclaiming his lost past. But a more important reason involved his idealization of the old middle-Georgia values of independence, resourcefulness, and agrarian pride that the parental homestead embodied. He seems to have made a conscious decision to bind his future to his beginnings, and in a more mysterious way to assume a paternalistic responsibility for himself and the welfare of the community by taking over where his father had left off. Fatherhood for Stephens, who never married and never had any children of his own, would always remain a symbolic condition, but it was a symbolism he apparently took to heart. In 1838, once his law practice had begun to prosper and after he had entered politics for good, he made the purchase. Though he never returned to live on the homestead, he maintained it as a working farm, and he wore a path to it by riding back and forth from Liberty Hall, the house he bought in 1845 to be his permanent residence in Crawfordville. Liberty Hall by itself, as an emblem of plainspoken purpose, deserves more than a passing glance in the overall design of Stephens' adult plan.

An unpretentious two-story frame building on a mildly elevated field of shade trees north of the town, the house was part of the estate of his stepmother's brother-in-law, the Rev. Williamson Bird, so in a sense it too was filled with family associations. Stephens, who lived in the house for several years as a boarder, first gave it the name Bachelor's Hall—an ironical way of undercutting any rough or bawdy remarks at his expense, of hearkening back to the high life of the eighteenth century in a spirit of humorous contrast that was wholly unnecessary for anyone who had even a passing acquaintance with Stephens. Everybody around him knew that he was far too puritanical to take advantage of his celibate status in the usual time-honored custom.

It was not a house built to hide or harbor secrets anyway, raised as it was on a hillside and in full view of anyone walking by on the short road into town, or congregating at the next-door church. Stephens could look down at the passengers on the slow-moving Georgia Railroad train that crossed in front of the property only a few hundred feet beyond the porch, and they could look up at him. This was the great appeal of the house to Stephens. It was open, approachable, and comforting in its situation and structure—close enough to the courthouse and the town center to give him a public forum (Crawfordville was the county seat) whenever he wanted and to involve him in the activities and affairs of the townspeople, and close enough to the country to satisfy all his fondness for the land as a committed farmer. The main north-south hall of the house pointed in a straight line back to the old homestead, and ahead in the direction of the town, the railroad, and the farther-flung political battlegrounds of the state and nation.

Liberty Hall combined to perfection Stephens' democratic convictions and his rising position in middle Georgia as an official guardian of law and liberty, so much so that it became in time a public institution itself, with something of the courthouse, the church, the school, and the local inn. For all his love of privacy and his taste for solitary meditation, Stephens thrived on company, and was widely known to be generous not only with his money but with his time and space as well. The house was never empty of friends, relatives, and miscellaneous boarders, many of whom lived there for months and years at a time. Law students whom Stephens taught for free were frequent guests, and so were various members of the Stephens clan who had come on hard times and who had been left, like Stephens himself in his youth, without a home or ready means of support. One of the most spacious rooms of the house was reserved for the often unannounced visits of Robert Toombs, the overbearing, hard-drinking, Falstaffian planter-senator from nearby Washington, Georgia, whose mismatched friendship with the frail, priestly Stephens (the Georgia bull and the Georgia scarecrow) became a favorite subject of journalists, and a legend of Georgia's political history.

Among the most visible beneficiaries of this wide-openness of spirit and house were Stephens' slaves. It was not unusual, of course, for the house slaves to live with the master and his family, but the paternalism that reigned both at Liberty Hall and at the homestead allowed the slaves there considerably more freedom of movement than was given other local slaves, who envied them. Stephens' slaves all had passes granting them permission to circulate beyond the limits of his property, and so were called "free niggers" by neighboring planters and farmers who disapproved of his liberal policy. Yet the relatively well-off condition of his slaves betrayed the most glaring blind spot in Stephens' vision of southern slavery—that treacherous loftiness of mind that Edmund Wilson described as characterizing Stephens' special brand of idealism. Because defend slavery he did, with some hesitation at the beginning of his political career, but with mounting conviction as the sectional struggle worsened. His defense was based on the standard religious, historical, and racial arguments (especially the latter). He believed in the inherent inferiority of blacks, as did most of the Western world, north and south, in the middle of the nineteenth century. He believed too that the slave system in the South was the best form of society responsible whites had yet devised to deal with a vulnerable race needing protection. He made Liberty Hall and his other slave-farmed holdings models of his creed. He did not hire overseers; he used the task system, whereby once the daily task was done the slave had the rest of the day to himself (as opposed to the more brutal dawn-to-dusk regime); and he absolutely refused to sell his slaves or to break up slave families.

But his benevolence made him defend the institution as a positive good when evidence to the contrary was over the next hill, and his idealism made him shut his eyes to the obvious neglect or outright abuse dealt out by less righteous planters while at the same time Stephens continued to pride himself on his rigid sense of realism. Two years after he was released from prison and had returned to Liberty Hall, he refused to give any credence to what he thought were wild rumors of white vigilante squads such as the Ku Klux Klan, until he witnessed several of their crimes himself. Stephens, like most people, had a gift for disavowing the existence of evil as long as it did its foul deeds downwind. When the whippings and murders reached Crawfordville, he finally took a stand, condemning them and the masked riders as a worse threat to the South than the corruptions of the Republican Radicals. During the early days of Reconstruction, this was not a comparison that would have been easy for him to make. It is worth noting that Stephens' own slaves chose to remain with him after the war, and lived on and around Liberty Hall until he died. And it is worth noting too that the passages in the prison diary that deal with slavery show him willing to grapple with his assumptions in a way that few other southern leaders at the time would have approved. He accepted the verdict of the war, at least as far as emancipation was concerned, and once more set himself apart from his peers, and many of his friends, by urging the right of blacks to representative suffrage.

Stephens lived in Liberty Hall until his death in 1883, leaving it for more than short visits only a few times during almost fifty years: when Congress was in session in Washington; when he felt he was needed in Richmond during the war years (less and less as his rift with the government widened); during his four months in prison; and for the brief period he spent in the official mansion in Atlanta as governor of Georgia the last few months of his life. Much of the prison diary might be said to be keyed to a single, hammering note of homecoming and return, not just to Georgia, but to Liberty Hall and all it signified, with Stephens repeating in his cell certain rituals such as the singing of a hymn before breakfast in order to conjure up the old atmosphere. He writes with passion that he is bound to his home by associations "tender as heartstrings and strong as hooks of steel," and over and over expresses the fear that he might never see it again. In the minds of most Georgians, especially the agrarian population of middle Georgia, Liberty Hall became in time identified with the owner, just as the owner, for the same reasons, identified Liberty Hall with his ideal of middle Georgia. It was proof to his electorate that one of their own could succeed in a hard world by virtue of the independent values they admired, and it was proof too that their chosen spokesman did not set himself above a past that had helped make him what he was.

As Stephens aged into a fixture of popular venerability, and came to be known and revered throughout Georgia as the "Sage of Liberty Hall," sitting high in his wheelchair on the front porch, the house did develop a patina of elevated dignity and may have risen a little off the ground in the process of public sanctification. But despite the increased paternal authority, Stephens remained his father's son. There was nothing that was patrician or aristocratic about the place or the owner, nothing that would have insulted or belittled the small farmer or field-school teacher of his youth. Architectural elegance or even grandeur could be found in middle Georgia in Stephens' day, flashing out from a brazen new plantation mansion or from one of the finer residences of a fast-growing market town, but Liberty Hall's modest glorification of a rural townhouse was more in keeping with the wary democratic bias of the region. Stephens organized barbecues in his backyard, and lit the road up to the front door with ceremonial bonfires. All other displays of magnificence were limited to the polished phrases of political oratory on the stump. No one felt it necessary to condemn a show of throwaway wealth when the giver lost nothing by the gift, and when the gift itself could be repeated and shared in a conversation in the grocery store or tavern.

Stephens' manners and ideology were always in full accord with the traditional anti-aristocratic instincts of his community. These were the same instincts, in fact, that made middle Georgia the original center of the southern humorist movement. Composed largely of professional men (lawyers, doctors, and newspaper editors), the movement had a short-lived but vigorous existence during the thirty years preceding the Civil War. It concentrated on depicting the eccentricities of southern life partly out of a taste for pure popular theater, and partly out of the conviction that the vitality of any self-respecting culture (with certain absolute standards to defend) depended on a willingness to look honestly and critically at the extremes that same culture generated. The movement was launched and led in the 1830s by Augustus Baldwin Longstreet with his series of satirical newspaper sketches first collected and published as a book in 1835 in Augusta, Georgia, under the title *Georgia Scenes*. A prison diary might appear to be the last place to search for parallels with the broad comedy favored by Longstreet and his disciples. The same moral standards and social values can serve more than one writer, however, and more than one mode of writing—especially (as was the case with these early middle Georgians) when these writers have all been taught from the cradle never to confuse the ripe and the robust with the merely rotten.

Longstreet's sketches derived much of their humor and high color from the rougher elements of the early river camps and frontier settlements. By the 1830s such communities had diminished in number, but had not yet disappeared, and a university-educated lawyer like Longstreet could describe these remnants of a more primitive age with the understanding that a superior civilization had made great strides in taking their place. When directed toward the backwoods man and woman, Longstreet's comic satire was not, however, without its sympathies and barely disguised regrets. He had grown up in that world himself, and to some extent missed its rawer codes of courage and crude directness. Like Longstreet, Stephens could be realistic in naming the ignorant ways of the poor whites living from hand to mouth on the edges of middle-Georgia society, and he could feel the same mixture of pity and amusement in noting their incurable grammar and fantastic turns of phrase. But even the lowest, most dismal wretch who had fallen completely outside the circle of the civic virtues and had given up all struggle to improve his lot had at least the excuse of his degrading poverty to mitigate the case against him.

For Longstreet and Stephens (and the majority of middle Georgians) there was little amusement, and no sympathy at all, when they turned their attention toward the false refinements and haughty mannerisms of those who lorded it over the less fortunate. They were the ones who deserved the democratic lash of derision. The worst examples could be found among those otherwise unexceptional citizens who did their best to imitate what they imagined to be aristocratic airs, or (worse still) among those actual planters who abused the advantages of their class. Whether they had been born to privilege, like the high-and-mighty John Randolph of Virginia—the prototypical "gentleman by the four descents," and proud of the distinction—or had pushed or married their way up, like James Henry Hammond of South Carolina, they were equally suspicious. For obvious reasons, Stephens did not always feel easy himself in the role of a wealthy landowner and slaveholder, and in the diary takes pains to distance himself from the northern caricature of the leisurely autocratic southerner who never had to work for a living. In a passage that seems to have affected Stephens deeply, he defends his good friend Robert Toombs, one of the richest planters of the region (thus an easy target for northern journalists) from accusations of the sort, and in so doing defends himself and middle Georgia in the same breath:

> As for Mr Toombs, it was a matter of pride with him, a thing of which he boasted on the stump and the hustings, that Georgia had sprung from paupers and "tack-landers," that she had made herself what she was by her own exertions; as she was dependent upon none save herself for her achievements in the past and present, so he wished her to be in the future. Few men of his real genius and intellect, whom I have ever met, placed lower estimate than he on descent and heraldry. Deeds and worth, with him, constituted manhood.

At the time Stephens wrote this, Toombs (who had held the office of Confederate secretary of state for five months before entering the army as a brigadier general) was an outlaw on the run, having escaped on horseback from the same Union officer who had been sent to arrest Stephens. Toombs eventually made his way to Cuba, and from there to Europe, before returning to Georgia in 1867. In the summer of 1865, though, Stephens in his prison cell could have well believed that he would never see his friend again, thus the impression he gives of making a final tribute.

The tribute is a long one, running to over four pages of concentrated praise in the latter part of the diary. It has its interest as a convincing portrait of Toombs, one of the extraordinary southerners of his day, and one who always seems a bit too large for life in most contemporary accounts. For readers of the diary, however, concerned first with the character of Stephens, the Toombs section has an added interest of self-revelation, and of turning attention back to Stephens' prison-cell recital (now intensified to a kind of exile's prayer) of the middle-Georgia virtues. There were innumerable good reasons to praise Toombs; as the often reelected senator from Georgia, he had been a powerful and effective voice in Washington for years; he was a brilliant lawyer and public speaker; he was an industrious and successful planter; and he was a generous and loyal friend in all weather, no matter how foul the winds blew. But to Stephens his most endearing qualities lay in his sense of individual justice, and in his steadfast refusal to curb (much less suppress) his freedom of thought and speech. Toombs embodied, to a degree that even Stephens could find excessive, an independent will and contempt of authority that knew no limits. One has the feeling that in Stephens' mind, Toombs raised middle-Georgia self-sufficiency to such a superior pitch that only another middle Georgian could appreciate it. He had his failings, but they were the honorable failings of manly passion and high spirits:

> He is open, bold, and frank to a fault. He has been, as he often says, his own greatest enemy in his freedom and extravagance of speech. His remarks are often pointed, cutting, and sarcastic, but there is no malice in his nature, not the slightest. Under impulse, he has often denounced in severest terms persons whom, when the excitement was passed, he would take cordially by the hand. There is not the least guile or hypocrisy in him; he speaks and acts just as he feels at the moment.

There is only one small qualification Stephens forgets to add. Toombs's temper did not always require the heat of the moment to make it flame and flare. When he felt his principles had been betrayed, his powers of damning invective were seldom diminished by a day or two, or more, of calm reflection. Every Georgia politician had this gift to some extent, but Toombs outstripped them all. A good example (there are hundreds more) can be found in one of his milder comments on former Georgia governor Joseph E. Brown, who had decided in 1868, against everything he had ever stood for in the past, to collaborate with the hated Republican Radicals: "What more can I say to commend this wretch to your detestation; he has fatigued public indignation, it is no longer equal to his crime. Ignoble villain, buoyant solely from corruption, he only rises where it rots."

There is genuine eloquence in these lines, but it is easy to see how Toombs could be carried away by his own fluency, and easy to understand why Stephens speaks of a lack of self-control as the flaw that cost Toombs the most in his political career. It probably cost him the Confederate presidency, a loss that had the unexpected result of thrusting the vice-presidency on his friend. Most historians agree that Stephens was made vice-president at the Montgomery convention held in February, 1861, as a peace token to the Georgia delegation, who had all assumed (including Stephens) that Toombs, and not Jefferson Davis or some other prominent figure, was one of the likeliest candidates for president.

From the moment their friendship began, in the mid-1830s, Toombs and Stephens were paired and compared in the political press and in the popular imagination. Toombs was big-boned and solidly fleshed. He was known to have a healthy thirst for strong drink. Stephens was small and fragile-looking and took his whiskey in spoonfuls (for medicinal purposes). When Toombs spoke, he thundered, commanding attention like the booming lower registers of a large bagpipe. Stephens' voice was a higher, shriller instrument, but could pierce a listener's brain to paralyzing depths. Stephens had the more private personality; when he felt his principles no longer convinced, he would regularly withdraw to Liberty Hall and brood in silence on the fearful powers of universal ignorance. Toombs, congenitally, could not be silent, and he loved to beat down a contentious audience. He had an indestructible confidence in his own opinions that sustained him long after he had fallen from national prominence. As the sovereign republic of Toombs, he never applied for a pardon after the Civil War, and refused to take an oath of allegiance to the United States. In 1881, four years before his death, he openly declared that he was "not loyal to the existing government of the United States and do not wish to be suspected of loyalty." This was the splendid all-or-nothingness that left Stephens and many other middle Georgians shaking their heads with affection (even when they had no intention of following Toombs down a road that everybody could see was a historical dead end).

For all his admiration of Toombs, and his love of the man as a friend, Stephens could not stand on independence alone as his sole principle of existence. Toombs probably would have been inclined to agree, but he did not always insist (as Stephens did) that independence without the freedom to act or to effect an influence was a kind of living death: politically, socially, and personally. An inanimate object might be said to possess independence—a solitary stone in the desert, for example. As Wilson argues in *Patriotic Gore,* Stephens could match anyone in the South in terms of idealism, pride, and hardheaded resistance. He was perfectly willing to die for a worthy cause. Independence without a minimum of free movement and exchange in the human community, however, meant sterility: an empty gesture in a dream. Stephens had disagreed with Toombs and the other prosecessionists over the wisdom of leaving the Union and the constitutional guarantees of individual freedom that held it together. A southern state within the Union could always appeal to the Constitution to argue its sovereign rights; outside the Union it became just another foreign entity to be ignored or crushed by a stronger force. There was something suicidal about a state leaving the Union before all other alternatives had been thoroughly tried and tested.

This is the same position Stephens maintained from within the Confederacy when he felt the roar for southern independence had all but silenced the southerner's individual voice. He never let anyone forget that the Confederacy could justify itself only by defending the constitutional rights it claimed the northern states had repudiated. In the prison diary he describes the original Constitution (replicated almost exactly in its Confederate version) as an "ark of covenant" to be "rescued" at all costs. In one of his strongest public statements as vice-president, he warned the Georgia assembly on March 16, 1864, that certain decisions and recommendations made by the Confederate government, including the suspension of habeas corpus and the call for involuntary conscription, threatened individual liberties from within as surely as the northern army threatened them from without. Stephens did not envy the independence of a despotic nation any more than he did the independence of a stone in the desert. To the assembly, he made his position powerfully clear:

> Never for a moment permit yourselves to look upon liberty, that constitutional liberty which you inherited as a birthright, as subordinate to independence. Let them stand together 'through weal and through woe,' and if such be our fate, let them and us all go down together in a common ruin. Without liberty, I would not turn upon my heel for independence. I scorn all independence which does not secure liberty.

To those who might think that the extending of executive power in the Confederate government was a necessary condition of holding off defeat, Stephens uses almost the same stinging battle-cry in his reply:

> I warn you also against another fatal delusion, commonly dressed up in the fascinating language of, "if we are to have a master, who would not prefer to have a southern one to a northern one?" Use no such language. . . . I would not turn upon my heel to choose between masters. I was not born to acknowledge a master from either the North or South.

Not surprisingly, all during the war Stephens was frequently denounced as a traitor by a whole range of extremist and not-so-extremist elements on both sides of the conflict. In the heart of middle Georgia, in and around Crawfordville, and in the small towns and crossroads nearby, the shock of the Georgia assembly speech (and others like it) would have barely registered. It merely confirmed what everyone had known for years. Little Aleck (as he was familiarly called throughout the state) could always be counted on to speak his mind on the side of the opposition, particularly when the opposition was weak and harried and underrepresented. It little mattered to him that he spoke as a member of the U.S. Congress, or as the vice-president of the Confederacy. The principle of fighting in the cause of the little man who refuses to be stampeded remained the same. For decades official southern doctrine had railed against the dangers of the federal government allowing majority rule to be wielded as a weapon against the democratic rights of the minority. Stephens had entered into the formulation of the doctrine with as much intellectual fervor as any other southern leader, and with more philosophical subtlety and sophistication than most. But for him the problem seems to reach beyond the issue of sectionalism or nationalism, beyond historical or political alternatives, and to lead back (and down) to a more mysterious protopathic source of passionate indignation. Certainly there was more at stake than abstract theory or ideological debate.

The statement he makes in the diary to mark his fundamental position is less a definition than an axiom or an article of faith, a divine inner law deeper than any man-made dogma, and too self-evident to explain: "The object of society's laws should not be the greatest good to the greatest number. Of all dogmas this, to my mind, is one of the most monstrous. The object of all laws should be the greatest good to the whole society, all its members, with injury to none." The words "with injury to none," in their context in the diary (they are repeated several days later in Stephens' letter to President Johnson), ring with the resonance of a primary truth, and should remind the reader of the letter that Stephens wrote to his brother Linton in 1851, the one Wilson cites with such great effect in *Patriotic Gore:*

> I have often had my whole soul instantly aroused with the fury of a lion and the ambition of a Caesar by . . . as *slight* a thing as a *look!* Oh what have I suffered from a look! What have I suffered from the tone of a remark . . . from a supposed injury? an

> intended injury? But each . . . such pang was the friction that brought out the latent fires.

The injury alluded to in these lines is almost certainly related to Stephens' anguished sense of himself as a physical grotesque, handicapped from childhood by his small size and freakish appearance, and preyed on all his life by a host of crippling illnesses and obscure nervous disorders. There seems to have been, in addition to all this (or perhaps the essential cause), a rare hormonal imbalance or deficiency that made him look late in his life like a shriveled young boy whose skin and hair had aged but whose features had never matured. Stephens once described himself as "a malformed ill-shaped half finished thing." He was probably sexually impotent, and he never married. Wifeless and childless, his lifelong celibacy alone made him a striking anomaly in the world of southern politics. There is a haunting photograph of Stephens just before his death that shows him slumped in a chair with two crutches leaning against his shoulder. He is ghostly white, and he gives the impression of a handful of sticks dressed in human clothes, but his face is the remarkably boyish face of a mummified adolescent.

This brings me to one final consideration of his character, and of the reputation he had forged among the middle Georgians by the time of the Civil War. In the career of lawyer and statesman he had chosen, there was no way he could escape public scrutiny; his every speech on the stump (at least at the beginning of his career) was made with the knowledge that before he uttered a word he would have been branded in everyone's mind as one of the most pathetic-looking human beings they had ever seen outside a sickroom or a sideshow. Even after he had become known as a brilliant orator and as a fearless opponent in a debate, his physical condition dominated public discussion. Stephens did not exaggerate the visual impact he made and had to struggle against. Rival journalists vied with each other in the luridness of their comparisons up until his death (which was predicted almost daily for forty years before it finally occurred), and every political contemporary, friend or enemy, had at least a word to say on the subject.

Robert Toombs recalled that Stephens "never looked as if he had two weeks' purchase on life." One typical newspaper account (favorable to Stephens' political opinions) portrayed him in 1857 as a "shrunken and emaciated figure, the shoulders contracted and drawn in, the face the color of ashes." Abraham Lincoln, with somewhat more humor, watched Stephens take off a huge overcoat on entering a room during their Hampton Roads meeting in February, 1865, and claimed he had never seen such a "small nubbin emerge from such an immense husk." Less friendly observers looked at him as a "refugee from the graveyard," or "doomed to speedy dissolution." During Stephens' notorious 1855 campaign against the Know-Nothing party (officially called the American party), an opposing paper called him "a hideous deformity of a man." The unrecorded insults were no doubt less restrained and less literate. One of the most vivid descriptions of Stephens as a barely animate ruin was written by an awestruck journalist in 1876, three years after Stephens had been reelected (at the age of sixty-one) as one of the Georgia representatives in Congress:

> A little way up the aisle sits a queer-looking bundle. An immense cloak, a high hat, and peering somewhere out of the middle a thin, pale, sad little face. This brain and eyes enrolled in countless thicknesses of flannel and broadcloth wrappings belong to Hon. Alexander H. Stephens, of Georgia. How anything so small and sick and sorrowful could get here all the way from Georgia is a wonder. If he were to draw his last breath at any instant you would not be surprised. If he were laid out in his coffin he need not look any different, only then the fires would have gone out in those burning eyes. Set as they are in the white-wax face, they seem to burn and blaze. Still, on the countenance is stamped that pathos of long continued suffering which goes to the heart.

During the first half of his political career, before the Civil War, Stephens built a reputation for being highly sensitive to verbal attacks. Not surprisingly, given all the attention his physical frailness attracted, he became extremely quick to pounce on the faintest suggestion that he could be insulted with impunity because of his size and disabilities. More often than not his response was made in the form of a direct and immediate challenge, and except for one celebrated encounter—Judge Cone's knife attack—these challenges were invariably refused or evaded. It was considered dangerous to enter into a duel with Stephens, not so much because of the threat of injury or death, but because of the political risk of being denounced as a bully who had taken advantage of a weaker man. There was no question that Stephens would fight if the challenge was accepted, and after the Cone affair, no one could ever doubt his physical courage.

The attack by Judge Cone occurred in the summer of 1848, not long after Stephens had helped table (and thus defeat) the Clayton bill in Congress. The bill had been proposed as a solution to the question of slavery in the territories, and the great majority of southern legislators had been in favor of it as furthering the overall cause of the South. Stephens, however, felt the bill was inadequate and potentially harmful for several reasons, chief of which was its decision to thrust the problem of slavery into the hands of the Supreme Court. On returning home to Georgia after his victory, he heard rumors that Judge Francis Cone, a Georgia Democrat and an old acquaintance of Stephens (who was a Whig at the time), had publicly cursed him as a traitor to the South. Stephens did nothing until he met Cone several days later at a political barbecue. When he asked Cone about the matter, Cone denied that he had said anything of the sort. Stephens replied that this was a good thing for everyone concerned, because otherwise he would have been obliged to slap the judge in the face. The affair was more or less forgotten for several days until Cone, a powerful man and normally a good-natured soul, began to react to taunts by his political opponents that he had been afraid to stand up to Stephens.

He confronted Stephens outside the Thompson Hotel in Atlanta; hot words were exchanged, and Stephens made good his threat, using his cane to strike Cone across the face. Furious, Cone rushed at Stephens with his knife drawn, cutting him deeply on the arms and body before he hurled him flat onto his back, held his head against the ground, and screamed in his face, "Retract or I'll cut your damned throat." Stephens' answer—"Never! Cut!"—enraged Cone even further, and he plunged down with the knife. Stephens caught the blade with his right hand, which was gashed to the bone and badly mangled, but he managed to keep up the struggle until Cone was pulled off by onlookers. Stephens never fully recovered the use of his hand, but proof of his fearlessness had been fixed in the public mind for good. The fact that he refused to prosecute the judge was remembered in Georgia long after the reasons for the fight were forgotten.

The best a political foe could do when challenged by Stephens was to turn the incident into a show of derision. Benjamin Hill (a young and vigorous candidate for the Know-Nothing party) did just this in 1856, when he engaged Stephens in an exchange of abusive letters and accusations published—to everyone's great delight—in the daily press. Hill refused to meet Stephens on the field of honor, where he had been grandly summoned by the older warrior, and replied instead with a final shoulder-shrugging dismissal that he had "a family to support and a soul to save, while Stephens has neither." We can safely assume that Stephens did not join in the laughter, but by this time no amount of ridicule, regardless of the accuracy of its aim or the violence of its thrust, could do much to lessen Stephens' lofty stature in middle Georgia.

At home at Liberty Hall after his return from prison, Stephens gradually reentered the world of Georgia politics, now in the position of the elder statesman who could do no wrong, at least as far as his local reputation was concerned. He occasionally stuck obstinately to an opinion that even his closest friends considered outrageous, such as his support for Ulysses S. Grant after the general had been elected president of the United States. The Augusta newspaper, the *Chronicle and Sentinel,* once commented on this particular aberration by writing that "just as a man might possess an abnormal taste for broiled buzzard," he was in no danger of losing his friends as long as he refrained from "making them partake of the delicacy." Stephens' support of President Grant was in character; that character had long been established and, in middle Georgia at least, accepted as a permanent quality. Alexander Stephens would not be himself had he ever failed to assert his essential right to an independent voice. Over the years Stephens had been affiliated with several political parties; he began in 1836 as a young member of the old Georgia States Rights party, joined the national Whigs in 1842, and eventually moved over (with some uneasiness) to the Democrats in the late 1850s. He also helped found the short-lived Constitutional Unionist party in Georgia. Perhaps his most notable, and most characteristic, political campaign, however, was the one he ran in 1855 against the Know-Nothings as the sole and solitary member of the "party of himself." This was the fiercest campaign he ever waged, the hardest to bear in its demands on his physical energy and stamina, and the one in which he had to endure the most vicious verbal attacks of his political career. His victory, narrow though it was, became part of the Stephens legend. Had the prison diary been published during his lifetime, it too would have fit the pattern of determined self-regeneration that middle Georgians had come to expect: that of facing up to a crisis, or a handicap, and of fighting his way through to some sort of resolution.

It is difficult to judge exactly why Stephens did not allow the diary to be published. Surely one reason was his consternation (perhaps some time after the fact) that it cut too closely to a secret throb of doubt, an uncertain sense of what he could absolutely rely on as an expression of his true nature, his true belief, and his true worth. That uncertainty, of course, is one of the reasons it has value for today's readers, not so much as another testimony to add to the heavy shelves of Civil War history and political controversy, but as the intensely "personal document" admired by Edmund Wilson. It belongs to that compelling category of writing (usually undertaken in prison, or elsewise under severe duress) that fascinates the reader by the simple fact of placing him directly at the center of a suffering human mind committed to an act of sustained consultation with itself. Stephens knows (this is part of the diary's honesty) that the mind can prey ravenously upon its own vital forces, with disastrous consequences. He possessed enormous respect for rational thought, for the power of the active intellect. All during his life he had relied upon his superior intelligence to compensate for the dispossessions of family, property, and health. His ability to think out loud and to reason under pressure could be disconcerting to his contemporaries. Popular journalists called him the "bodiless brain" so often that he tired of protesting. Even discriminating commentators resorted to much the same language when faced with the intellectual force he projected when speaking in public. The following newspaper account of his oratorical style (based on an important speech he had made in Washington in 1857) is typical of the impression he made:

> This very disdain for the externals of oratory had something imposing in it; one was made to feel that he was in the presence of a powerful mind that looked to itself alone, and one surrendered oneself more completely to its guidance from the conviction that no hackneyed artifice was employed to allure our confidence.

The diary, however, shows us a more complicated man than this. Stephens at one point declares to himself that one of the dangers of the human mind lies in its desire to "want all things to *square* with its own notions." The mind can help restore and strengthen the spirit; in Stephens' isolation in Fort Warren, it is the one instrument he can trust to assess his role in the plot of history, to explain his democratic principles, to meditate on a bedbug, to explore the mysteries of his human condition, within and without. But it cannot reach everywhere at once, and it cannot provide definitive answers. There are contradictions and unresolved tensions all through the diary, just as there had been in his political career (despite the raised shield of a defiant idealism), and just as there had been during the great human cataclysm of the Civil War. Alone in his cell, Stephens now refuses to ignore them, unlike many writers of his time and station. His is a rare mind, capable of rising above immediate historical fate and of addressing the perennial questions of man and meaning that have always been asked, from the ancients through the moderns, and that make such classical distinctions irrelevant. His prison diary is a powerful and memorable record of an exceptional individual writing his way triumphantly through the most critical moment of his life.

PART I

INTRODUCTION BY MYRTA LOCKETT AVARY

INTRODUCTION

ALEXANDER STEPHENS, a British lad, after fighting for Charles Stuart at Culloden, sought sanctuary from English vengeance in Pennsylvania. Here he married Catherine, daughter of James Baskins, a wealthy gentleman, who disinherited her for her choice. But her soldier of fortune fought in the French and Indian wars under Washington, and came out of the Revolution a captain. In 1784 he moved to Georgia, and on his rented farm on historic Kettle Creek, Catherine died and was buried. His older children scattered, and the old captain, ever a better hand at war than money-making, found his mainstay in Andrew Baskins, his youngest, a youth of unusual qualities. Andrew, with earnings made as a teacher while in his teens, bought a farm, nucleus of that "old homestead" which Mr. Stephens loved so well, settled thereon his father and sister and presently brought thither a fair wife, Margaret Grier. Margaret came of folk who had a liking for books, and a turn for law, war, and meteorology. Her brother Aaron was an Indian fighter and general of militia; her brother Robert was founder of Grier's Almanac; her cousin Robert became Justice of the Supreme Court of the United States. Her father was said to have "the largest library in all that part of the country" of mid-eastern Georgia where he lived. In her son's character was a marked blending of parental traits. He was thrifty, generous, progressive; one of the best lawyers in the land; a reader and collector of books; a close observer of the weather, and father of the Weather Bureau of the United States. He preached against war, but was quick to resent an insult by a challenge to a duel, his promptness in this respect being doubtless due to a disposition to show that he could give and take, and asked no quarter of strong men.

Margaret died in 1812, leaving him a month old, and so feeble an infant that it was a miracle he lived, bereft of her bosom and her care. In 1814, Andrew married Matilda, an excellent lady, daughter of Colonel John Lindsay, or "Old Silverfist," whose arm wore a silver cap in lieu of a hand lost in the Revolution.

Making a living was pioneer work for the Stephens family; all its members toiled, the head setting energetic example. Little Alex's devotion to his father stimulated his naturally industrious disposition. Like David, he tended sheep; he minded cattle, hoed the garden, gathered vegetables, picked up chips; was mill-boy and errand-boy; handed threads for his stepmother's loom; nursed her children; at ten, was a champion corn-dropper on his father's farm; at twelve, a regular ploughhand. Of this period he has left this pastoral: *

My duty in childhood was to tend the sheep. One evening, after a snowy day, I went to call them up, fold and feed them. I found all but one — a ewe. I called for some time but she did not come. The following evening she was still missing. Next morning, my father went with me. He did not see the ewe, and asked how long she had been missing. I told him. "Why did you say nothing of it before?" he asked sternly. I

*In several letters and in the memory of friends and relatives to whom he loved to talk of his childhood days. An extended statement of this and much else here given may be found in Johnston and Browne's "Life of Stephens."

could say nothing, for the true reason had been fear lest I be sent back in the dark and the snow. I had supposed she would come up in a day or two. We set out to search for the ewe, and found her dead, with a lamb she had borne dead beside her. It was a painful thought to me for a long time that "Mottle-face," as we called the ewe, had suffered and died through my neglect. No darkness, cold, or snow could have kept me from hunting her up if I had thought of her being in such a condition.

At fifteen, his schooling, a few months at a time as he could be spared from work, made a total of about two years in "old field schools." He writes:

I studied with intense interest by the light of blazing pine knots, the only light in our house for readers in those days. My stepmother had a candle in her room by which she sewed, patched, darned, and performed other domestic tasks. By the fire I read long after the whole household was asleep, and that after a hard day's work.

Of a May day in 1826 he said, years after:

Right along here I was ploughing when I was sent for to go to the house. Father was worse. It was the day before he died. Just up there I took out my horse, not dreaming it was for the last time.

In a week his stepmother died. Her children, John, Catherine, and Linton, were sent to her kin; Margaret's, Aaron Grier and Alexander, to their mother's brother, General Aaron Grier, near Raytown, Warren County. In Mr. Stephens's letters is this silhouette of his aunt, Betsy Grier:

Uncle Grier's sister, who lived with him, was a woman of unusually strong mind, and what in those days might have been called well read. She had a good library and made good use of it [his grandfather Grier's legacy].

At his Uncle Grier's, Alexander wrote his first letter.

It was, I think, the second Sunday after I went to our new home upon the breaking up of our little family circle on the death of father and ma. It was to Uncle James Stephens, of Pennsylvania, giving an account of our affliction. Uncle Aaron had gone to meeting. Brother Aaron Grier and I were both writing. We had a table in the middle of the big room. It was some time before we could get a pen apiece. At that time, no such thing as a pen of any kind but a goosequill was ever heard of, in those parts at least. Our inkstand was a little leather-covered vial Uncle Aaron used to take when he went from home; in it was some cotton that held the ink, and the pen was filled by pressing it against the cotton. I was all day at that letter. When Uncle Aaron came home, he looked over both letters, made some corrections, and then we had to write them over again. This, my first letter, was the utterance of the bitterest grief.

A Rev. Mr. Williams, wishing to start a Union Sunday School in Raytown, laid his plans before Miss Grier. Alexander helped to organize this school and taught in it. His renown as a Bible student quickly spread.

Of his first start to Sunday School by his father, he has said:

It was an epoch in my life. Then I first took a taste for reading. I was a little over twelve. All my reading had been limited to the spelling-book and the New Testament. I was put into a class beginning with Genesis. It was no task for me to get the lesson, though I had no other time for it but Sunday mornings and evenings, or at night by light of a pine-knot fire. My entrance into this school gave me a taste for reading, history, and chronology.

Comparing this with other epochs in his life:

One of the first that I remember was "dropping the slips" — a frock such as girls wear — and putting on breeches, an event giving me entirely new notions of myself. Starting to school was another. But I no more thought of this the morning my father gave me the beautiful new spelling-book with its rich blue cover, and told me to go to school and be a good boy, than I thought several years after that I was turning another point when he started me with a Bible to Powder Creek meeting-house.

After the first year at their uncle's, Aaron worked on the farm for wages. Alexander, to whom the same chance was offered, requested to continue his studies at Locust Grove Academy, where he and Aaron had been in faithful attendance as farmwork permitted. Of the close of the 1827 term, he writes:

I well remember my feelings the last evening; how I gathered up all my things — books, papers, slate-pencils and ink — put some in my basket and some under my arm, and then bade all good-bye. I reflected, as I walked the homeward path, that this was the last time I should ever tread its beaten track, and the last day I should ever go to school. The next week I was to go to Crawfordville to seek employment in a store. Next Sunday I went to Sunday School. Mr. Mills inquired how I was coming on at the Academy. I told him my term was out, and what I was going to do. He asked how I would like to go to Washington, Ga., and study Latin. I said I would like it very well, but had not the means. He proposed to send me. I said I would consult my uncle and aunt.

Aunt Betsy advised that the better his education the better he could repay Mr. Mills; she got his clothes ready and started him off. July 28, 1827, he was at Mr. Webster's academy and in Adam's Latin Grammar; August 18, he was reading *Historiæ Sacræ* in a class of a year's standing. His grammar had been his teacher's; in it he wrote, under "Alexander Hamilton Webster," "Alexander *Hamilton* Stephens," paying the donor the one tribute in his power by adopting the same middle name. He was troubled when told of a desire to educate him for the ministry: "Whether I should be fit to preach when I should grow up, I could not know. I could give no answer until I had consulted my aunt, my mentor." Mr. Webster and Aunt Betsy decided that he should complete his course under the Presbyterian Education Society, leaving the question of vocation in abeyance. August 6, 1828, he writes from the State University at Athens a letter to Aaron which quaintly reflects his own character and the turmoil of the day over the Tariff:

Dear Brother and Friend: I have now an opportunity of informing you of my situation. Early this morning, after you left me, I left Washington for Athens in a crowded stage; but we had a delightful journey, having good company and pleasant weather. About 5, we arrived in Athens. Thursday and Friday, I was engaged in nothing particular but walking about the streets, etc. Saturday my examination came off. After all my pains in reviewing at home, I was not examined on a single thing I had reviewed, but as good luck would have it, I missed none, and was admitted to the Freshman class. [Describes Commencement, etc.] The finest crops I have seen are between here and Washington.

Athens, I discover, is a very popular retreat for great people, especially about Commencement. To-day there is an innumerable number of people, horses, carriages, gigs, sulkies, wagons, cake-and-cider carts, etc. The Tariff is carried to a high degree here. It is sufficient for me to say that some of the people are so incensed against the Tariff that they wear their broadcloth every day and their homespun Sunday. Mr. McDuffie came to Athens last Sunday; he himself was dressed in homespun and his boy [Negro servant] in broadcloth. You can form an idea from the foregoing how the Tariff stands in the minds of the people here. The Colleges were illuminated last night, a candle to every pane of glass. I board at Mrs. Church's, and am much pleased both with Athens and the people. I must conclude, as I have nothing of importance and I have a very sore finger. So fare you well at the present,

And I ever remain your Friend,

A. H. Stephens

To all my friends
Who now do live
My compliments
I in love do give.

"Mr. McDuffie" was the Congressman who afterward became Governor of South Carolina. In 1828 the "Tariff of Abominations" was passed and the South, Carolina leading, protested violently. "Mrs. Church" was wife of Dr. Church, the later College President.

"My college days were my happiest days," Mr. Stephens has said. He was a favourite with faculty and students. His room was popular, a place of clean joviality, where wit and repartee and story-telling were cultivated, and refreshments, barring liquor and tobacco, were always on hand: "Boys met there who never met elsewhere — the most dissipated and the most ascetically pious" — "most were wealthy." Of his poverty he "seldom thought; no distinctions were there but of merit." In two years, deciding that the ministry was not his vocation, he repaid the Education Society's advances with funds borrowed from Aaron; and on his patrimony of about $400, completed his course. He then taught school in Madison for "four months of misery." He missed his college associations. And an experience which should have brought him life's joy brought him but sorrow. He loved. But he kept silent because of his poverty and ill health. So sacred he held this experience that only once or twice in after life did he mention it. All that tradition preserves of the object of his attachment is that she was lovely in person and character; was his pupil, and learned rapidly; and she had "dark eyes and curls and rosy cheeks." Years after, when in Congress, he loved again; the lady, a woman of beauty and distinction, was not indifferent to him; but again he kept silent; a woman's due, he thought, was a husband on whom she could lean and not an invalid whom she must nurse. From Madison he went to Dr. Le Conte's, Liberty County, as tutor to a few select pupils, among them John and Joseph Le Conte, the later eminent scientists. He was again a valued member of a scholarly and cultured circle, and life grew brighter, but he felt that he was not fulfilling his mission. Declining $1,500 for another year's stay, he began to study law at Crawfordville. Here he boarded with his stepmother's brother-in-law, the Rev. Williamson Bird, in the house which is now historic as Liberty Hall, this being the name Mr. Stephens gave to the property when he bought it, in 1845, on the death of Mr. Bird.

In his Prison Journal, he describes his admission to the bar. His first essay at "riding the circuit" was to Washington, twenty miles distant. He had no horse.

With saddlebags on his shoulders, he set out at dusk of a hot July day, walked to his uncle Aaron's, which was halfway; and next day, rode to court, clad in a neat white suit which he had retired to the woods to don just before entering town. At this court he met Robert Toombs, and their lifelong intimacy, second only to that between himself and his brother Linton, began. A partnership in Columbus at $1,500 or more a year was offered him by Swepston Jeffries, a leading lawyer, but he preferred Crawfordville and no prospects because nearby was the old homestead, over which he loved to roam, and which, in fulfilment of a cherished purpose, he bought in 1838. From his diary of 1834, the following condensed excerpts are taken:

May 2.—The other day, as I was coming from my boarding-house in a cheerful brisk walk, I was laid low in the dust by hearing the superintendent of a shoe-shop ask a workman, "Who is that little fellow that walks so fast by here every day?" with the reply in a sarcastic tone, "Why, *that's* a *lawyer!*"

May 8.— Read Jackson's Protest to the Senate. Am pleased with it in general . . . I feel interested for him . . . I see vile attempts made to fix infamy upon him. His Proclamation of December, 1832, I condemn. But for one error a man who has done much good for his country should not be abandoned. For where we find a president who will commit only one wrong, we shall find few who will not commit more.

May 12.—My desires do not stop short of the highest places of distinction. Yet how can I effect my purpose? Poor and without friends, time passing with rapid flight and I effecting nothing.

May 17.—Brother still with me. Had an introduction to a man who addressed me familiarly as "My son." Such often happens to me. My weight is 94 pounds, height 67 inches, and my whole appearance that of a youth of eighteen.

May 19. — Inferior Court sat; no business. Starvation to the whole race of lawyers!

May 30. — Examined some drawings of the ancient statues. With the Gladiator and Venus I am delighted. Pity but some of our fashionable belles would take a lesson from this elegant form of true grace, the Venus; they would change their present disgusting waspish taste.

June 3. — The railroad is the topic of the day. Railroads, it is true, are novel things. The greatest obstacle is the greatness of the enterprise. The stupendous thought of seeing steam-engines moving over our hills at the safe and rapid flight of fifteen miles an hour, produces a greater effect in dissuasion of the undertaking than any discovered defect in arguments in its favour.

June 6. — Read in *Southern Recorder* (the only paper I take, and devoted to States Rights) a chapter on cats, with which I was pleased.

June 7. — I believe I shall never be worth anything, and the thought is death to my soul. I am too boyish, unmanful, trifling, simple in my manners and address.

June 15. — Quarterly meeting. Pretty good sermon.

June 17. — Tried to borrow a horse to go to Uncle Grier's on business, but was so disappointed as to fill me with mortification and a due sense of my humble dependence. I had rather (and have often done it) walk than ask for a horse.

June 20. — Had a visit from Dr. Foster and promised to deliver an oration on the Fourth of July.

June 25. — Went to a party. Witnessed the new dance [the waltz] which disgusted me very much. Oh, the follies of man!

July 24. — Engaged for the first time, with a contingent fee of $180. May Providence look propitiously upon me!

He lived on $6 a month. In a letter, in after years, he wrote:

> No one can imagine how I worked, how I delved, how I laboured over books. Often I spent the whole night over a law-book, and went to bed at dawn. My business increased. My brother Aaron, who taught school in the Asbury settlement visited me often. Our excursions to the old homestead constituted most of my recreation except when I went to see him or Uncle Aaron or old Aunt Betsy.

On the Fourth of July, 1834, he made his first political speech, and it was on States Rights. Celebration of the Fourth was Crawfordville's great annual event, with people coming in from the country round and much feasting and barbecuing; a prominent citizen would serve as orator of the day and another as reader of the Declaration of Independence. From 1834 Stephens was in regular demand in one or the other of these capacities.

In his first important case, he did what he was often to do in Congress on great issues — carried a minority to victory. Isaac Battle, head of an influential clan, wished to retain possession of his grandchild, daughter of his son's widow who had married an intemperate man. A great crowd came to the trial of the case. After able counsel for the Battles had spoken, a pallid, unknown boy arose and pleaded for the mother the divine right of motherhood. A Battle reported next day: "When that little fellow began to argue and the judges fell to crying, I knew Isaac would have to give up Martha Ann." His practice grew rapidly. So much business came to him that he called Aaron Grier to his aid. When he took a Northern tour in 1838, he left his affairs in the hands of Toombs and Aaron. On this tour, he saw Fort Warren for the first time on May 25, the day on which he was to see it in 1865 as a prisoner. This was his second Northern trip; it included a visit to his father's brother James, in Pennsylvania, as had the first in 1835, of which an amusing incident has been preserved. At the family dinner, Uncle James, a worthy farmer, asked, "What business do you follow, Alex?" "I am a lawyer, Uncle." An ominous silence fell. Presently Uncle James asked huskily, "Alex, don't you have to tell lies?"

In 1835 Mr. Stephens had his first interview with a President of the United States. He found Andrew Jackson in dressing-gown and slippers, a silver pipe at his side, before a big fire in the White House. "What's the news from Georgia?" asked Old Hickory. Stephens told of the outbreak of the Creek Indians; the stage he boarded at Washington, Ga., was the only one of a train of coaches which had escaped capture with massacre of all passengers between Montgomery and Columbus. "I have a letter by the lower route telling something of this," said Jackson. "In God's name, where's Howard?" "I don't know. As Major Howard's are Georgia forces under control of the Georgia Legislature, there may be some question of jurisdiction"—"Jurisdiction by the Eternal! when the United States Mail is robbed and citizens murdered!" cried Old Hickory, springing to his feet. He kept Stephens for over an hour. In 1838, Mr. Stephens saw Congress in session; as he jotted down in a little note-book, he saw "Wise and Clay; a dull day; Webster, sullen, worn out, caged lion; Benton, arrogant, disgusting manner." He "walked way out on the commons N. W., where Washington will be in days to come." Baltimore was "first city going North that is lighted with gas"; and where he saw white servants. In Philadelphia at night in the Merchants' Hotel: "Startled in my room by cry of fire — mob set fire to Philadelphia or Pennsylvania Hall for its abolitionism."

Answering inquiries from a friend, Mr. Stephens, in 1871, gave some account of his political life to 1859, which is reproduced because of its spontaneity and because, as his own, it is authoritative, though it is by no means a complete statement:

I was brought up a Jeffersonian Democrat of the strictest sect — of the Crawford and Troup school in Georgia. All Georgians belonged to that school when I was a boy. The party divisions of the State, the Troup men and Clarke men, all supported Crawford for President in 1824, though Clarke was but lukewarm because Crawford was Troup's great leader; they barely ran no opposition; they sympathized in that contest with Mr. Calhoun, then becoming prominent, and between whom and Mr. Crawford no very kind feelings existed, the two being rivals in the same party.

My first vote was given in 1833, after the split on Nullification. The Troup-Crawford wing did not favour Nullification: they organized on a platform which they proclaimed as the true States Rights principles; while opposing Nullification as taught in South Carolina, they also opposed the doctrines of General Jackson's famous Proclamation; they held the right of Secession, but repudiated Nullification as a proper or peaceful remedy for a difference between a State and the United States Government. William H. Crawford was President of the organizing committee. Great numbers of the old Crawford-Troup-Jefferson party went with the Nullifiers. By these means, the old party in Georgia became demoralized. John Forsyth, then in the United States Senate, as a Troup-Crawford man, abandoned both wings. That is, he not only repudiated Nullification but also the States Rights doctrine announced by Crawford and Troup with their adherents. He organized what was called the Union party of the State, and took off enough of the old Crawford-Troup men to make with the Clarke men a majority, and for several years this Union-Jackson party, so-called, governed the State. In 1833, Wilson Lumpkin was their nominee for Governor, and the States Rights nominee was Major Joel Crawford (relative of W. H.). In this election, my first vote was given, and for Crawford.

In 1836, I was elected to the Legislature as a States Rights man. My county, Taliaferro, had been under the lead of Nullifiers; though they acted with the States Rights party in preference to the Forsyth party, they did not like to support one who did not accept the doctrine of Nullification — not even William H. Crawford and George M. Troup, their old leaders. I had bitter opposition in my first campaign because I was against Nullification. In 1836, the States Rights party in Georgia carried the electoral vote for President, casting it for Hugh L. White, of Tennessee. The Forsyth-Union-Jackson party ran Van Buren and were defeated in the State. In 1839, after the Harrisburg Convention nominated Harrison, I favoured the nomination by the States Rights party in Georgia of George M. Troup. A resolution to that effect was passed by the December Convention at Milledgeville. In the summer of 1840, when the Harrison fever raged high — when the storm was at its topmost pitch of "Tippecanoe and Tyler too!" the Georgia leaders became infected; another convention was held; Judge Berrien was the leading spirit; Troup's name was taken down and Harrison's run up.

I was young; and as it was shown that Harrison was a Jefferson Democrat, and as I felt it to be my duty to beat the corruptionists in power under Van Buren, I "went with my folks" and voted for Harrison. Whig had not then been introduced into Georgia as a party name. In 1842 the States Rights party in convention to nominate candidates for Congress, under the lead of

Richard Henry Wilde, assumed the name of Whig. Their ticket was defeated. In the Legislature of 1842 I, being in the Senate, made a long report on Federal relations; it became the Whig platform in Georgia. A vacancy occurred in the Congressional delegation elected as Democrats so-called the year before; in the summer of 1843, I was nominated to fill that vacancy by the Whigs, so-called on the principles of the report of 1842, and was elected by about 3,000 majority.

I took my seat in the House of Representatives, December, 1843. I stood nominally as a Whig, yet held few sentiments in common with the national party: was opposed to the protection policy; to the policy of receiving abolition petitions in Congress and to the Congressional jurisdiction in any form of the slavery question. I favoured the incorporation of Texas into the Union; not under the Tyler treaty — that I opposed — but under joint resolution for her admission as a State. This well-nigh severed my connection even in name with the Whig party at Washington as well as in Georgia. Judge Berrien had become thoroughly identified with Mr. Clay and the Whig party throughout the country, not only on the Protective Tariff but in opposition to Texan annexation. Indeed, he went further than Clay on the latter question.

I omitted to state at the right place that the Whig party of Georgia supported Clay for the Presidency in 1844, though differing widely with him on many questions. For instance, after Clay's Raleigh letter opposing annexation, our State Convention passed resolutions favouring that measure. These resolutions were drawn up by me in Washington and sent down to be adopted, as they were, by the State Convention nominating electoral candidates. I, however, gave Mr. Clay a warm support. I had urged him not to publish that anti-Texas Raleigh letter; he told me, as he was passing through the State, that he intended to come out with such a letter. I urged him not to. I believe he was influenced by considerations of policy. I knew from conversations with him that he was really in favour of the admission of Texas if it could be done without endangering the Union, and I believed that it would be a leading object of his administration, if elected, to bring Texas in without violent agitation. Texas was brought in as she was by my stand in the House. I got Milton Brown, of Tennessee, an old Member, and six or seven so-called Southern Whigs to stand with me. We, as the House was constituted, held the balance of power, and compelled the Democratic side so-called to come to our terms. Mr. Polk I regarded as a mere demagogue and a very bad man. He was elected by a political fraud on the people of Pennsylvania in the matter of his views on the Tariff; to save himself on that point, he resolved to get into a war with Mexico. The Texas question afforded opportunity. His course in relation to that war was what threw me into the ranks of the Whigs, the opposition. I denounced the war and its inauguration. I took the lead in this method of treating it in the House.

My first conversation with Mr. Calhoun was a day or two after my first speech on the war; in May, I think, 1846. It occurred in this way. Mr. Burt, of South Carolina, Member of the House and relative by marriage of Mr. Calhoun, said Mr. Calhoun had asked him to bring me to see him if agreeable to me; that he wanted to know me. We went. Mr. Calhoun stated that he had read my speech, was pleased with it, and wished to express his gratification; then he entered into a long conversation, in his peculiar and earnest style, on the whole subject; said he concurred with me fully in every view presented, but could say nothing then in the Senate, owing to his complications with the administration on the Oregon question; that he was exceedingly anxious to get that question settled without war with England; if he should denounce the administration as it ought to be denounced for its policy in bringing on the Mexican War, he would lose his influence with them on Oregon;

duty required silence for the present; but as soon as the controversy with England was ended, he should take the same position on Mexico in the Senate that I had taken in the House.

This I mention simply as an incident of my first acquaintance with Calhoun. Our conversation was full and free, but understood to be a matter, on his side, not to be talked of. He did, afterward in the Senate, follow the line he told me he would; it was after the Oregon question was settled, in February, I think, 1847. The only difference then between us was that he insisted that we ought to take a slip of country as indemnity, which seemed strange to me after his declaration in the same grand speech that "Mexico is the forbidden fruit."

My position on the mode of admission of Texas controlled that matter. This was during the second session of my first Congress. My action in the next Congress controlled the course the Mexican War finally took. The Whig party, in the Congress beginning 4th March, 1845, and ending 4th March, 1847, was in a minority of about 70. This was the Congress that recognized the war as the act of Mexico — a shameful lie! The Whigs, after war began, were all at sea. Winthrop, Joe Ingersoll, and the like knew not what to do; they were timid and fearful. No one, they would say, can oppose the war; the fate of all who opposed the War of 1812 was before their eyes; Crittenden in the Senate was of the same mind. Now, at this stage of the case (when the War party, Cass at their head in the Senate, was ready to swallow all Mexico, and really intended to do it, I verily believe), I drew up and submitted to our old leaders in the House, especially Winthrop and Ingersoll, a resolution which should properly present the position of the Whigs on the war. I told them it was essential in elections for the next Congress, to go before the country on a well-defined policy, and that that policy must be a true and patriotic one or we would be utterly defeated. It was embraced, I thought, in the resolutions. Ingersoll and Winthrop, as well as every other to whom I submitted it, not even excepting my colleague, Mr. Toombs, disapproved the policy of offering it; it would put us before the people as opposed to the vindication of the rights and honour of the country. I knew there was no hope of getting it in to be acted on but upon a motion to suspend the rules for its introduction; a vote could be had on that question and in this way it could be got before the House. I determined to offer it anyway, and did. At first, several prominent, aspiring, expediency Whigs dodged it, but when they saw that Cobb, of Georgia, a leading man on the other side, voted to suspend the rules for its introduction, they crawled out, like chickens that had been hiding in a bush from a hawk, and voted the same way. I finally got every, or nearly every, Whig vote in the House and a few Democrats, Cobb at the head. Cobb was an exceedingly quick and shrewd man; he saw the power in the resolution and foresaw its effect upon the public. The resolution became, as I intended it to be, the national Whig platform so far as the war was concerned. Upon it a majority was returned to the House in the face of a most brilliant war; and that majority by one vote arrested the war. It was all done on high and patriotic principles and on no base demagogical subterfuge.

The administration was greatly embarrassed by the change in the character of the House. Winthrop was Speaker, and the committees were all different from what they had been. Still, Mr. Polk attempted, by browbeating and charging us with disloyalty and with "giving aid and comfort to the enemy," to scare our weak-kneed into submission. Such treatment, I knew, had to be met with boldness and defiance. Hence, in February, 1848, while many Whigs were trembling in their shoes, the War party introduced for popular effect a resolution tendering the thanks of Congress to General Twiggs (I believe it was) for gallantry at Cerro Gordo. I joined in giving all the praise set forth to that brave officer and his men, but wished the resolution amended so as to read, "in a war unconstitutionally begun." When the time for offering the amendment came, Winthrop gave the floor to Ashmun, of Massachusetts, who offered it. A great sensation ensued. The War party was elated, they looked on triumph as certain; they did not think we would dare vote for it. Our weak-kneed trembled; many got up and walked out; I rallied all I could, presented an undaunted front, urged every one I could find to stand up square to the truth. The vote at first was close; but when the hidden chickens under the brush in the outside alleys saw that their votes would carry it, enough came up and voted "Aye" to pass it.

The War men looked aghast! That vote of the House — that expression of condemnation by a majority of the impeaching branch of the Government — ended the war, broke its backbone. Polk saw what was coming. In a few days, Trist was dispatched to Mexico to make the best terms of peace he could. This is the real origin of the celebrated "Treaty of Guadalupe Hidalgo."

The resolution thus amended was passed. The War party dropped it. John Quincy Adams died while it was pending. The House adjourned and the resolution was not again taken up. But that vote had done its work, as I knew it would when the shaft was sent.

For your question about my course toward General Taylor. It was I — no egotism in telling you the simple truth — who made him President. Soon after the first battles of the war at Resaca and Palo Alto, I urged on the anti-War party that Taylor was our man; I got his nomination in a Whig convention in Georgia in 1847. At the beginning of Congress in December, I was mainly instrumental in getting up a Taylor Club in Congress; it was known as the Young Indians. For months there were but seven of us: Truman Smith of Connecticut, Abraham Lincoln of Illinois, William Ballard Preston, Thomas S. Flournoy and John S. Pendleton, of Virginia, Toombs and myself of Georgia. Others came in afterward —

Cabell of Florida, Hilliard of Alabama, and some whose names I forget. It was confined to the House. Mr. Crittenden, of the Senate, fully concurred with us. While strongly attached to Mr. Clay personally, he did not think Clay could be elected. We opened an extensive correspondence and put the ball in motion. The contest between the Clay Whigs and the Taylor men for the nomination in Philadelphia was bitter and fierce. Many things I could tell which would entertain you, had I time. One incident I may mention — how I got a Taylor battery planted in New York City.

During the winter of 1847-48, we could get no hearing in New York, though we had some zealous men coöperating with us there, General Draper and others; and we had no Taylor paper there. Colonel Humphrey Marshall, of Buena Vista fame, had attempted to speak there for Taylor, but the roughs of the Whig party broke up all Taylor meetings. I saw that this must be changed; we must get a foothold by some means in the Metropolis. I devised a programme, choosing Toombs for speaker. Samuel J. Anderson, a clerk in the House and a very shrewd man whom I knew well, knew Isaiah Rhynders, captain among roughs and shoulder-hitters in New York — famous as the head of the Corbin [?] Club in the Clay-Polk contest of 1844; I knew he was sore at the manner in which he had been treated by the Polk administration and was in sympathy with the Taylor movement.

Now I told Toombs we must have a successful hearing in New York, and that he was the man to face any sort of crowd. My plan was for him to take Anderson with him; Anderson was to hunt up Rhynders (I believe that's the spelling) and bring him to Toombs. Toombs should tell Rhynders what he wanted — a fair and uninterrupted hearing from a New York audience in behalf of Taylor; and to ask Rhynders if he could see that he, Toombs, got it, and at what cost. I told him to pay Rhynders just what he would ask. The programme was carried out. Toombs and Anderson went on; Rhynders met Toombs at the Astor House, entered cheerfully into the engagement, and said it would cost $200: it would require that to secure the necessary force. Toombs closed with him. Rhynders said it would facilitate his work if Toombs would meet some of his "boy-hoys" at a certain noted saloon the evening before the speech and get acquainted with them. Toombs, who was able to make himself perfectly at home in such a crowd, went at the appointed hour and met the captain with his subalterns, Bill Ford, Sullivan, and other noted boxers. Nothing passed but such agreeable chat as Toombs knew how to give in his peculiar style, and the glass to his company. Rhynders, on parting, told Toombs it was all right; but that he must not get flurried or off his feet at any outburst that might happen at first; there might be some disorder at the start, but that he, Rhynders, would down it all right.

The meeting was duly announced. The hour arrived; a large audience assembled; the hall was brilliantly lighted. The most prominent Taylor men in the city presided; they knew nothing of Toombs's arrangement with Rhynders and were very uneasy. One of them introduced the orator of the evening. No sooner had Toombs with his fine and manly presence stepped forward and uttered the words, "Fellow citizens of New York —" than a yell rose from various parts of the house: "Slave-holder!" Slave-holder!" Toombs remained quiet and composed for a moment, and began again. Another yell went up: "Hurrah for Clay! Hurrah for Clay!" Toombs, in imperturbable temper, not seeming to be excited in the least, again commenced; again yells arose. Still unmoved, he began, when on repetition of the cries, "Slave-holder!" and the like, there was the greatest row you ever saw. "Put him out!" rang from one side of the hall to the other, and everywhere a stalwart arm was seen pitching some fellow out. Rhynders's men were at work. Some who were being pitched out exclaimed: "I made no noise!"

"You have chalk on your back!" was the reply; "and you've got to go."

In two minutes the hall was cleared of some forty "chalk-backs." Rhynders's plan, as he afterward told Toombs, had been to scatter his men through the audience; they were quietly to mark the backs of all who made interruptions; on the order, "Put them out!" they were to seize and put out by force all chalk-backs. He and they knew pretty well beforehand who were the brawlers sent to break up the meeting; but, to make certain, his plan was first to spot them. The hall was soon cleared of rowdies. The audience was quiet and orderly while Toombs gave them one of his masterly popular harangues. Before the conclusion, the wildest enthusiasm prevailed; loud shouts of applause went up; and then came "three cheers for old Zach!" given with a vim as Toombs took his seat. Our victory was complete; we had a foothold in New York; our battery in that stronghold of the enemy was well served afterward and did most effective work. Great events often turn on small ones. Now, as an active party in all these scenes, I tell you that that one little thing of getting a successful hearing in New York had powerful results.

This has taken up too much time for me to go on with other incidents. If I live to write a book, as I wish, on "Congressional Reminiscences," I may give more such incidents. Of course what I now write is only to afford you light on the points on which you question me. You will understand that in all I did, I was moved by a motive far higher than my own advantage or distinction. I have generally most cheerfully permitted others to reap the honours accruing from any line of policy I suggested.

When Taylor was elected, he sent for me immediately on his reaching Washington. Crittenden, then Governor of Kentucky, had advised him to consult me. Taylor asked me and Toombs to go into his Cabinet. I advised against this, and presented the names of George W. Crawford, of Georgia, and William Ballard Preston, of Virginia. The other names for Cabinet positions were submitted to me. I did not like Clayton for Secretary of State; Collamer for Postmaster General I approved; Meredith, of Pennsylvania, I knew nothing about; Reverdy Johnson for Attorney General, I thought well of.

Just at this time the seed of what ruined Taylor's administration was sowed in an alliance with William H. Seward, head of the Abolition party in New York. The saddest reflection for me was that this was effected through Preston. Preston was an able and true man; I had every confidence in him. He was a bold and active "Young Indian." He was the man who carried the Virginia Whigs against Botts. Somehow, strangely enough too, Seward, by some sort of blandishment, came it over him. Seward gave the strongest pledges that he, in the Senate, would drop the slavery agitation and give Taylor's administration a cordial support on a broad continental basis without stirring up sectional animosities. These promises were relied on by Preston, who looked on Seward as a great leader. Seward was put virtually in possession of the power of distributing the entire Federal patronage in New York. This was the state of things when I left Washington, March, 1849. I was not pleased, for I had no confidence in Seward.

When the new Congress assembled in December, 1849, I found that Seward as a charmer had complete control of Preston. He had got Webb, through whom his pledges had been given, sent as minister abroad. He had got Preston to believe that the Northern Whigs must hold on to their doctrine of Congressional exclusion of slavery from the Territories; that it would destroy them to abandon it; but the vexed question could be got rid of by what was known as the administration policy — non-action. I knew he was not sincere in this and that he only wanted Preston not to make war on the Wilmot Proviso. It was at the opening of this Congress that, as a touchstone of party principle, I insisted that the Whig or administration caucus, in nominating a candidate for Speaker, should define its position. Toombs and myself and six or seven other Southern Whigs so-called concurred in that view. The resolution (you can see more about it in Vol. II of my "War Between the States") was drawn up in my room and Toombs took charge of it. When the caucus met, he offered it. It embraced the idea that Congress ought not to abolish slavery in the District of Columbia nor prohibit it in the Territories. This resolution was laid on the table in the caucus on motion of Stanley of North Carolina. Toombs and myself and six or seven other Whigs so-called withdrew. That was the last time I ever met a Whig caucus so-called in Congress. Winthrop was again nominated for Speaker, but lost his election by defection of the Southern Whigs.

The lead I took in the adjustment measures of 1850 will be seen in Vol. II of "War Between the States." I controlled that settlement; that is, without the part I took at the time, it would never have been made. The rupture between me and Preston became open, and very painful to me. Taylor, under Preston's advice, still adhered to his non-action policy, while Seward was working with vim, just as he did long afterward with President Johnson, seeming to be with him but undermining him in all he did. I told Johnson of this, in 1866, but he no more heeded me than Taylor did. Taylor died in July, 1850, while all was at sea on the adjustment. A few days before his attack, I had a long and earnest interview with him and urged him to change his policy, which was at that time to send troops to Santa Fé, Texas, and take Federal occupation of territory against the claim of Texas — Seward's game, as I believed. I went to see Preston, Toombs with me. Preston was not at home; we met in front of the Treasury Building; we had a long talk; Toombs said little, that little on my side. I told Preston that if troops were ordered to Santa Fé, the President would be impeached. "Who will impeach him?" asked he. "I will if nobody else does," I replied. We turned and parted. That was our last interview until many years after, when, on other questions, we met cordially; and at the time of his death, we were again warm friends. The day after our street interview, there appeared a card from me in the *National Intelligencer*, which created a sensation in Washington; you will find it, if you see fit to look for it, in the issue on or about the Fourth.

With Taylor's death, Fillmore came in; a change took place in the Cabinet. Crawford had determined to resign if the order for marching the troops had been given. On 8th August, I think, I made a speech that did more than any other one speech that session, I think, to carry the famous adjustment measures; for it brought the Northern Wilmot Proviso men — Fillmore Whigs, I mean — to the conclusion that the Proviso must be abandoned. I was called home; I paired with a Free Soiler from Connecticut who was also called away, and I did not get back until the measure was passed. After this, I came home and stumped Georgia — travelled 3,000 miles by actual count — explaining the principles of the settlement and advising the people to accept them and remain in the Union under them. Our Legislature had called a Sovereign Convention of the People to assemble in case California should be admitted. I was against secession for that cause. Toombs and Cobb were both with me in this. The Whig Convention elected in the State was largely in favour of the settlement. I was in that Convention and on the Committee that drafted the celebrated Georgia Platform of 1850; these resolutions were on all turning points my work, though I did not figure before the public in them.

After that Convention, I returned to Washington, and gave Fillmore's administration my support. Before that Convention, I had gone to Washington to be present at the opening of Congress and especially to see Fillmore's message before it was delivered. I got an opportunity of seeing it through Mr. Crittenden, then in the Cabinet. On reading the latter part — the message was then in print; it was the Saturday night before Congress met — I did not like the conclusion, which spoke of some modification to be made in the adjustment measures. I told Mr. Crittenden that Mr. Fillmore ought to treat the settlement as final and to use the expression Mr. Webster had applied in a published letter in which he spoke of the measures as a settlement "in principle and in substance" of the subjects embraced in them. On my urgent entreaty, Mr. Crittenden took the message to Fillmore with the phraseology I had suggested substituted, and the change was made. This is how that important part of his message of December, 1850, came to be as it is.

I wanted Webster to be the candidate of the Constitutional Union party for 1852. The part I took in the Whig platform of that year, you will see in Vol. II. I did not, however, after 1849, meet a Whig caucus myself. I intended to be free of party trammels. If Scott, with whom I was on the most intimate terms of friendship, had endorsed that platform, I would have supported him. This he knew by direct message from me. When he refused to do it, I came out in a card in the *National Intelligencer*, signed by several others, giving my reasons for not voting for him. The result was as I expected. Pierce was elected. I acted with no party or parties organizing his administration. But on the assembling of the new Congress in 1855, I told Howell Cobb and J. Glancey Jones if they would in caucus adopt a resolution I would draw up, I would go in the House next day and not only vote for their nominee for Speaker but coöperate thoroughly with their party in the line of policy to be indicated in that resolution. This was in my room Sunday night; Congress was to meet next day. They asked for the resolution; I drew it up and handed it to them. They approved it; it went to the caucus and J. Glancey Jones offered it. It was passed unanimously. Upon that resolution, the party was organized. It was carried to Cincinnati and became part of the platform on which Buchanan was elected. Most of Buchanan's measures I supported; many I opposed. I deeply deplored his quarrel with Douglas. When I could not get him to abandon it, I quit Congress forever. As I told him in our last interview, if he persisted in his course a burst-up at Charleston [where the National Democratic Convention was to be held] would be inevitable; with that, war would come, the end of which I could not foresee, and as I did not care to be in at the death, I should retire. I told him in plain words that his policy would lead to disruption of the Government: "It will be as certain," I said, "as that you would break your neck if you should jump out of that window"; we were sitting by a window. He was inflexible. I wrote home saying I would not be a candidate for Congress again. I retired for good. Before leaving, I brought Oregon into the Union as a State. This was my last work in Congress. But for me, I am sure the bill for her admission would not have passed that term. I have given — in a brief and hurried way and as I recollect it — the personal data you asked for. This letter may sound egotistical to those who do not know me personally. It is not intended for anybody but you.

Yours truly,

ALEXANDER H. STEPHENS.

Some elaboration of the ground gone over in this fragmentary statement is essential to anything like a rounded view of Mr. Stephens's political life to 1859. Mr. Stephens mentions his minority positions on nullification and secession which his political opponents used against him in his race for the legislature in 1836. They also charged him with abolitionism because he opposed vigilance committees as proper tribunals for handling abolition agents sent South to incite Negroes to insurrection. He mentions framing the Whig platform in 1842. His legislative services extended far beyond this, and embraced matters of present-day value. His maiden speech in the legislature saved the measure for building the State Road, a project much ridiculed, railroads being then in the early experimental stage. The bill was nearly lost when he arose, in appearance an invalid boy with black eyes gleaming from an unearthly white face, and proved by indisputable data and argument the value and practicability of the road. His support saved the charter for the Macon Female College, the first in the world to confer on women the usual college degrees, and an enterprise, like the railroad, much ridiculed. He championed the cause of his *Alma Mater*, the State University, then in straits, and, as Chairman of the Committee on Education, advanced in many ways the cause of learning.

His first speech in Congress, against his own right to a seat, declared his lifelong creed that "the permanency of our institutions can only be preserved by confining the action of the State and Federal Governments each to its own proper sphere." He had been elected before Georgia's adoption of the district system as ordered by Congress. The right of Congress so to order being questioned, he upheld it on constitutional grounds. His political opponents at the South recited the scandal of how John Quincy Adams shook hands with him after the speech. Adams, who was not much given to listening to speeches, really paid the young Georgian marked attention. Till his death, Mr. Stephens preserved a poem written to him in Adams's cramped hand; the last stanza ran:

As strangers in this hall we met;
But now with one united heart,
Whate'er of life awaits us yet,
In cordial friendship let us part.

From this first speech in Congress to his last before the war, his straight line of endeavour was to preserve the Union under the Constitution. His opposition to Texan annexation was not pleasing to the South, but he was unwilling to receive Texas unless her slavery limits were first defined; as they were finally, and on his own plan based on the Missouri Compromise. His Texas speech,* the first to bring him into national prominence, contained the oft-quoted sentences which revived against him at the South the charges of abolitionism while at the North he was accused of labouring for slavery extension:

> My reason for wishing it [the slavery limit] settled in the beginning, I do not hesitate to make known. I fear the excitement growing out of the agitation hereafter may endanger the harmony and even existence of our present Union. . . . I am no defender of slavery in the abstract. I would rejoice to see all the sons of Adam's family in the enjoyment of those rights set forth in the Declaration of Independence as natural and inalienable, if a stern necessity, bearing the impress of the Creator, did not in some cases prevent.

The right of the Union to "acquire territory" and the wisdom of doing so were questioned. He declared for expansion but against imperialism:

> This [annexation] is an important step in settling the principle of our future extension. We are reminded of the growth of the Roman Empire which fell of its own weight; and of England, who is hardly able to keep together her extensive parts. Rome extended her dominions by conquest, she compelled provinces to bear the yoke; England extends hers upon the principle of colonization; her distant dependencies are subject to

* For the full text of the Texas speech, from which condensed excerpts are here made, see Cleveland's "Letters and Speeches of Stephens," 280-302.

her laws but are deprived of the rights of representation. With us, a new system has commenced, characteristic of the age. It is the system of a Republic formed by the union of separate independent States, yielding so much of their sovereign powers as are necessary for national and foreign purposes, and retaining all others for local and domestic objects. Who shall undertake to say how far this system may not go?

He said, speaking of Mexican territory:*

No principle is more dangerous than that of compelling other people to adopt our form of government. It is not only wrong in itself, but contrary to the whole spirit and genius of the liberty we enjoy.

Asking if the Mexican war was waged for conquest:

If so, I protest . . . I am no enemy to the extension of our domain. I trust the day is coming and is not far distant when the whole continent will be ours. That this is our ultimate destiny I believe, but it is not to be accomplished by the sword. We can only properly enlarge by voluntary accessions.

In his denunciation of Polk's abuse of power, we see the same jealous regard for the Constitution and the public rights which later inspired his arraignment of Davis and Lincoln for their usurpations:

Congress alone can constitutionally draw the sword. The President can not. The war was brought upon us while Congress was in session without our knowledge. The new and strange doctrine is put forth that Congress has nothing to do with the conduct of the war; that the President is entitled to its uncontrolled manage-

* For full text of the Mexican War speeches from which these condensed excerpts are made, see Cleveland's "Letters and Speeches of Stephens," 302-334.

ment; that we can do nothing but vote men and money to whatever extent his folly and caprice may dictate. Neighbouring States may be subjugated, extensive territories annexed, provincial governments erected, the rights of conscience violated, and the oath of allegiance administered at the point of the bayonet . . . and the Representatives of the people are to say nothing against these extraordinary outrages upon the fixed principles of their Government. For a very little further interference with discussion, Charles X. of France lost his crown, and for a very little greater stretch of royal prerogative, Charles I. of England lost his head. By reflecting on these examples, our Executive, without entertaining apprehensions of a fate similar to either, may yet learn some profitable lessons.

The description in this of the treatment of a conquered people in 1847 fits the case of the South during reconstruction with an aptness calling for remark. Emphasizing the peril of receiving Mexican territory without settling its slavery limits, Stephens said:

Who can sit here and listen to the debates and look unmoved on the prospect before us? . . . They show a fixed determination on the part of the North, which is now in the majority in this House and ever will be hereafter, that, if territory is acquired, the institutions of the South shall be forever excluded from its limits. What is to be the result? Will the South submit? Will the North yield? Or, shall these two great sections be arrayed against each other? If Mexico, "the forbidden fruit," is to be seized at every hazard, I fear that those who control public affairs, in their eager pursuit after the unenviable distinction of despoiling a sister republic, will have the still less enviable glory of looking back upon the shattered and broken fragments of their own confederacy.

The Mexican War resolutions, which were his masterpiece, offered in Congress when the war was at its height and national pride drunk with conquest, were so adroitly framed that the War party could vote neither for nor against them with safety, and refusal to vote at all placed them before the people as unable to say that the war "is not waged with a view to conquest or the dismemberment" of Mexico and that "it is the desire of the United States that hostilities should be terminated upon terms honourable to both parties." In making this issue, he relied upon the wisdom and conscience of the people; he was always ready to trust to that. His course led to the defeat of the War party at the polls and the election of a Whig President and Congress.

In his mention of making Zachary Taylor President, he neglects the "Allison Letter," the Whig platform, on which Taylor was elected. It was composed at the Rush House by Stephens, Toombs, and Crittenden, and despatched to Taylor at Baton Rouge; Taylor published it as a supplement, prepared on more mature reflection, to a letter to Captain Allison in which he had already avowed his position. Stephens's choice of Taylor was based on that great soldier's popularity. His disappointment in Taylor's administration caused him to declare that measures, not men or party, should thenceforth control his course; and he held to this when he refused to support Winfield Scott in 1852, though his friendship for Scott was as sincere and his appreciation of Scott's public services as great as in 1847, when he lent his effective exertions to Scott's investiture with the rank of lieutenant-general.

The "Three-million Bill," appropriating the first purchase-money for Mexican territory, passed in spite of his opposition. California, Utah, and New Mexico were acquired without settlement of their slavery limits, the South, eager for domain, voting with the North when the bill was stripped of the Wilmot Proviso. And now began the Union's death-struggle in the conflict between the sections over slavery in these lands. "It is the beginning of the end of the Union," he wrote.

For defeating the Clayton Compromise, an adjustment measure of 1848, he received doubtful thanks from Southern associates who clung to the belief that this measure was favourable to their section. While campaigning Georgia that fall he nearly paid for his course with his life. He was told that his friend, Judge Cone, had denounced him therefor as a traitor. Stephens said he could not believe this of Cone, but would slap Cone if Cone admitted it. In an amicable conversation with Stephens, Cone repudiated the remark reported of him; Stephens then told Cone what he himself had said, stating it in a way to rob the words of offense; they parted with mutual good feeling. But Cone's political foes taunted him with cowardice, until Cone, in heat and worry, wrote Stephens a demand for retraction. Stephens's amiable reply had not reached Cone before the two men met on the piazza of the Atlanta Hotel, and a personal encounter was precipitated by Cone's calling Stephens "traitor" and getting slapped in return. Cone, large and muscular, slashed at Stephens with a dirk-knife, bore him down, held the knife over his bare throat, shouting: "Retract! or I will cut your d—d throat!" "Never! Cut!" cried Stephens, catching the descending blade in his naked hand. As Cone was wrenching the knife away, the men were separated and Stephens was borne off with many wounds in his body, a severed artery, and his right hand so mutilated that he was never again able to write plainly. Cone's distress was deep; Stephens refused to prosecute him; and friendship was renewed. Stephens's next public appearance was at the head of a Taylor procession in a carriage drawn by men, while the people shouted, "Thank God for little Alex!" However the politicians might berate him, the people loved him from first to last.

He was Clay's coadjutor in securing the Compromise of 1850, which saved the Union then. That it carried its vital principle, non-intervention by Congress with slavery in the Territories, each Territory deciding for herself in framing her State constitution, was chiefly due to Stephens. In one of the most dramatic moments ever felt in the Senate, Webster cast his vote for non-intervention. Stephens's effort to hold both sections to it thereafter was no more inspired by a desire to perpetuate slavery than was Webster's vote; both desired to save the Union. The manifesto of 1851, signed by Clay and forty or more leading men from both Houses and irrespective of party, declaring for non-intervention as a final settlement of slavery agitation in Congress, was drawn up by Stephens. With Webster, he incorporated the same principle in the Whig platform of 1852. The great New Englander's "Union Speech," which closed Faneuil Hall against him, and his speech on the same line in the streets of Boston, all inspired, as Stephens felt, by selfless desire to save the Union, enshrined him in the Georgian's regard. Webster was Stephens's ideal statesman and perfect patriot. The tragedy of Webster's rejection by the Whigs in 1852 he felt keenly, and when he cast his vote for President, it was for Webster though Webster was dead. The card which he mentions as published by himself in the *National Intelligencer*, in 1852, is known in history as the card of the Whig leaders which disrupted the Whig party, defeated Scott and elected Pierce. The "Georgia Platform of 1850," his work, gave Georgia her title of "Union State of the South," and might have given her that of "Empire State," for by it she led sister States into line.

As Douglas's coadjutor, he sustained in the Kansas-Nebraska Bill of 1854 the settlement of 1850, to which "in principle and substance" both great parties stood pledged. He carried that bill through the House by a parliamentary manœuvre as brilliant and audacious as has ever been executed, and more than a match for that by which in 1850 he killed Doty's California resolution and saved the Compromise. The declaration in the bill that the Missouri restriction was void, drew from the abolitionists, the Sumner-Chase manifesto, calling the Missouri Compromise a "sacred pledge," and "solemn compact"; 3,000 New England clergymen, "assuming to speak in the name of Almighty God," as Mr. Stephens said, "joined in the chorus." His speeches on Kansas are clear history, showing, by analysis of the votes of the House, that the North in Congress had repeatedly repudiated the Missouri Compromise and so forced a new compromise or disunion. They reflect his own views that Congressional exclusion of slavery from the Territories, purchased with the blood and money of all the States, was unconstitutional, and that it was the virtual exclusion of the white Southerner, who, to settle in the common domain, must sell or free his slaves, however contrary either course might be to his interest and conscience and to their interest and desire, Negroes, in the patriarchal system of the day, being part of the master's family. He saw in it no mercy to the blacks, as it was their exclusion, emphasized in various States by statutes forbidding free Negroes to settle in them and by other discriminations against black labour. Now, and in later Kansas legislation, he urged on the North in Congress as Webster had urged: Why needlessly irritate the South by Congressional exclusion of slavery from lands where Nature's laws of climate, soil, and population prohibit it? And on the South: Why arouse fresh agitation by asking Congressional protection of slavery where Nature interdicts it? To both: As a practical issue, slavery in the Territories is a dead letter; the individuality of a State, the unity of the Nation, is a living one; and this is in your hands; stand by the Compromise of 1850.

Yet in one section he was reproached for leaning toward abolitionism and in the other condemned for advocating slavery extension. He was battling for a principle that he considered the bed-rock of the Republic's safety. The disposition of African slavery — though he did not minimize its gravity — was an incident as compared with the preservation of this principle, which, if adhered to, would preserve the Union, prevent war and bloodshed, and give the American people, whose wisdom and righteousness he never doubted, that security and peace of mind which is essential to sane deliberation and right enactments. He indicates in his Prison Journal his belief that but for outside agitation which prevented internal discussion, the South would have abolished or reformed the system of wardship in which she held her semi-savages. Before a Southern audience in 1859 he declared that slavery, if not best for both races, ought to be abolished. Yet he did not believe slavery wrong in itself; for the Bible, the religious and moral code of Christendom, upheld it.

A recent charge has been made that as an "emissary of the slave power," he corrupted the Supreme Court, unduly influencing its decision on the Missouri Compromise in the Dred Scott case,* his letters giving advance opinion on the decision being cited as proof. More natural explanation of his forecast is found in his long and close association with the justices, whose opinions he might be expected to know by inference, as well as by entirely proper conference, had there been any great secrecy about them, which there was not. He was not in accord with Chief Justice Taney's pronouncement on the Missouri Compromise, as his declared belief in its constitutionality before Congress, January 17, 1856, and his reference in his Prison Journal show. He did, as he stated in a letter "urge all the influences I could bring to bear" to hasten the action of the court, hoping its effect would be for the peace and preservation of the Union in quieting Southern fears of Squatter Sovereignty and Northern threats to abrogate the Compromise of 1850 by a revival of that of 1820.

When the Constitutional Union movement of 1850 in the South was wrecked in two years on the rock of old and petty party antagonisms, Mr. Stephens's anxiety as to the South's ability to establish separate existence under the leaders then guiding her was increased. His doubts had begun in Congress, where he had seen many

* See Dred Scott Case in Hill's "Decisive Battles of the Law"; — Curtis's "Life and Writings of B. R. Curtis"; — Tyler's "Memoir of Taney"; — Cleveland's "Letters and Speeches of Stephens," 416–31, 489–515.

vital points lost by lack of cohesion, shortness of vision and personal and party ambition in the Southern element; not that the Northern was free from these faults: but the Southern situation was more perilous and Southern need of statesmanship greater. An occasion when this lack of cohesion had profoundly impressed him was in the deadlock over the Speakership in 1849; then, had Southern Whigs and Democrats made common cause, they could, in his belief, have brought Northern associates to satisfactory terms; but, in his words, "the Democrats let go, elected their Speaker, and made all the capital they could out of the divisions in the Whig party." Again, on the "Three-million Bill," had the Southerners refused to vote the purchase-money, they could have prevented the acquisition of the Mexican territory unless Congressional protection of slavery, their constitutional right in the common domain, were pledged for it on the basis of the Missouri Compromise or some other line of division. This was the one occasion when he was willing to make a stand to the point of disunion, believing that without definite settlement then, disunion would result, as it did, from continued agitation in Congress; believing, too, that the settlement could be got and the Union preserved. After voting the money without bargaining for protection, he thought the South had lost her opportunity of power, and would be wise to hold on to non-intervention with all possible tenacity.

As the presidential year, 1860, approached, he saw more and more clearly that non-intervention was the one possible meeting-ground for the sections — all the North would grant, the least the South would accept; less though it was than the South's desire or her constitutional right, it had been attained by a struggle the intensity of which only those who made it could know; and these knew that more could not be won. He saw in Stephen A. Douglas, with his Western and Northern following, the one candidate favourable to the South who could lead the Democrats to victory; and that if Douglas were read out of the party, so would the North and West be. He tried to make Buchanan and Cobb, Buchanan's Cabinet officer and trusted adviser, see this as he saw it. But Buchanan could not forgive Douglas's defection on Kansas and his Squatter Sovereignty heresy; Buchanan wanted Cobb to succeed himself; and further, he was openly and honestly committed to protection. So, Mr. Stephens, foreseeing the end, left Washington. From the steamer, he looked back upon the receding Capitol. "I suppose you are thinking of your return next year as senator," said some one jocosely. He answered with emotion: "I never expect to see Washington again unless I am brought here a prisoner." As a prisoner on parole from Fort Warren, he next saw it.

In holding this sketch closely to the guiding principle of his political course, much that is valuable and picturesque has been omitted or but lightly touched upon. As for instance, his championship of new States. He said in his speech on the Missouri Compromise (December 14, 1854), when refuting the imputation that he was chiefly concerned to increase the number of slave States: "I have voted for the admission of every Northern State since I have occupied a seat upon this floor." His speeches for Minnesota and Oregon defended the alien suffrage clauses in their constitutions on a plea that, no matter what point was involved, called forth his utmost powers — the plea of a State's right under the Constitution of the United States.

He was an indefatigable worker; he performed official, professional, and social duties rigorously; read the papers; conducted a heavy correspondence; was the most approachable of men; people from everywhere wrote or talked to him about the "state of the country" — always with him a live topic, and about their troubles and everything else. He tried to answer every letter, to see every caller. Petitioners, whose own representatives would not heed them, appealed to him in their difficulties; and the patient, painstaking work performed by him in the Departments and elsewhere for people from all sections is almost beyond belief. The number of letters, sympathetic, information-giving, that he wrote with that maimed hand of his is almost incredible. For many of his services, charge was legitimate, but he made none.

It was his rule not to make a dollar beyond his salary when in Washington; and to accept no work at home that might conflict with his duties as a tribune of the people. When he entered Congress he was worth about $14,000; when he left, after sixteen years, about $16,000, the increase due to accumulation of interest. In 1859–61, he made $22,000 at his profession of law. At all times, his expenses were heavy. Simple in his own tastes and economical in expenditures on himself, he spent bountifully on others. He seemed unable to refuse his time or money to any in need. An ingrate would be helped anew. "He had power to forgive as long as any had power to wrong him," wrote "Dick Johnston." "Brother is like a ship otherwise stanch but eaten up by barnacles that he can not dislodge," said Linton. "He is kind to folks that nobody else will be kind to. Mars Alex is kinder to dogs than mos' folks is to folks," said his Negro body-servant. His hospitality at his rooms in Washington and at Liberty Hall was unbounded. Meal hours at the Hall were timed to suit the train hours. Distinguished visitors from everywhere sought the sage's dwelling; so did hungry tramps, black and white. Liberty Hall and its master belonged to the people. On the lot was a Baptist church; after the war, a Methodist church — Bird's Chapel, named in honour of the Rev. Mr. Bird — was added; when his Catholic sister-in-law, the second Mrs. Linton Stephens, visited him, a room in his house was converted into a Catholic chapel. So broad were his religious views that he was several times reported to be an atheist! The depth and intensity of his religious character, as revealed in his Journal, will be a surprise to many who knew him well, for so opposed was he to anything savouring of cant, that he erred, perhaps, on the side of too great reserve. Even in his letters to Linton, when Linton was a boy at school, his words of advice on spiritual matters are given with great hesitation — the hesitation of much reverence rather than of little faith.

He early began to help needy youths to an education. In Crawfordville, when a green country lad would step off the train, look timidly around, and ask: "Whar's the man that educates poor boys?" every finger would point to Liberty Hall. He was always ready to encourage struggling genius. He gave John A. Ward, the sculptor, his first paying commission, with $400 for its execution; he paid $600 to Count Sandors, the refugee artist, and through his influence with the Russian Minister, secured the exile's return to Poland.

During his first session in Congress, he supported the measure for testing the telegraph; and at a later session performed like services for the Atlantic cable. These enterprises, like the railroad and the higher education of women which he had advocated in the Georgia Legislature, were almost laughed out of court as being impractical and visionary. Our present mode of reckoning the Congressional year originated in a suggestion made by him in 1851 that it should begin with noon, March 4, instead of midnight, March 3, which was then the rule. His connection with one of our most useful branches of Government service is not a familiar fact, yet its nature was such that he may be justly called the Father of the Weather Bureau. This letter by him to F. G. Arnold, of the Treasury, written July 2, 1879, relates some interesting circumstances in the early history of the Bureau:

Your letter of Saturday was received this morning. I had not forgotten my promise to give you some points in my memory connected with the origin of our system of Weather Reports, from which sprang the present Signal Service Bureau. In the winter of 1853–4, I became acquainted with Mr. Espy, then styled the "Storm King." We boarded at the same house, kept by Mrs. Duncan. He was employed in the Meteorological Department of the Navy. As I took great interest in matters meteorological, we were soon well acquainted. His "Philosophy of Storms" was put into my hand by him, and I was informed that he had some years before submitted a paper embodying the same principles to an American association of scientists at New Haven, but it met with no favour. He submitted a similar paper to the Royal Society of London with like results, and then to the French Academy of Sciences at Paris, where it was referred to a committee consisting of MM. Arago, Pouillet, and Babinet. Their report concluded:

Mr. Espy's communication contains a great number of well-observed and well-described facts. His theory in the present state of science alone accounts for the phenomena, and when completed, as he intends, by a study of the action of electricity when it intervenes, will leave nothing to be desired. In a word, for physical geography, agriculture, navigation and meteorology, it gives us new explanations, indications useful for ulterior researches; and redresses many accredited errors. The Committee expresses then the wish that Mr. Espy should be placed by the Government of the United States in a position to continue his important investigations, and to complete his theory already so remarkable.

After this recommendation, he was placed in the office he held when I became acquainted with him. So satisfied was I with the correctness of his theory and the principles therein announced touching the formation of rainclouds, as well as great storms and tornadoes, that I urged immediate utilization. At that time the facts on which his theory rested, and, according to suggestion, on which their truth was to be established, were being collected by agents in different parts of the country, who sent monthly the result of their daily observations to him, which he embodied in an annual report to Congress. I urged the importance of daily telegraph announcements from all parts of the country. His reply was, want of money: his appropriation was only $2,000 per annum. I suggested that we go to the *National Intelligencer* and the *Union* and get them to publish short weather reports from distant points of the country as an item of news without charge. Messrs. Gales and Seaton, and Mr. Ritchie readily assented. A request to the telegraph companies to send such short messages without charge was granted. In this way, I think, the first telegraph weather reports were ever made or announced in this or any other country. The first appeared, as well as I can recollect, in the early summer of 1854. They were very meagre, simply announcing from New Orleans, Chicago, Boston, and other points, the course of the wind, state of the thermometer, and whether clear, rainy, snowing, cloudy, etc. Mr. Espy continued in his position as long as I remained in Congress. The appropriation for his salary was often assailed, but a few of us were able to save it.

He was a Pennsylvanian, and by profession a schoolmaster. He was an original thinker, but not a lucid speaker. Professor Henry [Secretary of the Smithsonian Institution] was one of the very few scientists of this country who entertained favourable views of his theory. The fashion was to snub him utterly with his entire system of philosophy. When we see the advantages arising from its developments and applications to commerce, navigation, and agriculture, in the saving of thousands of lives and millions of dollars' worth of property, is it assuming too much to say that the humble schoolmaster, comparatively unknown in his generation, will, at no distant day, be regarded as one of the greatest benefactors of mankind?

The force which Mr. Stephens made of his life is remarkable when we consider the difficulties he overcame. It is doubtful if any other man has achieved as striking eminence against as heavy odds. In addition to early orphanage and poverty, he was handicapped by a constitution so frail that his continued existence was a miracle. He never knew a well hour in his life. "He never looked as if he had two weeks' purchase on life," said Toombs. R. M. Johnston, a child at the time, saw him first when he was twenty-one: "His form was the most slight and slender I had ever seen; his chestnut hair was brushed away from a thin white brow and bloodless cheeks. The child looking at him felt sorry for another child." "Sonny, get up and give the gentleman a seat," his landlady at Charleston admonished him in 1839, when he was a delegate to the Southern Commercial Convention, where he crossed swords with Hayne, Hamilton, and Preston; with his "fondness for the humorous," he rose smilingly while his companions laughed. His weight was rarely over a hundred pounds and usually less.

In his earlier campaigns, he was often mistaken for a boy. But woe to the opponent who rated him by his size! Colquitt, judge and senator, and leading speaker and debater of the State, hearing how others had gone down before young Stephens, remarked casually that his "hands itched to get hold of him." When Stephens, with courtesy, humour, and facts (a store of which he always kept handy) demolished this Goliath, some wag in the crowd cried: "Your hands itch to let him go, Judge, don't they?" When he swept through Georgia like a cyclone, in 1855, in his campaign against the Know-nothing or American party with its "un-American secret-order organization" and "unconstitutional proscription of Catholics and foreigners," his hearers would exclaim, "He is nothing but lungs and brain!" Slight as he was in body, so forceful and effective were his denunciations that the party, or secret order, assailed, threatened to silence him by violence if he did not moderate his tone.

The *Pennsylvanian*, in 1854, when commenting on his Kansas-Nebraska speech and on him as "considered by many the ablest member of the House," who could "hold the congregated talent of the country spellbound for hours," describes his fragile appearance, and adds: "But the whole man is charged with the electricity of intellect — a touch would bring forth the divine spark." The Washington letter in the Charleston *Courier*, January 7, 1857, gives this dramatic picture of an hour in the House, with Stephens the figure dominant:

It had been rumoured throughout the city — told in drawing rooms, private parlours, and public saloons — that "Stephens of Georgia" was to speak on Tuesday. At an early hour the galleries filled to overflowing with the families of our distinguished statesmen, members of foreign legations, dashing belles, with a sprinkling here and there of our best residents. As we passed through the lobbies, we were struck with the deep and reverential quiet that pervaded the House. Where was the power that subdued the confusion of this always riotous assembly? Listening faces were turned toward a shrunken and emaciated figure, the shoulders contracted and drawn in, the face the colour of ashes. There was something grand in the spectacle of this shadowy figure binding up the very breath of the House! The speaker seemed the mere organ of some hidden power. He had little variety of gesture, and what he used seemed perfectly unstudied. He was so absorbed in his subject as to be unconscious that he had feet or hands to manage. His unearthly face seemed to brighten into fuller and ghostlier meaning; his eye shone like a sunken pit of fire suddenly disclosed; his attenuated form seemed to dilate to his dilating soul; his voice seemed exalted to a trumpet tone.

A picture by another writer:

A deathlike silence reigns over the Hall, broken only by the reverberating tones of the speaker's voice. Senators have deserted the other wing of the Capitol and are sitting as under a spell they cannot break. Mr. Speaker has thrown down his hammer.

But Stephens did not strive after oratory; in his belief, eloquence was a dangerous power, to be kept well in hand; it was the incident of his speeches; his first aim was to convince by fact and argument and not by a play upon the emotions. He never once made an appeal to sectional passions. It was the fashion to speak of him as "intellect incarnate" and a "bodiless brain." He could command always, it is said, the rapt attention of the House. He was an adviser of great leaders, a counsellor of presidents. Yet this is the man whom the Confederate Senate so humiliated on one occasion by a refusal to hear him speak, that he asked to resign his position as its presiding officer and the Vice-President of the Confederacy. He was a consummate parliamentarian; any one of the great games of state he played on the floor of the House would make a thrilling chapter. He was a bold and finished diplomat, an able and philosophical statesman. It is common for those who knew him to say, "He was a seer." His faculty of foresight seemed intuitive, mystical. This prophetic quality was in part the effect of illness upon his peculiar temperament, the result of protracted periods of physical quiescence and abnormal thought activity when, with attention focussed upon the problems of public life, he read the future by the past and by his knowledge of the minds of men. He was ambitious, but ambition was so slight a force in his character when compared with the grand passion of his life — love of country — that its voice was not even heard when patriotism spoke.

Socially, he was a man of much charm and magnetism. We wish he had left those "Congressional Reminiscences" with full record of the "Attic nights" at Mrs. Carter's, where he foregathered with a "mess" of which Justices Taney, Story, McLean, and McKinley, of the Supreme Court, and Jacob Collamer, of the House, were members; and of evenings at the Rush House where he lived with Toombs and Crittenden; and of those Sunday dinners at Sullivan's — Stephens objected that they were on Sunday, "but his company is generally select" — with Clay, Webster, Cobb, Hale, Stephens, Toombs, and Crittenden around the board. Among his papers are gilt-edged notes in Webster's hand relating to hospitalities between him and "Mr. Stephens and Mr. Toombs," with such other good companies present that we would like to play eavesdropper to their table-talk.

Stephens was popular in Government circles, where his labours to produce harmony between sectional factions were appreciated with some warmth even by those who knew they were vain and who helped to make them so. On his retirement from Congress, he was tendered the extraordinary compliment of a public dinner, both House and Senate to attend, irrespective of party, and headed by their presiding officers, the Vice-President and the Speaker. He was unable to accept it, but he was none the less pleased at the evidence of kind feeling.

The Speakership was more than once within his grasp. Toombs wrote, November 18, 1857:

I see a good deal about your running for Speaker. If you would accept the offer, I would like to know. I should very much like to see you in the Chair, especially as against Orr, who has conceived that what is called the ultraism of Carolina is obnoxious to the Nation.

Stephens wrote Linton, December 1, 1857:

Orr will be Speaker. I have forbidden the use of my name. I am for organizing the House with as much harmony as possible.

His reason in part for steadfast refusal when urged to stand for the Presidency was fear lest his physical strength was unequal to the canvass required and the duties which the position involved. He had some novel views of the office and its seeking. In 1858, disgusted over the mischievous scramble for the candidacy in an hour of imminent national peril, he exclaimed: "I had as lief be put on a list of suspected horse-thieves as in the number of those aspiring to the Presidency!" he had told a friend so to declare him. He was just back from a call on Buchanan:

> Perhaps Old Buck thought I was an insidious rival, slyly worming myself into his shoes. If so, alas, poor old fellow! how his views would change did he but know how I pitied him, as I looked upon him, with all his power!

He said in 1860:

> What amazes me in Douglas is his desire to be President. I have sometimes asked him what he desired the office for. It has never added to the reputation of a single man. You may look over the list: which made any reputation after becoming President? Four or eight years is too short a time to pursue a policy which will give this. If I had loved office, I would have continued in the House; I should be able to make a reputation faster in that place than in the other.

He refused to be put in nomination at Charleston in 1860 for President of the United States. At Montgomery, he declined to be considered for President of the Confederacy, and advised that it was not fitting for its first office to be conferred on him in preference to a leader of the secession movement which had created the new Government. The second position he accepted in the interests of harmony between the new Government and the anti-secession sentiment which he had led; and for other reasons, fully set forth in his Prison Journal.

He was about to become President, it seemed, in the order of succession, when, on several occasions, Mr. Davis was so ill that death was expected. In his sane view of the situation as expressed in a private letter, ambition played no part:

I should regard the President's death as the greatest possible calamity. . . . The general and profound shock would of itself gender and increase that spirit of dissension and faction, which at all times exists in a country situated as ours is. With us, it would almost certainly manifest itself in a formidable way from the fact that a large number of prominent and active men, who would probably soon form a party for concert of action, really and honestly distrust my ability to conduct affairs successfully. To what extent their demonstrations might go, I cannot conjecture; but far enough to cripple my efforts on any line of policy I might adopt, even assuming it might be for the best. The unhinging, upturning, and unsettling of things so little settled at present, the greater confounding of things even now confused, would render it one of the greatest calamities that could befall us, to say nothing of the correctness of the views of those who entertain such serious distrust of my ability to direct affairs. On that point, I assure you, I have the strongest distrust of myself.

While many would have welcomed his rule as leading to peace, a number believed his views inimical to Confederate success, and anonymous warnings were sent him that, if Davis died, he must resign or be assassinated. Such warnings or threats reached him on other occasions, accompanied with the charge of treachery to the Confederacy.

From this discussion of Mr. Stephens's views on office, we revert to the thread of our story with an extract from his last speech in Congress before the war and from his "Farewell Speech" in Augusta:

The immense territory to the West has to be peopled. It is now peopling; new States are fast springing up.

This is the sixteenth session I have been here, and within that brief space, we have added six States to the Union — lacking but one of being more than half of the original thirteen. Upward of twelve hundred thousand square miles of territory — a much larger area than was possessed by the whole United States at the time of the treaty of peace in 1783 — have been added. This progress is not to be arrested. There are persons now living who will see over a hundred million human beings within the present boundaries, to say nothing of future extensions, and perhaps double the number of States. For myself, I say to you, my Southern colleagues on this floor, that I do not apprehend any danger to our constitutional rights from the bare fact of increasing the number of States with institutions dissimilar to ours. The whole governmental fabric of the United States is based upon the idea of dissimilarity in the institutions of its respective members. Principles, not numbers, are our protection. By our system, each State, however great the number, has the absolute right to regulate all her internal affairs as she pleases, subject only to her obligations under the Constitution. Such is the theory of our machinery of self-government by the people. This is the great novelty of our peculiar system. It is for us and those who come after us to determine whether this grand experimental problem shall be worked out, not by quarrelling amongst ourselves, not by doing injustice to any, not by keeping out any particular class of States; but by each State remaining a separate and distinct organization within itself — all bound together for general objects under a common Federal head; as it were, a wheel within a wheel.*

At Augusta, July 2, 1859:

I deem it my duty to repeat what I said in 1850: Whatever abstract rights of expansion we may have secured

* The full text of the speech, from which this condensed excerpt is taken, may be found in Cleveland's "Letters and Speeches of Stephens," pp. 621-37.

in the settlement of that policy [non-intervention], you may not expect to see many of the Territories come into the Union as slave States unless we have an increase of African stock. The law of population will prevent. It is in full view of this, that I have stated that, if the present basis of settlement between the sections of the Union be adhered to, you have nothing to fear for your safety or security. For on these principles, one slave State by herself would be perfectly secure against encroachment on her domestic policy though all the rest were free.*

We catch, in these addresses, his idea of non-intervention as a policy whereby to make safe and peaceful end of the struggle between the sections, begun with the Union, to preserve their respective balances of power in Congress by equality in numbers, a struggle lost to the South with the admission of California. His purpose to quiet the South, to reassure her on the dangers of expansion, and at the same time to warn her as to her one path of safety, is plain; as is his intent to put the North on her Constitutional honour, now that numbers gave her power to oppress and harass her sister section who, as Thomas Jefferson described it, "had the wolf [slavery] by the ears and could neither safely hold him nor safely let him go." His Northern critics quoted his Augusta speech as proof that he advocated revival of the slave-trade with Africa; while his Southern critics began to ask anew if he was not unsound on abolition because he said this: "If slavery, as it exists with us, is not best, or cannot be made the best, for both races — the African as well as his master — it ought to be abolished."

His purpose when he left Washington in 1859 was

* The full text of Mr. Stephens's "Farewell Speech," from which this condensed excerpt is made, may be found in Cleveland's "Letters and Speeches of Stephens," pp. 637-51.

permanent retirement to private life. But the country's troubles drew him again into politics, and in 1860 we find him an Elector on the Douglas-Johnson ticket, campaigning Georgia for the "principles of 1850" and the Union. A letter of 1860, no day date, seems to have been hastily scrawled on the eve of his Union speech of Sept. 1, 1860, in Augusta, the John Forsyth mentioned being the publicist of that name:

Dear Brother: I am about to start to Augusta, all packed and ready to go. I feel sad, sad. I enclose a clip from John Forsyth's pen. When he, after his denunciations of disunionists in the summer, takes this position, what may be expected of others? This was sent me by Herring, of Atlanta, who has turned secessionist. We must do the best we can for the body politic — that is all. What is to be the result of the present malady or epidemic among our people, I don't know. But I am resolved to do the best I can for them. That is all I can do. The balance is with them and with God. Good-bye. Affectionately,

ALEX.

The severity of the malady is reflected in this, written by J. A. Hambleton, Atlanta, Ga., Oct. 25, to Mr. Stephens:

Mr. Toombs has just delivered a speech of the most abusive and inflammatory character of Judge Douglas. He spoke like a madman and acted like a fanatic. He told his hearers that Douglas is an incendiary and should not be permitted to speak here. The effect, I fear, will be that Douglas will be grossly insulted, a result that would be more than mortifying to me and to many, and hazardous to the aggressors. I sincerely hope you will be present, as, if there is a plan to insult Douglas, your presence will prevent its being carried out. I want you to introduce Douglas.

In his Augusta speech, Mr. Stephens condemned the action of those members of the Charleston Convention who withdrew from it because they failed to carry their demand for a plank in the party platform calling for Congressional protection of slavery in the Territories; and he made that prophecy for which some called him "insane":

I do not mean to say that the Secession movement at Charleston was a disunionist movement, or intended as such by all who joined in it, but I do mean to say that the movement tends to disunion, to civil strife; may lead to it, and most probably will, unless arrested by the virtue, intelligence and patriotism of the people. The signs of the time portend evil. You need not be surprised to see these States, now so peaceful, contented, prosperous, and happy, embroiled in civil war in less than twelve months.

The split in the Democratic party at Charleston and Baltimore, which put three candidates in the field against Lincoln, elected Lincoln on a platform declaring against Government toleration, in any form, of slavery in the Territories. South Carolina promptly seceded. Several States followed her. Georgia, trembling on the brink, was held back by Stephens as long as he had power to hold her. In his speech before her Legislature, Nov. 14, 1860, he pleaded eloquently for peace and the Union:

My object is not to stir up strife but to allay it. . . . It is said Mr. Lincoln's policy and principles are against the Constitution, and that if he carries them out, it will be destructive of our rights. The President is no emperor, no dictator. He can do nothing unless he is backed by Congress. The House is largely against him. In the Senate, he will also be powerless; there will be a majority of four against him. . . .

I am not of those who believe the Union has been a

curse. True men, men of integrity, entertain different views. I do not question their right; I would not impugn their motive. Nor will I undertake to say that this Government of our fathers is perfect, but that this Government of our fathers, with all its defects, comes nearer the objects of all good governments than any other on the face of the earth, is my settled conviction. The influence of the Government on us is like that of the atmosphere. Its benefits are so silent and unseen that they are seldom thought of or appreciated. . . .

Northern States have violated their plighted faith. What ought we to do? By the law of nations, you have a right to demand the carrying out of this article of agreement [Constitutional pledge for return of fugitive slaves], and in case it be not done, we would have the right to commit acts of reprisal on these faithless governments, and seize on their property or that of their citizens whereever found. The States of the Union stand upon the same footing with each other as foreign nations in this respect. But by the law of nations, we are equally bound, before proceeding to violent measures, to set forth our grievances before the offending governments, to give them an opportunity to redress the wrong. Let your Committee on the State of the Republic make out a bill of grievances; let it be sent by the Governor to these faithless States; and if reason and argument shall be tried in vain — if all shall fail — I would be for retaliatory measures. I advise the calling of a convention with the earnest desire to preserve peace. I am for exhausting all that patriotism demands before taking the last step.*

Toombs's speech the night before was as impassioned a plea for secession as Stephens's was an earnest argument against it. Yet after Stephens's speech, Toombs, who had bombarded it with interruptions, proposed

* For the full text of Mr. Stephens's "Union Speech," from which this condensed excerpt is made, see Cleveland's "Letters and Speeches of Stephens," pp. 694-713.

"Three cheers for Stephens!" "one of the brightest intellects and purest patriots that lives!" "That was well done," said some one to Toombs. "I always try to behave myself at a funeral," replied Toombs. A restraint grew up between the friends which was only dissipated when they met in the Confederate Congress at Montgomery. In his battle for the Union, Stephens, with Herschel V. Johnson and Benjamin H. Hill, led a forlorn hope against Toombs, the Cobb brothers, Governor Joe Brown, and many other men of might, who headed the swelling ranks of the secessionists. An idea expressed by Tom Cobb, "We can make better terms out of the Union than in it," turned the scale of fate, as Mr. Stephens believed. Boykin in his "Memorial" says the "voice and influence" of Howell Cobb caused Georgia to secede; and, had she declined to secede, "the other States would not have seceded." It has often been said that but for Cobb, Stephens could have kept Georgia in the Union.

Mr. Stephens's next Union speech was before the Georgia Secession Convention; in this he said:

> I have looked, and do look, upon our present Government as the best in the world. I have ever believed and do now believe that it is to the best interest of all the States to remain united under the Constitution. My judgment is against secession. We should not take this extreme step before some positive aggression upon our rights by the General Government, which may never occur; or before failure, after every effort made, to get a faithful performance on the part of those States which now stand so derelict to their plighted faith.

He received many letters from all parts of the country applauding his Union speech of November. A number of leading Northern and Western men, with whom he had been associated in Congress, approved his suggestion of remonstrance with the derelict States, and pledged their influence with their own States for a favourable hearing; some were already at work with their governors and legislatures. "All that the South has to do," wrote one, "is to appeal from the North drunk with fanaticism to the North sobered at the prospect of the dissolution of the Union." "All we ask of our Southern friends," wrote ex-Governor McClelland of Michigan, "is patience; and we hope they will forbear because we are truly suffering as much if not more than they are. The Constitutional men of the South have really more true friends in the North to-day, who understand and appreciate their grievances, than ever before, because our people did not until recently direct their attention to the subject, nor have very many of them yet had time to examine it in all its bearings." These letters gave Mr. Stephens a reasonable basis, if he had had no other, for his belief at this time, which was maintained during the war, that there was a hope for peaceful settlement through an alignment in common phalanx of the strict constructionists of the Constitution, North and South, and that Southern diplomacy should be directed toward the establishment of such an alignment.

Lincoln wrote to him for a copy of the Union Speech. In replying, Mr. Stephens said: "The country is in great peril, and no man ever had heavier or greater responsibilities resting upon him than you have in the present momentous crisis." This drew forth Lincoln's historic response, marked "For your eye only," an injunction observed by Stephens until after Lincoln's death and his own return from Fort Warren.

I fully appreciate the present peril the country is in, and the weight of the responsibility on me. Do the people of the South really entertain fears that a Republican administration would *directly or indirectly* interfere with their slaves? If they do, I wish to assure you, as once a friend, and still, I hope, not an enemy, that there is no cause for such fears. The South would be in no more danger in this respect than it was in the days of Washington. I suppose, however, this does not meet the case. You think slavery right and ought to be extended; while we think it is wrong and ought to be restricted. That, I suppose, is the rub. It certainly is the only substantial difference between us.

These sentences are from Mr. Stephens's lengthy reply, the main ideas of which, on slavery, are reiterated in the Journal:

Personally, I am not your enemy — far from it; and however widely we may differ politically, yet I trust we both have an earnest desire to preserve and maintain the Union. . . . When men come under the influence of fanaticism, there is no telling where their impulses or passions may drive them. This is what creates our discontent and apprehensions, not unreasonable when we see . . . such reckless exhibitions of madness as the John Brown raid into Virginia, which has received so much sympathy from many, and no open condemnation from any of the leading members of the dominant party. . . . In addressing you thus, I would have you understand me as being not a personal enemy, but as one who would have you do what you can to save our common country. A word fitly spoken by you now would be like "apples of gold in pictures of silver."

After the war, when Lincoln's picture was unveiled in Congress, and Stephens spoke as the South's representative, he said of his early connection with Lincoln:

I knew Mr. Lincoln well. We met in the House in December, 1847. We were together during the Thirtieth Congress. I was as intimate with him as with any other man of that Congress except perhaps one. That exception was my colleague, Mr. Toombs. Mr. Lincoln was warm-hearted; he was generous; he was magnanimous; he was most truly "with malice toward none, with charity for all."

Lincoln and Stephens had much in common. The boyhood of each had been a struggle with poverty; each had conned his lessons by a pine-knot fire. Both were lawyers. In Congress, both were Whigs and members of the same political club; they acted together on the Mexican War and in electing Taylor. Lincoln's early impression of Stephens appears in a letter to his law partner, Feb. 2, 1843: "I take up my pen to tell you that Mr. Stephens, of Georgia, a little slim pale-faced consumptive man, has just concluded the very best speech of an hour's length I ever heard. My old withered dry eyes are full of tears yet."

In his Journal, Mr. Stephens denies the truth of the report that Lincoln invited him to a position in his Cabinet. Lincoln seems to have considered doing so. Oberholtzer says in his "Life of Lincoln": "He wished to have the various sections represented. Montgomery Blair was taken from Maryland, after seriously discussing the availability of Alexander H. Stephens of Georgia." For Mr. Stephens's opinion of Lincoln's political course in the sixties, the reader is referred to that part of his "War Between the States" in which he fully reviews it and says: "Mr. Lincoln was kind-hearted (no man I ever knew was more so) but the same was true of Julius Cæsar"; "I do not think he intended to overthrow the

Institutions of the country. I do not think he understood them or the tendencies of his acts upon them. The Union, with him, in sentiment rose to the sublimity of a religious mysticism, while his ideas of its structure and formation, in logic, rested upon nothing but the subtleties of a sophism!" These strictures relate to Lincoln's encroachments on the Constitution.

Georgia seceded, and sent Stephens as delegate to the Provisional Congress of the Confederacy at Montgomery, first complying with the condition he required, that she should instruct her delegates to demand that any new government formed should be modelled on the old one. His object was to preserve to the States the American principles of self-government — the Constitution. He also plainly had in mind a reunion of the States under the old bond or the new. With like principles and machinery of government, the two confederacies would have no wide political chasm to cross for fusion — to which end he doubtless meant to direct his diplomatic energies. Should the new Constitution improve on the old, so much the better would be the chances for the Confederacy to become the absorbing Government.

His industry, knowledge of government, and parliamentary experience enabled him to be of great service in organizing the new republic. "The Rules for the Government of the Congress" was his work, and so to a large degree was the framing of the Confederate Constitution. A prohibition, in the latter instrument, of the slave-trade with Africa, is in itself refutation of the charge that he advocated revival of this trade. On February 11, his forty-ninth birthday, he was sworn in as Vice-President of the Confederacy. A week later, Jefferson Davis was inaugurated as President. The first mention of Mr. Davis in Stephens's letters is the following, written by Stephens when Chairman of the House Committee of Conference on the Kansas Bill:

May 1, 1858. — Every Southern Senator voted for it. Jefferson Davis had himself sent for to record his vote. He is in very bad health, has been extremely ill. I took the paper to him and got his approval of it before I would agree to report it. This is the way I worked the matter with all the leading men of the South.

And it was a tremendous labour, that of getting these men "present and ready to sustain it," as is shown in his notes of that time, with their refrain: "My heart is sad — sad. If we should separate, what is to become of us? Have we any future but miserable petty squabbles?" He and Davis were not usually in such accord as on this occasion. Davis came into Congress as a Democrat when Mr. Stephens was a Whig; Davis was for Polk, for the Mexican War, against Taylor, against the Compromise of 1850, and for Congressional protection of slavery in the Territories. The new plank in the Democrat platform which caused the "burst-up" at Charleston was, in substance, two of a series of resolutions offered by Davis, Feb. 2, 1860, in the Senate. This "plank" brought on the war, as Stephens felt. In character and temperament, the two men were as wide apart as in political views. Davis's education, of scholarly finish, had come to him without struggle; he was of aristocratic temper and bearing; a West Pointer and a stickler for military form and order. Stephens prided himself on being of the people; and as a lawyer, he was jealous for the civic power in any test between that and martial law.

As officers of the Confederacy, their early relations were harmonious. Davis sent for Stephens and consulted him to a considerable degree. In letters to Linton, Stephens soon expresses uneasiness about the "wisdom and discretion of the appointing power"; he presently mentions that the War Department "is badly managed. The Secretary is very inefficient. There were twenty thousand stand of arms offered us for sale. He postponed it until after the fall of Sumter; then tried to get them, but it was too late." This Cabinet officer, L. P. Walker, is he who made the unfortunate remark in a public speech after the fall of Sumter, that the Confederate flag should soon fly "over the Capitol at Washington" and "over Faneuil Hall itself," a boast not warranted by the purpose of the Confederacy, and one which did much to fan unfriendly feelings at the North.

Stephens's evident desire was to be useful in economics and diplomacy, to which fields his gifts and training fitted, and his physical infirmity limited him. His letters reflect his sharp sense of secession's business side, which "calls for great patience and forbearance by the people in sustaining the inconveniences and burdens incident to a change of government — derangement of mails and commerce, increase of taxes, and a thousand things not before thought of." "Independence will cost money as well as blood," he says, and is concerned as to how the people will meet the prosaic details of sacrifice. He promptly laid before the Government a plan by which, as he conceived, a sound basis of credit might be established through judicious employment of the South's staple — that King Cotton in whose powers her leaders had greatly confided when contemplating secession. This plan, as outlined in a speech at Crawfordville,

Nov. 1, 1862, his first on the subject which he allowed to be published, was as follows:

> I was in favour of the Government's taking all the cotton that would be subscribed for eight-per-cent. bonds at ten cents a pound. Two million bales of last year's crop might have been counted on. This would have cost the Government a hundred million bonds. With this cotton in hand and pledged, any number, short of fifty, of the best ironclad steamers could have been contracted for and built in Europe — steamers at two millions each could have been procured. Thirty millions would have got fifteen. Five might have been ready by the first of January last to open one of our blockaded ports. Three could have been left to keep the port open while two convoyed the cotton across if necessary. Thus, the debt could have been paid with cotton at a much higher price than it cost, and a channel of trade kept open until others could have been built and paid for in the same way. At less than one month's present expenditure on our army, our coast might have been cleared. Besides this, at least two million more bales of the old crop might have been counted on; this, with the other, making a debt in round numbers to the planters of $200,000,000. But this cotton held in Europe until the price shall be fifty cents a pound [it went higher] would constitute a fund of at least one billion dollars, which would not only have kept our finances in sound condition, but the clear profit of $800,000,000 would have met the entire expenses of the war for years to come.

Dr. Craven, in his "Prison Life of Jefferson Davis," reports Mr. Davis as describing a plan like this, which was urged on Mr. Memminger, by whom is not stated, and which Mr. Davis "privately approved but had not time to study and take the responsibility of directing until too late"; Davis said it would have maintained Southern credit, which "in itself would have insured victory." In her "Memoir" of her husband, Mrs. Davis makes slighting allusion to some such plan, as impractical and visionary and advised by critics of the Administration.

Mr. Memminger wrote Mr. Stephens, Sept. 17, 1867:

The scheme, as I understood it, never proposed a purchase of cotton with bonds but with money, or Confederate currency, which was then money. I enclose you a circular written at the time, which will put you in possession of the views then entertained. As for the notion since promulgated, of shipping cotton to England early in the war and holding it there as the basis of credit, that is completely negatived, as you know, by the fact that at the early stage of the war, no one expected the blockade or the war to last more than a year.

Mr. Stephens's letters and speeches of 1860-61 show that he feared a long war.

The circular says of the scheme:

The issue is to be paid in treasury notes, and therefore, if we put aside for the present the many and serious objections to the possession, transportation, and management of the crop by the Government, it becomes simply a question of amount.

Which amount was declared too large a burden for a new government "engaged in a gigantic war." The scheme was treated as a discrimination in favour of cotton planters. By the Loan or Memminger plan, the planter bound himself to pay into the Treasury a part of the proceeds from his cotton sales in exchange for interest-bearing bonds. Had Toombs been as careful as Stephens in preserving letters, we might reproduce the documents from Stephens which drew this from Toombs, June 21, 1861, when Secretary of State:

Dear Stephens: The Maryland Commissioners submitted nothing except to urge us to cross the Potomac as soon as possible with an army in order that they may join us. There is nothing in Harper's Ferry evacuation, except Johnston got strong enough to take the field and march forward to Martinsburg to meet the enemy rather than have leisurely to concentrate on him at the Ferry.

It is impossible to overestimate the importance of your present duty in procuring the Cotton Loan. I fear Tom Cobb got weary in well-doing too soon, and that interest may flag. Print your speeches, get the newspapers in Georgia to write on the subject and send to other States, chide the Southwest (Ala., Miss. and La.) for their tardiness. If we do not do this, the Loan will flag, and if that flags we shall see the worst times we have seen yet. With the Loan, we can do anything in time; without it, nothing. Push it to the last extremity. We have bought arms in Europe and are daily expecting them; the purchases were wholly below our wants from lack of comprehension in the War Department. Arrangements are enlarged, but it will take time to perfect them. Davis works slowly, too slowly for the crisis.

The scheme of taking the cotton at ten cents per pound won't do. We wish to borrow cotton or its proceeds, not to buy it. If it falls, it seems planters want to put the fall on the country. What sort of financial aid is that? If it were to happen that we could not get off the cotton, we would be utterly prostrated by flooding the country with credits we could not redeem, and for a commodity we could neither sell nor consume. It would be fatal to the whole scheme. I would rather condemn it to public use. I have taken up your letters and answered them as the items presented, and this letter therefore is without continuity of thought or subject.

I heard from England and France the twenty-first May. Both are very friendly, assure us they will buy our cotton this fall at all hazards, will observe strict neutrality for the present and acknowledge us formally as soon as either time or our decided success gives assurance of our power to maintain ourselves.

I think there will be very important developments in a few days at Philippi, Harper's Ferry, and Manassas Junction. It is impossible not to have a fight at one or all in a week. Virginia unanimously accepted the permanent Constitution yesterday, and is now in good.

Yours,

R. Toombs.

The Stephens plan seems to have received less attention from the Confederate Government than was its due by reason of authorship and merit. The rush and confusion of the times may have been partly responsible. Latter-day historians incline to treat it as lightly as Mrs. Davis does, yet Mr. Davis, according to Dr. Craven, believed it practical and that it would have "insured victory."

Mr. Stephens's views on other concurrent matters, as on this and on a somewhat similar use of tobacco which he suggested, are not those of the mere theorist and malcontent which he is often carelessly asserted to have been. As an example of the hard common sense he applied to business details of war, the following extract is made from a friendly letter, written by him, April 29, 1864, to Seddon, Confederate Secretary of War, on the conditions resulting from loss of public confidence in Confederate credit, and the consequent imperative necessity for honest and intelligent handling of the tithes, the army's one source of supply:

The greatest danger ahead is ultimate failure of subsistance. Our present reliance is upon our agricultural productions and not upon the credit of the Government. The tax in kind is the surest hope; that is abundant if properly managed. But under present management, it is wasting the substance of the country without supplying the army. In this country, small and poor as it is, thousands of bushels of tithe corn and a great amount of forage have been fed to poor cattle bought up in February and March for beef, while the tithe pork and bacon were uncollected. Had this pork and bacon been used now, the grasses of summer would fatten beef to be used then. This is a small matter, but what is being done here is doubtless being done elsewhere. Five thousand bushels of tithe corn just above me have been turned over to a party to distil into whisky, right on the railroad and in two days' transportation of Johnston's army. For this corn, he was to deliver five thousand gallons of whisky! One bushel, it is said, will make two gallons in winter, and the slops from the stills will fatten as much pork as the corn would. This contract is a small affair compared with others on the same principles. It is to all such contracts I call your attention. The army can do better without whiskey than bread; and if we have corn enough to put any into whiskey it ought to be in sections remote from railroads. So with all corn or forage fed to cattle and hogs for the army. The provision crop last year was abundant for the army and people at home this year if economically used. But I fear it will not be next year. The policy of impressing provisions without paying market price will greatly lessen production. Production will be greatly lessened by another cause — the general disarrangement of labour under the last military act.*

Under the uncertainty created by this act, which virtually conscripted the whole white male population and necessitated details from the army for agricultural and other domestic avocations, Mr. Stephens said, many persons were failing to plant usual crops; many plantations were being abandoned to Negroes with no white manager in charge; and the bare journeyings of men

* For full text ot letter from which this condensed excerpt is taken, see Cleveland's "Letters and Speeches of Stephens," pp. 786-90.

back and forth between home and camp to get papers made out or visaed would entail neglect of farm work. At the date of this letter, more men were in the army than the Government could arm or support. "The tithe," Mr. Stephens urges, "should be husbanded and guarded as gold; not a grain of corn or blade of grass should be wasted, lost, or misapplied." These are the reflections of an economist troubled by evil conditions and anxious for their remedy. In that awful time of starvation, war, and death, graft took as little heed as now of public peril and privation if only it might make profit for itself; among appointees who collected and distributed the tithes, some handled the precious grain and meat dishonestly, and some used it wastefully. In his address of March 16, 1864, before the Georgia Legislature, Mr. Stephens said:

Upon a moderate estimate, one within reasonable bounds, the tithes of wheat and corn for last year were not less, in the States east of the Mississippi (to say nothing of the other side), than eighteen million bushels. Kentucky and Tennessee are not included in this estimate. This would bread an army of five hundred thousand men and one hundred thousand horses for twelve months, and leave a considerable margin for waste or loss. This we have without buying or impressing a bushel or pound. Nor need a bushel be lost for want of transportation from points distant from railroads; it could be fed to animals, put into beef and pork. The tithe of meat for the last year will supply the army for at least six months. All that is wanting is men of business capacity, honesty, economy and industry in the management and control of that department.

Mr. Stephens's vital disagreement with the administration was based on a principle that was the "lode-star," as he says, of his political life. He condemned the conscript laws, martial law, impressments and suspension of habeas corpus not only as inexpedient but as infringing upon the constitutional rights of the people and not to be justified on the plea of "exigency of war," that ancient cry to which republics make their first strides to monarchy. He was not free from the fear, which has haunted our statesmen from Washington's presidency to Grant's, that a republic here might follow the fate of foreign predecessors; might, in time of revolution, become subject to its own military power and pass by the usual stages into empire with a Cæsar or Napoleon at the head. His public protests were not, as he declared at the time, to hamper or harass the administration or to lead a party opposition to it — this, he repeatedly refused to do— but to inspire the people to "guide and instruct their rulers aright." He had condemned like measures in Lincoln's government; and in his speech before the Georgia Legislature,* we hear the same voice, though in milder tone, that arraigned Polk in the Congress of the United States:

The suspension of the habeas corpus is the most important question. The first act on the subject was assented to on the twenty-seventh of February, 1862. This attempted to confer on the President the power not only to suspend the writ, but to declare martial law, etc. This was soon after amended. But no one can say that during the progress of these events I was silent. Conscription has been extended to embrace all between seventeen and fifty years of age. It cannot be possible that the object is to keep in the field all between these

* Full text of Mr. Stephens's speech from which condensed excerpts are here made, may be found in Cleveland's "Letters and Speeches of Stephens," pp. 761-86. For Linton Stephens's Habeas Corpus and Peace Resolutions, in support of which this speech was made, see 'War Between the States," II, 788-90, 532-36.

ages. The ruinous consequence is too apparent. Details are to be made [to perform the civil industries]. The effect is to put much the larger portion of the labour of the country, white and slave, under the control of the President. In this connection, take this habeas corpus suspension act by which attempt is made to confer upon him power to order the arrest and imprisonment of any man, woman, or child on bare charge unsupported by oath, of any of the acts for which arrests are allowed. Could the whole country be more completely under the control of one man? Could dictatorial powers be more complete? In this connection, consider the strong appeals made for some time past by leading journals for a dictator. In such times the most dangerous words that can be uttered are: Can you not trust the President? My answer is, Without any reflection or imputation against our Chief Magistrate, the measure of my confidence in him and all other public officers is the Constitution. My answer is the same I gave to one who submitted a plan for a dictatorship to me some months ago: "I am utterly opposed to everything looking to a dictatorship in this country. There is no man living, and not one of the illustrious dead, whom, if now living, I would so trust!"

You have been asked, What can you do? What did Virginia and Kentucky do in 1798–99? Though war was then threatening with France, though it was said then as now that all discussion of even obnoxious measures of Congress would be hurtful to the public cause, they did not hesitate by solemn resolves to declare the alien and sedition laws unconstitutional. Those acts of Congress were not more unconstitutional or dangerous to public liberty than this act. You can invoke its repeal.

In the "plan" submitted was this: "Let the President be proclaimed Dictator for a specified length of time and the Vice-President his successor." Referring to it in a letter of Nov. 6, 1863, Mr. Stephens says:

As this man's mind is running, other men's minds are running. I have heard such sentiments in so many quarters that I feel deep concern. Some of the newspapers — the Richmond *Enquirer*, for instance — have openly proclaimed sentiments of like character.

The Editor of the *Enquirer*, believed to be the organ of the administration, was John Mitchel, the Irish exile. Nat Tyler, Mitchel's associate, remarked in a letter to Mr. Davis, Jan. 15, 1885:

I remember Mr. Stephens coming to the office and lecturing the editors on their support of the measures for the public defense. . . . We gave to his person all respect and to his advice the least attention that was possible. I have always believed if you had assumed "absolute power," shot deserters and hung traitors, seized supplies and brought to the front every man capable of bearing arms, a different result of the war might have been obtained.

Thus contrary were the influences bearing upon the Confederate President. Tyler's letter throws a side-light upon Mr. Stephens's criticized absenteeism from Richmond and his stated reason that he could do no good there, but rather feared that his efforts to serve did harm by increasing dissension and division.

In his speech of March 16, he was supporting the Habeas Corpus and Peace Resolutions offered by Judge Stephens. Referring to what he believed to be the South's one hold on the world's sympathy, he said:

European governments have no sympathy with either side in this struggle. They are rejoiced to see professed Republicans cutting each other's throats. But we have friends there. No argument used by them heretofore has been more effectual than the contrast between the

Federals and Confederates on the subject of the writ of habeas corpus. Here, notwithstanding our dangers and perils, the military has always been kept subordinate to the civil authorities. Here, all the landmarks of English liberty have been preserved and maintained, while at the North scarcely a vestige is left. There, instead of courts of justice with open doors, the country is dotted over with bastiles.

The Resolutions contained this:

As constitutional liberty is the sole object which our people and our noble army have in our present terrible struggle with the Government of Mr. Lincoln, so also is a faithful adherence to it on the part of our Government through good fortunes in arms and through bad, one of the great elements of our final success: because the constant contrast of constitutional government on our part with the usurpations and tyrannies which characterize the government of our enemy under the ever-recurring and ever false plea of the necessities of war, will have the double effect of animating our people with an unconquerable zeal and of inspiring the people of the North more and more with a desire and determination to put an end to a contest which is waged by their Government openly against our liberty, but secretly and more covertly against their own. . . .

We earnestly recommend that our Government, immediately after signal successes of arms, and on other occasions when none can impute its action to alarm instead of a sincere desire for peace, shall make to the Government of our enemy an official offer of peace on the basis of the great principles declared by our common fathers in 1776.

He wrote of Lincoln's administration:

1861, April 1.—[Day blockade of Southern ports was declared.] The worst feature is the possibility that he has no real design, no settled policy; that he is, like the fool, scattering fire without any definite purpose. May 30.—[After suspension of habeas corpus in certain localities.] All Lincoln's Cabinet, except Blair, were opposed to the war at first, I think. The North, I believe, will go into anarchy. The Administration cannot stop the war. 1862, August 7.—The North is already a despotism. Blood will soon flow there as it did in France under the Directory. Winter of 1862.—If the South had not seceded, Lincoln's administration would have broken down in sixty days. 1863, March—Lincoln is no more a dictator now than he has been all the time. My opinion was, and still is, that it was better for all the States to remain in the Union under the Constitution. If the Northern Government would now acknowledge the Sovereignty of the States, war would instantly cease, and the great law of nature governing the proper union of States would work its results. But you might as well sing hymns to a dead horse as preach such doctrines to Mr. Lincoln and those who control his Government at this time. If we ever have peace on this line, it will be when other men are brought into power there. There are such men there—States Rights and State Sovereignty men of the Jefferson school.

The organization of the Peace party at the North "may justly be claimed as part of the fruits" of the Georgia resolutions, Mr. Stephens says in a letter of Sept. 22, 1864; the movement in the Chicago Convention, which nominated McClellan, for a peace convocation of all the States, he hails as "the first ray of real light from the North." He listened eagerly for some expression of sympathy with this movement from Mr. Davis. Their difference of opinion at this time led to a painful correspondence, initiated by a note from Davis, December, 1864, calling on Stephens to explain this passage in his published letter to Senator Semmes:

I know there are many persons amongst us whose opinions are entitled to high consideration who do not agree with me on the question of McClellan's election. They prefer Lincoln to McClellan. Perhaps the President belongs to that class. Judging from his acts, I should think that he did.

Mr. Stephens, in his explanations, said:

The Peace party at the North had planted themselves at Chicago on a States Rights platform. McClellan was their candidate. They announced, as their purpose, if brought into power, to propose a convention of all the States. This proposition, in your Columbia speech, you opposed. How could their leading men urge their people to rally with any prospect of success, in opposition to the potent argument of their adversaries that the Chief Magistrate of the Confederate States had declared in advance that he would not entertain any such proposition? The rejection was accompanied by words that must have grated very harshly, that there was no prospect of peace but by the sword, that the "only way to make spaniels civil is to whip them." The natural tendency was not only to dampen the ardour of the peace men but to excite bitterness. Who would be willing to subject himself to the taunts of the war champions that he had been "whipped" into his conciliatory mood, and, in the estimate of our Chief was no better than a spaniel, and a whipped spaniel at that?

Mr. Davis replied·

My speech was not such as you represent it, and I now quote the passage from which you have torn a few words. I said, "Does any one believe that the Yankees are to be conciliated by retreating before them, or do you not all know that the way to make spaniels civil is to whip them?" I plainly intimated my desire for the success of the Peace party in the words, "Let fresh victories crown our arms, and the Peace party, if there be such at the North, can elect its candidate." The speech is an appeal to the people to trust to their own courage and fortitude for the maintenance of their rights. It was delivered after the publication of McClellan's letter avowing his purpose to force reunion by war if we declined reconstruction when offered.

Mr. Stephens explains further the Semmes letter:

There was nothing in it intended to be offensive to you, or to any one who differed from me, no desire to impeach their motives, integrity, or patriotism. Very few of our public men or presses agreed with me. I stood almost solitary and alone. I had been grossly assailed; my objects were misunderstood by some, misrepresented by others, while my motives were openly impugned by many. It was in vindication of myself that I gave these views.

He had been called a traitor. He said in the Semmes letter:

I know that many of our people think that any allusion to peace on our side is injurious to our cause. Some maintain that we cannot entertain any propositions unless they be based upon our Independence. I concur in none of this reasoning. Nothing would give us more strength at home or abroad, with our armies and the world, than to keep constantly before the public what we are fighting for, and the terms upon which the contest forced upon us may be ended.

In January, 1865, resolutions by Stephens, encouraging the idea of a convention of the States and of peace measures based on "the principles of 1776," had nearly passed the Confederate Congress when Francis P. Blair's visits to Richmond created a diversion that led to the Hampton Roads Peace Conference.

Mr. Stephens's first connection with a peace conference was in 1863. Lee's victory at Chancellorsville and Grant's repulses at Vicksburg had discouraged the North, where large peace meetings were held and the papers preached peace. Indications that exchange of prisoners was to be suspended gave Stephens his opening. He wrote Davis, June 12, offering to go to Washington to treat on exchange; if an interview could be had with authorities there, he hoped so to conduct it as to initiate peace measures; or, in any event, to make it, in publication, a moral argument for the South. June 19, Davis called him by wire to Richmond; he responded instantly. Learning that Lee was now invading Pennsylvania and Grant pressing Pemberton at Vicksburg, he told the President and Cabinet that he had no hope, under changed conditions, of being received by Lincoln. They were doubtful, as was he, of his reception under any circumstances, but thought chances increased by Lee's position. He was gotten to City Point, July 4; detained there two days while Admiral Lee, U. S. N., waited to hear from his telegram to Washington stating Stephens's request for conference; July 1–3, Gettysburg was fought; July 4, Vicksburg fell; July 6, Admiral Lee informed him that his request was refused.

Sherman sent him a verbal invitation, September, 1864, to conference at Atlanta on peace, under the impression that he might act without reference to Davis. Stephens's written reply assured Sherman that the object was so dear to him that he would make any sacrifice short of honour for its sake:

But the entire absence of power on my part to enter into any such negotiations, and the like on his, as appears from his message, preclude my acceptance. If he is of opinion that there is any prospect of our agreeing upon terms of adjustment to be submitted to the action of our respective governments, and will make this known to me in some formal and authoritative manner, I would most cheerfully and willingly, with the consent of our authorities, accede to his request.

After Blair's visits in 1865, Davis told Stephens that Blair had proposed, with Lincoln's knowledge as was understood, a "secret military convention between belligerents" with a view to their sustaining jointly the Monroe doctrine, then threatened in Mexico by Napoleon; the armistice that would be necessary and engagement in a common cause would tend to cool sectional rancours and pave the way to peace. Stephens advised a meeting between Davis and Lincoln near City Point with only Grant and Lee in the secret. Davis insisted on a commission of three, naming Stephens, R. M. T. Hunter, and Judge J. A. Campbell. Stephens objected that the absence of both himself and Hunter — Chairman and Chairman pro tem — from the Senate would imperil the secrecy which Blair had said was essential. The appointments held. The Commissioners' departure was heralded in the papers, and by the time they reached City Point, the North was in a stir. There, Grant received them on his own authority, pending advices from Washington. Stephens says of his first impression of Grant:

I was struck with the great simplicity and naturalness of his manners. He was plainly attired, sitting in a log-cabin, busily writing on a small table by a kerosene lamp. There was nothing in his appearance or surroundings which indicated his official rank. There were neither guards nor aids about him. Upon Colonel

Babcock [of Grant's staff, their escort] rapping at his door, the response, "Come in," was given by himself. We were with General Grant two days. He furnished us with comfortable quarters on one of his despatch boats; met us frequently, and conversed freely upon various subjects, not much upon our mission. I saw, however, very plainly that he was anxious for the proposed conference to take place. He was, without doubt, anxious for a termination of the war, and the return of peace and harmony. It was through his instrumentality mainly that Mr. Lincoln finally consented to meet us at Fortress Monroe.

To contrast with this Mr. Stephens's first impression of the South's great captain, Lee, is a digression justified by its interest. Mr. Stephens first saw Lee in the Capitol at Richmond at his installation as Commander-in-chief of the Armies of Virginia, a dignified and imposing ceremony through which Lee, handsome and polished to the last degree, bore himself with a simplicity not surpassed by Grant's in the log-cabin. Mr. Stephens was in Richmond to invite Virginia's alliance with the Confederacy. He knew that Lee could defeat the measure by "a look." That night in his rooms at the Ballard House, he sounded Lee, and found that Lee desired that no consideration for himself should enter into the question of alliance, though he knew it would reduce his rank, subordinating him to the Confederacy's chief officer. In discussing Lee at different times in 1862–63, Mr. Stephens said:

I have always regarded him as the ablest man in our army; indeed, the first military man on the continent. The last time Mr. Davis consulted me on any question was about who should be sent to command at Charleston. I urged him to send Lee. Lee was sent. This was in

November, 1861. . . . I was wonderfully taken with Lee in our first interview. I saw him put to the test that tries character. He came out of the crucible, pure and refined gold.

The Commissioners met Lincoln and Seward aboard the *River Queen*, in Hampton Roads. Stephens opened the conference with some pleasant remarks to Lincoln on their association in Congress and as Young Indians. Lincoln responded cordially; inquiries concerning old comrades were exchanged. Then political discussion began, during which no one entered the saloon, "except a coloured servant to bring water, cigars, and other refreshments." Seward promised that there should be no clerk, no records. The military convention, Monroe doctrine, armistice, emancipation, compensation for slaves and status of seceded States if war were abandoned, were reviewed. Lincoln's "opinion" was that the States would be instantly "restored to their practical relations to the Union"; that his Emancipation Proclamation, as a war measure, would only apply to such slaves as had come under its operation; he favoured voluntary emancipation by the States, the Government paying indemnity. But he promised nothing, except liberal exercise of Executive clemency in the enforcement of penalties. "Restoration of the Union is a *sine qua non* with me," he said. His letter to Davis by Blair had referred to "our common country"; Davis's reply, to "the two countries." Stephens brought up the question of exchange. Lincoln said he would refer that whole matter to Grant with whom the visitors could confer. Stephens relates:

I then said, "I wish, Mr. President, that you would reconsider the subject of an armistice on the basis which has been suggested. If, upon so doing, you shall change your mind, you can make it known through the military." "Well," said he, as he was taking my hand for a farewell leave, and with a peculiar manner very characteristic of him—"Well, Stephens, I will reconsider it, but I do not think my mind will change; but I will reconsider."

So ended the one interview the Confederate Government was able to obtain with Lincoln, though it had sought many, and in matters of form, Davis had made every concession except that embraced in the term, "the two countries." A pleasant incident occurred when Lincoln said: "Well, Stephens, it seems we can do nothing for our country. Is there anything I can do for you?" Stephens replied that he would like to secure the exchange of his nephew, who had been in prison nearly two years, being sixteen months of this time on Johnson's Island. Lincoln said he would be glad to attend to the matter personally, and on reaching Washington, he telegraphed to Johnson's Island for Lieut. John A. Stephens to be sent to him. John Stephens, ignorant of the cause of his summons, was ushered, at the White House, into Lincoln's presence. Lincoln, who was sitting on a table in a half-reclining posture and talking to Seward, arose, and greeted the young man cordially, remarking in substance: "I saw your uncle, the Honourable Alexander H. Stephens, recently, at Hampton Roads and I promised to send you to him, Lieutenant." In the conversation that ensued, Lincoln gave John what was virtually his first direct news from home, carefully imparting all that could be recalled from what Mr. Stephens had said at Hampton Roads; he spoke warmly of Mr. Stephens, and closed the interview by telling young Stephens that the freedom of the city was his as long as he chose to remain in Washington, and, "When you want to go home, let me know and I will pass you through our lines." Weak and ill from long imprisonment, John Stephens was glad of the privilege, and stayed in Washington for nearly a week. On his farewell call at the White House, Lincoln, after a pleasant chat, gave him a letter to his uncle, and then his own autographed photograph, saying in his droll way: "You had better take that along; it is considered quite a curiosity down your way, I believe."

Another incident of the interview is given here because of a reference made to it in the Journal. Hunter called attention to the sufferings which immediate emancipation would entail upon the Negroes, especially on the aged and the infirm, the women and children of the race, who would be unable to support themselves. Lincoln replied with this anecdote:

An Illinois farmer was congratulating himself with a neighbour concerning a discovery he had made which would save time and labour in gathering a food crop for his hogs. "What is it?" asked the neighbour. "Why, plant plenty of potatoes, and when they mature, turn the hogs in and let them get their food as they want it." "But how will they do when the ground is frozen?" "Let 'em root!"

Stephens advised Davis against a public report of the conference; spoke of Lincoln's promise to "reconsider"; thought Davis might hear from it in a quiet way after the "hubbub" over the conference had subsided; the publicity which had attended the mission was enough to account for its failure, if Blair's representations were correct. Davis insisted on the public report, which was made to the Confederate Congress, February 6th, stating that no terms were offered the South except unconditional surrender and Lincoln's pledge of Executive clemency. Resolutions of indignation and purpose to fight on naturally followed. Impassioned addresses of like tone were made in the Old African Church* and in the Capitol Square by Davis, Benjamin, Hunter, and others. The United States Congress called on Lincoln (February 8th) for information concerning the Congress, and it was given.

Stephens's distress at the turn of affairs is so pronounced in his Journal and in his letter to Seward as to suggest that something more than is published was said about secrecy. There may have been passes of a purely personal nature between himself and Lincoln as old friends and as men, in which each expressed desire to coöperate for peace, and which each felt bound in honour never to reveal. Seward, as a man, may have spoken in some such way. There may have been a tacit understanding, on Stephens's initiative, that the conference should at least not be used to foment public wrath. It is almost impossible to conceive of Stephens as having that interview with Lincoln and not making in his personal character some appeal to the merciful side of his friend in behalf of a suffering people. Yet on the basis of what is known, he might feel acutely that Northern resentment would tie Lincoln's hands and prevent "reconsidering."

Admiral Porter relates of the conference held by Lincoln, Grant, and Sherman on March 27: "Lincoln wanted peace on almost any terms. He did, in fact, arrange the (so-called liberal) terms offered General Joe Johnston." These terms, in Lincoln's words to the Peace Commissioners, "restored the States to their

* Richmond's largest auditorium, built by the whites as a place of worship for their slaves.

practical relations to the Union." Sherman says in his "Memoirs": "Mr. Lincoln exclaimed more than once that there had been enough blood shed." In all this, may there not have been some "reconsidering" of that talk at Hampton Roads between the two old friends, neither of whom doubted the goodness and patriotism of the other and both of whom were deeply humane?

Mr. Stephens declined to make a speech in line with the speeches of the Administration: "I could not undertake to impress upon the people the idea that they could do what I believed impossible, or to inspire in them hopes which could never be realized. It was then that I withdrew from Richmond." In their last interview he told Mr. Davis that he would keep silent as to his views of the situation. They parted in the "same friendship that had always marked our intercourse," Mr. Stephens says. It can be understood how each regarded the other as having obstructed Confederate success. In his "War Between the States," the ablest defence of the Confederacy ever given, Mr. Stephens gives a mellowed view of his Chief, but it is not inconsistent with that of the Journal, given when the sore was raw; when the South was in ruins, her public men in prisons, and threatened with hanging; and when he felt that none of this need have come to pass. From his last interview with Mr. Davis he went to Liberty Hall, where he remained quietly, awaiting arrest and probable execution. Their next meeting was when they were both prisoners; Stephens tried to avoid it, as a painful trial for himself and as doubtless the same for Mr. Davis.

It is now in order to give some account of his family ties and surroundings at Liberty Hall, thus making clear his relation with various people mentioned in the Journal.

When Mr. Stephens's half-brother, John, died in 1856, he left his wife, children, and estate to Mr. Stephens, who installed "Sister Elizabeth," as he called her, and her family at the old homestead, and cared for them faithfully. Her sons, John A., Linton Andrew, and William Grier, served in the Confederate Army, though the two last were but youths; Clarence, the youngest, attended day school at Crawfordville. Her widowed daughter, Mrs. Reid, afterward Mrs. Corry, lived with her. At Sparta, some twenty miles distant, resided Judge Linton Stephens with his three little daughters, Becky, Em, and Claude; their mother, Emmeline, daughter of Judge Thomas, died in 1857. Sparta also was the home of Richard Malcolm Johnston, a friend much beloved by Mr. Stephens and his brother Linton; he is best known to the public as the author of the "Dukesborough Tales" and as Mr. Stephens's biographer. Mollie and William A. Greer of the Journal were children of Mr. Stephens's half-sister Catherine, who died in 1857, he was long the mainstay of her and her family; and he was a kind and thoughtful brother to "Sister Sarah," widow of Aaron Grier, his only full brother. Aaron, the patient yokefellow of his poverty and orphanage and for a time the sharer of his better fortunes, died in 1843, just as Mr. Stephens entered Congress.

Mr. Stephens had many relatives and friends who were his constant visitors. One room at the Hall, called the "Parson's Room," was sacred to Mr. Quinea O'Neal, dubbed "The Parson" because of his amiable mentorship to the young men of the neighbourhood. He died at the Hall, after the war, at the age of ninety. "G. F.

Bristow," of the Journal, was probably the lawyer of that name, who at one time lived at the Hall and read law under Mr. Stephens.

Liberty Hall was so named, Mr. Stephens said, "because I do as I please here and expect my guests to do the same." During the war, it was known, too, as the "Wayside Home" because it sheltered so many sick and crippled soldiers. In that day of scant food supplies, it was, as at all other times a seat of free hospitality. In the master's absence, as in his presence, open house was kept, his servants, Harry and Eliza, doing the honours. Harry was Mr. Stephens's body-servant, butler, and man-of-affairs generally; Eliza, Harry's wife, was cook and feminine superintendent. Their children, Ellen, Fanny, Dora, Tim, and Quin, engaged themselves about the place in work or amusement as convenient. From Washington Mr. Stephens, in the toil and moil of getting the Compromise of 1850 through the House, wrote Linton:

I forgot to reply, in my letter from the House to-day, to the request of Googer's Harry to take Eliza for his wife. Say to him I have no objection. And tell Eliza to go to Solomon & Henry's and get a wedding dress, including a fine pair of shoes, etc., and to have a decent wedding of it. Let them cook a supper and have such of their friends as they wish. Tell them to get some "parson man" and be married like Christian folks. Let the wedding come off when you are at home so that you can keep order among them. Buy a pig, and let them have a good supper. Let Eliza bake some pound-cake and set a good wedding supper.

He bought Harry for Eliza's sake. At the homestead and the Hall, he kept a number of aged black pensioners; "Aunt Mat," of the Journal, was one of these; her office was to feed the chickens and *not* to do violence to Binks, the dog, when he worried them. Residents of no small importance were Mr. Stephens's dogs. A deceased favourite, Rio, mentioned in the Journal, became a public character through much travel with his master; he was a beautiful creature of almost human intelligence, seeming to understand his master's speech and to enter into all his moods. In 1859, Mr. Stephens writes Linton: "A part of my daily duties is to doctor Rio. Poor fellow, he is blind!" He writes of a dark and wintry afternoon in 1861, which closed a day spent in reading letters advocating secession:

> I felt as if I wanted to get away from all company. I took my poor old blind dog, string in hand, and sought solitude. I went through the old fields, and through the pines, sighing in the chill wind, until I came to the place your grandmother settled. What a wreck was before me! I went to the spot where I met you on my first visit to your grandmother's after you went there to live. You were then a very little boy. You ran out to the gate to meet me. Do you remember the time and the spot? . . . Emotions, deep and strong, swelled my breast. Rio whined in sympathy and raised a mournful howl.

Mr. Stephens's affection for his brother Linton was of unusual depth and tenderness, and almost maternal in solicitude. As soon as his own problem of poverty was conquered, he assumed the care of this young half-brother and sent him by turns to his own *alma mater*, to Virginia University, and Harvard College. When in 1859, Linton became a judge of the Supreme Court of Georgia, Mr. Stephens's gratification was less that the honour had been conferred on him than that he was so equal to it. Judge Stephens, at the time of his visit to

Fort Warren, was a handsome man of forty-two. During Mr. Stephens's imprisonment, the brothers received few letters from each other. What became of the many written is a mystery explained in part by uncertain mail facilities in the South and official interference with suspected letters in transit, letters between the brothers coming perhaps more readily under this head than Mr. Stephens's other mail. It is true, too, that Judge Stephens did not write so often as was his custom, being doubtful if his brother would get his letters and fearful lest something he might say would be so construed as to increase his brother's peril and attract undue attention to himself and the family property at a time when sudden arrests and confiscations were the order of the day. In previous separations, the brothers had exchanged letters almost daily. These letters usually discussed men and measures, and the "state of the country." Valuable as they are, one of another type is preferred here to reflect the relationship between these men, neither of whom had known a mother's care and one of whom had denied himself love and marriage. Linton, just before his wedding, in 1852, wrote from Milledgeville, then Capital of Georgia, to Mr. Stephens in Washington:

Dear Brother: I wrote you no letter last night because it was so late when I returned from the House. I went into the Executive Office, and the Governor, Mr. Bartow, and myself figured up the State's finances; then all went to Mercer's and took an oyster supper.

A favour I want you to do me; it is to give me the benefit of your taste in a little matter. I find that it has grown into a sort of common law for all brides about Sparta to receive a bridal present from the intended; and I am inclined to suspect that my sweetheart would not like to be obliged to admit that she is an exception.

Women have a pride to gratify, or at least, to save; and though I think *she* cares as little about such things as anybody else, yet I fear that even *she* might feel a shade of mortification if when asked by her friends to show the accustomed token, she should be obliged to tell them she had none. Therefore, I want to make her a present, and I want *your* judgment as to what it shall be; and as you will readily know from what I have before written you, I want it very soon. Now, I have an idea of a breast-pin with my daguerreotype in it. What think you of that? Or, a bracelet with my likeness? An objection to either is that she already has my daguerreotype in a fine locket; and she has a very fine bracelet. How would a *ring* do? What think you of a *chain?* wouldn't there be a *meaning* in that? If the chain should strike you, couldn't you find in Washington one with some fanciful significance yet in good taste? If Mrs. Toombs is with you, couldn't you get an idea from her? Not that she would certainly be *right,* but she is a *woman* and might give a valuable suggestion. It is a thing of much consideration and great difficulty with me, and I expect something strikingly original and appropriate from you. I will bid you good night with the hope that you will not *burn* this letter, provided always you will keep it *safe.* I may like to look over it some of these days and to show it to *somebody.*

Yours affectionately,

LINTON.

The original of the Prison Journal is owned by Alex. W. Stephens, Robert Grier Stephens, and Mrs. Robert Lee Avary, all of Atlanta, Ga. They are the children of John A. Stephens, who died in 1887. He was the executor of his uncle's will by the terms of which he acquired title to the Journal. His daughter, in transcribing it, had to choose among several readings possible for some expressions. My work in editing has consisted mainly in reducing matter to publication limits. Mr.

Stephens, in the effort to keep his mind from feeding on itself, copied into his diary copious extracts from the Bible, hymn-book, and the classics. Grave impression of his situation and his endeavour to surmount it is gained in turning page after page of such copy in his painful writing, particularly when he notes in accompanying entries that his eyesight is failing, his hand cramps, and his hair has turned white. He reviews books, gives his every *menu*, and all weather and thermometric changes. The extracts and such matters as these are largely omitted from this publication. Other reduction is made in small points of style, as in substituting his briefest for his most diffuse form in giving dates, mail arrivals, and other routine incidents. Asterisks to denote omissions are dispensed with for the most part in abridgement of the diary as well as in speeches and letters in this sketch. It was his habit to repeat himself in letters, writing the same thing in slightly different form to several persons. In selection from original documents, the shorter forms are preferred here; for fuller versions of several condensations, the reader is referred to Johnston and Browne's "Life of Stephens." For Mr. Stephens's speeches in full, he is referred to Cleveland's "Letters and Speeches of Stephens"; and for complete elucidation of Mr. Stephens's political views to his own "War Between the States." For sympathetic aid and cooperation in her work, the editor hereby acknowledges her indebtedness to Mr. John M. Graham and Mr. T. K. Oglesby, formerly secretaries to Mr. Stephens.

Mr. Stephens was in close confinement from May 25 to July 29; until August 20, was in a cell where constant fire was needed to "keep the room dry"; he was troubled with evil odours from the sink, and with vermin. He transfer to better quarters was, as he publishes in his "War Between the States," through the kind offices of Senator Wilson, of Massachusetts, whom he had known in Congress: "He visited me, and seeing my situation, went to Washington and interceded in my behalf. The order came from President Johnson himself; it seemed that Mr. Stanton would not give his consent to it to the last." By officers and men at Fort Warren, he says, "I was treated with the utmost respect and kindness consistent with their orders"; and, "The many acts of kindness I received from the good people of Boston can never be forgotten by me." Among his papers is a petition to President Johnson for his release, carrying the original signatures of a number of prominent Boston men; Mr. Dawson sent it to him after submitting it to Seward. Johnston, in his "Life of Stephens," says Stephens's release was largely due to John W. Garrett and W. Prescott Smith, officers of the Baltimore and Ohio Railroad. Smith, after a visit to Stephens, reported to Garrett that Stephens's death was imminent unless he were set free; Garrett hurried to Washington and let Seward have no peace until the order for release was signed.

Mr. Stephens resented his imprisonment as an act of tyranny, but his tone is free from querulous complaint of minor prison hardships, to which he exhibits remarkable powers of adaptation and a saving sense of humour, with quick responsiveness to the least kindness. July 19, after eight weeks in prison, he writes: "Lieut. Newton approached me and shook hands. This was the first civility of the sort extended me since I have been in this cell." July 22, he says of his escort during the daily walk allowed, who is "a sort of familiar acquaintance, the only one I have here": "Lieut. Woodman sat down and talked with me — the first time he has sat down and talked." Such chronicle betrays how utterly lonely has been this man who was so preëminently social and sympathetic in temperament. He breaks down weeping as Woodman talks. Dr. Seaverns, the fort surgeon, is brought. The ice melts quickly now. The post people are very human and their prisoner is lovable and rare good company too. The underground cell soon becomes a point of attraction for the officers of the fort, and the children find their way to it.

As the story of Mr. Stephens's prison life, the Journal has a very appealing human interest. In its exquisite unfoldment of a rare fraternal love, it is a drama, a classic. As a revelation, unguarded and intimate, of himself and of his opinion of the great events in which he was an actor, and of public men who were his associates, it is a valuable political and historical document. These events were of tremendous import, the most tragic in our national existence, costing thousands of lives and billions of dollars' worth of property, with anguish and rancours that cannot be measured; and these are the views of the second officer of the Confederacy and of a man who, when in the service of the Union, was pronounced the "ablest Member of the House," a House that has never been surpassed in its weight of intellect, character, and brilliancy. The views of none of the other great actors in these events are preserved to us in such form as this — a diary in which the man is talking as if to himself. We are sure that we have here Mr. Stephens's ideas, as they actually were, of Mr. Davis, Mr. Lincoln, the Confederacy, the war, and the Negro question. His views of Negro suffrage, expressed before its trial was decided upon, are peculiarly interesting as coming from the then leading statesman of the South and one who was not allowed in 1866 to take his seat in the Senate.

The cause he had at heart, and for which the South had gone to war, was the preservation of the principles of the Constitution. When he saw those principles violated by the Northern and Southern Governments, he raised his voice in warning to both peoples against their greatest peril. At the South, he gave expression to the apprehensions of many who were not in a position to make themselves heard, even as Seymour, Curtis, Winthrop, Vallandigham, and others did at the North. He believed that if the Confederate administration would relieve these fears, its army would be strengthened, and its people newly inspired, while fraternity of sentiment might be revived or awakened at the North. Few men of his day or ours have made such study of the American form of Government, and none have been better equipped to speak with authority on public measures as they were related to it. What he says merits careful consideration, for, in principle, it is not inapt to our times.

The era in which he lived was the most important the world has seen in its trial of republican form of government. His participation in it was effective in the maintenance of the principles upon which our republicanism is founded, and hence, of the Republic as it is to-day. For survival through this trial of the constitutional liberties of the American people, this country owes her Commoner — not merely Georgia's or the South's — a debt not yet paid in that coin due to one who so loved the people, so believed in them — popular acknowledgment. The man who urges men forward is the man whose part is conspicuous and easily recognized; the man who holds men back is the man whose part is not quick to be seen or valued, but it often requires the highest kind of courage. Our country has had her season of praise, almost of worship, for those who led men on. It is time she should at least turn clear eyes of scrutiny upon her sons who in the terrible sixties, held their brothers back from what might else have been done. At the head of these defenders of her Constitution, she will see Alexander H. Stephens. Lincoln stood for the Union, Davis for the Confederacy; Stephens for the Constitution, the code of the liberties of the American people; to save the Union or the Confederacy at the cost of the Constitution was to save the house by blasting the rock upon which it was builded. Each man suffered for his faith; Lincoln was slain, Davis was chained; Stephens was stoned by public opinion — and he is still stoned.

If we consider the present travail of Russia to win a constitution; and reflect upon what most peoples endure before they secure such an instrument — a constitution of unknown, untried qualities — we may better appraise the gift our fathers gave us in our own code of liberty and law, and the anxiety of those statesmen who have sought to preserve it to us. In his Texas speech, Jan. 25, 1845, Mr. Stephens said of "this richest inheritance ever bequeathed by patriot sires": "If idolatry could ever be excused, it seems to me it would be in allowing an American citizen a holy devotion to the Constitution of his country." In 1858, when striving to preserve the "Constitutional Union," he exclaimed in a letter to Linton: "My country — what is to become of it — it is the idol of my life!" In his Union Speech of 1860, he said: "This Government of our fathers comes nearer the objects of all good government than any other on earth. The influence of the Government on us is like the atmosphere: its benefits are so silent and unseen that they are seldom thought of or appreciated." To Linton, Aug. 31, 1862: "This generation of men seems to have looked upon the Constitution as a matter of course, without knowing anything of its original cost, its constant hazards, and the only securities for its perpetuation."

He was the one public man of his day who remained throughout the war neither Northern nor Southern but American. He arraigned both Governments for usurpations, but he no more uttered a bitter word against the Northern than against the Southern people. He never seemed able to separate these peoples in his affection, his care, and his desire that the Constitution be preserved as their common heritage. He never ceased to believe that if the true issue of the war — not slavery, not the independence of the Confederacy, but the supremacy of the Constitution — were brought home to them, they would see that the cause of the Southern States was the cause of all, they would render righteous judgment and peace would follow.

During the war, his work for the hospitals, the sick and the wounded, and the prisoners of both armies, was unremitting. "Whenever I see a head at an iron grate, my heart is interested," he wrote from Richmond in 1864. We are now to see himself behind an iron grate, a prisoner of so gentle and sweet a spirit that he makes his dungeon walls a home of good influences for our thoughts.

MYRTA LOCKETT AVARY.

PART II

PRISON JOURNAL OF ALEXANDER H. STEPHENS

Prison Journal of Alexander H. Stephens

CHAPTER I

FORT WARREN, Near Boston, Mass., May 27, 1865. —This book was purchased this day of A. J. Hall, Sutler at the Post, by Alexander H. Stephens, a prisoner at the Fort, with a view of preserving in it some regular record of the incidents of his imprisonment and prison life. It may be of interest to himself hereafter, should he be permitted to refer to it; and if his own life should not be spared, it may be of interest to some of his relatives and friends. He knows it will be of interest to his dear and only brother, the Hon. Linton Stephens, of Sparta, Ga., should this brother ever be permitted to see it. He feels sure that all his relatives would be exceedingly glad to peruse it, especially in the event that they never see him again. For these reasons the book has been purchased. In it, he will first transcribe his notes made in pencil from the time of leaving home; that done, he intends to continue it as a daily journal of such things as he may feel disposed to record.

Liberty Hall, Georgia, Thursday, May 11, 1865.— This was a most beautiful and charming morning. After refreshing sleep, I arose early. Robert Hull, a youth, son of Henry Hull, of Athens, Ga., had spent the night at my house. I wrote some letters for the mail, my custom being to attend to such business soon as breakfast was over; and Robert and I were amusing ourselves at casino, when Tim [a negro servant] came running into the parlour saying: "Master! more Yankees have come! a whole heap are in town, galloping all about with guns." Suspecting what it meant, I rose, told Robert I expected they had come for me, and entered my bedroom to make arrangements for leaving, should my apprehensions prove true. Soon, I saw an officer with soldiers under arms approaching the house. The doors were all open. I met him in the library. He asked if my name was Stephens. I replied that it was. "Alexander H. Stephens?" said he. I told him that was my name. He said he had orders to arrest me. I asked his name and to see his orders. He said he was Captain Saint of the 4th Iowa Cavalry, or mounted infantry, attached to General Nelson's command; he was then under General Upton: he showed me the order by General Upton, at Atlanta, directing my arrest and that of Robert Toombs; no charge was specified; he was instructed to go to Crawfordville, arrest me, proceed to Washington and arrest Mr. Toombs, and then carry both to General Upton's headquarters.

I told him I had been looking for something of this kind; at least, for some weeks had thought it not improbable; and hence had not left home; General Upton need not have sent any force for me; had he simply notified me that he wished me at his headquarters, I should have gone. I asked how I was to travel. He said: "On the cars." I then learned that his party had come down on the train arriving just before Tim's announcement. I asked if I would be permitted to carry any clothing.

He said, "Yes." I asked how long I might have for packing. He said: "A few minutes — as long as necessary." I set to packing. Harry came in, evincing great surprise and regret, to pack for me. The Captain then said: "You may take a servant with you if you wish." I asked if he knew my destination. He said: "First, Atlanta; then, Washington City." I called in Anthony, a black boy from Richmond who had been waiting on me several years, and inquired if he wished to go; I told him I would send him from Washington to his mother in Richmond. He was willing, so I bade him be ready soon as possible.

In the meantime, Mr. Hidell [his secretary] had come in; he was living with me and had gone out after breakfast. None of my brother John's family residing at the old homestead happened to be with me; however, Clarence, who was going to school at the Academy, hearing of what had occurred (I suppose), came over with some friends from town. It was about 10 A. M. when Captain Saint arrived. In about fifteen minutes — not much over—we started for the depot, Anthony and I with the Captain and squad; friends, servants, and Clarence following, most of them crying. My own heart was full — too full for tears.

While Anthony was getting ready, I had asked Captain Saint if I might write a letter or two to some friends, to my brother and to my sister-in-law's family. He said I might. My brother and his children had left me two days before, after a visit of nearly a week. I wrote him a note in about these words:

Dear Brother: I have just been arrested by Captain Saint of the 4th Iowa Cavalry. The order embraces General Toombs. We are both to be carried to Atlanta, and thence to Washington City it seems. When I shall see you again, if ever, I don't know. May God enable you to be as well prepared for whatever fate may await me as I trust He will enable me to bear it. May His blessings ever attend you and yours. My kindest regards to Cosby, Dick Johnston, and all friends. I have not time to say more. My tenderest love to your dear little ones. Yours most affectionately,

ALEXANDER H. STEPHENS.

This I sealed and addressed to Linton and told Harry to send it over to Sparta immediately after I should leave. The Captain said he preferred that I should not send the note then; we should come back, and then I might send it. I told him it simply announced my arrest and destination; he might read it. I opened and handed it to him. He still objected, and I tore it up. Supposing similar objection would be made to my sending any other, I did not write to my sister-in-law's family. I knew that Mr. Hidell, Clarence, servants, and all present would give them full information. At the cars a great many people had assembled. All seemed deeply oppressed and grieved. Many wept bitterly. To me the parting was exceedingly sorrowful. Hidell was to leave for his home in Memphis on this day. He was all packed up and ready to start on the down train.

When we left the depot, the train backed up several hundred yards and took on some soldiers who seemed to have been put out there as scouts. While we were standing, I saw Mr. Singleton Harris and, by the Captain's permission, sent word to Hidell not to leave my house until he should hear from me. When all the soldiers were on the cars the train moved down the road again, not stopping until we reached Barnett, where we took another engine and started to Washington, Ga. About four miles from that town, the train slowed up at a shanty occupied by a track supervisor. Here, I was put off with about twenty soldiers to guard me. The Captain and the others went on to Washington. He said he expected to be back in an hour. He did not return until after dark. During his absence there was a heavy fall of rain, which was much needed as it had not rained for several weeks. The man of the house gave me dinner: fried meat and corn bread. He said it was the best he had. I was not hungry, but to show my gratitude for his hospitality, I shared his homely meal. Night came. The Captain had not returned. The good man asked me to partake of his supper; I accepted as before; his lady was kind, and apologized for having no better fare to offer.

Soon after dark, the engine was heard. I was anxious to know the result of Captain Saint's trip. What we supposed was the train proved to be the engine only: the Captain was bringing his men commissary stores. He went back immediately, but not before I had asked the cause of the detention. What had occurred? was General Toombs at home? He answered evasively, and left me in doubt and perplexity. About nine the engine was heard again. It brought the train. I was put aboard, Anthony looking after the baggage. The ground was wet and I got my feet damp; this, with the chill of the night air gave me a sore throat with severe hoarseness. When the train was under way for Barnett, I asked the Captain if he had Mr. Toombs. "No," he replied, "Mr. Toombs flanked us."* This was said in

*Toombs was in his front door when Captain Saint entered his yard; he went out at the back and escaped to the woods.

a rather disappointed and irate tone, and I made no further inquires. Reaching Barnett about eleven, we remained for some time and then took the train for Atlanta. Some panes of glass were broken out of the car windows, and I was further chilled.

Atlanta, Georgia, May 12. — This is one of the most eventful days of my life. Never before was I deprived of my liberty or under arrest. Reached Atlanta about eight-thirty. Quite unwell. Carried to General Upton's headquarters. The first person I saw that I knew was Felix, a coloured man who was a servant to Mr. Toombs and myself when we lived together in Washington City. He was very glad to see me and I gave him a hearty handshake. He was our cook in Washington, and a good cook he was. General Upton had gone to Macon but was expected back that night. Captain Gilpin, of his staff, received me and assigned me a room. Anthony made me a fire; Captain Gilpin ordered breakfast and Felix soon had it ready: fried ham and coffee. Walked about the city under guard. The desolation and havoc of war here are soul-rending. Several persons called to see me, Gip Grier [his cousin A. G. Grier] the first; my heart almost burst when I saw him, but I suppressed all show of emotion. General Ira R. Foster* was allowed to write me a note and I to answer it, but no interview was permitted. Colonel G. W. Lee was permitted to speak to me, but not to hold conversation. John W. Duncan was permitted to visit my room and remain as long as he pleased; so, too, was Gip Grier: both made me several

* Confederate Quartermaster-General of Georgia during the war. Other visitors, except those specified as from the North or as belonging to General Upton's staff, were Confederates.

visits during the day. Captain Saint called and said he would send the surgeon of his regiment to prescribe for my hoarseness. The surgeon came, and his remedies did me good. Major Cooper called and gave me a bottle of whisky.

I started from home with about $590 in gold which had been laid up for a long time for such a contingency. I got Gip Grier to exchange $20 of it for greenbacks and small silver. I had first asked Captain Gilpin if this would be allowed and he made no objection. Gip offered me $100 additional in gold if I wished it. I declined it. Duncan offered any amount I might want. I told him I hoped I had enough. All this was in the presence of the officers. General Foster, in his note, offered any funds I might need. I informed him in my answer that I had plenty for present use and hoped I should need no more.

May 13. — General Upton called early. I was so hoarse I could hardly talk. He informed me that he had removed all guards, that I was on my parole. I told him I should not violate it. He was very courteous and agreeable; told me my destination was Washington. I learned from him that Mr. Davis had been captured, that Clement C. Clay * had surrendered himself, and that Mr. Davis and party would be in Atlanta to-night on their way to Washington. He gave me choice of route: by Dalton and the lines of railroads northwest and north, or by sea from Savannah. I selected the sea route, but told him I did not wish to go with Mr. Davis. He

* Confederate Senator; member of mission sent, 1864, by President Davis to Canada; charged by President Johnson with complicity in Lincoln's assassination; a reward of $25,000 was offered for his arrest.

said he would send me in a special train to-night to Augusta, but from there to Savannah I should have to travel on the boat with Mr. Davis and party; there was but one boat at Augusta. From Savannah to Hilton Head and on he would try to have me sent by separate packet if it could be done. I had frequent talks with General Upton during the day and was well pleased with him. Some friends called; Gip Grier and Duncan several times. Duncan gave me a bottle of Scotch ale which I put in my trunk. He told me of a banking-house in Europe in which he has funds, authorizing me to draw on his account for any amount I might need. I am truly grateful, but I trust I shall never be brought to the necessity of availing myself of his generous tender. He said he would write the house to cash any draft by me. Major Cooper called, Dr. Powell, Dr. Simmons and others; and some ladies, who wept in parting with me. Mrs. Powell sent refreshments; and Mrs. Thrasher the mattress and covers which form my comfortable bed.

Felix informs me that after he was cook for Mr. Toombs and myself in Washington, he was sold by Mr. Wallack to Senator Sebastian, of Arkansas, and was the Senator's cook until the war broke out. Senator Sebastian now lives in Memphis, has freed all his people, and Felix has been for some time the servant of Dr. Little, U. S. A. He inquired after Pierce, my servant boy who was with me in Washington. I told him I had let Pierce go where he pleased and do as he pleased for several years, and when last heard from, he was in Macon; if he would write Pierce there I thought the letter would reach Pierce, who would be glad to hear from him and much gladder to see him. They were very intimate in Washington.

Anthony said Felix was going to try to go with me to Washington. I did not encourage this idea as I know Dr. Little would not like to have Felix quit him so suddenly, and then I am not certain of my ultimate destination.

This evening Colonel Peters, of Iowa, came to renew acquaintance with me. He was introduced to me in Washington City many years ago by Senator G. W. Jones, of Iowa. He seemed glad to renew the acquaintance. We talked agreeably of old events and associations.

From my window, just before night, I took a bird's-eye survey of the ruins of this place. I saw where the Trout House stood, where Douglas spoke in 1860 — I thought of the scenes of that day, and my deep forebodings of all these troubles; and how sorely oppressed I was at heart, not much less so than now, in their full realization with myself among the victims. How strange it seems to me that I should thus suffer, I who did everything in the power of man to prevent them. I could but rest my eye for a time upon the ruins of the Atlanta Hotel, while the mind was crowded with associations brought to life in gazing upon it. There, on the fourth Sept., 1848, I was near losing my life for resenting the charge of being a traitor to the South: and now I am here, a prisoner under charge, I suppose, of being a traitor to the Union. In all, I have done nothing but what I thought was right. The result, be it what it may, I shall endeavour to meet with resignation.

9 P. M. — General Upton informed me that my train starts at eleven; that I may stop at home, take breakfast, and get more clothing: the train carrying Mr. Davis and party leaves here two hours later than mine; I may remain home until it overtakes me. I immediately wrote

Hidell. I hoped my brother might be in Crawfordville. I was anxious to see him and doubted not that word had been sent him of my arrest. Gip took the letter to the mail-train at ten-thirty, returned, and remained with me until near the hour for my departure, as did Duncan. I requested both to write Linton, giving him the particulars of my situation and destination as far as known.

I told General Upton that there was another coloured boy at my house, Henry, Anthony's brother, whose mother is in Richmond and whom I should like, if there is no objection, to take to Fortress Monroe whence I could send him to her. He consented. Captain Gilpin requested my autograph, which I gave. A little past eleven, we were off.

Crawfordville, May 14. — This is an ever memorable day to me. It is the anniversary of my stepmother's death, the day on which was severed the last tie that kept the family circle around the hearthstone at the old homestead. My father died one week before, on the 7th, 1826. The date, to make this anniversary more impressive, falls now, as then, on Sunday.

At eleven-thirty this morning, the cars reached Crawfordville. Hidell had gotten my letter. A large crowd was at the depot to see me. I hastened to my house as I had much to do and not much time to do it in. Church was just out, preaching over, and the congregation leaving. I could but give a parting shake of the hand to many whose eyes were filled with tears. Nearly all my servants from the homestead were at church, but none of my sister-in-law's family, except my nephew, Linton Andrew. Hidell had not had time to send them word I was coming. My nephew, John, was gone to Washington,

Ga. First, he had gone to Sparta and informed my brother Linton of my arrest. Hidell said John had reported Linton as ill. What a pang that struck to my heart!

I ordered breakfast for myself, Captain Kennedy, and two others who had accompanied me on invitation. I had a hurried repacking of clothes into a larger trunk I borrowed from my true friend, Mr. Joseph Myers. Everything I could think of that I might need — that I had — was put in; besides clothing, two large bed-blankets and one large afghan. Henry and Anthony were soon ready. Such hurried directions as I could give were given to the servants on the lot and to those from the homestead. Harry was told what to do in taking care of things; Fountain and George were told how to manage the farm. I did not have as much talk with my nephew, Linton Andrew, as I wished, nor with Hidell. Leave-takings were hurried and confused. The servants all wept. My grief at leaving them and home was too burning, withering, scorching for tears. At the depot was an immense crowd, old friends, black and white, who came in great numbers and shook hands. That parting and that scene I can never forget. I could not stand it until the other train arrived, and I requested the Captain to move off. This he did.

Augusta, Ga. — At Barnett, we waited for the other train. General Upton came in and suggested that I would be more comfortable in the car he had on that train. I told him, if he had no objection, I should prefer to remain where I was. He said he had none, and I remained. Mr. Davis and party were on the other train. In a short time we were under way again. Reached

Augusta before sundown. General Upton had a carriage to take me to the boat, four or five miles down the river. The other train came up a half-hour behind us. Mr. and Mrs. Davis were put in a carriage, and some officer with them. Mr. and Mrs. Clay were in a carriage to themselves; as our vehicles passed, I, for the first time, saw them; they bowed to me and I to them. Mr. Davis did not see me until we reached the boat. Anthony rode in the carriage with me. Henry went with and took care of the baggage, consisting of Myers's trunk with my things in it, my trunk with Anthony's things, and Henry's box. My carpet-bag, shawl, greatcoat, umbrella, cane, and small overcoat I kept with me; Anthony kept his and Henry's carpet-bags. It was some time before all things were ready; all was under military arrangement. Mr. Davis's party, twelve in number, were placed foremost in vehicles that I could not see; then Mr. Davis's carriage, then Mr. Clay's; I brought up the rear. A major from Indiana was with me. Just before we started, Mrs. Davis's white nurse came and asked to ride in our carriage. The Major let her in. She had Mrs. Davis's infant* with her. Guards rode in front, at the sides, and in the rear, some on horse-back, some in wagons, all well armed. When the cortège, which looked much like a funeral procession, had gotten away from the depot, we found the streets lined on both sides with immense crowds. Occasionally I heard some one say, "There goes Stephens"; but I recognized only one person, Morse of the *Chronicle and Sentinel*. I bowed to several who bowed to me, but whose faces I did not know. Everybody looked sad and depressed.

We moved slowly. It was dark long before we reached

* "Winnie," afterward known as the "Daughter of the Confederacy"; born in 1864.

the boat-landing. Outside the city, the Major requested Anthony to ride his horse, which some friend, who wished to return, had ridden to that point. Anthony acted the horseman better than I feared he could. After we reached the landing, it was a long time before we got the boat. The walk to the river-edge was rough; deep ravines without bridges had to be crossed. It was with great difficulty, even though assisted, that I was able to get along. The Major helped me. He was agreeable and cheerful in conversation, but I was suffering too much from headache to take interest in conversation. To board the boat, we had to walk a narrow plank, descending at that. This I could not do. Several helped me across. Here, we waited until the baggage was all aboard. I felt relieved when Anthony reported everything safe and Henry on board. The boat was a miserable affair, a river tug without cabin. There were a few berths which the ladies occupied; the rest of us were put on deck, except Mr. Davis, who staid in the part of the boat occupied by the ladies. A covering was overhead but the sides of the deck were open.

We found General Joe Wheeler and four of his men on board. They had been captured near Athens some days before and had been sent down in advance of us. Our whole party now, Mr. Davis and those captured with him, Mr. and Mrs. Clay, myself, General Wheeler and his men, numbered over twenty. I don't know exactly how many were in Mr. Davis's party. I recognized Governor Lubbock and Colonel Johnston of his staff, Mr. Harrison, his private secretary, and Postmaster-General J. H. Reagan. Mr. Davis had with him one man-servant, Bob, a woman, Ellen Bond, coloured, and a white woman, also a little mulatto boy. His children, Jeff, Maggie, and Willie, I recognized, also Mrs. Davis, her sister, Miss Howell, and her brother, Jefferson Davis Howell. A young Mr. Monroe, grandson of Judge Monroe, of Kentucky, was also with Mr. Davis, but I did not see him after the party got on the boat.

Mrs. Davis and Mrs. Clay came on deck where we were. Our meeting was the first that the Davis party knew of my arrest. Mr. Clay had seen me at the depot and knew it from the fact of my situation, but had not heard of it before. General Wheeler had not heard of the arrest of any of us. Mr. Clay told me he had been on parole all the way, and had not come on in the procession with the rest of us, but had been permitted to drive with his wife about the city and visit some of her acquaintances. He gave me the particulars of his surrender.

Before taking leave of me, General Upton turned me over to Colonel Pritchard of the 4th Michigan Cavalry, who had captured Mr. Davis and who now took charge of all the prisoners. The General told Colonel Pritchard that Mr. Clay and I were on parole, and he allowed us the run of the boat. I asked him to grant me permission to write to my brother. He said he supposed this privilege would not be denied whenever I got to a place where I could write.

On the cars from Barnett to Augusta I had travelled with General Elzy [C. S. A.], who had been paroled, and had requested him to write John A. Stephens at Crawfordville that I wished him to remain with his mother until he should hear from me. I deeply regret that I did not meet John at home as I passed there.

My feelings this night on this boat are past all description. We were all crowded together in a small space on the deck. The night was cool, the air on the water damp, and I was suffering, as I had been for hours, from a severe headache. No mention was made of supper, but I thought not of supper. I had taken breakfast at noon, and did not feel now as if I should ever want to eat again. Clay and I combined our cloaks, coats, shawls, etc.; General Wheeler sent us a blanket; Mrs. Davis sent us a mattress, and we made a joint bed in the open air on deck. I put the carpet-bags under our heads. Strange to say, I slept sweetly and soundly, and rose much refreshed next morning. The boat had raised steam and left the bluff, not the wharf, about nine that night. Reagan, Wheeler, and the rest, including Bob, Anthony, Henry, and the other servants, had stretched themselves on the open space the best way they could, all except one little boy, with covering of some sort. Just before I fell asleep, I witnessed this scene: A little black boy, ragged and woe-begone, lay in the passway. Whose he was or where going, I know not. An officer came along, gave him a shove and a push, and in harsh language ordered him to get away. The boy raised up, roused from his sleep, and replied plaintively: "I have no lodging, sir." That scene and that reply were vividly on my mind with all my personal cares when merciful slumber drowned them, as I was borne away from home and all dear to me, on the broad smooth bosom of the Savannah.

May 15.—I awoke much refreshed. Morning beautiful. Got a rough soldier's breakfast. Mr. Davis came out on deck soon after I got up. It was our first meeting since our parting the night after my return from Hampton Roads Conference to Richmond. Much as

I had disagreed with him and much as I deplored the ruin which, I think, his acts helped to bring upon the whole country, as well as on himself, I could but deeply sympathize with him in his present condition. His salutation was not unfriendly, but it was far from cordial. We passed but few words; these were commonplace. Talked to-day a good deal with Clay, Reagan, and Wheeler, but spent most of my time in lonely meditation on the side of the boat, looking out upon the willows along the margin of the sluggish, muddy, crooked stream. My thoughts were filled with home scenes and Sparta scenes and scenes of kindred association. Colonel Pritchard introduced to me Captain Hudson of his regiment, and a Mr. Stribling (I think the name is), a correspondent of the New York *Herald*. We talked a good deal on the state of the country, etc.

Savannah to Hilton Head, May 16. — I omitted to note yesterday that we got dinner and tea at the usual hours: potatoes and beef stewed for dinner; at tea, a good cup of black tea that suited me well. There was hardtack, which some preferred, but I chose baker's bread. The table seated only four at once. It took some time for all to eat. We reached Savannah this morning at four; were transferred from the tug to a coast steamer, bound to Hilton Head. On it we got a good breakfast. Witnessed a scene at the breakfast table, in which Mr. Davis was chief actor, that I can never forget. About eleven a. m., we anchored in the harbour off Hilton Head and were transferred to the *Clyde*, a new steamer, bound for Fortress Monroe. There were several good berths in the cabin below and a number of staterooms on deck above. The ladies and most of the gentlemen selected staterooms. I preferred a berth below; which I found on the voyage an excellent choice. After we boarded, a number of officers and other persons came on the *Clyde*. They brought New York papers, *Harper's Weekly* and *Frank Leslie's Illustrated News*. It had been a long time since I had seen these prints. Here, for the first time, I heard of the Military Commission trying Mr. Lincoln's assassins.

On the *Clyde*. — The officers came down in the cabin where I was and we talked for some time on the state of the country. They were all courteous and agreeable. Captain Kelly, who formerly knew me in Washington City, told me he was now in the quartermaster's department at Hilton Head. He was pleased to refer kindly to his recollection of me; alluded to my Milledgeville "Union speech" of November, 1860; spoke highly of it and expressed regret that I had not adhered to it. I told him I had. In that speech I had, with all my ability, urged our people not to secede; the present consequences I then seriously apprehended; I told them that if, in solemn convention, the State should determine to resume her delegated powers and assert her sovereign and independent rights, I should be bound to go with her: to her I owed ultimate allegiance; her cause would be my cause, her destiny mine. I thought the step a wrong one — it might be fatal; and exerted my utmost power to prevent it; but when it was taken, even though against my judgment and counsel, I, as a good citizen, could but share the common fate, whatever it might be. I did, as a patriot, what I thought best before secession. I did the same after. Captain Kelly had not recollected that part of the speech acknowledging my ultimate allegiance as due to the State of Georgia.

The whole conversation was quite friendly. He manifested a good deal of personal regard for me.

About four, the *Clyde* put out to sea. Before leaving, Mrs. Davis addressed a note to General Saxton, who has charge of colonization in South Carolina, consigning to him the little mulatto boy she had with her. The parting of the boy with the family was quite a scene. He was about seven years old, and little Jeff's playfellow; they were always together; it was "Jeff" and "Jimmy" between them. When Jeff knew that Jimmy was to be left behind, he wailed, and so did Jimmy. Maggie cried and Billy cried, and the coloured woman (Ellen) cried. Mrs. Davis said the boy's mother had been dead a number of years and Ellen had been a mother to him. As the boat taking Jimmy moved off, he screamed. He had to be held to prevent his jumping overboard. He tried his best to get away from those holding him. At this, Jeff and Maggie and Billy screamed almost as loudly as Jimmy. Ellen wept aloud. Mrs. Davis shed tears. Mrs. Clay threw Jimmy some money but this had no effect. Some one on the deck of his boat picked it up and handed it to him; he paid no attention to it but kept on scuffling to get loose; he was wailing as long as he could be heard or seen by us.

The sloop-of-war, *Tuscarora*, a steam propeller, put to sea soon after we left. We understood from Colonel Pritchard that she is bound to Fortress Monroe. The *Clyde* is long and narrow, and rolls very much. The purser, Mr. Moore, the captain's son, expressed some kind personal regard for me this evening; told me he was from Philadelphia; gave me a copy of *Harper's Weekly:* and said if I had any little thing that I could spare to give him as a memento, he would feel very much obliged. I was puzzled to think of anything I had that would answer his purpose. I chanced to have in my pocket a chess-piece of a set that was very prettily made. It was a bishop. I took it out, and asked him how that would do. He seemed highly pleased, and I was gratified that I was able to comply with his wishes.

There was some misunderstanding about dinner. Nothing was said about it until we had left Hilton Head. It was getting late and several of our party expressed themselves as being hungry. I inquired about it of the steward, a coloured man from Washington City, who knew me. He said the captain had no provisions for us; our rations were on board but no arrangements had been made between Colonel Pritchard and the captain about cooking them. I gave him twenty-five cents in silver and told him to bring me some bread. This, with water, made my meal; I ate in the cabin below. The engineer, who in passing saw me, brought me some whisky. I knew from his manner and from what he said that, personally, he is a friend to me. I told the steward, Lucas, to give Anthony and Henry their dinners, and I would pay.

Near night, a message came to me that dinner was ready. I went up on deck where I found a table set between two staterooms with several of our party, as many as could get at it, seated. It was a very good dinner. A remark by Mrs. Davis caused me to inquire about it afterward. She said we were indebted to her for it; she had ordered it. This led me to believe that we were each to pay for his meal, or that each ought to pay a ratable part. She did not say she had ordered it on private account. I inquired of the purser how it was. He said the captain, at the request of Mrs. Davis, had prepared dinner out of ship's stores and that it was furnished at seventy-five cents each. I paid him my part, and all the rest did likewise, I believe. Clear, beautiful night, but the vessel rolls very much.

May 17. — Did not sleep much; not seasick, yet with symptoms strongly marked. This morning I told Anthony to come into the cabin with me. He was sick, seemingly almost unto death. I directed him to lie down, and remained with him. It seemed to do him good to have some one with him. He said Henry was forward and not sick much. Gave the steward fifty cents for breakfast, which I took myself in the cabin. Anthony could eat nothing. Saw Henry on deck. He seemed to be doing pretty well. Found General Wheeler on deck where he had spent the night; he was very seasick. Few of the party were out. Reagan had taken a berth in the lower cabin with me. He kept it closely. Mr. Clay was on deck; the sea never affects him, he told me. Mr. Davis was out. Did not seem to be much sick. He and Mr. Clay came into the lower cabin during the day, not together but separately. I had a long and friendly talk with each. Breakfast was served for the party at nine. I heard that a few were at table. The purser, during the morning, stripped bedclothes from all berths but mine in the cabin below. He indignantly said the occupants had gone to bed with their boots on. Reagan told me this was not the case with him. How it was with the others, I do not know. I had taken off my shoes but no other part of my clothing. The purser told me about one o'clock that Colonel Pritchard had arranged for our meals hereafter, and that they would be furnished without pay. About two dinner was announced. Mr. Davis, Mrs. Davis, Mr. Reagan, and myself were present, and some others. It was a good dinner for those who had appetites; I had none. The *Tuscarora* all day near us, sometimes in the rear, sometimes on the side, sometimes ahead. She spoke to our ship during the evening, giving the position at noon. Anthony continued very sick; I felt truly sorry for him.

May 18. — Passed Cape Hatteras, the pilot told me, about one. Paid steward for cup of coffee and dry toast, which I took early. Anthony still very sick. Gave him some coffee and toast. He seemed to relish it but soon threw it up. Henry about on deck, not sick at all. General Wheeler still on deck, quite seasick. Lubbock keeps close in his stateroom. So does Mrs. Clay. I called to see her with Mr. Clay. She seems to suffer severely. But no one seems so sick as Anthony. He can neither walk nor stand. Still in the cabin with me, where I can be with him.

Dinner; present: Mr. Davis, Mr. Clay, Mr. Reagan and myself, with others. Mr. Davis's children, Jeff, Maggie, and Billy, do not appear to be seasick at all. Both nurses are ill. Mrs. Davis takes charge of the infant, relieved by Mr. Davis, Mr. Howell, her brother, and others. Jeff lost his hat somehow; it fell overboard; he wears General Wheeler's, as the General keeps stretched on deck in the shade and has no use for it. Grows cloudy toward night. Some entertain serious apprehensions that the *Clyde* could not weather a storm. She is too high and has too much exposure with her line of staterooms on deck.

Tea at seven. Present: same as at dinner. Mr. Davis sits at the head of the table. All wait until he and

Mrs. Davis are seated. He bows his head and asks a blessing, but not audibly. All wait until this is over; then the steward helps those seated, always beginning with Mr. Davis. About eight P. M. the *Tuscarora* came alongside and spoke to us, told the pilot our position and that we would enter Hampton Roads in the morning; to go about five knots an hour, no more.

Hampton Roads, May 19. — On rising, was told by Lucas, that we were in sight of land. Cape Charles Lighthouse was quite visible when I went on deck. Breakfast for the party at nine. Mr. Davis looked quite well. Mrs. Davis well. Mrs. Clay now up. Governor Lubbock at the table, General Wheeler also. All the sick seem recovering except Miss Howell, whose illness is said to be more than seasickness. Anthony revives, walks out, gets his breakfast and seems all right again.

Pilot boat meets us. We are asked where we wish to pilot to. "To Washington" is the reply. A pilot comes aboard. The *Tuscarora* leads the way. Arrive at Hampton Roads. Colonel Pritchard goes to Fortress Monroe. Returns and says we must await orders from Washington. I had asked him to inquire if I might be permitted to telegraph or write home. He could bring no information on that point. We anchored in the harbour. *Tuscarora*, close by, anchored also. We see near us the iron steamer, *Atlanta*, captured at Savannah. Dinner at usual hour. All hands at table except Miss Howell, and all with good appetites except myself. My throat still sore, but much better than when I left Hilton Head; I had no cough last night. Sent for New York papers by the purser, who went ashore. He brought the Richmond *Enquirer;* said he could get no other paper.

All anxious to know our destination; all desire to go to Washington.

May 20. — Still at anchor in the Roads. Colonel Pritchard tells us that a telegram last night informed him that General Halleck will be at the Fort at noon, and give him further orders. The day is dull; nothing to enliven it but the passing of steamboats and small sails. A British man-of-war and a French corvette lie near.

Called Henry into the cabin. Told him he would go from here to Richmond; sent my remembrance to his mother and Travis,* gave him $10 and told him to be a good, industrious, honest and upright boy; not to gamble and never to bet. He promised to comply with my injunctions. Told him to tell Travis to come to see me if I should be sent to Washington. I told him Anthony would go with me for the present, if permitted.

8 P. M. — Colonel Pritchard came to the cabin and told Judge Reagan and myself that some officers in the captain's room wished to see us there. We found Captain Frailey of the *Tuscarora* and Captain Parker of another war steamer. Captain Frailey received us courteously and told us he had orders to take Reagan and myself aboard the *Tuscarora* next day at ten; he had come to give notice that we might be prepared. "What place is our destination, Captain?" I asked. "Boston," he replied. I knew then that Fort Warren was to be my place of imprisonment. I told him I feared the climate would be too cool and damp for me; I should greatly have preferred Washington if the authorities had so decided. I asked him how about Anthony's

* A negro servant, probably Henry's brother.

going with me. Told him the facts relating to Anthony. He could give no information but said he would inquire and let me know before ten in the morning. Before we left the captain's office, General Wheeler entered with his party. His conference was with Captain Parker. Captain Parker was to take them in his steamer to Fort Delaware. Reagan and I left Wheeler in the office. I sent for Captain Moody, now a fellow prisoner with Mr. Davis, and who had been a prisoner at Fort Warren, to learn something of regulations there. He spoke in favourable terms of them; said he had been in several prisons and had been better treated at Fort Warren than anywhere else. Being relieved of the suspense we had been in for several days, Reagan and I went to our berths at an early hour. I slept little. Thought of home, sweet home. Saw plainly that I was not to be permitted to communicate with any one there; this was the most crushing thought. Death, I felt, I could meet with resignation, if such was to be my fate, might I but communicate with Linton and other loved ones while life should last.

Sunday. — Rose early. Took a towel bath, changed underclothes. Anthony rubbed me down for the last time. I told him I should leave him. Gave him five dollars and the same advice and instructions I had given Henry. I added that I was going to Fort Warren. Told him to ask Mr. Baskerville to write this to Linton at Sparta and to John A. Stephens and George F. Bristow at Crawfordville, hoping that some one of them, if not all, might get the letters. Colonel Pritchard told me that all the coloured servants who should be left at this place, he would send to Richmond without charge.

This I told Anthony, and bade him take care of his money, he might need it. I gave him my leather trunk that he had brought his clothes in.

Saw Mrs. Clay and requested her to write Linton and Mrs. Dudley M. DuBose* my destination and present condition. We do not know what is to be done with Mr. Clay, or where he is to be sent. After that shall be made known, it is Mrs. Clay's intention to go North if allowed; that is, if her husband shall be confined in prison. Yesterday we got New York papers. Saw the progress of the trial of the assassins. Mr. Clay expressed to me the fullest confidence that nothing could be brought out against him in such a crime; he spoke of the assassination in strongest terms of regret; said how deeply he deplored it; repeated his exclamation to that effect when he first heard the news. We had a long talk this morning.

General Wheeler and those who went with him left at six A. M. I was up and took my leave of them. The parting all around was sad. At ten Captain Frailey came up in a tug, and boarded the *Clyde*. Reagan and I were ready. We took leave of all. Anthony and Henry looked very sad. Anthony stood by me to the last. Mrs. Davis asked Captain Frailey if Anthony might not go with me. He said he had inquired of the officer commanding the fleet and had been informed that his orders related to only two persons. This closed the matter just as I had anticipated. I bade Anthony good-bye the last one. Mr. and Mrs. Davis, Mr. and Mrs. Clay, and Mr. Harrison, I had taken leave of.

On my taking leave of Mr. Davis, he seemed more affected than I had ever seen him. He said nothing but

* General Toombs's daughter, wife of General DuBose, prisoner at Fort Warren.

good-bye, and gave my hand a cordial squeeze; his tone evinced deep feeling and emotion. With assistance, I descended the rope-ladder to the tug's deck. All baggage being on, off we steamed to the *Tuscarora.* We stopped a short distance from her and took her lifeboat, as the tug could not well go alongside of her where the steps were let down for us to ascend by. The tide was running in fast, so that by the time we were in the oarboat and ready for the oarsmen, we had drifted farther from the *Tuscarora* than we were when we left the *Clyde.* The tide was coming right ahead of us at about six miles an hour and it was all that the stout seamen with their oars could do to make any head against it. Captain Frailey called twice, "Send the tug!" but he was not heard on the *Tuscarora.* After a long while we reached the ship, but not without some wetting from splashing of waves over the sides of the lifeboat. Right glad was I when we reached the steps on the ship's side.

On the *Tuscarora.* — On deck, we were introduced to several officers, Lieut. Blue, Purser Painter, and others. The captain showed us our quarters; we were to be in the cabin with him. There was but one berth or state-room in it. This, he said, he would assign to me, and he and Reagan would sleep on the circular sofa which ran around the cabin. I declined depriving him of his room and bed. He said it was no deprivation, that he generally slept on the sofa or in a chair; that he resigned it to me "in consideration of my age and past services to the country." These were his words. He was very polite and courteous.

When boarding the *Clyde* that morning, he had brought some strawberries to Mrs. Davis, Mrs. Clay, and Mrs.

Davis's children. He said he had known Mrs. Davis and Mrs. Clay before. The morning we entered Hampton Roads, he had come aboard to give orders to Colonel Pritchard. I did not see him then, but Mrs. Clay told me he had inquired for her; was very courteous to her, etc., and asked if there was any little delicacy he had that she needed, such as preserved or canned vegetables, etc. If so, he would take pleasure in sending her some. She declined; so the strawberries, I suppose, he thought would be acceptable. He had gotten them at Norfolk that morning.

About eleven, anchor was weighed, and we were off. Our fellow prisoners on the *Clyde* stood on deck watching us. When we were fairly under way, we saw a white handkerchief waved toward us. This I felt was by Mrs. Clay, though we were too far off to see distinctly. Reagan and I waved handkerchiefs in return; thus bidding final adieu to them all, I went into the cabin below. Soon out of sight of land, with a clear sky over us, and nothing but the deep blue sea around.

Took lunch with Captain Frailey: strawberries, cheese, etc. He lives to himself; the other officers mess to themselves. Dinner at three; soup, fish, roast beef, asparagus, etc. Tea at eight.

May 22. — Last night I undressed and went to bed, as was my custom at home, for the first time since the night of the 10th, when I occupied my own bed for the last time. Slept sweetly and soundly. Breakfasted at eight; better appetite than for a week or more. Took a smoke in a room on upper deck. Met Lieut. Blue, Mr. Griffin, Mr. Painter, Mr. Mallard, officers of the ship and others. Spent a pleasant time in conversation with them. The captain joined us. The day passed off pleasantly. Lunch, dinner and tea as yesterday.

May 23. — This morning thick fog. Captain made for Block Island to get a pilot. A signal gun was fired. Pilot came and took us to Newport. Reached there about twelve, and anchored in the harbour. The sun shone out. Lieut. Blue went ashore. Sent us papers. Captain's son, in the naval school, came aboard and spent some time with his father. I passed the day, as yesterday, in the cabin and in the smoking-room above with officers. All courteous and agreeable.

May 24. — Mr. Griffin knew Judge Hillyer,* of Georgia, and spoke kindly of him.

We left Newport early this morning for Boston, with new pilot to take us through the sound, leaving Martha's Vineyard and Nantucket to the right. Lieut. Blue told me that he met a lady, relative of Governor Lawrence of Rhode Island, last evening, who expressed sentiments of personal kindness toward me. For this I felt profoundly grateful. It is a consolation to know and feel, as I do, that thousands in all sections of the earth sympathize with me, personally at least. We reached Boston Harbour at eleven p. m. and anchored just below Fort Warren.

* Junius Hillyer, former Congressman and Solicitor U. S. Treasury.

CHAPTER II

FORT WARREN, May 25.—I rose early. Saw Boston in the distance; Fort Warren just ahead. We took our last breakfast with Captain Frailey. He informed us that General Dix was at the Fort and would come aboard to receive us at ten. The gunners got ready to fire a salute in the General's honour. Ten came. General Dix sent two officers, Colonel McMahon of his staff, to represent him, and Lieut. Ray, adjutant of the Post. They said they would take me first. A tug was brought alongside. Our steward, a Frenchman, and Isaac, the coloured cook who had attended to me well, had my baggage ready. I paid them for their attentions. I bade Judge Reagan good-bye in the cabin. Took my leave of all the boat's officers except the Captain, who accompanied the fort officers and myself. I expected we would go to General Dix, but was disappointed. Lieutenant Woodman, of the Fort, met us at the landing. To him I was turned over. Captain Frailey was with the officers who had brought me: before I was aware of it, we were separated, and I did not see him again; this I deeply regretted, inasmuch as I wished to say farewell and express again my sense of obligation for his many acts of kindness. Lieutenant Woodman brought me immediately inside the Fort; after going through the sally port and descending some steps, he stopped at the first room to the left, saying, "This is your room," or "These are your quarters," I forget which. I asked if I could not see Captain Frailey again. I asked if I could not see General Dix; I wished very much to see him about sending word to Linton and about my diet and conditions of prison life. He said "No," and left.

I surveyed the room. A coal fire was burning; a table and chair were in the centre; a narrow, iron, bunk-like bedstead with mattress and covering was in a corner. The floor was stone — large square blocks. The door was locked. For the first time in my life I had the full realization of being a prisoner. I was alone.

Not long after I saw Lieutenant Woodman with Judge Reagan pass my windows (there are two fronting southeast). They went farther front to the left on the same level which is one story below ground-level in front. In half an hour, Lieut. Woodman returned, unlocked the door, and had my trunk and other baggage brought in. He said it was necessary to examine it. I opened the trunk, showed all that was in it; amongst other things the bottle of ale Duncan gave me, and the bottle of whisky Harry put up for me. He said whisky was prohibited. I told him I used it only as medicine; it was necessary sometimes; he said nothing further on that point. He asked if I had any funds. I told him I had. He said it was necessary for him to deposit them with an officer of the Fort, who would receipt and account to me. I counted out to him $560 in gold — all I had left. During the evening, he brought me a receipt from Lieut. Wm. Ray. He told me I would be permitted to walk out with an officer one hour every day; when I wanted anything, I could call to the guard at the window and ask for the orderly, who would attend to my needs; if I wished to communicate with my friends or other persons, I would have to do so by letter through

General Dix at New York. I asked for water, which was brought in a pitcher. I walked the room until three, when dinner came: ten ounces of fresh beef, cooked I don't know how, and sixteen ounces of baker's bread, in a basin or pan of metal something like tin or pewter; an old knife and fork came with it. I ate little.

Called for orderly. He sent me a corporal, whose name is Geary. Asked Geary to request Lieut. Woodman to come to see me. The Lieutenant came. I inquired if I might have a bowl or basin and a washstand; if these could not be furnished, might I supply them out of my funds? He said he would send in a washstand and basin; I might buy any other little things I might desire from the sutler. I made out a bill of articles, gave them to the corporal, and requested him to order for me the *Herald*, *Times*, and *Tribune*, of New York, and *Journal*, of Boston. The papers he soon brought. In the Boston *Herald*, which he also handed me, I saw an account of a conversation with me at Hilton Head by some reporter, who states that I said my reason for going for secession was disinclination to clash with Toombs. I gave no such reason. I went with my State after she resumed the full exercise of her sovereign powers in her Ordinance of Secession (which I had opposed with all my power and had voted against) because I considered my ultimate allegiance due her. To have further or longer opposed her, I should have been amenable to her laws as a traitor. But I had no inclination to disobey her mandate. Toombs, for whom I ever had a warm regard, and I had frequently clashed on many grave questions. We had clashed upon the candidacy of Douglas; and pointedly upon this very question of secession. I could afford, and had afforded, to clash with him but not with the State of Georgia.

May 26. — Suffered intensely last night in feeling. I see a statement in a Boston paper about my saying, on my way to Fortress Monroe, that I would have gone to Washington to be hung on notification from authorities there, etc. This is a mistake; I said, as I had said to General Upton, that there was no necessity to send an armed force for my arrest; on notice or request, I should have gone to Washington without arrest or guard, though I might have been certain that hanging would follow; I had no inclination to avoid a full and speedy investigation of my whole conduct, or to evade the result, whatever it might be; I had no disposition to make or attempt an escape, and should not, let my fate be what it might. This is the substance of what I have said on this subject on all occasions. May the great God above enable me to make it good! Oh, my brother! my brother! and dear ones at home! would to that same great God I could know how you are, and that you, Linton, are well again! My greatest suffering and agony of soul, which are almost more than I can bear, are mainly on your account. Wrote letters to General Dix, and to Dick Johnston, Sparta, Ga., of which the following are copies:

MAJOR-GENERAL JOHN A. DIX: I desired exceedingly to have a personal interview with you yesterday while you were here. As that could not be, I now address you this note. I wish you to have forwarded, if you please, the enclosed letter. Its object is simply to inform my relatives and friends where and how I am. They, of course, are very anxious to know. General Upton was of the opinion, when I left him, that this privilege would be allowed. They are expecting it. I could make other earnest requests as to the nature of my confinement, diet, etc., in consideration of my feeble health, etc., but I forbear. I will, however, give you the assurance of a man of honour, that I would not escape if I could; and if proof were needed to establish the sincerity of this declaration, I have but to refer to the facts attending my capture and my well-known position in regard to it long before. All I desire is such comforts as are consistent with imprisonment and necessary to my health. So much for myself. As for my country, I will add that my constant desire is for its speedy pacification and well-being. My whole efforts, were I permitted to make them, would be devoted to that object.

Yours most respectfully,
ALEXANDER H. STEPHENS.

PROF. R. M. JOHNSTON,

My Dear Sir: I am here in about the same state of health as when you last saw me. The sea voyage I stood better than I expected. Please let this be made known to my dear relatives and friends. All communications they have with me, if any are allowed, must be through Major-General John A. Dix, of New York City. I am exceedingly anxious to hear from them. Tell Mr. Myers to see to it, for my sake, that none of them at home suffer for food. My kindest regards attend you and yours. My tenderest love to Linton and the little ones.

Yours truly,
ALEXANDER H. STEPHENS.

These letters I handed Lieutenant Woodman, requesting that they be forwarded. I sincerely wish they may, but I am in doubt. I have been more overcome with mental torture to-day than for many years; more heavily weighted down than since the death of my father. That blow left pangs that can never be forgotten; so did the death of my dear brother in 1843.

Six P. M. — My letter to Johnston returned. Lieut. Woodman says Major H. A. Allen, 2nd U. S. Artillery, who commands this Post, has forwarded to General Dix the letter addressed to him, but from previous orders did not feel at liberty to forward its enclosure. I do still hope that General Dix will allow it to be sent.

May 27. — Took short walk out this morning with Lieut. Woodman. Rain drove me in. Greatly depressed about home and the dear ones there, though I have not suffered such agony as yesterday. Gave an order on Lieut. Ray in payment for certain articles which have been brought me. These, with prices are as follows:

1 lb. coffee, 80 cts; teaspoon, 37 cts; condensed milk, 75 cts; 1 lb. B. sugar, 25 cts; 1 lb. W. sugar, 30 cts; 1 lb. B. tea, $2; matches, 4 cts; scissors, $1; pitcher, 75 cts; mirror, 50 cts; candlestick, 37 cts; blankbook, $2; vial ink, 15 cts; steel pens, 15 cts; lead pencil, 20 cts; spittoon, 75 cts; 1 pk. Irish potatoes, 50 cts; cup and saucer, 50 cts; box for potatoes, 25 cts; coffee-pot, $2; washstand, $2; 1 lb. candles, 60 cts; in all, $16.23. The sutler's name is A. J. Hall.

Have been looking over a catalogue of books in the Post library, which prisoners may use. Lieut. Woodman was kind enough to get it for me. He left to-day for Boston, turning me over to Lieut. Croak in his absence; will be gone until Monday. I inquired of him this morning if Mr. Reagan was well. He replied in the affirmative. I asked if Mr. Reagan was able to be up.

He said, "Yes." I said nothing more about Mr. Reagan. Before I got the catalogue, I had ordered from the sutler, Greeley's "American Conflict," Prescott's "Ferdinand and Isabella" and "Conquest of Mexico," and Savage's "Representative Men." After seeing that Prescott's histories are in the library, I countermanded the order for his works.

I see in the evening Boston *Journal* that Mr. Davis has been put in irons at Fortress Monroe. This I deeply grieve to learn. Most profoundly do I sympathize with him in his present condition. Widely as I differed from him on public policy before and after secession, ruinous to our cause as I have thought his aims and objects, much as I attribute the condition of our country to his errors, yet I do now most deeply pity him and commiserate his condition. Got from sutler, Greeley's "American Conflict." Read it till time to put out lights, nine-thirty.

Sunday — The horrors of imprisonment, close confinement, no one to see or to talk to, with the reflection of being cut off for I know not how long — perhaps forever — from communication with dear ones at home, are beyond description. Words utterly fail to express the soul's anguish. This day I wept bitterly. Nerves and spirit utterly forsook me. O God, if it be possible, let this cup pass from me! Yet Thy will be done.

Walked out; a northeaster blowing, with mists of rain; felt weak and sick; returned in ten minutes, Lieut. Croak with me. Sent for the surgeon, Dr. Seaverns. Was too full to talk much with him without bursting into tears. He allowed me to have a bottle of ale, which I requested. My affliction, I know, is more of mind than body. Thoughts of home, my brother, and all the dear ones there, black and white, almost kills, almost crazes me.

May 29. — Cloudy and misty. Walked out at nine with Lieut. Croak. Spent my time afterward the best way I could; mostly in transcribing previous notes to these pages. Got the papers. Lieut. Woodman returned. Was quite glad to see him. No reply yet from General Dix.

May 30. — Took a towel bath this morning, changed underclothes. Washing put out the day I came was returned Sunday morning. Had an interview with Lieut. Woodman. Asked if General H. R. Jackson and General DuBose were here yet. He said they were. Asked if they were well. He said they were. Asked about Judge Reagan. He said Reagan was well.

P. M.—Lieut. W. read a reply to me from General Dix. It was in substance that General Dix would have seen me on my arrival here had he known such was my desire; that I would be permitted to purchase such articles of diet as I might wish, under some general regulations previously made and referred to. What these are I don't know. I wrote General Dix again:

Dear Sir: Will you be pleased to make known to the President or the Secretary of War my earnest desire and request that I be allowed to communicate by letter with friends at home? It is a matter of very great importance to quite a number of persons who are dependent upon me, that I should. This is apart from their desire and expectation barely to hear where and how I am. I left a brother's widow with a large family, all dependent on me for subsistence, with supplies on hand for but a short time. I had made arrangements for providing more, of which they know nothing. I wish to give them this information. I have but one brother living. He was quite ill when I left. I wish, earnestly wish, to hear from him, and to let him know how I am. What I request of the President is that privilege of communicating with these friends, through the War Department, upon these matters exclusively private, may be extended to me. Besides my deceased brother's children, I am guardian for a number of other minors, for whose private interest it is important that I should be permitted to write to some one in their behalf. I repeat my assurance, as a man of honour, that under no circumstances should this privilege be abused; but, indeed, it could not be, as all letters from and to me would pass your inspection or that of the War Department, as may be thought proper. I would be greatly obliged to you if you would submit this letter to the President or Secretary of War, and let me know as early as possible through Major Allen whether this request is granted or not. So much for myself. As for my country, I repeat what I said before: "My earnest desire is for its speedy pacification and well-being. My whole efforts, were I permitted to make them, would be directed to that object." I have just had read to me the reply made to my former communication, for which I feel truly obliged.

Yours most respectfully,
ALEXANDER H. STEPHENS.

This morning I saw the President's Proclamation of Amnesty, of 29th May. My brother is justly entitled to its benefits, though he was in the war for a short time as Lieut.-Colonel of the 15th Ga. Regt., and was later in the militia. He was opposed to secession, and voted with me against it. Like me, he felt it his duty after the Ordinance was passed, to go with his State, but his leading object at all times was merely to vindicate the principles of State Sovereignty. He was, as his course in the Legislature shows, for peace upon the American principles of 1776, leaving the future relations of the States to be regulated by themselves. The Peace Resolutions of the Georgia Legislature were drawn up by him. He was utterly opposed, as I was, to the leading ideas and policy of the authorities at Richmond in the conduct and object of the war. So far as concerns slavery in the proclamation, I don't think that individually, or so far as relates to his private interest, he would care a straw for that. I know I do not. I own, or have bought, a number of Negroes; some have been born on my premises; in all, those who by our laws have been my slaves, I believe, are about thirty-five; I have spent for them and their comfort at least $20,000 of my own earnings, perhaps more. I am perfectly willing that they shall be free. I feel assured that Linton feels as I do. Whether he will apply for a special amnesty or not, I do not know, or whether he need ask amnesty under the present proclamation. I am greatly distressed on his account, more than on my own.

May 31.—Was threatened with *nephritic calculi*, or feared, from symptoms, one of those terrible attacks. Informed Lieut. W. and asked that the orderly might be in hearing should I call out in the night. What I should have done in this cell with a severe attack of this most painful affliction, I do not know. But I got relief before midnight; Lieut. W. came at eleven, very kindly, to inquire how I was getting along. I was then comfortable. Was out this morning with him, rested under the shed for the band. We passed the drill of the Battalion, 1st Mass. Artillery. He told me that he belonged to Company A of the Battalion. Saw, in the New York *Herald*, Mr. Toombs's letter of 24th March; also Carpenter's version of President Lincoln's pig anecdote at the Conference in Hampton Roads. It is incorrect. The mistake arises, I doubt not, in Mr. Carpenter's recollection. The anecdote was not in reply to anything I had said, but to Mr. Hunter's remarks concerning effects on the coloured race of general and immediate emancipation, and the destitute condition that would ensue to a large number of its women and children who would be unable to provide subsistence for themselves. In reply to this the President, in a good-humoured, jocose style, told the story, the substance of which Mr. Carpenter gives. Mr. Lincoln's conclusion was simply, "Let 'em root!" the reply of the farmer. To this I said, "That, Mr. President, must be the origin of the adage, 'Root, pig, or perish.'" I did not think then, nor do I now, that the moral of the story, in its application was very good or humane. Still it amounted to only this: that in Mr. Lincoln's opinion there would be no difficulty in that class of people's taking care of themselves.

Had hot rolls, cup of coffee, fried ham and an egg from sutler for breakfast. Geary told me there were no rations in the cook's room but bread; and I ordered of sutler, who did not send the bill. What I am to pay, I do not know. I requested Geary to go for the bill and I expected it. Whether I shall indulge in such luxuries will depend somewhat on the cost. I have eaten but little here; the camp ration does not suit me. Sutler, several days ago, sent Prescott's histories, six volumes, saying they were bought before my order countermanding purchase was received. To my request to return them he sent word that he could not. How much of my money will be lost by this purchase, I do not know. Greeley's "American Conflict," which I received with the other books, I find interesting. In the main, Greeley has put the issues preceding the conflict as fairly as could any Northern writer of this generation. Wherein I differ from him, and essentially, it is not now my purpose to state. I wish, if my life is spared and my health permits, to leave a memorial on the subject of this war and these troubles.*

Five P. M. — Spent the day reading, and in walking my room or cell, whichever it may be called. It is, estimated by steps, about 24 by 18 feet. It is a consolation to realize that, hard as is my confinement, it might be a great deal worse. How much better is my condition than was that of Lafayette at Olmutz; yet he stood it for five years. My case and his seem dissimilar only in the less rigorous severity of my situation. He seemed a creature of destiny, victim of the policy of others. In all he did, he aimed only at the advancement and security of constitutional liberty for his country. This has been my sole object. His counsels were not heeded. From the most patriotic motives, he suffered himself to be put in a position which swept him into a vortex, beyond his powers of resistance, escape, or control. So with me.

How much better is my condition than was his! I have a large, airy room; plenty of Heaven's precious light; a comfortable bunk with shuck mattress, on which, with my blankets, I get along with tolerable comfort; pure water, though not cool; and enough food, if it were only suited to my habits and state of health. I am permitted to purchase what suits if I possess the means.

* He left it in his "War Between the States."

I have the privilege of seeing daily papers and reading books. What abundant cause for consolation! How much more miserable and horrible might not my condition be! It is true I suffer intensely; my anguish is unutterable. This arises from no self-accusation, no apprehension of the future, nor fear of death. I feel as if I can meet death, if such fate as a punishment awaits me, with as much calmness as did Seneca or Socrates. My suffering springs from confinement and from being cut off from all communication with home and its dear ones. No mortal ever had stronger attachments for his home than I for mine. That old homestead and that quiet lot, Liberty Hall, in Crawfordville, sterile and desolate as they may seem to others, are bound to me by associations tender as heartstrings and strong as hooks of steel; there I wish to live and there to die.

Am anxious to hear from General Dix. The papers say General Howell Cobb has been arrested. I regret to see Bates's testimony before the Military Court at Washington. I can not believe it true; but this statement of what Mr. Davis said in Charlotte, N. C., on receipt of the telegram informing him of Mr. Lincoln's assassination and of what he said to General Breckinridge* on the same subject will, I fear, whether true or false, make a very unfavourable impression against him. While it in no way connects him with the affairs, yet it will make the impression upon the popular mind that one who could utter such sentiments possesses a bad heart; and this will lessen that sympathy which his condition naturally inspires. For the honour of my beloved South, I do trust that no such foul stigma shall ever rest on her

* See Mr. Davis's own statement in his "Rise and Fall of the Confederate Government," II, 683. For statement of courier who handed him the telegram, see Avary's "Dixie After the War," 84. The false testimony, to which Stephens refers, represents Davis as expressing gratification.

escutcheon as even an approbation or countenance of that deed by one holding high position in her councils and in the trust of her people, would, by the common consent of civilized nations, place there. Whatever be our fate, whatever else we may lose, rights, property, even life, I wish our honour and that of our rulers preserved untarnished. In the worst possible contingency, let us be able to say, as Louis did at Pavia, "We have lost all but honour." I see that Mr. Davis is about to be carried to Washington for trial. I am glad of this. Hope he will have a speedy and a fair trial. My earnest wish in regard to myself is a speedy settling of my fate, whatever it may be.

CHAPTER III

THURSDAY, June 1. — Dreamed of home last night. O Dreams! Visions! Shadows of the brain! What are you? My whole consciousness, since I heard of President Lincoln's assassination, seems nothing but a horrid dream.

It is a week since I entered these walls; three weeks since I was arrested at my home; and just four, I think, since all of the Stephens blood and name in Georgia, accidently, or providentially rather, met at the old homestead. That was a remarkable meeting. Linton and his three children were on a visit to me. We went down to the homestead; there, the widow of my brother, John L., and her family reside. Her three sons, John A., Linton Andrew, and William Grier, had just returned from the army. John had just got home from Johnson's Island where he had been a prisoner a long time; had been captured at Port Hudson in 1863. Mr. Lincoln, at my request, had granted him a special parole, for which I was truly obliged; this parole he had promised me at Hampton Roads, and had complied with his promise. He had written me a letter by John which I never saw until after his assassination. I almost wept over the letter when I saw it. He had sent to Johnson's Island for John. Had a personal interview with him [in Washington], treated him very kindly, spoke in kindly terms of his former acquaintance with me, all the particulars of which John gave me in detail. He let John remain in Washington as long as he chose, which was five days, I believe.

Linton A. had just gotten home from the army in North Carolina; William G., wounded in the leg, had been home some days from the same army. James Clarence, 15 years old, was at home; he had never been in the army. Mary Reid, their sister, with her little son, Leidy Stephens Reid, who lived with Sister Elizabeth, my brother John's widow, were at home. So all of our name and blood in the South were met together. All but William walked out to the old burying-ground; we stood by the graves of my father and grandfather. The occasion was a solemn one, and the more so that it was near the anniversary of my dear father's death and the dispersion of his little family circle. Will such a meeting ever take place again? I have often reflected upon the fact that many of the most important events of my life have happened in the early part of May; so much so that I have a sort of superstition on the subject. On the 12th of May, 1812, my mother died; on the 7th May, 1826, my father, on the 14th, my stepmother, and in a few days, the family were dispersed. Now, on the 4th, all who were living and their descendants were gathered together for the first time after the dispersion, thirty-nine years before, on or near the same spot. It seemed ominous.

Rose early. As it is fast day and mourning in memory of Mr. Lincoln, I had requested Mr. Geary, the corporal, to bring me from sutler's nothing but a cup of hot coffee and rolls. These he brought at seven. I noticed he brought the rolls on an earthen plate. This is an improvement in kindness and attention.

On the 7th of May last, Sunday, and the anniversary

of my father's death, Harry came into my room about day and told me "The Yankees are here." "Where?" I asked. "All about in the yard and in the lot," he replied. "Well," said I, getting up, "Harry, I expect they have come for me, they will probably take me away; you may never see me after to-day. I want you to take care of my things and to do as I have told you in all particulars as far as you can. Have they asked for me? "No," he replied; "they only said they wanted breakfast and corn for their horses." "Give them what they want," I said, and dressed myself in readiness to leave in case I should be arrested. That dress was unchanged — pants, coat, and vest — until this morning when I put on a thinner suit. But to return to the scenes of that Sunday morning. Harry reappeared and told me that the officer in command said he wished to see me; that I need be under no apprehension of arrest, all he wanted was breakfast and feed for his horses; he expressed high regard for me personally. I went out and met him in the passage. He announced himself as Lieutenant White of the 13th Tennessee, of General Stoneman's command. We talked in a friendly way until breakfast. He and four of his men sat down with me to my table. My brother and his family were also present.

During the day Lieut.-Colonel Stacy, in command of the 13th Tenn. Cav. Reg., came into town with a battalion, and sent his adjutant to say he would be glad to see and take tea with me. My response was for him to "come, I should be glad to see him." In the evening he, his adjutant, and Dr. Cameron, surgeon of the regiment, called, spent some time and took tea. Conversation was agreeable. I invited them to stay all night; they declined but accepted my invitation for breakfast.

They gave me to understand that they were in pursuit of Mr. Davis. Monday, after breakfast, they all left by the Sparta road. Monday night, Major Dyer with a battalion arrived; he left Tuesday morning.

Tuesday morning my brother and his three children, and little Emmie Stevens, daughter of Rev. Carlos W. Stevens, of Sparta, left for home. That was my last sight of Linton, perhaps forever. Soon after his departure, considering it most probable that I should be arrested and at an early day, about which we had talked and agreed, I went to the homestead to see my servants there; I gave them all the information I could regarding the condition of public affairs and my own situation. I told them they were now free, at which I was perfectly contented and satisfied; that I might and probably should be taken away from them soon and perhaps hung; that I wished them, if they saw fit, to remain there and finish the crop. I thought this would be best for them; they should have half of what was made and be subsisted out of supplies on hand; at the end of the year, if I were in life and permitted, I would furnish lands to such as wished to remain for the future, dividing the plantation into small farms or settlements which they could occupy, paying rent. I took a parting and affectionate leave of them. That is the last time I have seen them all together.

At home. I called in Harry, my ever true and faithful servant on the lot, and made him a bill of sale for the mules and buggy horses there. He had deposited with me for several years his private earnings; these amounted, I think, with interest to $662. I sold him the mules and horses, to which he was attached, for the debt; he was perfectly willing. They were worth more, but I gave him the difference. I gave him general instructions how to manage, in event of my arrest, until he should hear from me. Subsistence for the summer was the main point. My corn was scarce, not enough on hand. I had some conversation with Mary Reid and John on the same subject but not so full as I wished. We were interrupted by company. The conversation with her, I think, was on Wednesday. I staid at home, not wishing by absence to seem to be avoiding arrest, which from the time I left Richmond, I considered my ultimate fate. I felt distressed and pained at the use made and turn given by the authorities at Richmond to the report of the Commissioners of their conference with President Lincoln and Mr. Seward at Hampton Roads. It seems they were controlled by the genii of fatality. "*Quos Deus vult perdere prius dementat*" seems strongly to apply to them.

At the close of the last sentence, Lieut. W. entered for the usual morning walk. We went on the parapet; looked at target shooting by a company; rested under music-band arbour. He informed me that my room had never been occupied by any prisoner except Captain Webb of the *Atlanta* and some of his men; this in reply to my question prompted by writings on the wall.

A favourite maxim in my life has been, "The world treats a man very much as he treats it," or, "Whoever kicks the world will be apt to be kicked in turn." This was given me soon after my majority, by a man of experience, while I was chafing under some ill usage. I have repeated it to many young persons since. It recurs to me often since I have been here, obtruding itself upon the mind as Job's comforters pressed their consolations on him. The inquiry springs up: "Do you hold to your maxim? If so, must you not admit that you have acted a very bad part toward the world?" With the firmness of Job, I neither make the admission nor repudiate the maxim.

I do know that my acts toward the whole human family have been marked by kindness. In all that I have done from the beginning of the political troubles which have brought me here, I have been governed solely by a sense of duty to do the most good to my fellow men that I could under the circumstances. Personal ambition had no part in anything I have done; nor had prejudice toward the people of the North; I never entertained to them any feeling of unkindness. My earnest desire from the first has been that the conflict might end in the speediest way possible for the interest and well-being of both sections of the country; for their advancement in prosperity and happiness and for the preservation and perpetuation of their Constitutional liberty. This, I thought, and still think, could be better effected by maintenance of the principles of the ultimate, absolute sovereignty of the States, than in any other way, In these principlès I was reared. They constitute the polestar of my political life. I am not prepared to admit that I erred in entertaining them, and to govern my conduct accordingly, because I suffer as I do. Why I thus suffer I do not know, but I feel an internal assurance that all will ultimately be right, let the sequel be as it may.

In the Boston *Journal* I see that Gen. Howell Cobb was permitted to visit his family, while Mr. Mallory [Confederate Secretary of Navy] and Senator Hill (B. H., of Georgia, I suppose) had been sent the day before to this place of confinement. I am truly glad Cobb has been permitted to visit his family. Would to God I might be permitted so much as to write and to hear from my dear ones at home! I should be exceedingly gratified to see Mr. Mallory and Mr. Hill when they reach here, but take it for granted that this privilege and pleasure will be denied. It is announced from Washington that though Mr. Davis is about to be removed to the barracks there, his trial is not expected to come off in a month. This I regret. I earnestly wish all trials and results quickly over. Particularly do I wish my own fate determined.

It is a matter of perplexity with me whether or not I should make special application to President Johnson for amnesty. I am willing to comply with the requirements made of others. But how the application might be received, I do not know. Should it be considered as emanating from a desire to evade the responsibility of my acts and to avoid punishment, this would cause me mortification and pain. On the other hand, should I fail to apply, might it not be regarded as evidence of a defiant spirit of protest against the existing state of things resulting from the fate of war? I should regret to be so interpreted. I think I shall wait to hear the result of my request through General Dix for permission to communicate with my relatives and friends.

Much is said in the papers about "loyalty" and "disloyalty," "Union men" and "traitors." What is meant by "loyalty," as thus commonly used, I do not exactly comprehend. No one ever lived with stronger feelings of devotion to the Constitution of the United States and the Union under it than myself. I regarded it as embodying the best system of government on earth. My views on this subject have been often expressed. For the Union barely, without the rights and guarantees secured by the Constitution, I never entertained or professed any attachment.

My devotion and my loyalty were to the Union under the Constitution with the civil and religious rights it secured — not to the Union *per se*. This devotion was felt and expressed by me until the powers that made the Union unmade it; or, at least, until Georgia, one of the parties to the compact, withdrew from it. I opposed that action of the State, in which I was born and of which I was a citizen, to the last. I conformed my conduct to hers not because of less loyalty to the principles of the old Constitution, but because that Power which had transferred the allegiance of its citizens under limitations to the United States had withdrawn this allegiance. It was by Georgia's act as a party to the Compact of Union set forth in the Constitution, that I had owed even a qualified allegiance to the Government of the United States, and it was by her act that I considered that allegiance withdrawn. But my "loyalty" to the principles of Constitutional liberty remained unshaken. My effort was to rescue and save the Constitution — the great principles of self-government therein set forth — to the people of Georgia though the Union had been abandoned by them. Never for one instant has a sentiment of "disloyalty" to these great essential, cardinal principles of American constitutional liberty entered my breast. So much on the point of my "loyalty."

As for the "atrocious rebellion and conspiracy against the life of the Nation" in which I am charged by the press with having taken part, I here state that I always considered the "life" and very *soul* of the "Nation" to be the Constitution and the principles of popular self-government therein set forth and thereby secured. Never did and never can rebel throb enter my breast against these. The "Nation" without these principles never had any proper or legitimate life. The only oath of allegiance the Constitution requires or ever required was and is to itself — to support and defend itself. This, I did to the utmost of my ability *in* the *Union* so long as Georgia acknowledged herself a party to it; and never since her withdrawal have I swerved from the oath, often taken before that event, to support and defend the same sacred principles. This I have done with more hazard and risk and under heavier denunciations than most men are willing to encounter. In doing it, I looked to nothing but the public good, to the welfare of those who without my solicitation had confided high trusts to me.

P. M. — Corporal Geary brought sutler's bill: 6 vols. Prescott's Histories, $21; Greeley's American Conflict, $7; tea canister, 75 cts; tea pot, $1; sugar bowl, $1; 2 qts. ale, 50 cts; in all now presented, $31.25: making my expenditures this one week $47.48. This summation is frightful! I must curtail, even if I suffer physically. This does not include my newspapers. I had no idea the books would have been at such prices, or I should not have thought of buying them. My funds will soon give out at this rate; then what shall I do?

5 P. M. — Just got a sight of Reagan as he passed my window, returning from his evening walk, I suppose, Lieut. W. with him. He looked well and stepped firmly. How I should have liked to speak to him!

A correspondent from Hilton Head to a New York paper says I did not look when there as if I considered myself a prisoner, or as if I had any idea of the estimation in which I was held by the people of the North. I *felt* myself a prisoner, however I may have looked; but I did not consider myself a *culprit*, or so feel, whatever may be the opinion of any one else on that point.

June 2. — Another improvement in attention this morning at breakfast — a silver fork and an ivory-handled knife. The breakfast was palatable but the little I ate tasted no better than with the black knife and fork. The attention I duly appreciated; it may have been accidental, but I am inclined to think not. Lieut. W., at nine, brought Lieut. William Longly to walk with me; had long conversation with him. He told me he was living in Macon, Ga., when the war broke out, was clerking in a mercantile house, Bond & Co.; knew many of my acquaintances; was in Macon in 1860 when Douglas and I spoke there; heard H. R. Jackson's speech that night before the bonfire in the street, against us. We had a long talk, the whole hour, about the state of the country. On the whole, perhaps my most agreeable walk here. It was a source of some pleasure to see and converse with one who had lived in Georgia. Anything from Georgia, however remotely, cheers my heart. What delight it would be to get a paper from Augusta, Macon, Atlanta, or Columbus! What intense delight to get a letter from Linton, or home!

2.30. — As I was walking my room just now, a number of persons — men, women, and children — appeared on the stone walk directly in front of my windows. This walk is on a solid wall about eight feet from the wall of my cell, allowing a passage for the guards. The guards' beat is on the same level with my floor, but the level of the walk is that of the drill-ground and on the same plane with the top of my windows. By peeping down, these persons could see me as in each round I approached and passed my windows. Some were old and some were young; all were attired as if on a jaunt for amusement, particularly the ladies and children. I felt no indisposition to gratify their curiosity and continued my walk, giving them such sight as they could get of me when I passed the windows; occasionally, I gave them a good steady look in return. Who they were, or whether friendly toward me personally or otherwise, I do not know. They are, I suppose, visitors to the fort, who, on having my cell pointed out to them, came to get a peep at me. This is the first time I have been gazed at by any persons with only a view to gratify curiosity, since my arrest.

Geary tells me the sutler will charge $1.40 per week for coffee, rolls, etc., such as I have been getting for breakfast. This causes me reflection; how to do without them I don't know, and yet if I incur this expense my funds will soon run low. I may need other essentials much more, and I may not be permitted to have other funds sent me. My condition would then be bad indeed. I told Geary to continue the breakfast a week; meantime, I will endeavour to ascertain whether I shall be permitted to receive further funds when present supply is out. If I am not satisfied that I shall, I must curtail this expense. Had I looked for such a state of things, I should have accepted Gip Grier's and General Foster's offers.

5 P. M.—Kind and attentive Geary brought the Boston *Journal*. I see that Governor Brown [of Georgia] has been released on parole. I am glad others are permitted to go at large, if I cannot be. Could I but correspond with home people, how much better I should feel! The

world's justice is strange. While thousands who contributed all their influence to bring these troubles upon the country are at large, I, who did my utmost to avert them, am confined in a cell, cut off from communication with relatives and friends and deprived of comforts essential to life in my enfeebled condition. May the Lord God mercifully sustain me and enable me to bear with resignation what His Providence permits! Have I unconsciously committed some great wrong in His sight?

9 P. M.—Lieut. W., who calls every night at this hour, informs me that, in reply to my letter to General Dix, I may, through General Dix, write letters home on private business. This is a great relief. Whether I shall be permitted to receive letters, I do not know yet.

Lights have to be put out at nine-thirty; a tap of the drum or blast from a bugle is the signal. Took up my Bible ——

June 3.—At "Bible," the bugle note sounded. My pen was instantly dropped and the candle blown out. What I was about to put down was this: Took up my Bible with a desire to find in it something on which the soul could rely for comfort and hope. The book opened at Isaiah 38. Was it accident? Believing all things are under the direction of the Ruler of the Universe, by whom even the hairs of our heads are numbered, I secured consolation from this chapter. As has been my custom for the last twenty years or more, before committing myself to sleep, I committed my body, soul, and spirit to His keeping, praying devoutly that His will "be done on earth as in Heaven." This fact I here record mainly because religion is a subject on which I seldom speak or write. Perhaps in this I have done wrong. It has arisen from a very deep aversion to what I consider "cant."

P. M.—Spent the day reading the papers, particularly therein Sumner's eulogy on Lincoln; and in writing letters home. This is a copy of my letter to Linton:

My dear Brother: This little messenger of love, by the permission of the authorities, is about to be dispatched from the quarters of my present confinement. It goes as the embodiment of the tenderest and strongest affections of my heart to the dearest one to me on earth; so receive it and cherish it. I am in about the same state of health as when you saw me last. I stood the sea voyage better than I expected. I reached here on the 25th of May. As I passed by my home on Sunday the 14th, I heard that you were quite ill the day before at your home. This caused me great pain, the more from the sad reflection that it was the ever memorable anniversary of the death of the only surviving parent of our household, whose life kept our little family circle happily together around the paternal hearthstone; that never-to-be-forgotten 14th day of May, 1826 — that, too, was on Sunday. My greatest mental disquietude, my greatest sufferings, have been on your account. Would to God I could know this day how you are, and that you are well again. Do write immediately, if you get this, and let me know. Inclose your letter to Maj.-General John A. Dix, New York, with request that it be forwarded to me, and I think it will be promptly done. All communications must be through him and open to his inspection. I wish simply to know how you and all the dear ones are. This is all that is allowed. I have no communications here with any persons but the guard and officers in charge. I am permitted to walk out on the grounds inside the Fort accompanied by an officer one hour every day. No rudeness has been exhibited toward me, but on the contrary I have received every proper courtesy and attention, considering my condition. I have access to books and the daily papers. My room is large and well ventilated, all usual necessaries are supplied, and I get such extras as I need by purchase. These are great privileges and comforts which are highly appreciated by me.

[I left the court papers in the case of Barksdale and his sister, which we were to settle, with Harry, and requested him to hand them to Judge Reese. See that the Judge gets them. In my table drawer, I left some private papers for Prof. R. M. Johnston, which I wish you to hand him.] May you speedily get this letter. May I soon hear from you and know that you are well. That we may once more meet, and at no distant day, is the earnest wish with which I now take my farewell leave. God bless you and yours now and forever. A kiss to all the children. Kind remembrance to Cosby, Carlos' family, Simpson, Lane, Evans, Harris, the Alfriends, and all the rest, especially Judge Thomas — be sure in your letter to let me know how he is; tell him I send my special regards to him, Sallie Baker, Henry, and their little ones. And last though not least to Dick Johnston and his family.

Yours most affectionately,
ALEXANDER H. STEPHENS.

I rewrote this, omitting lines in brackets, fearing the officers might think the papers some I wished removed and concealed. The other letters were to George F. Bristow, John A. and Elizabeth M. Stephens.

Unusually depressed; reaction perhaps from elate feelings animating me while writing letters home with the thought that they would soon be received and I should soon have answers. Now that I think on obstacles, perhaps insuperable, in the way of my letters ever reaching their destination, gloom comes over me. All will depend on the officers, even to get them to Augusta;

no mail open through the Carolinas yet, I think; when one will be open, who can tell? If they reach Augusta, perhaps no mail on the Ga. R. R., if on that, perhaps none to Sparta. All is dark as to when I shall ever hear from home.

Dinner: tough green beef; the cook seems to have done his best with it, but it was beyond his skill. If it had not been for my potatoes, I should have suffered for food; the cook boiled two for me, and on these I fared.

5 P. M. — More low-spirited; feel as if I had had an interview in reality with homefolks and they had left me. Wrote to Dr. Paterson, of Augusta. My morning walk was with Lieut. Longly. We had but little talk; I was too full of the idea of holding converse by letter with the dear ones at home. Paid fifty cents for postage stamps. All expenses paid up to this time, $47.98.

June 4. — Sunday again. This day four weeks ago, where was I? Oh, the scenes and faces then surrounding me! Now, nothing but these white sepulchral walls! My letters did not get off last night. Lieut. W. did not call in time. This I deeply regret. I wished not a moment's unnecessary delay to attend their going. He called this morning at nine-thirty for them. They start by the fort tugboat; then go by mail to New York to-night, I hope. May Providence in mercy expedite them!

This is a strange world; it presents striking inconsistencies. One of the most notable is the difference between profession and practice in religion. New England and the United States boast of their religious principles; yet in this fort the fife, the drum, the bugle, and the drill go on with no difference between Saturday,

Sunday, or Monday. To the soldier there is really no Sabbath, no sacred day of rest and worship, in field or garrison. A number of the bloodiest battles of the late war were fought on Sunday. It is claimed that this most fiendish, deadly, Sunday work, this mutual slaughter of men (who personally bore each other no ill will) was the work of God to advance civilization and Christianity. There are not wanting those, on either side, to preach such doctrines to congregations every Lord's Day.

Again the drum-beats, and the soldiers are summoned to their tasks. Slavery! Liberty! What are ye? What is the difference between camp, factory, and cotton field? Casuists, moralists, statesmen, philanthropists, humanists, sage philosophers, evangelists, Christianizers, and world-reformers, answer me. Orders must be obeyed. Where is room for discretion or for exercise of conscience to the poor soldier any more than to the poor Negro or the poor labourer in a factory? The great problem of human wrong has not yet been solved. Perhaps the best thing that can be done by the wisest and the best is not to war against nature, not to find fault, but to take things as they are and do all that can be done, under circumstances as they arise, for the good of every fellow-being. Often more mischief and misery attend well-meant efforts to right apparent and gross wrongs by rashly uptearing old systems than would ensue from letting them alone. Human society is not unlike the human organism. However badly it may be constituted, however diseased from hereditary or other causes, yet, as David said of man, its great prototype, it is "wonderfully" as well as "fearfully made." It has nervous fibres running all through its most diseased parts. The rude touch of a probe in the hands of a rash operator may cause deeper injury and more suffering to the invalid than that which he before endured.

I do not mean that no effort should be made to eradicate causes of evil and wrong, but only that all such efforts should be wisely made; reason guided by justice and general benevolence should govern, not passion incited by prejudice and bent on making conditions square with some favourite preconceived theory. It seems a law of the human mind to want all things to *square* with its own notions. But *squares* of all sorts are artificial. They are not met with in phases of the natural universe. Throughout cosmos, we see nothing in forms, changes, or motions approaching squares or direct lines. Light, heat, and electricity are swerved by the media through which they pass. Squaring is not nature's process either in the material or mental world. No human society or government can be wisely or safely built upon any one general, unalterable principle fixing permanent status for all its members.

As gravitation is the general fixed law of the material universe, so justice should be the fundamental law of all political or social organizations. How society is to be constituted so that all can attain justice; that is the vexed question. While I confess myself unable to see how it is to be perfectly done, I am equally well satisfied how, in some particulars, it cannot be. It cannot be done, for instance, by any such dogma (not well understood by its advocates) as that all members of society are equal, for this settles nothing.

Equal in what? In age? Facts answer, "No." In feature and appearance? Facts answer, "No." In bodily size or strength? Facts answer, "No." In mental strength or vigour? Facts answer, "No."

In moral qualities? Facts answer, "No." In acquirements or accumulations? Facts continue to answer, "No." In not a single one of these particulars can any two amongst millions be found with the dogma of equality. In what then are all men by nature equal, or in what ought they to be held to be equal? Is the dogma utterly false and absurd, or is there in it a latent truth which some superficial and rash spirits, not perceiving, ignore in their misapplication, thus disgusting sincere inquirers?

The dogmatists must admit that all men are not equal in any of the particulars here stated. When asked in what way they are equal or ought to be recognized as equal, one dogmatist will reply one thing and one another, hardly any two agreeing. This shows the vague ideas entertained on the subject. One will say, equal in the eye of law; another, equal before the law; another, equal in all political rights; another, in all political and social rights. Now, that all men are not equal in the eye of the law is apparent from the fact that the law properly pronounces many persons morally disqualified for membership in society. That all are not and should not be equal in political rights, is apparent from the fact that some must, for the time at least, govern, administer, and execute the law while the rest must obey. Between these there is no equality in political power or rights. The right to govern and punish is entirely political; it is not personal or individual. It is impossible, therefore, for all men to be recognized as having equal political rights. What is meant by social rights is too vague and uncertain to define.

Now, I hold that as gravitation is the law governing the material universe, so justice should govern the political or moral; and in all human societies be the controlling principle. As every part of matter, small or great, an atom or a world, is equally impressed and influenced by gravitation, according to its size and density (which constitutes its own specific gravity and weight), so every human being in society, whether small or great, low or high, black or white, should come under the influence of this universal law of justice. In the organization of society upon this principle and in the administration of government after organization, every member should be perfectly *equal* in this; that justice should be equally dispensed to all according to position, merit, or demerit. There should be perfect equality in right to have justice rendered in all cases, and perfect equality in the securities for the enforcement of the right to have justice administered. All men may truly be said to be created equal in their rights to justice in their relations and conditions of life.

Then comes the question: What is justice? These random reflections, penned in my solitude, suggest a much wider range of thought and a much greater enlargement than I can now enter upon.

Society, in its government, should be so organized that as a whole it should govern itself, not that the bare majority should govern the rest at will and pleasure for any time or length of time, but that the consentient will of the whole mass, as nearly as possible, should be expressed in its laws. The object of its laws should not be the greatest good to the greatest number. Of all dogmas this, to my mind, is one of the most monstrous. The object of all laws should be the greatest good to the whole society, all its members, with injury to none. Society in its government of itself should never inflict an injury on any one of its members; that is, it should not deprive any one of its members of his or her natural acquirements, or do anything calculated or intended to oppose or obstruct any member or component part in the pursuit of happiness and the development of the highest attainable point of culture.

What constitutes happiness? What constitutes vice and immorality? How far shall subordination of certain component elements of society, such as minors, those *non compos mentis*, women, and other classes, for a term of years, or other probationary trial, or absolutely, be deemed proper? These questions should be settled by society, some of them in its organization, by fundamental rules, founded on reason, looking solely to the best interest of all without injury to any. The entire structure, in organization and laws, should be based upon the principle that society should, in the government of the whole, never injure an unoffending member even for the public good without making fair and adequate compensation. This justice requires. The natural rights of man in society, or out of it, consist in this one right of all unoffenders not to be injured by others whether in organized social compact or out of such organization. The fulfilling of the law of justice is that which worketh no wrong to another. I do not here speak of the rights of society over offenders, those who by violating the right of others have forfeited their own. Injuries to them, by way of punishment and reform and to deter others from perpetrating like acts, are founded on principles of the strictest justice.

As society cannot meet *en masse* either to form general rules for its government or for particular acts of legislation, representation of some sort must be agreed upon. On what principles or under what limitations this should be fixed, depends upon the circumstances of the case. The right to participate in the choice of those who are to make or execute the laws, is not a natural right; it is a conventional right, springing from the organization of society. Enlightened reason, looking to ultimate justice as the great end, should determine its investiture and exercise. Reason teaches that no one rule can be properly laid down for all times, persons, and places. Nor has a bare majority any natural right to govern the rest. Society has no moral or natural right to govern itself except upon the principles of justice as stated. With society so established and its government so administered, every member, whether man, woman, or child, of whatever race or colour, is *equal* in this: that he or she has an equal right, with equal security for the right, to have justice rendered. Perfect justice in all cases need not be expected. In administration all that the best of mortals can do is to attain the nearest approximation possible to this Divine attribute; reason and a sense of justice based upon the Golden Rule laid down by Him who spake as never man spake — of doing to others as you would have others do to you — must be the guide. This rule, in my judgment, means that man in all circumstances should do to others as he would have others do to him, positions being reversed.

The Corporal with dinner stops these reflections. Dinner over. Had a mess of green peas from sutler's; what he will charge I do not know. Thought of home, Harry, the garden, the beautiful plot of ground we had in peas, so promising when I left.

Lieut. W. walked out with me this morning. He pointed out General Jackson, dressed in gray, walking on N. E. parapet. We were on S. E., several hundred yards away. He told me that Dr. Willis, of Savannah, supplies Jackson and other officers, prisoners here, with funds; he supposed I would be allowed to receive funds from friends. This gave me relief. He informed me that General DuBose is in excellent health and spirits, always pleasant and jovial. Reagan, he said, was well. General DuBose writes to Mrs. DuBose through General Wilson at Macon. I inquired if he knew if General DuBose had received any letters lately from Mrs. DuBose. He said he did not know. Jackson walked with quickness, great elasticity, and firmness of step.

Corporal brought my wash bill. I paid it, Sunday as it is; the rate is $1.25 per dozen; for 16 pieces, $1.56. Whole expenses thus far paid, $49.56.

For the first time in four weeks I became conscious of smiling. It was on reading Artemus Ward in Richmond *Enquirer*. For the humorous I ever had a relish, even when at my own expense or that of my friends. The impulse to laugh was succeeded instantly by a sense of my situation, thoughts of friends and of the condition of the country. All risible inclinations were banished; sadness ensued.

CHAPTER IV

JUNE 5. — Thunder and lightning after candles were out. First thunder since I left Hampton Roads. The warmest night since I have been here. Rose after a refreshing sleep. As has been my custom for many years on arising at home, I commenced singing, in my way, whatever happened to occur to me. This morning I began Moore's hymn:

> This world is all a fleeting show
>   For man's illusion given;
> The smiles of joy, the tears of woe,
> Deceitful shine, deceitful flow —
>   There's nothing true but Heaven!

The very unmusical noise I made, or something else, seemed to excite much astonishment in the guard passing my window, just as the same discordant notes used to excite the mirth of Mr. O'Neal when he lived with me at Liberty Hall. He was a very grave man usually, and seldom I saw him seem to laugh internally at anything more than at my attempts to sing.

Breakfast: No meat; coffee and rolls from sutler's — that's all he sent. I ordered a half-pint of syrup: this Geary brought.

With all my intense distress on Linton's account, I have not once dreamed about him. Last night, I dreamed of little Becky [Linton's daughter]; thought I was at home in a room writing, and she ran in and told me "The Yankees have come!" I saw them with guns at the window. I was not discomforted, nor was the dream unpleasant. Becky did not seem frightened. I awoke. The vision was gone and I was lying on my bunk — far away from the scenes where my sleeping thoughts had roamed.

Paid newspaper bill, $2.03; all expenses paid to date, $51.59. Lieut. W. walked out with me. Spent the full hour walking and talking. Wrote two letters: one to Mr. Henry C. Baskerville, Richmond, Va., and one to Dr. Francis T. Willis or Dr. Richard Arnold, Savannah, Ga. That to Mr. B. was about Hidell's business — to know if he had heard from Hidell—and if Henry and Anthony had got safely home and how they are. The letter to Willis or Arnold was to get from either information, if possible, about Linton and home in case my letters to Linton and others at home should fail for any cause to reach them. Lieut. W. is to call at one-thirty for letters. Hear a piano overhead. This may be an offset to my music of this morning.

10.30 — Got New York papers of Saturday. They are not brought down on Sunday. The name of the *Herald's* correspondent who travelled with me from Augusta to Fortress Monroe, is Theodore T. Scribner; it appears in the *Herald's* announcement of his having sent the Secretary of War the original draft on parchment of Alabama's Ordinance of Secession. He took it from the walls of the Capitol in Montgomery when General Wilson's forces were in that city. Mr. Stanton acknowledges its receipt and says it has been deposited in his office at Washington. The Boston *Post* publishes testimony, heretofore suppressed, in the Court Martial in Washington. If this testimony be true or half true, there was a most diabolical plot, deeply involving the honour and good name of my country. I cannot believe it is true. The statements are vague; the witnesses do not seem to have been cross-examined. Clay, from what they say, was in Canada in February last. He left before that time. From his solemn declarations to me, I cannot believe that he was engaged in or had knowledge even of such a hellish plot.

Wonder and surprise have been expressed in a number of papers at the suddenness and completeness of the collapse of the Confederate Cause, etc. This wonder and surprise proceed from lack of accurate knowledge of public sentiment in the South. Resistance to the last extremity, it is said, was expected, and yet, more than 100,000 men-in-arms yielded the contest, abandoned the conflict, quit the field, surrendered on parole and went home.

The facts are these as I understand them: No people on earth were ever more united, earnest, resolved to resist to the last extremity, than the Southern people at the outbreak of the war and during its first two years. They were ready to sacrifice property, life, everything, for the Cause, which was then simply the right of self-government. They conscientiously believed that the old Union was a compact between Sovereign Independent States; only certain powers named in the Constitution had been delegated by the States separately to the Central Government; among these was not ultimate absolute Sovereignty, this being retained by the States separately in the reserved powers; each State had the right to withdraw from the Central Government the powers delegated by repealing the ordinance that conferred them and herself resuming their full exercise as a free Independent Sovereign State, such as she was when the compact oı the Union under the Constitution was formed. These principles and doctrines the great majority cherished as sacred and as underlying the whole framework of American constitutional liberty. Thousands who disapproved Secession as a measure of policy did not question it as a matter of right. The war waged by the Central Government against these States, striking at their Sovereignty and causing as it would, if successful, their complete subjugation, these people considered unconstitutional, monstrously aggressive, and utterly destructive to everything dear to them as freemen.

The slavery question had but little influence with the masses. Many even of the large slave-holders, to my personal knowledge, were willing from the first years of the war to give up that institution for peace on recognition of the doctrine of ultimate Sovereignty of the separate States, allowing upon this basis the formation of any new Union that the several Independent Parties in convention, or otherwise, might determine upon. Few sensible men of the South ever expected or desired a distinct Independent Nation embracing none but the slave States. The view of the great mass was that with the recognition of the principle of State Sovereignty as a basis of adjustment, the future might well be left to take care of itself; the States would soon assume relations to each other in such political bonds as would be most conducive to the interest, peace, happiness, and prosperity of all. These views and principles were what mainly animated the breasts of an overwhelming majority at the South. In their views not only their own domestic institution of the subordination of the African race amongst them was involved in the issue, but the very essence of constitutional liberty. So long as these principles were the watchword in the camp and at home, the people were ready to sacrifice everything in maintenance of the cause.

When the Government at Richmond itself commenced to violate some of these great cardinal principles for which hundreds of thousands had volunteered their lives, the ardour of many at home and in the army was dampened. The first great blow was conscription! With this came impressments, suspension of habeas corpus, military arrests and imprisonments, martial law. The effect upon the minds of the Southern people was fatal to the Confederate Cause. Besides in the management of the finances, the line of policy pursued by the Executive and Congress in almost every department of government soon led the most sensible men of the country to believe that there was not enough wisdom or statesmanship in control to afford reasonable hope for ultimate success. The course of the Administration during the last year toward the peace sentiment in the Northern States and toward the States Rights men influenced many to believe that Mr. Davis did not desire and was not looking for success upon the principle of State Sovereignty — the only real issue in the war — but was aiming at the establishment of a dynasty of his own.

Apprehensions were increased by the tone of the press known to be most in the confidence of the Administration; and by the avowed sentiments of some near the President and standing highest in his favour; by these, State Rights and State Sovereignty was ridiculed, sneered at, scoffed at. Many, with misgivings and forebodings, continued to support the Cause as the best they could do, hoping that the election in the Northern States might bring about a change of administration there, and with it some offer of negotiation or settlement leading to peace on the principle of State Sovereignty. The spirit of the army, though greatly dampened, was still resolute to maintain the Cause during that campaign, hoping for some change of policy at both Richmond and Washington by the coming fall. Such were the conditions during the summer and up to the meeting of the Confederate Congress in Richmond in November, 1863.

Mr. Davis's message * at the opening of the session produced a sensation throughout the country, even in the circle of his hitherto most zealous defenders. With many reflective people, the feeling was little short of consternation. This feeling extended to the masses. The policy foreshadowed in that message, if carried out, would lead to a centralized, consolidated, military despotism, as absolute and execrable as that of Russia or Turkey. This, men in the army and men elsewhere saw. The question was asked by many, What will be the fruits of success on this line? No answer satisfactory to a friend of constitutional liberty could be given. The only reply pretended to be given was, Independence. Sensible men knew, in the first place, that independence could never be achieved on that line; they knew too much of the men who constituted the armies, and of the objects and purposes for which they entered the fight. But secondly and mainly, they loathed, detested, and abhorred any such independence as that policy would secure.

These feelings spread and increased; the tone of the press only gave them new impulse. Thousands enter-

* See Messages and Papers of the Confederacy Richardson, I, 345–472; and Mr. Stephens's speech, March 16, 1864, in Cleveland's "Letters and Speeches of Stephens," 761-86.

tained them who would not venture to express them except in a private and most confidential way. Amongst friends it became common to say: Is it of any use to prolong the conflict? Why sacrifice more lives? Will ultimate success be any better in any view of the subject, even so far as the institution of slavery is concerned, than subjugation? Mr. Davis in his message virtually yields that institution forever. His principles announced in relation to it are as unconstitutional as those of Mr. Lincoln in his Emancipation Proclamation. No difference in principle between the utterances of these men; both make necessity of war override constitutional limitations of power. What interest, therefore, have we, looking to the guarantee of rights either of person or property, in prosecution of the war? Will not independence, if achieved by Davis under his line of policy, bring with it almost necessarily a far worse despotism than any yet foreshadowed by Lincoln? Lincoln, it is true, utterly ignores the doctrine of the Sovereignty of the States; Davis in his message, though not avowedly, yet in effect does the same. His recommendation for general and universal conscription, not exempting governors, judges, and legislators of States except by his special grant of favour, strikes for all practical purposes as deadly a blow at independent State organization, States Rights, or State Sovereignty, as anything Lincoln has done or can do. Thus men argued within themselves; thus talked among themselves, many even of those who had been ardent, zealous advocates of secession. Thus the masses and the army felt.* Thus the cause was given

* Mr. Davis, in his Macon speech of September, 1864, said: "If one-half the men now absent from the field would return to duty, we can defeat the enemy." James Seddon, Confederate Secretary of War, said in 1863 that "the effective force of the army was not more than one-half, never two-thirds, of the soldiers in the ranks."

up: it was not lost because the great body of soldiers were not as ready to resist to the last extremity and as willing to die in the maintenance of their principles as when they put their armour on, but because they saw and felt that the cause in which they had enlisted was not that in which they were now called to risk their lives and shed their blood. This is the real and true reason why the great masses of the Southern people have so generally and quietly accepted the present state of things. This is the explanation of what strikes so many at the North with wonder and surprise.

A more intelligent, patriotic, or braver body of men than those who filled the Southern armies never went to battle for their country's cause in any age or clime; and never were any men animated by loftier, purer principles and sentiments; it was with no view of aggression upon others but simply to defend their own rights; not to make war on the Union but to maintain the Sovereignty of their own States, which had quit the Union but had rescued the Constitution. This ark of the covenant of their fathers was in their hands; and it was to preserve this (containing the life-giving principles of self-government) from destruction and pollution that they rushed to the ranks as soldiers never did before — not even in the days of Peter the Hermit and the Crusades. It was for their ancient rights, customs and institutions, their liberties achieved and bequeathed to them by their ancestors, that they fought.

The idea set forth by Mr. Greeley in his "American Conflict" and by Senator Sumner in his late eulogy on Lincoln, that this noble band of warriors was nothing but a set of reckless-spirited rebels, disloyal to the Constitution of the United States and conspiring to overthrow it and to establish on its ruins a Slave Oligarchy, is utterly unfounded. The ruling motive of these armed hosts was to maintain and perpetuate the principles of the Constitution, even out of the Union when they could no longer maintain them in it. I speak of the ideas and sentiments prevailing among our people at the time, and not of the correctness of their judgment as to whether their constitutional rights could or would have been maintained in the Union. What I affirm is, that the Southern people were actuated by no disloyalty to the Constitution, to the principles it contained, or to the form of government thereby established.

Nor were the men who met at Montgomery and framed the Confederate States Constitution governed by any such motives as have been ascribed; the work of their hands show this. "By their fruits ye shall know them." The new Constitution was but an embodiment of all the essential principles of liberty contained in the old. Some changes were made on minor points; all were of conservative character; most only settling clearly points in the old that gave rise to doubt, cavil, and conflicting construction. The great essential principles of Anglo-Saxon liberty, dating back to the Magna Charta, were reaffirmed and guaranteed. Nothing savouring of the slightest spirit of disloyalty to these principles is to be found in it.

When Georgia had seceded against my wish, judgment, and vote, my greatest apprehension was lest liberty be lost in the confusion that might follow. To guard against such an event, I myself, looking to the future, introduced a resolution, which was passed by the seceding convention, instructing Georgia delegates to a proposed Convention in Montgomery of seceding States, to adopt the old Constitution as basis for any new one that might be formed. Such was my admiration of the wisdom of the fathers, such my loyalty and devotion to the principles they had established. At Montgomery, no delegate from any State evinced in any debate the slightest disinclination to conform strictly to this policy. Even on African slavery in the South, no change from the old was made in the new Constitution save in clearly defining those points on which disputes had arisen — all of which points had been decided by the highest judicial tribunals of the old Government as they were now set forth in the fundamental law of the new. The only striking difference between the old Constitution and the new was the immediate and perpetual prohibition of the African slave-trade in the latter, whereas continuance of this traffic for twenty years had been provided for in the former. I speak from memory, but I think I am correct.

As for my Savannah speech, about which so much has been said and in regard to which I am represented as setting forth "slavery" as the "corner-stone" of the Confederacy, it is proper for me to state that that speech was extemporaneous. The reporter's notes, which were very imperfect, were hastily corrected by me; and were published without further revision and with several glaring errors. The substance of what I said on slavery was, that on the points under the old Constitution out of which so much discussion, agitation, and strife between the States had arisen, no future contention could arise, as these had been put to rest by clear language. I did not say, nor do I think the reporter represented me as saying, that there was the slightest change in the new Constitution from the old regarding the status of the

African race amongst us. (Slavery was without doubt the occasion of secession; out of it rose the breach of compact, for instance, on the part of several Northern States in refusing to comply with Constitutional obligations as to rendition of fugitives from service, a course betraying total disregard for all constitutional barriers and guarantees.)

I admitted that the fathers, both of the North and the South, who framed the old Constitution, while recognizing existing slavery and guaranteeing its continuance under the Constitution so long as the States should severally see fit to tolerate it in their respective limits, were perhaps all opposed to the principle. Jefferson, Madison, Washington, all looked for its early extinction throughout the United States. But on the subject of slavery — so called — (which was with us, or should be, nothing but the proper subordination of the inferior African race to the superior white) great and radical changes had taken place in the realm of thought; many eminent latter-day statesmen, philosophers, and philanthropists held different views from the fathers.

The patriotism of the fathers was not questioned, nor their ability and wisdom, but it devolved on the public men and statesmen of each generation to grapple with and solve the problems of their own times.

The relation of the black to the white race, or the proper status of the coloured population amongst us, was a question now of vastly more importance than when the old Constitution was formed. The order of subordination was nature's great law; philosophy taught that order as the normal condition of the African amongst European races. Upon this recognized principle of a proper subordination, let it be called slavery or what not, our State institutions were formed and rested. The new Confederation was entered into with this distinct understanding. This principle of the subordination of the inferior to the superior was the "corner-stone" on which it was formed. I used this metaphor merely to illustrate the firm convictions of the framers of the new Constitution that this relation of the black to the white race, which existed in 1787, was not wrong in itself, either morally or politically; that it was in conformity to nature and best for both races. I alluded not to the principles of the new Government on this subject, but to public sentiment in regard to these principles. The status of the African race in the new Constitution was left just where it was in the old; I affirmed and meant to affirm nothing else in this Savannah speech.

My own opinion on slavery, as often expressed, was that if the institution was not the best, or could not be made the best, for both races, looking to the advancement and progress of both, physically and morally, it ought to be abolished. It was far from being what it might and ought to have been. Education was denied. This was wrong. I ever condemned the wrong. Marriage was not recognized. This was a wrong that I condemned. Many things connected with it did not meet my approval but excited my disgust, abhorrence, and detestation. The same I may say of things connected with the best institutions in the best communities in which my lot has been cast. Great improvements were, however, going on in the condition of blacks in the South. Their general physical condition not only as to necessaries but as to comforts was better in my own neighbourhood in 1860, than was that of the whites when I can first recollect, say 1820. Much greater would have been made, I verily believe, but for outside agitation. I have but small doubt that education would have been allowed long ago in Georgia, except for outside pressure which stopped internal reform.

P. M. —The hours for my meals are seven for breakfast and three for dinner. This morning I had no meat. At dinner, the cold corned beef being very uninviting, I ordered something from the sutler's. Geary brought asparagus and warm roast. The tendency seems to throw the cost of my living upon me. My ration of beef could as easily have been sent warm as cold; besides, it was sent in in such plight as seemed designed to force me to ask for something better. I have not usually taken any supper; sometimes have eaten some remnants of bread left from dinner, washing it down with water.

To-night I thought I would try my hand at making tea. Tea and tea-pot, sugar, etc., I have had on the window-sill since soon after my arrival. So I set to work. How to effect my object I hardly knew. I had a fire — have had a fire all the time day and night since I have been here — but it is of anthracite coal and not suitable for cooking. I had no kettle for boiling water. Necessity is the suggester of expedients as well as the mother of inventions. I resolved to fill my tin cup with water, put it on the fire until the water should boil, then pour the water boiling hot into the pot with as much of the dried tea-leaves as I thought would do. Here was another knotty problem, for I had never noticed how much leaf was used in making any given quantity of beverage. I wanted only one cup. Concluding it better to be on the safe side, to put in too much than too little, to have it too strong than too weak, I took up between thumb and forefinger as much as I guessed would make a cup and put it in. The water in the cup boiled in due time; I poured it on the tea in the tea-pot, set the pot at the foot of the grate and let it remain some time for the tea to draw. On pouring it out, I found I had a most excellent cup of tea, which I relished well. I may try it again. While at the operation I was closely watched by a guard, who, peeping between the iron bars of the window every once in a while, evinced strong curiosity to see what I was at. When he saw how the land lay, his countenance assumed a vacant expression of "Is that all?"

June 6. — Since I have been permitted to write home and thus to have hope of hearing from home, a great burden has been lifted from my spirits. I am more comfortable in mind as well as body. Could I have had communication with my dear ones and have known that they were well and doing well, I should have borne all that has fallen to my lot with perfect composure; nay more, with such communication I feel internal assurance, that through Divine mercy, I could meet any fate that might or may await me with fortitude, even hanging unto death. There has not been the slightest shrinking of the nerves from contemplations on that score. My whole public as well as private life has been inspired by a consciousness of rectitude of motive and sense of duty that would bear and sustain me by the mercy of God triumphantly through the dark valley and shadow of death though the gallows be the way. I do not pretend that I have done right in all things, still I feel that from my youth up my earnest desire and prayer has been to be guided by Divine Wisdom, to see the right and to pursue it. My errors, whatever they have been, have sprung from infirmities of human nature in not perceiving the right rather than from inclination to do wrong knowing it to be wrong.

In looking back upon my public conduct, closely and critically as I have done since I have been in this cell, I do not see that I could have acted more rightly or more in accord with duty, or that I should act differently under like circumstances if my life was to go over again, even in full view of my present situation and prospect. Therefore I can meet my fate, so far as it involves me personally, with as much meekness, philosophy, and firmness as Socrates met his.

Lieut. Croak walked with me. Lieut. W. gone to Boston. I asked him some days ago to let me know in advance of his next trip; I wished to send for some things; also, to get him to inquire at the post-office there for letters for me; I think Mr. Baskerville or Travis must have written as I directed Anthony to request them to do. Lieut. W. promised to let me know. He did not. I have requested him repeatedly to get from Adjutant Ray a statement of my account; I wish to see at what rate he is disposing of my gold. This he always promises to do, but he has not done it. Thus, I am somewhat annoyed by little matters as well as great. The current of life no more than the "course of true love" runs smooth. Governor Brown, I see by the papers, has been allowed to go home on parole. I hear nothing further of Cobb, Mallory, or Hill. What has become of them? I have been thinking about making special application for amnesty for myself. The question presents embarrassing complications. How would I feel to make it and have it rejected? In what estimation would the President hold me were I seemingly to neglect or spurn what he would willingly grant?

For dinner, beef utterly unfit to eat, almost as tough as whitleather. It cannot be that the Government feeds the soldiers here on such meat. If so, the poor men fare worse than nine-tenths of the slaves in my country have fared since I can remember. My opinion is that the sending of such food is the cook's trick to drive me to the sutler's. A profit somewhere is probably the object: "Money makes the mare go," the world over. The sutler sent a cup of English peas, some strawberries and milk; on these and bread I made my dinner, and to settle it took a drink of whisky from Harry's bottle. This reminds me of what Clay told me when he took a drink with me on the *Clyde* out of Major Corbin's bottle; which was that he had been told by somebody, during his recent sojourn in Georgia, that I was killing myself with liquor. The only impression this news made on me was to excite my wonder as to how such rumours ever start.

I was never drunk in my life, and I question if all the spirits I ever drank would amount to three gallons. Before 1842, I had not drank altogether as much as a pint. Brandy was then recommended as a medicine, a tablespoonful daily after dinner. This, I continued for some time regularly, and then occasionally. Since the war, when I could not get brandy I have used whisky in the same way — never except a small portion after dinner or when I had got wet or been exposed, or was exhausted in speaking. When I canvassed the State or made long speeches, I always, after 1843, took brandy, a spoonful or so, during the speech or after. I have not been without brandy or whisky to use in this way since 1842. A drink with me is about a tablespoonful, rarely more, often less; but frequently whole months have passed without my having tasted liquor. My habits in this particular can be better judged from this detailed statement, than from the assertion that I have never been drunk. Have just written a letter of which this is a copy:

MAJOR H. A. ALLEN, COM'D'G. MAJ:

Can I be allowed to commute the ration daily furnished and have the amount of commutation in money turned over to the sutler on my account? Please let me know and oblige

Yours most respectfully,

ALEXANDER H. STEPHENS, Prisoner.

I have had on my table ever since I have been here a novel, which was handed me "to read on the way," by Mrs. Alfred Cumming at Barnett on the Sunday I came from Atlanta to Augusta. Governor* and Mrs. Cumming got on the train at Union Point on their way from Athens to Washington, Ga. We were together from Union Point to Barnett. She was much affected at seeing me under arrest; she wept. I let Colonel Johnston read the book as we came on to Fortress Monroe; he told me it was interesting but had a sad ending. I do not wish to read anything sad now. My object is to divert the mind. But I treasure the book as a memento.

8 P. M. — Lieut. W. informs me, in reply to my note to Major Allen, that no commutation can be allowed; but he will arrange with the sutler to take my rations by the month in bulk and account to me for their value. He also informs me that he had received a letter for me which he had sent to General Dix at New York. It was, he said, from a Mr. Myers, but contained nothing important. How anxious I am to see it! It is from Joe Myers, Crawfordville, I have no doubt.

* A Georgian; Governor of Utah, 1857-61.

June 7. — Rose with my usual discordant notes of song. Spirits oppressed but a vast burden removed by assurance that I shall soon hear from home. Took a pretty good bath by standing tiptoe in the wash-bucket and pouring water from the tin pan over the body; rubbed down with a towel, thinking all the time of my room at home, of Anthony, Tim, and Binks.*

Got a good cup of coffee from the sutler's, with hot rolls and a slice of ham from the cook. Feel refreshed, and am now ready for my morning's work. How much better I should feel if I did but know that Linton is well; that all are well at home and that all is going smoothly. My sufferings I can bear with unflinching fortitude, but the thought of the suffering of others, particularly my brother, on my account unmans me, touches the quick, the very nerve-strings of the soul. Wounds in the mind, as in the body, must have vent or they diffuse poison throughout the system. The troubled mind must have vent or the heart breaks and the spirit dies, withered and blasted. The natural vent is in the soul's outpourings to some sympathizing friend. When this is denied, as it is to me, other expedients must be sought. One of these with me is indulgence of a cherished hope that some day hereafter this outpouring may take place; that I can yet talk over all my present trials, incidents of prison life, as well as the general troubles of the times and the oppression and deep afflictions of our country, with him who is the light of my life, with my dear brother; and if that should never be, that he may at least some day with sympathizing eye peruse the jottings on these pages.

* At home, his Negro servant, Anthony, rubbed him down; Tim, a little Negro (Harry's son), assisted at his toilet and sported with Binks, the dog.

Lieut. W. walked with me; he left me, part of the time, to walk on at my pleasure. Have been thinking more of the amnesty matter; penned some ideas for application if I should make one.

Dinner: the bacon ration was about half as much meat as I usually eat when I eat meat at all; and I am but a moderate eater. This bacon and beans does not suit me. The fault is perhaps with the cook. I have not yet been able to see him. I asked them that he be allowed to see me, but the petition was denied. I wanted to give directions about the proportions of my meals, and tell him how I liked them. Sometimes I think he may be a fellow-citizen of African descent with prejudices against me; if so, I feel sure these would be overcome on acquaintance. I never yet knew one of the coloured race who did not like me. Toward coloured people I have always felt cordial sympathy and it has never failed to be reciprocated. Geary got me a can of tomatoes to-day, but too late for dinner; the price was $1.

My eyesight is growing dimmer. I had to use my eye-glasses to-day in separating the sound beans from the unsound. The looking-glass shows that my hair grows white very fast.

5 P. M. — Just finished reading in the New York *Times* the official publication of the suppressed testimony before the Military Commission; that of Montgomery, Dr. Merritt, and Conover.* Merritt is certainly mistaken about seeing Clay in Canada in February last; his is the strongest testimony against Clay; he is mistaken

* See Turner's report on "the matter of witnesses who had sworn falsely in relation to the complicity of Jeff. Davis and others in the assassination of President Lincoln," O. R. War of the Rebellion, S. N., 121, pp. 921–23.

or he swore falsely. I am confident that nothing as regards assassination can be proven against Clay. The whole testimony tends to leave the impression on almost any mind that the capture and removal by strategy and violence of Mr. Lincoln and other heads of the Government at Washington was discussed by confidential Confederate agents in Canada,* and connived at by them with assurance of approval at Richmond. But the testimony is not conclusive on this point; far from it. I cannot yet give my assent to a supposition even that Clay was privy to any such scheme or policy; and the whole testimony may be utterly false.

When this Canada mission was established, I supposed its object was to bring about some friendly understanding with leading men of the States Rights School of politics at the North, in order — if peace could not be otherwise and sooner obtained — to organize a party there for carrying the fall elections on the basis of peace; leaving all questions of old Union and new Union to be settled amicably in convention on the principle of "mutual convenience and reciprocal advantage," this being the only secure basis of permanent peace between the States, and one which soon would have brought harmonious adjustment upon the recognized principle of the Sovereignty of each State. Last winter I stated to Governor Graham [Confederate Senator from North Carolina] my desire to know more about this mission. From what I saw in the papers, I was apprehensive that our agents were doing no good but rather injury to our cause, and I advised him to call for all correspondence, to move

* In July, 1864, the mission, consisting of Clay, Thompson, and Holcombe, in Niagara, Canada, sought through Horace Greeley a peace conference with Lincoln, which Lincoln declined. The other part of their purpose was somewhat as stated by Stephens, according to Davis in "Rise and Fall of the Confederate Government," II, 611; also to liberate Confederates in prison near the border and to aid escaped Confederates to return South. See So. Hist. papers; VII, 99, 132–39, 293.

an inquiry in the Senate as to who these agents were and what they were about; I asked General Wigfall [Senator from Texas] to do the same, or gave him the same views I had given Graham; but neither moved in the matter. When, on return of the Commissioners from Hampton Roads, Mr. Davis said, in the public meeting in the African Church, that before the summer solstice we should have the North suing us, as their masters, for terms of peace, perhaps the misguided man was looking to the success of some of these Canadian schemes, either the uprising of the people of the North or the abduction of the heads of their Government. At the time he uttered the sentiment, it seemed to me the emanation of a demented brain, but he may have been relying on something I and the world generally knew nothing about; the declaration produced astonishment in the minds of all sensible men who spoke to me of it. But I have no idea Mr. Davis ever countenanced assassination. No!

I see by the Boston paper that the Hon. Joshua Hill has reached Washington. As a Provisional Governor is to be appointed for Georgia, I do hope he will be the man. He is a gentleman of high tone and honour, a man of inflexible principle and integrity.

June 8. — Breakfast: from the cook's room, a piece of bread and the worst piece of meat yet sent me. Could not think of attempting to eat it. From sutler's could get nothing but a cup of cold coffee. Took my Bible, stretched myself on bunk to rest while reading. With a fervent prayer to Almighty God to be directed to some chapter of His Word from which I could derive comfort, opened at Lamentations V. Was it accident? Every word was a fit channel for my soul's outpouring.

I have been in this cell two weeks; for four I have been a prisoner. How long those weeks seem in some views, in others how short! Sometimes it seems an age since I left home; at other times the brief moment of a horrid dream. Sometimes it seems impossible that my surroundings are reality; I feel as if I must be waking from the frightful delusion of disturbed slumber on my own bed in my own room at my beloved home. The human mind is a complicated piece of mechanism, the least aberration of its workings disturbs its proper balance. Is it marvellous that so many are pronounced insane? Insanity is only a question of degree. The operation of no human mind is morally and intellectually perfect; the orbit of none is in perfect circle. The orbits of all are more or less elliptical, as are those of the greater and lesser worlds in space. Truth and Right constitute the gravitating centre of the mind's orbit. In astronomy those bodies whose motions discard not only the circle but the ellipse, assuming the parabolic curve and never returning in the same path, or sphere, are known as comets. Minds which become so eccentric in their motions as to wheel out of all regular orbits are considered lunatic. Lunatics are only mental comets. But none, no not one, moves around the true great centre in a perfect circle; all aberrate more or less. What constitutes insanity is only a question of degree.

Lieut. W. walked out with me. Has not arranged with sutler about taking my rations and furnishing me meals from the mess with charge for difference. Everything I wish done here seems slowly done, when done at all. Began letter to President Johnson, making special application for amnesty. Wrote to Linton; Lieut. W. was to call for letter for evening's mail, but did not.

Large concourse of strangers visited the fort to-day; the convention of physicians now assembled in Boston, I believe, with ladies, friends, etc. Several visitors took a peep into my cell, but not many satisfied their curiosity if a good sight of me was what they wanted. I was eating my dinner — the worst yet sent — and was, for the first time lately, really hungry. I had tried the beef but could make little impression on it by gnawing; cut it, I could not. This beef and some of my potatoes was set before me. I had expected something from sutler's. Geary presently brought in a tin cup some of my tomatoes. I was fishing these up as well as I could with a knife — the old rusty cookroom knife before mentioned. Such was the situation when the crowd darkened my windows. Not wishing to be, under these conditions, the observed of all observers, I withdrew to the far end of my cell, where eyes could not reach me. The tomatoes were not good. Ordered a small wooden tub to-day for bathing: Price $2, Geary said.

8 P. M. — Lieut. W. called for my letter to Linton, but too late to mail it. Apologized, said the crowd of visitors detained him.

CHAPTER V

JUNE 9. — Lieutenant Longly walked out with me. Day clear and hot; raised my umbrella, the one I bought last year for $20, Confederate money. Saw the mowers cutting grass on the grounds. Thought of George and Vincent in our experiments in the same line last year and the year before on the bottoms at the Nunn and River places. Sniffed the pleasant odour of new-mown hay, and returned to my cell.

11 A. M. — Got a letter from Joe Myers of Crawfordville, the same Lieut. W. told me of some days ago. Dated Augusta, 24th May; it gave me great relief and comfort. A thousand thanks to Myers for that letter! All well at home. Harry gone with Linton to the Jefferson place. I do not understand this. Who will take care of my affairs on the lot in Harry's absence? Good rains, and corn growing nicely. This is good news. Again, a thousand thanks to Myers for that letter! Answered it immediately. Hope he may get the answer. See in N. Y. *Tribune* that it was currently reported in Augusta that Mr. Toombs had committed suicide to prevent arrest by Federal forces. Can't give my assent to the truth of that! Breckinridge [Confederate Secretary of War] had escaped by ship from some point in Florida.

Another crowd of visitors, and music. A salute, of I don't know how many guns, was fired. I did not think to count when the firing began. A jar was felt in my cell. Heard broken glass falling in some place not far off, and cry of children as if alarmed. My cell is under officers' quarters; some of these officers have families.

Great shouts and huzzas are heard from Confederate soldiers; those under the rank of major are about to be released and paroled under late order to that effect. Would that I were going with them!

Crowds of strangers, visiting men and women, peep into my windows, trying to get a look at me. I write at my table, and let them make the best observation they can. My only objection is that they stand so thick as to obscure my light in some degree.

Finished letter to the President. Wish Linton were here; should like to know what he would think of it. This is a copy.

HIS EXCELLENCY, ANDREW JOHNSON,
President of the United States;

Mr. President: You will, I trust, excuse if not pardon, this communication if it should be deemed obtrusive. It is under great embarrassment I make it, but I feel it to be my duty to myself, to my country, as well as to Your Excellency.

Several days have elapsed since your Proclamation of Amnesty and Pardon, dated Washington the 29th of May, reached me in my present confinement, through the medium of the newspaper publications. Having been connected with the Confederate States Cause in the late armed conflict between the States, by accepting and holding a high though inactive civil position in their organization, and being now in prison on account (I suppose) of that connection, I come clearly within the 1st and 12th of the enumerated classes excepted from the benefit of that Proclamation, and, but for the terms of the Proviso, "that special application may be made to the President for pardon by any person belonging to the excepted classes, and such clemency will be liberally extended as may be consistent with the facts of the case and the peace and dignity of the United States," I should have felt no inclination to do anything but silently and patiently as possible await results and meet my fate, whatever it might be, under the regular Judicial Tribunals, with that resignation, firmness, and fortitude which seldom fails to sustain, under all circumstances, those who have within them the consciousness of rectitude of motive and integrity of purpose.

The embarrassment under which I now address you arises from considerations of a twofold character, which, upon statement, you will doubtless readily perceive and, I trust, duly appreciate. First, it is due in candour to make known to you, as I now do, that I am perfectly willing to comply, and in good faith too, with the conditions and requirements of the Amnesty set forth as to all outside the excepted classes. But how a special application in my case for the benefits of the Amnesty liberally tendered in the Proviso, might be received or considered by you, even with the assurance expressed, is altogether uncertain to me. I am without grounds to form any satisfactory conjecture. If you should look upon such application as presumptuous in itself, or as implying any confession of a sense of guilt on my part for anything that I have done in the late most lamentable conflict through which our country has passed, this would be a source of deep regret and personal chagrin to me. Were I to remain silent and say nothing, might you not be led to construe this as an evidence of persistent defiance and a persistent disinclination to accept and abide by the issues of war as now settled and determined? Might you not look upon it as evidence at least of a disregard on my part for that liberal tender of Executive clemency without inquiry as to past, which you have been pleased so graciously to make? To be considered presumptuous in seeking to avail myself of what was never intended for me on the one side; or on the other to subject myself, by silence, to the inference that I am indifferent and insensible to the clemency thus liberally tendered, would be equally hurtful to me. Hoping I am fully understood, I proceed briefly to make to you, however it may be received, a special application for amnesty in my case under the terms prescribed for others not embraced in the excepted classes, and to submit for your consideration some reasons why the promised clemency should be extended.

No man living, I think, exerted his powers to a greater extent according to his ability to prevent these troubles and the late deplorable war than I did; and no man in the United States is less responsible by any intentional act for the consequences than I feel myself to be. In Georgia, I opposed secession to the utmost of my ability, in private and public, in conversations, and votes. My appeal to the Legislature in November, 1860, may not be unknown to you. After that, I was in the State Convention that passed the Ordinance of Secession. I opposed and voted against that Ordinance. This I did, however, viewing the question solely as one of policy involving the peace, happiness, prosperity, and best interests of the entire country, and not one of Right on the part of the State. After Georgia had passed that Ordinance in the most solemn form by a Convention of her people, regularly and legally chosen and assembled, thereby rescinding her Ordinance, similarly adopted in 1788, by which the Constitution of the United States was adopted and her membership of the Union was enacted, my connection with the new Confederation of States that was formed, and my subsequent course and conduct has this explanation, if not excuse and justification: I was brought up in the straightest sect of the Crawford, Troup, and Jefferson States Rights School of Politics. The first lessons of my political creed from earliest youth were the Kentucky and Virginia resolutions of 1778 and

1799, the former drawn up by Mr. Jefferson himself. In these Resolutions it is declared:

Resolved, That the several States composing the United States of America are not united on the principle of unlimited submission to their General Government, but that by compact under the style and title of a Constitution for the United States, and of amendments thereto, they constituted a General Government for special purposes, delegated to that Government certain definite powers, reserving, each State to itself, the residuary mass of rights to their own self-government; and that whensoever the General Government assumes undelegated powers, its acts are unauthoritative, void, and of no force: that to the Compact each State acceded as a State, and as an integral party, its co-States forming as to itself the other party: that the Government enacted by this compact was not made the exclusive or final judge of the extent of the powers delegated to itself, since that would have made its discretion and not the Constitution the measure of its powers: but that, as in all other cases of Compact, amongst Powers having no common judge, each party has an equal right to judge for itself, as well of infractions as of the mode and measure of redress.

These principles were taught me in my youth; in them I was reared. In whatever party associations I have acted throughout life upon other questions or measures, these principles and their associates in these time-honoured resolves have stood forth as the polestar of my guidance on all questions referring to the true relations existing between the several States and the Federal Government under the Compact of Union set forth in the Constitution of the United States. My convictions were strong that under the Compact of Union of 1787, reserved sovereignty resided with the people of each State, not only to judge of infractions or breaches of the Compact by the other party to it, but to adopt such "mode and measure of redress" for any real or supposed infractions or breaches as they, in their sovereign capacity, might determine for themselves, subject to no authority for their actions in the premises but to that great moral law governing the intercourse between Independent States, peoples, and nations.

The reservation of Sovereignty to the several States was clearly set forth in their first articles of Union under the old Confederation. In the succeeding Compact for a "more perfect union" of 1787, all powers not expressly delegated, or such as are incident to, or proper and necessary for, the execution of those expressly delegated, are expressly reserved to the States. That Sovereignty expressly set forth as retained in the several States in the articles of Confederation is not, most certainly, parted with by any expressed terms in any part of the Compact or Constitution of 1787. Nor could I ever see how its transfer or delegation could ever be justly implied from anything in that instrument. If carried by implication, it must be upon the assumption that it is an incident only of some one or all of these specific and specially enumerated powers expressly granted. This cannot be, as that would be making the incident greater than the object, for Sovereignty is the highest and greatest of all political powers; the embodiment of all, great as well as small: all emanate and proceed from it. All the great powers specifically and expressly delegated in the Constitution, such as the power to declare and make war, to raise and support armies, to tax and lay excise and import duties, etc., are but the incidents to Sovereignty. If this great embodiment of all powers was parted with, why were any minor specifications made? Was it not as useless as absurd?

If then, this ultimate, absolute, Sovereignty did reside with the several States, as without doubt it did up to the formation of the "more perfect Union" of 1787; and if, in the Constitution then made, setting forth specifically the new and additional powers therein delegated for the purpose of forming that "more perfect Union" aimed at and established thereby, this Sovereignty is not delegated, surrendered, or parted with in expressed terms; and if, further, the greatest of all political powers cannot be justly claimed as incidents to lesser ones and thereby carried by implication: then, of course, was it not most clearly still reserved to the people of the several States in that "mass of residuary Rights" (in the language of Mr. Jefferson) which was reserved in express terms in the very Compact itself for the "more perfect Union" of 1787?—the language of the Constitution being to the effect (I cite from memory, not having it before me) that "all the powers not delegated to the United States by the Constitution nor prohibited by it to the States, are reserved to the States respectively, or to the people." To my mind it seemed to be clearly so. And if so, was not this reserved Sovereignty still existing and residing with the people of the several States in 1861—the new States as well as the old—since the new came in and were admitted upon an equal footing with the original Parties to the Compact? To me, this seemed to be equally clear. Such were my firm and most conscientious convictions.

When Georgia, in her sovereign capacity in 1861, seceded from that Compact of Union of 1787 to which she had, in the language of Mr. Jefferson, "acceded" in 1788, I considered my allegiance due her. In that State I was born; of that State I was a citizen. In no sense was I ever a citizen of the United States except as a citizen of Georgia—one of the "States united" under the Compact of Union of 1787. So long as Georgia was one of the United States, by being one of her citizens, I thereby became a citizen of the United States, of which title, name, or distinction, I had ever been proud. But when Georgia resumed her Sovereign power as an Independent State amongst the nations of the earth, as I considered she had a clear and perfect right both morally and legally to do, however unwisely (in my judgment) it was for her to do it, I felt bound to obey her behests—to bow my will to hers, as the only power to which I owed ultimate allegiance. By her act she had seceded from the Compact of the Union; she was no longer one of the United States. I was, by being a citizen of Georgia, no longer thereby a citizen of the United States. I thought it the duty of all citizens of the State to do as I did. All who might have been inclined to do otherwise would, by so doing, have rendered themselves amenable to her laws against treason to the State. I felt no such inclination myself but bowed submissively, as I had at all times said I would, to the will of her people expressed in their most august sovereign capacity. This I did from no change of views, or approval of what had been done, but solely from a sense of duty.

My subsequent connection with the movement thus inaugurated was not of my seeking. It was not to gratify any personal ambition or aspiration that I yielded to the unanimous wish of her Convention, as expressed in their appointment of me to be one of the delegates to represent her people in the Montgomery Convention. It was from a sense of duty. On this point I deliberated two days: the times were ominous and perilous, society was wavering and rocking to its foundations, general wreck and ruin seemed imminent. Georgia, my native State, whose people I had served so long and loved so well, had by her authoritative voice (spoken through those with whom I had acted in the great issue just settled as well as by most of those with whom I had so widely and radically differed) called on me not to withhold the aid of my counsels in providing for her welfare in the future on the line of policy she had adopted. Was it, or was it not, my duty to obey this call? that was the question. I concluded that it was.

If further considerations than the above stated be necessary for excusing, if not justifying, that conclusion, let these be added: The President of the United States [Buchanan] had, in his annual message of December, 1860, declared and proclaimed to the world, in substance, that there was no rightful or Constitutional power in the Government of the United States, or any branch thereof, to coerce or to attempt to coerce a seceding

State. The Attorney General, the law officer of the Government, had given an elaborate opinion to the same effect. Moreover, such a leading organ of the popular sentiment of the incoming administration (the election of which was one of the chief causes of Secession) as the New York *Tribune* (a journal considered to be of great candour, integrity, and unsurpassed ability) had, after the results of that election were known, and in view of the expected course which certain States, Georgia of the number, would take in consequence, put forth in an elaborate article this declaration:

> Nay: we hold with Jefferson to the unalienable right of Communities to alter or abolish forms of Government that have become oppressive and injurious; and, if the Cotton States shall decide that they can do better out of the Union than in it, we insist on letting them depart in peace. The right to secede may be a Revolutionary one, but it exists nevertheless; and we do not see how one party can have a right to do what another party has a right to prevent. And whenever a considerable section of our Union shall deliberately resolve to go out, we shall resist all coercive measures designed to keep it in.

The *Tribune* was not alone amongst influential journals of the same party in putting forth such sentiments as indices of the policy of the incoming administration on the questions then pressing for solution. Others had similar courage. It is true the President-elect had given no public declaration of his own views, or the policy he should feel it his duty to pursue in case of Secession by any State. Nothing from him either approving or disapproving the sentiments of the incumbent in the message referred to, reached the public. Under these circumstances, might not a good and true man be excused, even in an error, on the grounds of misguided patriotism, in going with his people, espousing their cause as his cause, and linking his destiny with their destiny, although he might not have as strong convictions as I had that his people had not erred as a matter of right, however much they had erred as a matter of policy? If so, how much more should he be who had such convictions?

I affirm that no sentiment of disloyalty to the Constitution of the United States, to the principles it contained, or the form of Government thereby established, ever entered my breast. The controlling motive with me in accepting the new trust assigned me was an earnest desire to rescue, secure, and perpetuate these in the convulsions about to ensue. My greatest apprehensions from secession, as appears from a published letter from me about this time to a secessionist living in New York, was that the result would be the loss, both North and South, of these great essential principles of American Constitutional Liberty. Hence, in the State Convention, I drew up a resolution which passed that body, instructing the delegates from Georgia to the Montgomery Convention, to form a new Confederation on the basis as nearly as practicable of the United States Constitution.

It was with these views and feelings, I finally consented to go to Montgomery. There my object was achieved almost to the letter. Such changes as were made looked mainly to the more clearly settling of disputed points in the old Constitution, so as to more surely close and bar the door against those constructions and discussions which had so unfortunately agitated and distracted the public mind and so seriously disturbed the public tranquillity throughout the land under the old Government. All changes were of a conservative character and tendency. If the old Confederation was to be abandoned, as seemed to be resolved upon by the Southern people and not seriously or forcibly to be objected to by the Northern, I wished, in that event, the same principles of liberty to be preserved and perpetuated in the new one about to be formed. Against these sacred principles, I repeat, no disloyal or traitorous throb ever beat in heart or breast of mine. "To maintain the Union upon these principles, to promote its advancement, development, power, glory, and renown," I had declared on a memorable occasion in the House of Representatives [Jan. 6, 1857] was my earnest desire, my highest aspiration.

> "All thoughts, all passions, all delights,
> Whatever stirs this mortal frame,
> All are but ministers of love
> To feed this sacred flame."

"But," I had added, "the Constitutional Rights and Equality of the States must be preserved." In my judgment, this was the only way in which the Union could be maintained and these principles preserved. Such was my loyalty to these principles expressed in the Capitol of the Union; it was not questioned then. Such it was at Montgomery.

After the formation of the new Constitution there adopted, the position assigned me in the new Government instituted under it was likewise conferred upon me unanimously and without any solicitation on my part. But for the unanimity with which it was conferred, I should not have accepted it. Conferred as it was, it was accepted partly as a high compliment to my integrity of purpose in the maintenance of those principles, as it evidently was, coming as it did from those with a large majority of whom I had differed so widely and radically and so recently upon vital questions of public policy; but chiefly from a sense of duty I accepted this evidence of confidence reposed in me, in the hope that I might be able to contribute some aid and exert some influence that I could not otherwise, in controlling events the best way possible to secure the best results possible, not only for the peace and welfare of Georgia and her new Confederates, but for the peace, welfare, and prosperity of the people of all the States. My object was in all things so patriotically to act as to secure the surest settlement of difficulties between the States upon such terms and on such basis as reason and justice, not arms, should discover for the best interest, quiet, happiness, peace, tranquillity, and prosperity of the whole country. This has been my object, the controlling motive of my course and conduct throughout. I have been wedded to no ideas as a basis of such settlement save one alone: the recognition of the ultimate absolute Sovereignty of each of the several States as the surest foundation of permanent peace in such a Republic as ours — such a Confederation of States with such diversity of interests, stretching over a vast extent of territory, and, with peace and prosperity, likely to stretch so much farther.

My opinion was, that if this principle should be acknowledged, all other matters of difference and difficulty would soon adjust themselves. It would prove to be the self-adjusting principle of our system. It would become the Continental Regulator of all the North American States to whatever limits their boundaries might go, or to whatever extent their numbers might swell. I know the objection to this doctrine is that a Union or Government formed upon such a principle would have no adhesion between its parts or members; government, to be anything, must be strong; its parts must be held together by force; a Union formed upon the principle of permitting any member to quit it at pleasure would be held together by nothing better than a rope of sand. The reply to this with me has ever been, that the strongest force that can hold the parts or members of a Government together is the affection of the people. Government, to be strong and powerful, must indeed be held together by force. The force in the material world, which binds and holds in indissoluble union all the parts in their respective and distant spheres throughout the limitable regions of space, is the simple law of attraction. So should it be with Government, especially with a republic formed by States united or confederated in any sort of compact, agreement, or constitution with a view to "mutual convenience and reciprocal advantage." The only force that should keep them in bonds, should be that which brought them together in the beginning: the law of attraction, affinity, affection, and devotion. This is the true principle of the strongest adhesion between States thus united. It springs from considerations of interests, safety, security, and welfare. When these are left untrammelled, in the light and under the guidance of dispassionate reason, no union would remain long dissevered that was really beneficial to its members. None, it is true, would stand that was inherently and permanently injurious to any; nor ought such to stand.

These are some of the views by which I was actuated in being thus wedded to the maintenance of this doctrine of the Sovereignty of the States as the basis of a general adjustment and settlement of the questions involved in our late troubles. Whether under an adjustment thus made, the old Union should be immediately or ultimately restored, or whether new confederations should be formed as might be deemed most conducive to the best interest of the parties concerned, was a matter of much less importance and consideration with me than the maintenance of the principle which lies, as I conceived, at the foundation of all American Institutions of Self-Government. You will please excuse this rather lengthened exposition. It was, and is, necessary for a correct understanding of my conduct and the motives by which I have been governed throughout.

As for slavery, or the relation of the Black race to the White, so far as concerns the pecuniary view of the subject, I would personally have been willing any day to give that up for recognition of the other great principle. Slavery, in the abstract, I ever abhorred and detested. Slavery in the concrete, being, as it existed with us, the subordination of an inferior to a superior race, was ever considered by me more in reference to its features as a social problem than one barely of capital and labour. In this view, it always presented itself to my mind as one of the greatest and most difficult questions to adjust upon the principles of reason and justice, to which the attention of statesmen, philosophers, philanthropists, and Christians was ever directed.

My judgment and convictions, after much thought and reflection, were that a proper subordination of the inferior to the superior race was the natural and normal condition of the former in relation to the latter. I thought the assignment of that position in the structure of society to the African race amongst us was the best for both races and in accordance with the ordinance of the Creator as manifested in His works. In His Word, given through his Inspired Oracles, there is nothing against this view, but much which clearly sanctions it. Our system was not perfect, as what human systems are, ever were, or ever will be? Many things connected with it not only did not meet my approval but excited my strongest aversion and deepest sympathy and commiseration. The same I may say of many things connected with the best institutions in the best regulated communities in which I have ever had the good or bad fortune to cast my lot. Whenever I have been up North or out in the far West, as well as down in the far South, I have met with many things in the workings of the best systems which caused me to feel if not to exclaim:

> Alas! what crowds in every land
> Are wretched and forlorn.
> Man's inhumanity to man
> Makes countless thousands mourn.

If our system on the subject of the proper relation between the two races was not the best for both, or could not be made the best for both, looking to the progress and advancement of both in civilization, physically, morally, and intellectually; then I ever held it to be radically wrong, and freely admitted that it ought to be abolished, and some other system adopted that would allow the accomplishment of these ends. All government, I ever maintained, should be so constructed and administered as to promote the interests and welfare of all its constituent elements without injury to any. The principle that might gives right never received approval by me on this or any other subject. The dogma of the greatest good to the greatest number, I, on many public occasions, openly repudiated in reference to this very subject of slavery as it existed amongst us. Instead, I maintained the true principle to be the greatest good to all without detriment or injury to any. The pecuniary view of the subject was ever with me but the dust in the balance compared with others connected with it. After this struggle commenced, I was willing to give up the whole system (its difficulties to be left for adjustment, upon the best basis attainable for the best interest and welfare of both races, to those on whom the high trust of solving these questions might devolve) for the recognition, as I have stated, of the other great principle — the Sovereignty of the several States.

If my position in the Confederate Government was still retained after I clearly saw that the great objects I had in view when accepting it were not likely to be obtained even by the success of Confederate arms, and after I saw that the Administration was pursuing a line of policy leading to decidedly opposite results to those I was aiming at, and to which I was not only strongly opposed but exceedingly hostile — it was mainly with the view and in the hope that some occasion might arise when my counsels might be of more avail than they had been. Owing to my hostility to the measures of that Government, my loyalty to its cause was more than suspected; I was by many denounced as a traitor; my loyalty, however, my whole soul and heart, was ever true to that cause with the aims and objects therein set forth, as it had been to the old cause of the old Union with the same. If I was a traitor to either, then in heart I was equally traitor to both.

Throughout the struggle, my heart bled over the sufferings of the people, both North and South, from the atrocities of war. The condition of suffering prisoners on both sides was one that awakened in me deepest interest and most active sympathies. My efforts to mitigate them need not be stated. Many are already known to the world; others not known, of not much less importance, would have been attended with great good had they been successful. Suffice it to say, that all that I could do on that line was done.

The conclusion of this whole statement then, is this: The war was inaugurated against my judgment. It was conducted on our side against my judgment. I do not feel myself morally responsible or accountable in any way for any of the appalling evils attending it. Its results are not what I desired, the Sovereignty of the several States has not been maintained. Thus, regularly constituted Governments have been displaced, as part of its results. Slavery has been completely abolished. If any other system or measure can be devised for the better amelioration of the condition of the coloured portion of our population, consistent with the best interest of both races, then I shall be content. The conflict is over; all further contest has been abandoned — abandoned not so soon as I wished it to be, but abandoned when it was, with my entire approbation for reasons I need not state; and in full view of the consequences, I accept the issues and results as they exist, and declare my entire willingness in the most perfect good faith to abide by them accordingly.

If, upon this statement of my case and of these reasons or of any others, you shall be pleased to extend to me the benefits of that amnesty awarded to others, it shall be as cordially accepted as it has been liberally tendered. Not from any weakness of nature prompting a desire to shun the full legal responsibilities of my acts under the Constitution and laws of the country, nor any dread of meeting and bearing the consequences even though the end should be the scaffold or the gallows; but because, feeling as I do, I think I should do you, as well as myself, a wrong in not thus accepting it if the case stated is embraced in the tender. If, upon a review of the case thus presented, you should be of opinion that it is not so embraced, that it would not be "consistent with the peace and dignity of the United States" to embrace me in this liberal offer set forth in the proviso in the proclamation; or if you should think best not to decide the question hastily, or without mature deliberation; then I have this request to make of you: that in the interim I be released from my present confinement on my parole of honour to report myself at any stated place and time upon due notice to meet any charge that may be legally established against me.

I have been now four weeks in custody; two in this place in close confinement, permitted to speak to no one except the guard and officers in charge, with liberty to walk out one hour every day on the grounds accompanied by an officer. My physical condition is feeble. The diet furnished is not such as the state of my health, and previous habits, require for its preservation. I am permitted, it is true, to supply necessary extras at my own cost. This is consuming the small stock of means I possess.

The whole of my personal effects will not more than pay my debts and provide education for orphan nephews under my charge and dependent on me. I have much to do at home in arranging for supplies for a number of other persons also dependent on me for subsistence, and in settling estates of which I have direction and management. I wish, moreover, in the new order of things to make suitable provision for those who have heretofore stood in the relation of slaves to me under our laws. I have lands on which I wish to make them as comfortable as possible. I had told them, upon the surrender of the Army of Virginia, what I supposed would be the result of the war as to their condition, and the terms on which they could remain at the old homestead, if they wished. To these terms they all most cheerfully assented. I was arrested and brought away before arrangements, which involved surveys, allotments, etc., were perfected; my presence is necessary for their consummation.

I have but one brother living. His position toward the war, in opinion and sentiment, has been almost identical with my own. The most marked difference between our cases is, he held no office that excludes him from the general amnesty of the Proclamation. He was reported to be quite ill at his home a day or two after my arrest and before I left the State. I have heard nothing directly from him since. I am exceedingly anxious not only to hear from, but to see and be with, him. These, to say nothing of divers other considerations under the privations and sufferings of prison life, urge me to request of you this enlargement, at least, until charges shall be legally instituted.

My pledge of honour was never broken and never will be. Others have been similarly released; why should not I? Whatever conditions may be required, touching my intercourse with others during my enlargement, will be most strictly conformed to. On this subject, it may be proper to state that if I were permitted to exert them, all my influence and power would be directed to a restoration of quiet, order, and government in Georgia upon the basis of accepting and abiding by the issues of war as proclaimed by the Executive. I should certainly say or do nothing intended to check or thwart the policy indicated by the administration in bringing the seceded States back into practical relations with the General Government. But I have no desire to take any active part in these matters; not even to exercise the franchise of a citizen is any object with me. Personal liberty is what I chiefly want. Should my real estate, which is, perhaps, worth about ten thousand dollars, be also spared me, it would add a great deal to my comfort while I live. As for the franchise or having any voice hereafter in the administration of government or the election of rulers, I care but little. The last election I ever took part in was the election of delegates to the State Convention in 1861. My vote was then cast against secession. I am perfectly willing that that shall stand as the last vote ever cast by me.

And now, Mr. President: If it does not consist with your views either to grant the special application as made in the foremost part of this communication, or the request for the release on parole just made, then I have one other still smaller request to make: and that is, that my imprisonment here shall not be *close*, that, during the day, the door of my apartment shall not be locked; that I may be permitted to walk out and in at pleasure, between sunrise and sunset; that I may not be debarred from holding communications with friends in and out of the Fort in the presence of officers, or subject only to the instruction of the officer commanding at the Post. Instructions from a distance necessarily cause unnecessary delay.

May I presume to ask that this communication be answered and that the answer, whatever it may be, may be sent as soon as your manifold duties will conveniently allow?

All of which is most respectfully submitted to Your Excellency's thoughtful, clement, and patriotic consideration by

Alexander H. Stephens.

June 10. — Did not finish copying letter to the President before extinguishment of lights. Rose soon, finished, and handed it to Lieut. W. for morning mail. Last night, woke from a dream in which Henry and Anthony appeared; both were in bad condition, Anthony in particular; both wanted to go back to Liberty Hall. Poor Anthony! I fear he is in trouble. Wish I could hear from Mr. Baskerville. Did not walk out this morning; Lieut. W. was too busy, he said, getting off prisoners of war discharged by late orders. He told me a prisoner named Hardin is going to Georgia, after being in prison at least two years. I wanted to send a message by him but could not. I asked Lieut. W. to tell him I wished he would go to Crawfordville and see my people, or would write Linton that I am tolerably well and how to communicate with me. Whether the Lieutenant will do it or not, I do not know. He promised to come and walk with me this evening before sundown.

Been thinking of my letter, debating over again the propriety of what I have done. Do wish Linton were here to advise with me. I would rather have his opinion than anybody else's. I think of many things that would have improved it — but it was too long anyhow. How shall I feel if it is rejected or unnoticed? I feel that there is nothing in it but what is right, and therefore I shall be better able to bear what follows. I might have made it better, that is true, but let it go.

Thunder shower. Did not walk out until late. Lieut. W. told me my letter did not go off to-day. Major Allen had not got through reading it.

CHAPTER VI

JUNE 11. — But for the close confinement in this sort of underground place, I think my health would have improved somewhat. If I were here with liberty, comfortable quarters, and privilege to hear from home, I should not object to spending a month or two on the island. The salt air and generally mild temperature seem to suit me.

9 A. M. — Lieut. W. called for the walk but, as it was hot, asked if I would prefer to postpone it until evening.

I was in a railroad wreck near Macon in 1853, when a poor brakeman did what he could at his post to stay the smash-up, losing his life in his effort to save others. In the country's troubles, I did but act as he; did but seize the brake to arrest, as far as possible, impending mischief; my efforts have been no more availing than were his. Perhaps in the end I shall fare no better; if not by sentence of law, by disease and death from imprisonment.

Had a very sick spell to-day. The bowels have not been in proper condition. I became prostrate over the urinal, could barely get on my bunk; perspiration pouring over the whole body, head perfectly wet. Called to the guard several times, but could not make myself heard. I wanted cool water badly; half an hour went by before I could see any one pass the windows. Then a guard passed. His attention I was able to arrest, and

I asked for Lieut. W., who came and went immediately for the surgeon, Dr. or Major Seaverns. I told the doctor I was only suffering from a sick spell such as I was subject to, and that it would soon be over. All I wanted was some cool water; a little ale might do me good. Lieut. W. brought me a glass of ice water, the first I have drank this season. It relieved me very much. The Doctor remained some time, then left, promising to send some medicine. I told him the liver was not performing its functions properly; my remedy was a preparation of nitric acid which I had with me, but I needed a glass tube in taking it. He had no tube; would send some straws. In an hour or more I was able to sit up at my window.

I see in the Boston *Herald* that there was a riot yesterday in Washington, D. C., between Federal soldiers and Negroes; attack by the former upon the latter; 150 or 200 soldiers engaged. The military, or provost, guard was called on to suppress it. Several were wounded and some killed on both sides. Is this but the beginning of deplorable conflicts hereafter to be enacted between the races, until one or the other is extinguished? Sad forebodings haunt me. I apprehend intestine strifes, riots, bloodshed, wars of the most furious character, springing from antipathies of castes and races. Equality does not exist between blacks and whites. The one race is by nature inferior in many respects, physically and mentally, to the other. This should be received as a fixed invincible fact in all dealings with the subject. It is useless to war against the decrees of nature in attempting to make things equal which the Creator has made unequal; the wise, humane, and philosophic statesman will deal with facts as he finds them. In the new order of things, I shall hope and, if permitted, strive, for the best; yet I cannot divest myself of forebodings of many evils. Whether there will be greater ones than these freely admitted to be incident to the former system, time alone will determine.

God knows my views on slavery never rose from any disposition to lord it over any human being or to see anybody else so lord it. In my whole intercourse with the black race, those by our laws recognized as my slaves and all others, I sought to be governed by the Golden Rule; taking this rule in its true sense of doing unto others as I would have others do unto me were positions reversed. I never owned one that I would have held a day without his or her free will and consent. One of the greatest perplexities of my life was what disposition to make of my Negroes by will. Our laws against manumission I looked on as unwise and impolitic. Some Negroes of mine, I knew from conversations with them, wished to be free when I should be gone. This I provided for as far as I could by will under our laws. To all the rest, I secured the right of choosing their future masters. My own judgment was that those who elected to go to a free State would not be so well off as those who should remain at home with masters of their choice. Still, that was with me a matter for their own decision and which I did not feel at liberty to control. So far as my own Negroes are concerned, there is nothing now that would give me more pleasure, under the changed order of things, than to try the experiment and see what can be done for them in their new condition.

Read Gerrit Smith's lecture in New York on Treason and punishment of traitors as reported in the *Tribune*. It is about what I should have expected from him. I knew him personally in Congress; formed there a very favourable opinion of his general generous impulses of philanthropy. He was considered by most Southern people as a monster. But few Southern members would recognize or speak to him at first. This prejudice wore off, I believe, before the termination of the Congress of which he was a member. I entertained none of it myself; met him socially as I would any other intelligent, courteous gentleman. I dined with him at his own house, and we talked over in a friendly spirit all those questions which were agitating the country to its foundations, questions on which we radically differed in many respects and which have ended in such bloody deeds.

My arrangement with sutler for meals has commenced. I fare better.

Dinner to-day: salmon, broiled turkey, asparagus, potatoes, and pudding, all well cooked and palatable; having little appetite, I ate little. The Doctor recommended a stimulant, so I took a drink from Harry's bottle. Paid sutler $4 for "sundries"; what "sundries" are I do not know.

7 P. M. — From the parapet on the eastern bastion had a magnificent view of the ocean; as far as the eye could reach, its wide green plain stretched out, placid as the bosom of a lake. I thought of my first view of the great deep. It was near Sunbury, Ga., on the 2d March, 1833, one of my Saturday holidays. I had gone 12 or 15 miles for no other purpose than to behold it. Where I stood this evening is a favourable point for a sea-view; 70 feet above high-water mark, enabling one to look much further out than from any place I have ever been before. On the N. W. bastion got a full, clear outline of Boston, Bunker Hill Monument, etc.

Did not walk much, strolled slowly, rested under musician's arbour. I was feebler than at any walk since I have been here.

In Boston *Herald* is a statement that the President has refused to allow my friends to communicate with me. I hope it is not true. I once said, before the Georgia Legislature, in March, 1864, on the Habeas Corpus Resolutions, that "I was never born to acknowledge a master." I am now in the hands of the President. I cannot even have the opportunity of suing out a writ of habeas corpus. It may be said that I have a master now, whether born to acknowledge one or not. This is but too lamentably true. I did not mean to say, however, that I never was born to be in the power of one from whose oppression I could not extricate myself, but meant that I was never born to acknowledge myself the willing subject of any man on earth, or to yield to an unconstitutional authority oppressively used, acknowledging it to be right. I have the same spirit I had then. Whatever outrages may be perpetrated against my rights as a freeman under the Constitution and the laws, I shall never *acknowledge* him to be my master who commits them, or orders them committed. Superior force, as fate, has to be *yielded* to.

I asked Lieut. W. if he thought the *Herald* statement correct, or if he had any reason to think so. He said he did not think it true; the privilege to send or receive communications under which I had written home and had received Myers's letter, came, as he had informed me, from Washington; and no change of that order had been received here.

Another glimpse of Judge Reagan this evening as he passed my window on his return from walking. He did not see me. He looked pale but stepped firmly. Dr. Seaverns called, and sent by Lieut. W. some medicine for me. Lieut. W. told me to-day that he saw a letter from Mrs. DuBose to the General. It was dated the 27th of May, and said all were well.

June 12. — When I awoke, about 6, the sun was shining in at my window. The phantom of a dream was left upon the memory. In that dream I seemed to be in Atlanta on my way home. Pierce [a Negro servant], well dressed, in good spirits, joined me there; said he had come to go with me and we would spend the balance of our lives together; he intended never to leave me, I had been the best friend he ever had and he should never forget it. Sportive fancy enlivened the scene with a puppy Pierce had picked up somewhere. Its capers excited Pierce's indignation, but in me a disposition to laugh. For dogs I ever had a fondness; they ever seemed to like me. If to err, on the part of men, be but human, what ought to be expected of dogs — even grown-up dogs with all the culture and improvements that dog education and training can impart? and what should be expected of a puppy? So in my sleep I said to Pierce, "Let the puppy alone, he knows no better." When I awoke from sweet sleep with this ludicrous dream lingering upon memory, sad reflections sprang from my actual surroundings — far from my home, my friends, my servants, not allowed even the companionship of my faithful dogs, Troup, Frank, and Binks. Lying on a straw mattress upon my narrow iron bunk in this lonely cell of thick walls, stone floor, strong locks, bolts and bars — I thus situated, who have laboured all my life, feeble and frail as I have been from the cradle up, more for the comfort and happiness of others than for my own!

SCENE IN CELL, 10 A.M.

[*Prisoner* reading. Door unlocked; *Surgeon Seaverns* enters.]

Surgeon. Well, how do you feel this morning?

Prisoner. Good morning, Major. Much better, thank you.

Surgeon. Did you like the medicine I sent you?

Prisoner. Yes, sir: took a dose this morning. Were you able to get any straws for my use with the nitric acid?

Surgeon. Not yet. Those obtainable are too broken or mashed. I will try and get some. [Looking about on the table and mantel-piece.] I see you have some books here.

Prisoner. I see by the library catalogue that the library will furnish me abundant reading matter. I did not know of it when I purchased the "American Conflict" and Prescott's works.

Surgeon. [Looking at Greeley's book.] I have never seen this work before; I have never read it.

Prisoner. I have read it with a great deal of interest. It is one of the fairest as well as one of the ablest one-sided histories I ever read.

Surgeon. I have not read much from Greeley lately. He has been rather vacillating during the war. You know him, do you?

Prisoner. Oh yes, I have met him often. He served a term in Congress while I was there. I was on very good terms with him in our personal relations. I always regarded him as a man of inflexible purpose, principle, and integrity on his line. He is, in many points of view, a real philosopher. His paper, the *Tribune*, I always read with a great deal of interest — as I have read his book — however much I disagree with him in his premises and conclusions. He is always fair in statements, open and bold in purpose, and has a vigour, force, and perspicuity in style rarely equalled. Like most philosophers, he has many eccentricities in ideas as well as in manners.

Surgeon. Even in dress. His coat and hat are quite famous.

Prisoner. Yes; no one thinks of Greeley without the coat and hat. These seem part of the physical man, no less characteristic than his long stride and shambling gait.

Surgeon. Well, sir, I am glad to see you so well this morning. I will try and get you the straws or the quill; and if there is anything else I can do for you, let me know. Good morning, sir.

Prisoner. Thank you. Good morning, Major.

Geary brought dinner. For dessert, a cold custard such as I got at a Mr. Palmer's in East Haddam in 1838. I had called to see Mr. Palmer on business for some orphan children in Georgia; Mrs. Palmer brought refreshments, and such a custard in such a cup! Obeyed the Doctor's directions in finishing with some whisky — from the bottle Harry put up for me. I have never taken that bottle from my trunk without thinking of how Harry looked when he got it and handed it to me. It was just before the trunk was locked; all had gone out of my room but him and me. He looked sad. I hastily gave him all the directions I could, in rather confused order; told him, amongst other things that I wished him to remember if I never saw him again, to be sure and send his children to school, to give them an education if he could.

His sorrowful face at that last interview is daguerreotyped upon my memory, and I never see the bottle but association brings it out in its distinct impression.

The papers state that Hunter, Campbell, and Seddon are prisoners in Fort Pulaski. Walked at 6.15. Saw several stalks of green rye growing in the angles and about the walls of the Fort. They were large-headed and I thought might answer my purpose for taking the acid, so cut some. Geary brought sea-water and poured it in my tub. I wish to try a salt-water bath; as the water might be too cold, taken from the bay in the morning, I arranged to have it sit in the room all night. The temperature of my room I should think is about 75 degrees. I wrote the sutler to-day to get me a small thermometer.

June 13. — Another clear, brilliant, glorious day. When I awoke, the sun was peeping into my otherwise dark and gloomy cell, with one of the most radiant and joyous countenances he ever wears. Dimpling, beaming smiles covered his whole broad face. Oh, how I should have enjoyed this morning could I but have gone out, caught the inspiration of "incense-breathing morn," and joined in the chorus of nature's responsive welcome to its sun, her *Te Deum* to the advent of this most glorious day! As it was, I could but rise from my bunk of iron and straw, and while taking my salt-water bath, chant in not very musical notes:

> Alas, and did my Saviour bleed,
> And did my Sovereign die?
> Would he devote that sacred head
> For such a worm as I?

My thoughts wandered far, far away; to Georgia, Liberty Hall, and the old homestead. Read several chapters in

Job. Was reading when Geary brought breakfast: good coffee, hot rolls, mutton chops, and cornbread.

In the N. Y. *Times* I see a letter of some importance from Hon. J. Minor Botts. It sets forth many truths; but what appears therein as an extract from my speech in the Georgia Secession Convention is incorrect. I opposed the Ordinance of Secession and made a speech against it, but used very different language from that attributed to me. Where he could have got such a report of my speech, I cannot imagine. None such ever met my eye before; I never saw but one report of it. That was in the Southern *Recorder*, of Milledgeville, a few days after I made it. I could not have spoken of secession as a crime, for, however much I was opposed to it, I did not so consider it. I considered that the State had a perfect right to secede; her act was fully justified on the grounds of breach of compact by several of the Northern States in the matter of the rendition of fugitives from service, by which open, palpable, and avowed breach of faith, she was released from all moral obligation to continue in bonds of union with them. A contract broken by one party is dissolved as to all, if the others so choose to consider it. But I did not consider it politic or wise for the State to adopt that mode of redress, though she had a perfect right morally and politically to do so. Nations or States are not bound, even in honour, to adopt the *ultima ratio regum*, for everything that would justify it. This was my position which seemed so hard for the mass of mankind to comprehend. This breach of covenant on the part of several of the Northern Confederates, was in my judgment the only ground that fully justified the State, in view of the moral obligations resting upon her under the Compact of Union, in taking the course she did. But what is fully justifiable, morally and legally, is not always wise and expedient.

An important card from W. W. Cleary on Conover's testimony in the Assassination trial is in the N. Y. *World*, copied from the Toronto *Leader*. And an extract from the Charlotte *Democrat* on Bates's testimony as to what Mr. Davis said on receiving telegram of Mr. Lincoln's death. According to this, Bates's testimony is utterly worthless. This I thought most probable at first. The N. Y. *Times* has an editorial on "The Doom of Treason." I look on this as more important from the fact that the *Times* is said to reflect Mr. Seward's sentiments. It says:

> The trial of Davis, Breckinridge, Cobb, Thompson, Stephens, Benjamin, Slidell, Mason, etc., for treason is demanded by every consideration which concerns the dignity of the Government, the majesty of the law, and the safety of her people. The tears of weeping millions and the blood of slaughtered thousands demand, at least, this measure of atonement. Nor will it be denied. And when tried, if lawfully convicted, the President of the United States will determine whether their execution or banishment will best comport with the nature of their crime, the spirit of the age, and the judgment of the world.

If such be the sentiments of Mr. Seward, such will probably be the result; so far from shrinking from a trial, all I ask so far as concerns myself is a speedy trial, public, with such time only as shall be necessary for preparation, and such conveniences during its progress as will afford me access to the authorities and documents I may desire. With this, God mercifully giving me health and strength of body and usual vigour of mind,

I shall be prepared to pass the ordeal with an unquailing spirit, let the end be anything but exile. Exile I could not stand! Nor could I well stand life-time close confinement; at least, I think, under it my life would be short. That spirit within me which could meet death on the gallows with steady nerves, would it stand by me or sink and break within me under sentence of exile or long imprisonment? I am inclined to look on this editorial with the more interest from the fact that it appeared after time had elapsed for my letter to the President to reach Washington.

I see from the N. Y. *Herald* that the Boston *Traveller's* account of the Medical Convention's visit to the fort last week, states that Judge Reagan occupies a room adjoining mine; that he appeared at his window once and bowed to an acquaintance; but that my windows were curtained and I was not to be seen. This Medical Convention was the great mass of visitors noticed by me on the 8th, and my account of it is correct. There are no curtains to my windows.

Walked out at 5.45 with Lieut. W. Saw a number of Confederate officers, prisoners, walking on opposite parapet, but could not recognize any of them. Found thermometer on table when I returned and paid for it, $1.25, making all expenses $61.48. It stands at 77 degrees. Geary brought tea, strawberries, and sweet cakes.

CHAPTER VII

JUNE 14. — Another bright morning out. Rose at 6.30. Thermometer 72. This thermometer is to be a sort of pet with me, I expect. Read Jeremiah 30, and all of Lamentations. The wailing of Israel's poet over the subjugation, desolation, and ruin of his Zion, meet a sympathetic response in my breast over a like condition of my own dear Georgia. How truly is our condition set forth:

> Our inheritance is turned to strangers, our houses to aliens. We are orphans and fatherless, our mothers are as widows. Our necks are under persecution: we labour and have no rest. The elders have ceased from the gate, the young men from their music. The joy of our heart is ceased; our dance is turned into mourning. For this our heart is faint; for these things our eyes are dim. . . . For thus said the Lord; we have heard a voice of trembling, of fear and not of peace. Ask ye now, and see whether a man doth travail with child? Wherefore do I see every man with his hands on his loins, as a woman in travail, and all faces are turned into paleness?

How vividly return to my mind the feelings with which I went from a sick-bed to address a vast concourse of people at Dalton, in 1860; in that address, with all due reverence, I exclaimed: "O Jerusalem, Jerusalem, thou that killest the prophets and stonest them which are sent unto thee, how often would I have gathered thy children together, even as a hen gathereth her chickens under her wings, and ye would not." This speech was made in prophecy of impending ruin; amidst interruptions and attempts to prevent my counsels trom having effect, I warned our people to stay these calamities while they might.

I see a statement in the New York *Tribune* that the President has granted unconditional pardon, accompanying it with a letter, to Hon. W. W. Boyce, of South Carolina. This I was glad to see, not from any encouragement I may be supposed to take that similar grant may be made me, but because I think well of Mr. Boyce; think he deserved what he is reported to have received, notwithstanding he was so much more responsible for this war than I; notwithstanding his speech in Columbia, November, 5, 1860, in which he is reported to have said:

> The question then is, what are we to do? In my opinion the South ought not to submit. If you intend to resist, the way to resist in earnest is to act — the way to avert revolution is to stem it in the face. The only policy for us is to take up arms as soon as we receive authentic intelligence of the election of Lincoln; it is for South Carolina, in the quickest manner and by the most direct means, to withdraw from the Union. Thus, we will not submit, whether the other Southern States will act with us or with our enemies.

At this time, my utmost exertions were in the other direction. His impulses, I doubt not, were prompted by apprehension of danger to the Constitutional Rights of his State from Mr. Lincoln's election. I have no question that this was the case with Governor Joe Brown, Governor (then Judge) Magrath, and great numbers of other leading men whose actions and counsels "precipitated" the war. I was "precipitated" by them against my judgment and protest, and am suffering in consequence. I rejoice to see that these men — Boyce, Brown, Magrath, Smith (Governor of Virginia) and Cobb, with thousands of others who followed like course — at large enjoying on parole their personal liberty. Such liberty would be to me a great boon also, but perhaps it is better for me to suffer, if so be some few must suffer to satisfy public vengeance. Isolated and almost alone in the world, a strange creature of destiny at best, with but few ties to life, why should not I be one of the victims? My fate may be a hard one, but it has been a hard one throughout life.

Walked my room and thought of home — of Linton; smoked my pipe, the meerschaum Girardey gave me. This has been a great source of comfort to me. How often I have thought of him, Camille Girardey of Augusta, Ga., when I have puffed that meerschaum in this dungeon. Walked out at 6.15. Saw Jackson and DuBose on the opposite bastion — too far to recognize them. Lieut. W. told me who they were. Saw General Ewell on his crutches. He was walking on parapet. I remarked that I thought Ewell had an artificial leg; wondered he did not use it. Lieut. W. replied that Ewell said he was waiting before getting an artificial leg to see if the authorities were going to hang him; if he was going to be hung, he did not care to go to the expense; intended to wait and make out on his crutches until that matter was decided. Ewell has a sense of humour.

We heard a cannon. Turning toward the point from which the sound came, we saw smoke near a small craft lying at the wharf of a little town, called Hull, near by. Lieut. W. said, "Oh, it's Dexter Follet's yacht." "Who is he?" asked I. "A young man of Boston, son of a rich father. He keeps this yacht to sail about as he likes. Carries a gun on board, and always fires it off upon landing or leaving, upon heaving or hoisting anchor." We saw the yacht pass on its way to Boston.

Geary brought tea, toast, and strawberries. I thought of Dick Johnston's extensive bed of strawberries and of what an abundance of berries he must have had this spring. All gone by this time, I suppose.

June 15. — Rose at 6.45. Was disturbed by dreams. Richmond was the scene. I seemed to be roaming amid ruins, looking for Mr. Baskerville's house; was on my way home, and had stopped to see after Henry and Anthony. The house — in my dream — had been burned, not a vestige remained of it, nor of other houses that had stood around it; Mrs. Stanard's and all were swept away by fire. I could find nobody I knew and could learn nothing about Henry and Anthony; could hear nothing of Nancy, their mother. Read Bible until 8.15. Geary brought breakfast: fresh fish, beef-steak, hot rolls, coffee, fried potatoes, and cornbread. The cornbread I ate. Breakfast good enough, but I had no appetite for it, due, perhaps, to its late coming. It is essential to my health for me to have breakfast as soon as I can get ready after rising. Half an hour is my usual time for dressing. I can fast an hour after rising, but beyond that I cannot go with impunity. I want my breakfast at this season at seven; for several days I had it at this hour, but since Sunday — Geary saying he could not get it so soon — 8.15 is the hour fixed. This morning it did not reach me until 8.45, a half-hour past the time for which I arranged my rising and dressing.

The Boston *Post* says, "The health of A. H. Stephens is said to be precarious." A letter from Charleston, in the N. Y. *Herald*, gives an account of Governor Aikens's return from Washington. I did not know that he had been in custody. The New York *Times* reports Breckinridge and Trenholm [of the Confederate Cabinet] as safely arrived in Bermuda. I am almost certain that this cannot in part be true. Trenholm, I have reason to believe, has not even attempted to leave his State.

Dinner at 2.45: salmon, beef-heels, mutton, vegetables, and gooseberry pie — no uncertainty about it to-day; it was gooseberry, the same as that of yesterday. Upon my inquiry, Geary said so; that settled it. Besides this, there was a saucer of cream and jelly. My diet now is as much over the proper mark for me as it was too low before. The *juste milieu* is in everything the most difficult point to attain. Could I get meals served in half the quantity and variety, to say nothing of some reduction in quality, with corresponding reduction in cost, I should feel myself as well off as possible in respect of food.

5 P. M. — Walked the room, exercising the whole body as much as I could by swinging my arms and giving them all sorts of motions. This has been my habit for several days, particularly after extinction of lights. I have a notion to get a rubber ball to play with. That would afford better exercise than I can take otherwise. During my walk I thought a great deal about home. Am beginning to doubt whether any of my letters have reached their destination. It is certainly time I heard from Mr. Baskerville, if he was in Richmond and got my letter. How relieved I should be by only a few lines from Linton, giving assurance that he is well! Could I but have the assurance that he is bearing

up under my imprisonment with firmness and without too great uneasiness, I could stand all that is before me without a murmur. Wrote to Dr. Berckmans, Augusta, Ga.

Took overcoat for my walk at Lieut. W.'s suggestion; he said it was rather raw out. Did not feel well; pain in the side. Rested under music-stand and returned before hour expired. Saw Confederate prisoners on opposite bastion. I have a pretty large fire of anthracite coal in the grate. The fire in that grate has not gone out since I have been here; it has been kept up, day and night. A grate of this coal put on at 7 p. m. will burn until 6 a. m.

June 16.—Before I got up, Geary brought in a wooden box on legs. I suppose that I will not be stating a matter of indifference to those sympathizing friends for whom these entries are made, when I tell them that I *live* in this cell except during the hour of my daily walk on the grounds. Whatever functions of nature are performed in eating, drinking, sleeping, or otherwise, are performed herein. At my request Geary got the carpenter to make this commode; price $1.83. While on this point, I will add that Geary is very attentive to my room; keeps it well swept and dusted; and makes up the bed every morning, that is, beats up the straw and arranges the covering, which, besides the sheets, are the blankets and afghan I brought with me. He brings cool water as often as I desire it; it is cistern water, clear and pure, about 65° in temperature. I see in the papers an account of John Mitchel's arrest in New York. Mitchel is a rare character, an eccentric genius. I was sorry, not only on his own account, but on account of the South and her cause, when I saw some weeks ago that he was in New York writing for the *News*. He is a man of too much violence of temper, too much extravagance, and too little discretion, to be identified, to its advantage, as a leading exponent of any cause.

When Smith O'Brien* was in this country on a visit to Washington, he stopped with Mitchel† who had a house there. I was on friendly relations with Mitchel. At his invitation, I called to see O'Brien and was well pleased with this far-famed "patriot and rebel." His bearing, as well as his high intelligence and virtue, could not fail to impress any one coming in contact with him. I assumed the discharge of the office, very agreeable to myself, of introducing him to President Buchanan; Mr. Mitchel accompanied us. As we were returning to our carriage, speaking of Mitchel in his presence to O'Brien, I said that Mitchel's greatest difficulty lay in extravagance of feeling and expression; that he seemed to forget that there were three degrees of comparison in language; he dealt almost exclusively in superlatives.

O'Brien nodded assent with a smile, while Mitchel did not seem to dissent from the justness of the criticism. Afterward, while O'Brien was on a visit to me at Liberty Hall, on his tour through the South, Mitchel was often the subject of our conversation. O'Brien, it was evident, was devotedly attached to him personally, while deeply regretting some of his eccentricities and extravagances. I am truly sorry for Mitchel. He did a great deal in bringing on the war. He has suffered severely for it. A son of his, of great promise, bearing, I think, his father's name, fell in defending Fort Sumter. The

*† Mitchel and O'Brien, as leaders of the "Young Ireland Rebellion," had been banished from Great Britain in the 'forties. Mitchel edited by turns several papers in this country, and during the war, the Richmond *Enquirer*, reputed organ of the Confederate administration.

father seems, by nature, one of those restless spirits born to stir up strife, and to become the sport, football, and victim of adverse fortunes.

I get no letters; hear nothing from my application to the President, see no allusion to it in any of the papers. It must have reached Washington before this, but perhaps it is filed away in some pigeon-hole to be taken up in its turn, which may not be for weeks or months. Who in that busy crowd cares for me? A man in prison is soon forgot, almost as completely as if he were in his grave. With the great active living mass, in their pursuits of business or pleasure, or borne down with their own afflictions, the world moves on as before. The daily papers are sought by the merchant, the banker, the ship-owner, the politician, and the devotee of fashion, to see the state of the markets, the prices of stocks, the arrivals and departures of all sorts of water-craft, the progress of reconstruction, the new concerts and other amusements, marriages, and deaths, and what not. But who in all this turmoil thinks of me? A brother, a few relatives and friends and faithful domestics and, perhaps, three devoted dogs, are, in creation's range, the only beings that think once of me in a week or a month. Read Jeremiah. I can exclaim with him:

Oh that my head were waters, and mine eyes a fountain of tears, that I might weep for the slain of the daughter of my people!

I turned to Job; my Bible opened at this:

If I did despise the cause of my manservant or of my maidservant, when they contended with me; If I have withheld the poor from their desire, or have caused the eyes of the widow to fail; Or have eaten my morsel myself alone, and the fatherless hath not eaten thereof; If I have seen any perish for want of clothing, or any poor without covering; If his loins have not blessed me and if he were not warmed with the fleece of my sheep; If I have lifted up my hand against the fatherless, when I saw my help in the gate; Then let mine arm fall from my shoulder-blade, and mine arm be broken from the bone. If I rejoiced at the destruction of him that hated me, or lifted up myself when evil found him: Neither have I suffered my mouth to sin by wishing a curse to his soul. The stranger did not lodge in the street: but I opened my doors to the traveller.

Most truly can I repeat this, if I know myself. When has suffering humanity appealed to me for assistance or redress that was not rendered if in my power? When have the poor, even the unfortunate blacks, driven from their abodes in winter cold and snow, appealed to me that they did not receive food and shelter? When has the voice of distress, from high or low, ever reached my ears unheard or unrelieved, if relief was in my power? I do feel that I have laboured more during my feeble, suffering life for the comfort and happiness of others than for my own.

I have aided between thirty and forty young men, poor and indigent or without present means, to get an education; the number I do not exactly recollect. Many of these I took through a regular collegiate course, or offered them the means for such a course. My assistance of this character has not been confined to young men; orphan and indigent girls have received liberally of my bounty. I have spent many thousands of dollars for the accommodation and comfort of those recognized as my slaves by our law, over and above all returns they ever made to me. This was of my own earnings. I commenced life without a cent; indeed I was in debt for my own education: as I had been assisted when in need, so I ever afterward assisted those in like circumstances, as far as I could. In all my troubles and trials, and they have not been few or small, I never cherished malice against those from whom I had received wrong. Never did I "rejoice at the destruction of him that hated me or lifted up myself when evil found him."

Finished "Ferdinand and Isabella." Whether the great heroine and heroes are not glossed over too much by glowing rhetoric, giving the work somewhat the character of a romance, may be suspected. And whether the benefits of the consolidation of the separate kingdoms of Spain into one government, which is a leading idea, are not over estimated, may be more than suspected. Many evils, to which Prescott alludes as following the consolidation, may be traced to it. Whether the conquest of Granada, Navarre, and Naples, and the consolidation of the Spanish Empire which enabled it to assume such grandeur amongst the powers of Europe at the close of Ferdinand's life, contributed anything to the real happiness of the people of Aragon and Castile may be more than questioned. It certainly resulted in the loss of many of their liberties, and it is difficult to see how it added to their progress in civilization and refinement. Might not those anterior causes, which prompted such heroic exertions and grand exhibitions of virtue in the reign of Ferdinand and Isabella, have led to far higher results under different guidance, results which would not have been attended, and almost necessarily, with the consequences that ensued under the reign of Charles V., and which ultimately ended in the present state of things in Spain?

Prescott pays too little attention to the old constitutions of Castile and Aragon, particularly the latter. The most important principle of this constitution which had lasted for nearly two centuries, required unanimity in both branches of the Cortes, as well as the sanction of the crown, to give validity to any legislative act. Any member of either branch by simply interposing his veto could arrest action, a very remarkable fact. The workings of any system established on such a principle deserve thorough consideration. Prescott passes over it with little more than incidental mention. Yet under this system, Aragon had risen from almost barbarism to that high state of culture, civilization, and liberty which had produced a Mena, Villena, and Santillanna, literary lights not surpassed by any in Spain since their day. In that state of vigorous development in all that ennobles nations and peoples, Ferdinand found her when her future became subject to his influence as her sovereign according to the well-settled principles of this time-honoured constitution. Had he more carefully studied and conformed to its principles, looking more to internal policy than external acquisition, how vastly different might be the condition of things in Spain to-day! The world needs full exposition of the workings of these ancient systems of Aragon and Castile, these early germs of representative government in Spain. Whatever else the reign of Ferdinand and Isabella did, it led to the overthrow of these systems of liberty and to the establishment of despotism in their stead. Had the Cortes been consulted, as it ought to have been under the old constitution, who can believe that Torquemada could ever have introduced the Inquisition into Castile? And how much more difficult and even impossible would it have been for this most iniquitous institution to get foothold in Aragon if unanimity in each branch of the Cortes had been necessary.

I see in the New York *Times* a short notice referring to the nature of my confinement, state of health, etc. I am weary in spirit and sick at heart waiting for letters from home. I begin to fear the officers do not transmit my letters with much dispatch. I should certainly have heard from Mr. Hill* at Washington City. I cannot believe he would be neglectful or remiss in writing to me. Why has not Mr. Baskerville answered my letter? Why have not I received some reply from the President? These things set heavily upon me.

Read Prescott's "Conquest of Mexico," until Geary brought evening paper. I see a telegram from Washington in reference to my application. It has me intimating, as a reason for acceding to secession, a belief that there would be no war. I did no such thing, and intended no such thing. My opinion from the beginning was that there would be war and a bloody war.

Walked out with Lieut. W. The warmest evening yet on the parapet. Geary brought tea.

Sunday — Rose at seven. Read Psalms; this came in order:

By the rivers of Babylon, there we sat down; yea, we wept, when we remembered Zion. We hanged our harps upon the willows in the midst thereof. For there they that carried us away captive required of us a song; and they that wasted us required of us mirth, saying,

* Joshua Hill, of Georgia; Member of Congress, 1857–61; Unionist throughout the war; U. S Senator, 1868–73.

"Sing us one of the songs of Zion." How shall we sing the Lord's song in a strange land? If I forget thee, O Jerusalem, let my right hand forget her cunning. If I do not remember thee, let my tongue cleave to the roof of my mouth; if I prefer not Jerusalem above my chief joy.

With "Georgia" for "Zion" and "Jerusalem," these words might be the outpourings of my own heart. I remembered Georgia in her desolation; thought of home, its sweet endearments, of my brother and his little ones.

In the Boston *Herald*, I see that James Johnson, of Columbus, has been appointed Provisional Governor of Georgia. I know him well. He was my classmate in college, and contested the highest distinction with me. No honours were awarded by the faculty: but Johnson, William Crawford (son of the once-candidate for President of the United States) and myself were selected to deliver three orations: salutatory in Latin to the audience, trustees, and faculty; valedictory to the same and the class; and a philosophical oration to the audience. "Salutatory," "Valedictory," "Philosophical Oration" were written on separate slips of paper and put in a hat held by Dr. Church; he called Crawford who stepped forward and drew "Valedictory"; Johnson drew "Oration." Of course, "Salutatory" was left to me. The faculty allowed me to make also an address in English to the audience. The valedictory by college usage was always assigned as first honour, the Latin salutatory as second, and the philosophical oration as third; but as the faculty were prohibited from conferring honours, they fell upon this expedient of arranging for Commencement. Had honours been assigned according to roll of merit or class standing, the first would have been mine.

Johnson and Crawford, I think, stood equal, two marks only below me. Johnson, like myself, was poor. He taught school, raised means thus, and was admitted to the bar. He is, by nature, of vigorous mind, adapted to the law. He rose rapidly at the bar, and has long stood amongst the best in his section of the State; has had little to do with politics, was generally on the unpopular side of agitating questions; was elected to Congress once and served out his term with distinction, but had no inclination to return, or at least, did not return. His election was during the excitement over the settlement of 1850; he was a strong Union man and was elected on that issue; he has remained in retirement since, pursuing his profession. He was a strong Union man in 1860, but when the storm of secession lowered and no man could advocate the Union without subjecting himself to sneers and insults if nothing worse, he gave in and went with the crowd, as I was informed; even made a speech in favour of secession and voted a secession ticket. I have but little doubt that that speech and vote were against his better judgment. His greatest defect is want of firmness and decision; so great is it that it may be said to amount to timidity. He is a man, however, of strong sense and good principles. How he will succeed as Executive in restoring order and bringing Georgia into the Union at this trying time and on this trying basis is to be seen. He has my best wishes, personally and officially, but I envy him not his task. We have always been friends. There was at college a little estrangement but it was soon over. In politics, we have differed at times, but this never interfered with our personal relations. He was brought up a Clarke*

*The party divisions, Clarke and Troup, took their names from the Governors — Clarke (1819–23), and Troup (1823–27), the "Great States Rights Governor."

man, while I was brought up a Troup man. When Nullification became the issue, he went with that faction of the Clarke party which espoused this doctrine, while I went with that portion of the Troup party, led by Troup and Crawford, which repudiated Nullification but stood on the doctrine of States Rights as proclaimed in Milledgeville, Nov. 13, 1833. Johnson went for Van Buren and I for Harrison in 1840. In 1850 we both went for the Union. In 1855 he went with the American Party while on the issues of that day I was with the Democratic. In 1860 I sustained Douglas while, I think, he was for Bell, though he sympathized with the friends of Douglas and would gladly have seen him elected. I am not sure that he gave the secession speech and vote as above stated, but such were the current rumours, and I never heard them denied.

Walked out with Lieut. W. Saw ships going out to sea, and one beautiful steamboat moving toward the summer resort at Hull.

June 19. — Read Psalms. Newly impressed with this: "The fear of the Lord is the beginning of wisdom, a good understanding have all they that do His commandments." It recalled to my mind the words of Solomon that my father, when I was a small boy, often repeated to me and made me repeat to him: "Fear God and keep His commandments: for this is the whole duty of man."

8.15 — Breakfast. All good; coffee not quite as good as usual, being not quite so hot; still, far above the average standard furnished in the best hotels that I was ever at. The coffee here is of most excellent quality. Coffee is one of three things of which I have long considered myself a judge; the other two are lizards and watches. I do not mean to say these are the only things I think myself capable of forming correct opinion upon; but they are three that I do claim, especially, to be a good judge of.

Read "Conquest of Mexico" until Geary, ever punctual, brought daily papers. Confirmation of yesterday's despatch about my application; and what purports to be an official report of the death of Federal prisoners at Andersonville, Georgia, during 1864. Upon this subject — treatment by Confederates of Federals in prison at Andersonville and other places and the great mortality amongst them — this remark may not be inappropriate: Their sufferings, and what is called the inhumanity of their treatment, were in great measure an unavoidable necessity.* Confederates had not means to make their prisoners comfortable or to furnish suitable diet; they were pressed for their own subsistence; many of the necessaries of life, to say nothing of luxuries, were cut off from the soldiers and the body of the people; they were themselves subject to privations from which many not only suffered, but contracted disease and died; soldiers in the field were often on very short rations and of a very unwholesome quality. My nephew, Wm. A. Greer, of the Fourth Georgia Regulars, wrote me last winter from near Petersburg, Virginia, that he had had nothing to eat for twenty-four hours but two small biscuit. He was writing at night, and said he did not know when the troops would get any rations; he had eaten nothing but the biscuit since the morning before, and was sick from hunger. His was not a single instance.

* See Southern Hist. Papers, I, 113–327; XXX, 77–104; Stevenson's Southern Side of Andersonville; Davis's Rise and Fall of the Confederate Government, II, 584–608; Haley's true story of Andersonville Prison; Evans's Military History, XII, 147.

From every quarter, news reached me of the suffering of our soldiers for food.

At Andersonville, there were crowded together on a small piece of ground, enclosed by a stockade, upward of 30,000 prisoners. The space occupied by this large number was, I believe, about ten acres; in this small compass this large body of men had to live, exposed to sun, rain, and all sorts of weather. What could be expected, even with an abundance of substantial food, but disease and death to great numbers? But whose fault was this? Was it entirely chargeable to Confederate authorities? The Confederates were ever anxious to exchange prisoners of war. This, the Federals refused to do. The Confederates could not separate their prissoners, or provide a number of places so as to have fewer men crowded together. They had not the means. They had not men to spare to build prisons or stockades in which to secure their many prisoners. Nor had they sufficient force in the field to spare men from it for guard duty even if they had been provided with proper places in plenty for the safe confinement of prisoners. The Federals were well advised of the conditions. May not the suffering, disease, and death of thousands who fell victims in these miserable places be, in part, charged to the conduct of their own Government which they had served so well and in whose cause they so mournfully and pitifully fell?

When I heard of the conditions at Andersonville, my feelings were excited to the highest degree of commiseration — just as much as when the sufferings of the Confederates captured in Arkansas were detailed to me by some one who had passed, still living, but shattered forever in health, through the dread ordeal which was their lamentable lot. When I was satisfied of the inability of the Confederate Government to provide for its prisoners as humanity required, I wished them all (or at least all in such places as Andersonville) to be released and sent home on parole. My policy was for Mr. Davis to address them, setting forth the cause for which we were contending, the great principle of States Rights and Self-Government for which their ancestors had pledged life and honour in 1776; and that we viewed this war, waged against us with such fearful odds on their side, as altogether wrong, aggressive, and utterly at conflict with these great fundamental principles of American constitutional liberty; that though the fortune of battle had placed them in our hands; though their own officials refused such exchange as was usual in civilized warfare; yet, as we could not supply them with such quarters or food as humanity dictated, we, with that magnanimity which ever characterizes those who take up arms nerved with a full sense of the justice of their cause, released them on their parole of honour not to engage further in the struggle until duly exchanged. To this policy, objection was made that it was necessary to hold these prisoners as hostages for our own men in prison, who, if we dismissed them, would be killed. Confederates escaping from Camp Chase and other Northern prisons represented their treatment in these places to be as bad as any now described in exaggerated statements going the rounds about barbarities at Andersonville, Salisbury, Belle Isle, and Libby. There were barbarities, no doubt, and atrocities on both sides horrible enough, if brought to light, to unnerve the stoutest heart and to cause the most cruel and vindictive to sigh over human depravity. War is at best a savage business. Yea, it is worse; it transforms the noblest work of God, His image, into a devil incarnate. All the outrages on humanity, the cruelties, the vile exhibitions of the most malignant passions that have attended this late lamentable war, are not confined to our side. Even the asserted project for firing cities, poisoning reservoirs of water, and assassination,* hellish as they are, have actual, not merely asserted, counterparts in the depopulation of Atlanta,† the sacking and burning of Columbia,‡ and the daring though unsuccessful attempt of Dahlgren on Richmond,|| in which general robbery, arson, and the assassination of Davis and his Cabinet were said to be combined objects. If the Confederates, or any of them, were demons, certainly all of the Federals were not angels.

Dinner: The first snap-beans I have seen this season; the potatoes were new; these and the beets carried my mind back home. I thought of Harry's garden and what a plentiful crop of all these things he must have had long before now. I ate sparingly, and still thinking of scenes about Liberty Hall, and of Harry, I finished with a drink from the bottle of whisky he put in my trunk just before I took my last departure from my own room in my own dearly beloved home.

---

* Charged against the Canadian Mission. † Hood's Advance and Retreat, 229–242. Sherman's Memoirs, II, 11–29. ‡ Southern Hist. Papers, VII, 156–57, 185–92, 249; VIII, 202–14; X, 92–3, 109–19; XII, 233. S. Carolina Women in the Confederacy, 247–54, 261–72, 288–335; Pendleton's "Stephens," 283–89. || So. Hist. Papers, III, 219–21; XIII, 516–59.

CHAPTER VIII

JUNE 20. — At every reading of Scripture I find something fitting my condition. This morning: "How long will thou forget me, O Lord? Forever? How long shall mine enemy be exalted over me?"

Scene in Prisoner's Room, 19th of June

Prisoner intensely interested in a great battle by Cortes, as described by Prescott, with Cortes in the hottest of the fight, when the bugle-blast sounded notice that all lights must be put out. Instantly, prisoner blew out his candle, leaving himself in darkness and in perfect bewilderment as to the result of the battle. He paced his room. Over what regions of time and space did not his thoughts wander? Their flights no walls or bars or bolts could restrain! The treasured meerschaum, gift of Camille E. Girardey, of Augusta, lay upon the table. He picks it up, fills it with some of the weed he brought from home; holds the small end of the poker in the fire until it becomes red, then applies it to the weed. This expedient after the candle is out is usual; he can not resort to match or paper without violating orders, and what might be the consequences of such indiscretion, even in the small matter of lighting a pipe, he does not know. He feels himself subject to rules neither definite nor prescribed. He paces on, indulging his roaming thoughts. On, time also moves. He goes to the wall where hangs his watch; the crystal being broken, he can not wear it in his fob; takes it down, and by the glare from the full grate of anthracite coal all aglow, he sees with the aid of his glasses that an hour has rolled around since he dropped his book and put out his candle. Still not wearied, he lays his meerschaum on the table, and resumes his walk.

He goes to one of his windows facing southeast and looks out upon the heavens. The sky is clear, the stars shine brightly. Prisoner gazes upon them as upon old acquaintances; theirs are the only familiar faces, save the sun's and moon's, that he has seen for many days. His heart is somewhat comforted as he watches the heavenly hosts move on in their far-off nightly courses, just as when he watched them from his own front porch at home. Home, and that porch with its two settees! a thousand thoughts and images of the past rush upon him. There, so many pleasant starlit summer nights have been spent. The refreshing, cooling southern winds seldom failed there. There, the silvery sheen of moonlight on the grass was chequered with the deep shade of cedar, oak, hickory, and other trees. In his mind, as he stood by his prison window, not only images of inanimate things arose, but the well-known forms of persons beloved and dear; among these Linton's.

All around was still; nothing to be seen without save dark outlines of the granite wall; above, the bright luminaries twinkling and sparkling in the high, bending arch of the heavens. Nothing was to be heard save the heavy tread of the guard in his solitary beat on the stone pavement. Prisoner turned and resumed his rounds; on, on, he walks while his thoughts still roam afar. Again, he consults his watch and sees that another hour has passed. He sets the blower as a screen before his grate so as to shut off the heat, takes the end of his bunk and turns it so as to make the length range as nearly north and south as he can guess (this has been done by him ever since he has been here); then spreads before his chair, a newspaper (New York *Herald* as it chanced to be), four sheets double on the stone floor, as is his custom, thus making a mat for his feet; he undresses and stretches himself on his bunk. Here, with soul devout, he endeavours through prayer to put himself in communion with God. To the Eternal, Prisoner in weakness and with full consciousness of his own frailty, commits himself, saying from the heart, "Thy will and not mine be done." With thoughts embracing the well-being of absent dear ones and all the world of mankind besides, whether friend or foe, he sinks into that sweet and long sleep from which he arose this morning.

I see in the papers that Erskine, of Atlanta, will probably be District Judge of the State; a good appointment. See several allusions to myself. No two agree, and not one except that in the Boston *Post* is true, and that may not be. It states that my voluminous document has been committed to Secretary Seward for his examination and report.

Took up the last volume of "Conquest of Mexico." But first and foremost, took a seat on my bunk and, with penknife in hand, went deliberately to work and cut all the leaves so as to have an open field for reading. Uncut leaves impede my progress in reading. Why any publisher should send forth a book with the leaves uncut, I cannot imagine. But so it is; they do it greatly to the annoyance of the reader. After getting through with this work, I resumed the narrative with as much eager interest as I ever felt in a novel.

Dinner was not brought until 3.30. All cold; seemed to be scraps. This all grew out of Geary's absence. The orderly substituting him, Massury, said Geary was gone to town. I asked no further questions; I concluded that in Geary's absence I had been forgotten temporarily, and that such fragments of dinner, some time over, as could be gathered together, were sent me. An incident occurred under my observation just before this dinner was brought, which I should like to mention here, but as these entries may fall into other hands than those for whom intended, and as my motives in mentioning it might be misconstrued, I think proper to let it pass without record.

6.15 — Walked out with Lieut. W. He told me he had sent off all prisoners from this place, except 33 including Reagan and myself. DuBose and Jackson are still here. All here have applied for amnesty.

Massury brought the cup of tea with dry toast, sweet cakes, and strawberries. I miss Geary, however.

June 21. — The little incident and some other matters, all small but seemingly cognate to it, or something else kept me from sleeping much. I was awake nearly all night, my mind dwelling on the little incident, or the combination of incidents. I may hereafter feel free to give an explanation; but, at present, can say no more. I miss Geary. My slop-bucket was not emptied and no fresh water was brought this morning. I made out the best I could, humming my usual unmusical chant. Read in Jeremiah and Psalms.

Finished "Conquest of Mexico." Nothing else I have read, purporting to be history, has struck me as being so marvellous. Few of the wildest romances are more wonderful than Cortes's life.

Lieut. Woodman called to let me know he was going up to Boston; I had requested him to give me notice; I wished him to take my watch and have the broken crystal replaced. I asked him to get me an almanac. This is the 21st of June, the summer solstice. To-day, the great Monarch of the Seasons stops his northward march. This is the day predicted by Mr. Davis in his speech at Richmond, on the report of the Commissioners from Hampton Roads Conference, as that by which the authorities at Washington would be suing those at Richmond for peace on their own terms as their masters. Instead, alas! our cause has collapsed, our Government is dispersed, our armies are disbanded; members of the Cabinet and of the higher grades of generals are under arrest, while Mr. Davis lies in a dungeon, manacled, perhaps awaiting trial for treason. His condition awakens my deepest sympathy and commiseration. But when he made that speech in Richmond, brilliant though it was, I looked upon it as not much short of dementation. I then thought that, unless his policy was speedily and rapidly changed, by the summer solstice there would hardly be a vestige of the Confederacy left. I felt assured that there would be no change in his policy. I am, with him and thousands of others, a victim of the wreck.

The solstice is upon us. But as the sun this day stops his progress North, and turns Southward in his course, may it not be hoped that there will be some corresponding turn of fortune toward the States of the

South? May it not be hoped that they have reached the solstice of their desolation, ruin, and woe? May it not be hoped that Mr. Davis has reached the solstice of his own troubles, grief, sufferings, and anguish, and that henceforth, brighter prospects may open up even for him as well as for all the rest of us?

Massury brought daily papers. Hon. H. C. Burnett was arrested yesterday at Willard's Hotel in Washington. He was Senator in the United States Congress from Kentucky; remained there until after the Bull Run fight, July 1861; then left Washington, and later represented Kentucky in the Confederate Senate. I suppose he will in due time be pardoned and released. According to Washington letters, applications for pardon pour in like a flood from all quarters of the South. Too many entirely for careful disposition by detail. I think it would be well for the President to dispose of them in lump somehow. When the good Catholic father Ximenes, Archbishop of Toledo, found it impossible to administer baptism singly to thousands of applicants (rushing almost *en masse* for it upon the conversion of the Moors as effected by the conquest of Granada), he fell upon the expedient of using a mop, by which means water was rapidly sprinkled with a few twirls of the hand over the vast multitude, constituting no inconsiderable portion of a once mighty nation. Now, in this matter of the absolution or purification of the South, I think it would be well to adopt some means like unto the good old father's mop, some short method of accomplishing the object wholesale. A general and universal amnesty should be proclaimed. In the *Times* I see Hon. Reverdy Johnson's argument against the constitutionality of the Military Commission now sitting on trial of the conspirators in the assassination; the argument is long; I have laid it away for perusal.

I got very hungry before dinner was brought. Hunger is unusual with me here. I seldom think of dinner until it appears. To-day I concluded that the hour had passed, and that the new orderly was neglecting me again. My watch was gone and I could not even guess the time, for the sun had passed out of range of my window: I could see no shadow by which to judge. I decided to call up Massury. So I went to the window, where the guard is always walking to and fro, night and day, with musket and bayonet. I said, "Guard, I wish to see the orderly." The guard instantly cried out, "Corporal of the Guard! Post Number 24!" Presently he reported through the window that the corporal was at the Adjutant's office, and would be here directly. I threw myself on the bunk to wait patiently. After awhile, the corporal made his appearance at the same place with the inquiry, "What is wanting?" I told him I wanted the orderly. Presently, Massury appeared, not at the window but in the door, which he had unlocked. I asked, "What time is it?" He said, "Twenty minutes to three." I asked, "When will you bring dinner?" He replied, "I was going after it at three, but will go now, if you wish it." I said, "I wish you would; I am hungry; but bring some cool fresh water first, if you please." He brought me water; had got it out of some standing vessel; it was not cool as that Geary brings. He then brought dinner: all cold, which caused me to think my suspicions as to time correct. But cold as it was, hunger gave sauce to it. I ate heartily, and finished with a drink from Harry's bottle. I wish Geary would come back. I miss him very much. He begins to look and feel to me like homefolks. He attends to me diligently and promptly. Massury says he expects Geary to-night.

I see by the Boston *Journal* that it is telegraphed from Washington to-day that General Lee and myself, according to report, are to be pardoned on condition of leaving the country. I shall never accept pardon on such conditions. Georgia is my country; within her limits I shall live, and at the old homestead I shall be buried. In no event will I ever by election become an exile from Georgia. Whether in prison or by the hands of the executioner, I prefer to die where some kind friends may take charge of and deposit my earthly remains in Georgia.

5.30 — Lieut. W. brought my watch with new crystal. No charge. The workman, he said, on being informed whose watch it was, would make none. I feel truly obliged to this unknown friend. A shower postponed my evening walk. Geary returned at six. Very glad to see him.

6.30 — Shower ceased. Lieut. W. came for walk. We went on the terreplein, but it was too wet; went up on parapet; but the grass, which is heavy set on it, was too wet. We stood on the bastion and enjoyed the fine southern breeze. Looked over the harbour and saw several showers passing around us. Boston was immersed in one, and the rays of the sinking sun, beyond the city and coming through the falling rain, not thick enough to shut them out, gave a beautiful appearance to glistening domes and steeples. We saw Confederate prisoners on the bastion nearest that on which we stood. One, Lieut. W. said, was Jackson. I could not recognize him. DuBose was not among them. Lieut. W.

told me that a gentleman, named Nourse, in Boston, told him to tell me, if I wanted clothing, money, or anything else, to call on him and he would let me have it. I asked the Lieutenant to return my thanks and say that I stood in need of nothing yet; if I were kept here long, I might require assistance; at present, was getting along comfortably. We came down without having walked much; I took three or four turns on the stone pavement and then came in. Geary brought my tea, toast, and sweet cakes. He had also brought sea-water for my bath in the morning. I found my room very neatly done up.

While on the bastion, I saw a row of men, about twenty, walking, two together. They were moving from the entrance to the inside of the fort and toward some underground apartments formed by a sort of mound near the water's edge. I asked if these were soldiers going to their quarters for the night. They looked dejected as they walked along. "No," said the Lieutenant. "They are the chain-gang, the criminals, deserters, etc. They are made to work on the fort. They are going to their quarters for the night." I felt sorry for the poor fellows, and thought of Jean Valjean.

June 22.—I barely got through Bible reading when breakfast was brought in by Geary; everything good. An incident took me back to Georgia. Geary in cleaning up yesterday carried away all cups and saucers. His usual plan is to bring coffee hot in some vessel and pour it into a cup kept here; he washes this cup in the adjoining orderly and corporal's room, as it seems to be. Cups and saucers had accumulated; these he took back to the sutler's. When coffee was to be poured this morning, there was no cup. It was too far to the sutler's, so he served it in a tumbler. I found I could not drink it, good as it was. Then recurred to me a remark made last winter by Mrs. Lou Stevens that she couldn't drink tea out of anything but china. The philosophy I cannot explain, but the fact is, I could not drink coffee out of glass. I took it from a cream pot. I have long known that water drinks better out of a gourd than out of tin, and out of glass than earthenware. But why coffee should reverse this and taste better out of earthenware than glass, I do not understand. Perhaps it is nothing but association of the same sort that makes hock wines taste better in greenish glasses and claret in reddish or brownish ones; while the clear crystal ones seem best for sherry and Madeira. This trifling incident brought in its train many memories of home.

In the *Tribune*, an item in reference to myself contains more truth than many other notices not half so long. It has some show of truth in it. My singing I do not think so good as one might believe on reading this account. Then, I think, I am free from anything like "a proud and haughty air." There is nothing of that in my nature or bearing. I have ever endeavoured to be correct and courteous to all, superiors as well as inferiors; neither sycophantic to the one class nor haughty toward the other. The bearing, which springs from the principle of doing to others as I would have them under like circumstances do to me, and which in my estimation is the stamp of true gentility, or the mark of the true gentleman, has ever been my standard, and I hope has characterized my intercourse with mankind.

I see Hidell has reached Nashville and taken the amnesty oath. I am glad to hear even indirectly from him. See that Breckinridge and party reached Cuba. What has become of Benjamin?* Trenholm, I see, is at Hilton Head under arrest to be sent to Fortress Monroe. Cobb, it is stated, is still in Macon. Crops, the report from Augusta says, are good in that part of the State. I hope this is true, and that the same good condition extends up to my place. See account of a horrible accident below Shreveport to a steamboat loaded with paroled Confederate prisoners. The boat snagged, sunk, and over two hundred lives were lost. Mrs. Seward died yesterday in Washington. This I regret, not only from sympathy with Mr. Seward in such a severe affliction, but from fear that it will delay action on my application, which, as the papers report, was submitted to him. General Dix has been ordered to Montreal on business. His absence from New York may delay letters for me.

I dreamed of Judge James Thomas last night. Linton and several others figured; Linton only incidently. I did not see him; knew he was present. The scene was his house. Strange I have had no dream about himself since I saw him; none in which he has distinctly figured; and yet he has occupied more of my waking thoughts than all other persons besides. It is four weeks to-day since my imprisonment here. It seems to me, if I had then known that I should not hear from Linton or home before this time, I should have been crushed. And how I would now feel but for the few lines received from Mr. Myers, affording such indirect information as they did, I do not know. That little missive, that short letter, gave me great relief, and the more from hope created

* Judah P., Confederate Secretary of State; escaped to England; became Queen's Counsel.

that it was pioneer of others soon to follow from those on whom my thoughts were most intent. But "hope deferred maketh the heart sick." Sometimes I have apprehensions that friends at home are keeping from me news they think would cause me distress. How long, O how long, shall I be doomed to this suspense?

SOMEWHAT OF A FANCY SKETCH AND YET NOT ALTOGETHER FANCY:

[Cell at Fort Warren. Alexander H. Stephens, *prisoner.* R. M. Johnston, *visitant* through window of imagination.]

Visitant. Well, what do you think of public affairs now? Only what you have told me for the last four or five years? Has the "pessimus" point not yet been reached?

Prisoner. Hardly, or as Jenkins* says in one of his decisions, "Scarcely. No, not yet." Things are truly in evil state; still they may get worse before they get better; and wise men, while hoping for better, should be prepared for worse. Over two years ago, William F. Fluker asked me if I didn't think the darkest hour of our troubles upon us, that hour which precedes light and cheer. I told him, No, that so far from having reached the darkest hour — the hour before the dawn — we were not even in the night of the war, the sun was not gone down. Last year, after Atlanta fell, he asked if I did not think the darkest hour had come. I told him the sun had set; we were in the night of our woes, but far from the midnight. "Well," asked he, "what is to become of us?" I said, it was a painful reflection to me that our people

* Charles J. Jenkins, Judge of Supreme Court of Georgia.

were so unconscious of their pending doom, of the great desolation coming upon them before their darkest hour would be passed, and before that dawn of better times for which all were so anxiously looking, would greet their eyes. I am not prepared to say that our people have reached their darkest hour.

Visitant. Why, what can be worse? The States are subjugated, their governments overthrown, their whole social system and internal policy uprooted and demolished, and most of their public men in prison, as you are, or in exile. How can matters be worse?

Prisoner. In many ways: internal strife, insurrection, and wars between races, ending in the extermination of one of the two now constituting the South's population, would make conditions, bad as they are, infinitely worse.

Visitant. What, in your opinion, is to be the remedy or end?

Prisoner. It is one thing to see threatening evils and a different one to prescribe measures for ending them, or to prejudge the extent to which they may go.

You may remember what I said to Bishop Elliott* last year when we dined with him at Mr. Stanard's. I told him that in my judgment abolition was the moving spirit of the war at the North; I did not think the war, end when or how it might, would leave slavery as it found it; while I looked on the institution recognized amongst us by our laws (which, so far as the spirit of the law was concerned, was only subordination of an inferior to a superior race) as sanctioned by God, yet I thought great wrongs had been perpetrated under it; as with all human institutions in accordance with the sanction of the Creator, there were reciprocal duties and obliga-

* Stephen Elliott, first Protestant Episcopal Bishop of Georgia.

tions; when these were faithfully performed on both sides, reciprocal and mutual benefits were the results: in our system, the superior race had looked too much to the benefits received from the relation, and too little to its obligations to the inferior, and the benefits to which that inferior was entitled; the moral and intellectual culture of the inferior race, to which it was entitled to the extent of its capacity and condition, had been greatly neglected: the Negro had been made to perform his part of the obligation while the white man had failed to fully perform his: this was, in my judgment, one of the great sins for which our people were brought to trial. The status of the Negro would not be left by war where war found it. But if the principles of President Lincoln's Emancipation Proclamation — the ultimate policy therein indicated of attempting to establish perfect political and social equality between the races — should be carried out to its final results, it would end in the extermination or the driving from the country of one or the other of the races. That policy, I regarded as against nature, against the ordinances of God; it never could be practically worked. This and much more on the same line I said to the bishop at that time; I repeat the views then expressed.

If the principles of the Radicals, who are determined on the levelling system of making the black man in the South equal politically and socially to the white, are to be carried out, I see no end to it all but the ultimate extermination of one or the other of the races, so unfortunately, to both in this view, interspersed with each other. Will events take this course? I cannot answer; that is why I cannot say whether we have reached the darkest hour in our troubles. There are other courses events might take which could possibly bring about a better state of things for both races than existed under our slave system, yet not better than might have been attained under it with wise and philanthropic legislation. The long night of darkness has no promising dawn as yet to my vision.

Visitant. I come to you for comfort as for four years past, but you give no more when war is over than when it began. How do you feel as to yourself? What will they do with you, do you suppose?

Prisoner. All opinions are speculative. I look on my present confinement as a great outrage. Six weeks to-day I was arrested at my own home and have been in custody ever since. For four, I have been in close confinement in this cell or dungeon or room, call it what you may, without any warrant or oath or any charge legally alleged against me. This is done by those who profess to be the guardians and defenders of the Constitution. Indeed, to add mockery and insult to wrong, if called on for the reason of their course toward me, I suppose they would declare that their object is to uphold the Constitution against an atrocious rebellion designed to overthrow it, with which I was connected. That is, they openly trample under foot the most sacred guarantees of the Constitution for the purpose of upholding it. What worse treason can there be in any free country than that which strikes a blow at the principles of its fundamental law? These constitute the life and soul of a free people. How any man can feel himself justified in violating my most sacred rights under the Constitution, if I am amenable to it, on the pretense of its being his sworn duty to support that Constitution, I cannot perceive. It is simply absurd and shameful! If, as alleged in the newspapers, I had violated the laws of the country, had desired to overthrow its Constitution; had committed an act of treason and had become connected with the most atrocious rebellion on earth; yet, I was quietly at my home; the charge could have been made and the arrest as prescribed by law, and I should have been entitled to all the rights of a speedy and public trial on presentment or indictment by a grand jury as set forth in that great charter of constitutional liberty which, it is said, I was endeavouring to upset and overthrow. But, instead, all these securities and rights thus guaranteed have been denied me, and by those who have the unblushing effrontry in this very denial to pretend that thereby they maintain the Constitution!

Visitant. The papers say you have applied for amnesty. Is that so?

Prisoner. Yes. I thought perhaps it was but proper for me to do so. My case was a peculiar one. The more I thought of it the more I was inclined to that view, and I finally wrote to the President, going fully into details, and asking amnesty if my case came within the purview of his tender; in case that were not granted, for release on parole until charges could legally be preferred, and if not this, then that my confinement be somewhat mitigated in rigour and restrictions. As to whether my letter shall be answered favourably in whole or in part, I have no idea. I try not to let myself dwell on the subject. I am anxious to have a reply one way or the other. If the response is entirely unfavourable, I shall ask speedy trial. Whether that will be granted, I don't know. There is nothing so depressing to me as the prospect of continued close confinement in this or any place, cut off virtually from free communication with home; cut off from all communication, free and full communication, I mean, with Linton, the light of my life. This is not much short of a living death.

Visitant. The papers say the President is going to pardon you on condition that you leave the country.

Prisoner. I will not accept pardon on those terms. I am willing to die if I cannot return to my home and be with Linton while our joint lives last. As for dreading trial for treason, or its consequences, I care but little. My conscience is void of offense toward God and man. I should feel no shame in being executed for anything I have done; and if I cannot be permitted to spend the balance of my days at home, with the dear ones there, on my farm, in my gardens, orchards, and vineyards, and amongst my books, then let me die, even on the gallows though it be. My greatest sufferings, for many years at least, have been since I came here. At first I was almost overwhelmed. They spring from being cut off from communication with Linton and the rest at a time above all others when I want to be with him and consult with him on public as well as private affairs. Exile would be but continuation of this. No, give me death in preference! let my days be brought to an end in my own native land! let my last breath be of my own native air! My native land, my country, the only one that is country to me, is Georgia. The winds that sweep over her hills are my native air. There, I wish to live and there to die, and if I am not permitted to die there, I wish at least to die somewhere, whether in prison or on the gallows, within reach of some kind friends who may gather up my remains and commit them to that last resting-place which I have prepared for them in the walled enclosure at the old homestead.

Visitant. What do you think we all had better do in Georgia, take the oath or not?

Prisoner. Conform to the existing order, accept the issues of the war; take things as you find them, and do the best you can with them as they arise. There is nothing in the oath* that any man ought to hesitate in swearing to now that the Confederacy has failed, except what relates to the Emancipation Proclamation and the laws of Congress on the subjects alluded to therein. But these are the results of the war; conformity follows as a matter of course. Swearing conformity does not add to the obligation that most men would feel they had incurred in accepting the issues without the oath. Slavery is abolished. Let every good citizen abide by this fact. Let every one who has had slaves do the best he can with them, working to their future interest as well as to his own. Let every suggestion as to the best policy in regard to the relation hereafter to be maintained between the races be listened to, and the wisest and most judicious adopted. If one experiment fails, let another be tried, and let the future, with honest exertions on the part of all for the best, be left to take care of itself. In this way, "sufficient unto the day is the evil thereof." Let no evils be unnecessarily anticipated, but let all have firm faith in God that all things will work out right in the end, whether it be according to their liking or not.

Visitant. Have you as strong confidence as ever in Democratic institutions? Do not late events shake your old ideas?

Prisoner. Not in the least. I still have unshaken

* Oath of Allegiance to the United States, prescribed in Johnson's Amnesty Proclamation.

confidence in the people under the providence of God. They do not always do right. The late horrible war on both sides may be attributed to considerable extent to popular passions spurred to excess; but reaction will come sooner or later. I have strong hopes that, after this generation shall have passed away, if not before, a new order will arise, from which still further progress in civilization will be made and a still higher and grander career entered upon by the people of this continent. The people in their passion often vibrate from one extreme to another until they settle down at the right point. What will be the state of things in twenty-five years on questions now agitating the public mind and which have produced so much suffering, desolation, and ruin, no one can predict. If the people of the United States can be kept true to the principles of their Constitution, all will yet be well. That they will prove true when the passions of the times have passed away with this generation, I cannot permit myself to doubt. I retain my confidence and faith, unshaken and undiminished by anything that has happened yet, in the people and their capacity for self-government. I have never believed that progress and civilization can be effected by arms. Reason and Justice are the principles through which reformations are to be made and by which all real and true progress is to be effected. A worse ordeal than any they have experienced may be in store for this generation, and yet a grand future may await and award that generation coming after. What shall be the form of our resurrected society, we know not; but hope, sustained by reason, looks forward to one on a higher, better, and grander scale. To this end, at least, I look and hope—though my eyes shall never see it — provided the people — the white people, I mean — be always left to govern themselves and provided they do not surrender their power. [Here, the *Visitant*, with countenance betokening deep thought, and without another word, vanished through the window.]

Took short walk, but was driven in by another shower. Lieut. W. gave the name of the gentleman who offered any assistance I might need in funds — Benjamin F. Nourse, of Boston; and of the man who put the crystal in my watch — Isaac H. Tower. I wish to remember both. Geary brought from the library a book I sent for — Cicero on the Gods, Fates, etc. Got another pound of candles; six in a pound. The first pound lasted four weeks; I have a piece long enough to burn to-night.

CHAPTER IX

JUNE 23.—I have just walked a mile and upward in my room; that is, 1,900 steps, which, with my stride, I have no doubt would make a mile in a direct line. I counted the steps by hundreds; at the end of each hundred I put a piece of straw on the corner of the table. When I had walked half an hour, I found the number of straws to be 19. The room or cell, 24 x 20 feet, offers space for a good walk by moving in a circle. If I had a rubber ball, I could exercise myself very well, not only in bouncing it on the floor and catching it, but in playing a game of fives *solus* against the walls.

Dinner: salmon, lamb, peas, snap-beans, turnips, potatoes, bread, ice-cream and other confections about which I can give no other information than that they were palatable, though I barely tasted of them. The ice-cream was my first this season; being a little apprehensive of bad effects, I finished with a pretty stiff drink from Harry's bottle — about two tablespoonfuls.

Walked out with Lieut. W. Rested under music arbour. He pointed out Jackson and DuBose on opposite bastion. They were walking together, walking fast. DuBose wore neither coat nor vest; was in shirt-sleeves. Returned without going on the ramparts; not well; oppressed at no news from home. Stood by the window and gazed at passing clouds: thought of home and Linton. Geary brought supper — many dainties — while I was at the window. Ate the strawberries.

June 24. — Put on my prunella shoes. The leather shoes I have been wearing are hard and producing corns. The change, I fear, will give me cold. To prevent that as far as I could, I put on a pair of thick woollen socks, which, by the way, is the only pair of the kind I brought from home. How this happened I cannot imagine. These prunella shoes I bought in Montgomery in 1861; they have lasted for summer wear ever since.

Breakfast at 8.30. Ate but little. In thinking of home, I found a flood of tears gushing from my eyes, rolling down into my plate. I turned from the table, and with my handkerchief stanched the current as best I could; I had, however, little more control over it than I should have had over a current of blood issuing from the nose. Home! home! sweet, sweet home! Nothing but news from home and Linton can allay my disquietude, and satisfy the cravings of my heart.

Finished Cicero on Divination and Fate. As in his treatise on the gods, he arrives at no certain truth or conclusion. Much he says on dreams commands reason's assent. Yet who does not feel that in his own experience there has been impressed upon his mind or soul — the thinking principle within him — presentiments of coming events? The usual explanation of dreams, such as Cicero gives has always been about as satisfactory to me as explanations in our schools of the tides and other obscure matters in natural philosophy. The mind assents to these as probably correct in the absence of better. Some dreams seem to carry the unmistakable impress of an agency other than that known in ordinary workings of the mind. Impressed on consciousness are matters on which the mind had never before indulged a thought, but which come to pass in almost exact accordance with the vision. What I say is mainly from my own experience. I have had many such dreams.

Reason cannot explain some of the many impressions and fixed conclusions of the mind. Neither should it exclude them as phantoms or the bare results of what is called superstition. There are subjects connected with human existence which appear not properly to come within the sphere of what is called reason. Reason is an intellectual faculty. But man is a triune being; there is in his composition matter, mind, and soul. The laws governing the third essential, its operations and aptitudes, are as different from those governing the intellect barely, as the latter from the physical laws governing the material part. Therefore in spiritual matters, it should be expected by reason that many things will arise which cannot be compassed, comprehended, or explained by itself even in its highest attainable development.

I am no disciple of the modern school of Spiritualists; I neither affirm nor disaffirm belief in their teachings. I know not enough about them to do so. From what I have seen and heard, I doubt not that much deception is practised by them, as it has been in all ages by professed fortune-tellers, soothsayers, conjurers, and diviners. All I mean to affirm is, that reason in its pride should not reject all spiritual operations, convictions, and manifestations, barely because they are beyond its power of understanding or accounting for.

Cicero, though he had demolished, in his own judgment, such things as presentiments or divine intimations to men through oracles, dreams, agencies, or prodigies, admits, after a survey of the whole field, that there is "a true religion." He says, "The beauty of the world and the order of all celestial things compels us to confess that there is an excellent and eternal nature which deserves to be worshipped and admired by all mankind." What is this but God? If he is to be worshipped, how but in soul and spirit? How can human reason undertake to prescribe the manner of these spiritual approaches? or the manner in which the Great Father may commune with his children? Who can be so bold as to say there can be no such communications because human reason cannot explain their operation? These remarks have been extended much farther than I purposed. Having said so much, I should say more; that is necessary to rebut an inference as to my own faith and creed. I must however defer it.

The N. Y. *Herald* gives an account of some who were my fellow prisoners on the way here, Governor Lubbock, General Wheeler, and others. It appears that Wheeler has been released, and that all prisoners at Fort Delaware will be released soon. When will the general jail-delivery extend to Fort Warren, I wonder?

5.30. — Lieut. W. brought me a letter from Mr. Baskerville, dated Richmond, 19th inst., in answer to mine of the 5th. Correspondence is certainly slow between here and there. He says he got mine on the 19th. I was much relieved by this letter; Henry and Anthony had got home safely. Mr. Stanard had suffered from the fire of April 3d,* but had repaired his property and was getting on comfortably. Mr. Thomas had lost his eldest daughter. Travis was in Richmond and well. Hamilton Baskerville was in the country at school. The letter did me good. I hope it will be the breaking up of the ice. In the Boston *Journal*, a telegram from

* The burning of Richmond at the Confederate evacuation.

Washington says President Johnson intends to pardon no more prominent leaders of the late conflict. If this is so, my case is settled.

6.15. — Stood on western bastion and looked toward Boston. Saw the State House cupola, Bunker Hill Monument, and other prominent objects. As my eyes rested on the outlines of where I supposed Cambridge to be, my thought of Linton, his sojourn there at the law school in 1845, riveted me to the spot. The eyes soon filled with tears. I instantly wheeled, not wishing my condition to be seen by the Lieutenant, and we renewed our walk, going back to my cell. Silence was observed on my part for some time; I could not have uttered a word without faltering; with that, I should have burst into weeping.

June 25. — Have been ill all morning; was taken about two with violent pain in the bowels. I called the guard and asked for Lieut. W.; I wanted some one to be in the room with me and hand me water and some whisky; was suffering too much to do this for myself. Lieut. W. came and attended to my wants himself. I took a pretty large drink of Harry's whisky, which gave me temporary relief; also, some cool water which Lieut. W. brought me. He inquired if I would have the surgeon; I told him "No." Dr. Seaverns called this morning; something he has sent gives partial relief. If I could but hear from home and know that they were all well! I could then bear pain and sickness and privation better. Lieut. W. has just called to see and inquire after me.

2.30. — Geary brought excellent dinner. I ate a little bread and a bit of turkey. Finished Jeremiah and read Cicero on "Laws."

6.15. — Walked out with Lieut. W. He told me he had seen a letter to a person here which stated that all were well at my home on the 7th. This is comfort and relief. It was a beautiful evening, and I looked closely for the new moon but could get no glimpse of her; the sun was too high. I did not walk much; rested under the music arbour.

Geary brought tea, dry toast, sweet cakes, and strawberries. I took a little tea and toast and a few berries. Why he continues to bring sweet cakes, I do not know, except for show. I have told him I never eat sweet cakes. To prevent any bad effects from the berries, I took a drink from Harry's bottle.

June 26. — My before-breakfast reading was from Job — a favourite book with me. I have read Job oftener than any other book in the Bible, except perhaps St. John. After breakfast took up Cicero. It is to be regretted that the treatises on the Commonwealth and the laws are so fragmentary. The phases of each subject to me most interesting, those relating to changes in the constitution and laws of Rome growing out of the withdrawal of the people or the great secession of the Tribunes, are wanting. One thing is striking. His opinion, when questioned by Atticus regarding auguries and divinations, is adverse to that expressed to his brother Quintus in the treatise on Divination. He shows that he was a believer in immortality. On all moral subjects, including man's duties to his fellows as well as to his Maker, he seems to have attained the highest round of reason's ladder. In expressing the opinion that God does sometimes communicate with man by inspiration or otherwise, he gives some of the very reasons I gave in my criticism the other day upon his anterior and opposite conclusion. Scipio's dream, a purely fancy sketch, presents some wonderful thoughts. I was not aware before that philosophy had attained such heights, either in physical, moral, or spiritual matters in that age.

This reminds me of something in Prescott's Conquest of Mexico: the extraordinary character of Nezahualcoyotl, Prince of Tezcuco. He was born about 1399, and died about 1470; his reign was therefore more than half a century before the arrival of European adventurers in the walls of Mexico. He was a wonderful man in the government of his country and the advancement of those arts and sciences through which the highest order of civilization and refinement are attained; but in nothing does he seem to me to be so wonderful as in his moral or spiritual side. Here is a specimen — a few sentences —from one of his moral essays:

> All things on earth have their time, and in the most joyous career of their vanity and splendour, their strength fails, and they sink into the dust. The great, the wise, the valiant, the beautiful — alas! where are they now? They are mingled with the clod, and that which has befallen them shall happen to us and to those that shall come after us. Yet let us take courage, illustrious nobles and chief captains, true friends and loyal subjects. Let us aspire to that Heaven where all is eternal and temptation cannot come. The horrors of the tomb are but the cradle of the Sun and the dark shadows of death are brilliant lights for the stars.

Wherein is this inferior to anything left by Socrates, Plato, or Cicero? Nay, wherein is it inferior, in a moral point of view, to the best things ever written by the wisest princes who ever ruled the chosen people of God? Is there not much in it that looks toward immortality? He built a temple and dedicated it "To the Unknown God, The Cause of Causes."

Cicero's attitude on canvassing for suffrage, I think subject to many grave objections; it can only be accounted for by the prevailing ideas and corruptions of the times. Some things in his letter to his brother Quintus, then candidate for the consulship, are excellent; but others, such as justifying the solicitation of votes and the making by the candidates of promises never intended to be fulfilled, are abominable.

Morning papers at usual time. A statement in the Boston *Post*, copied from the Augusta [Ga.] *Chronicle and Sentinel* of the 7th, on the Hampton Roads Conference, is a discordant jumble of facts which presents almost anything but the truth. The *Post's* editorial comment that it is understood that this statement was prepared at my instance surprises me. It was not nor is it true that I ever saw the editor of the *Chronicle and Sentinel* after my return from the Conference. His remark that, "We will now give the history of the Conference, as nearly as we can remember it, from the statement of Mr. Stephens to *us* directly after his return," has not a single leg to stand on. It is true I spoke freely of the Conference to a number of friends, but refused to put in writing anything for the public except what appears in the Commissioner's report. The subject-matter of that conference was not for the public. What really *led to it* is not known to the public at all, and what passed on those matters that led to it has never yet reached the public on either side. It was called a Peace Conference. The country on both sides so understood it, but the first object of the mission was a truce or armistice, to which, as was supposed by us, authorities at Washington might be induced to accede by questions exterior.* This supposition was founded entirely on representations made by Mr. Blair to Mr. Davis. It is true that while I had strong hopes of effecting an armistice, which I looked upon as most desirable in every respect, and while this was the sole purpose for which we were sent on the mission, I availed myself of the opportunity to sound the Washington authorities upon the subject of general peace. We had no authority, however, to treat for peace. Now most, if not all, of what is jumbled up in this statement in the *Chronicle* I have said in private conversations, in connection, however, with a great deal which is not stated, and not in the connection that is here given. I suppose the editor must have made up his report from what some person repeated to him as what I had been heard to say. But that any editor should have put such an account over the official signatures of Hunter, Campbell, and myself is strange; it is especially annoying to me as I am here in prison and powerless to correct misrepresentation.

Dinner: good, but I ate sparingly. Sitting at my window, smoking my meerschaum, my mind went into reverie on my present situation; especially the absurdity and foolery of it. This was suggested by the passing of the guard to and fro, with his loaded musket and glistening bayonet, peeping in occasionally, to see if I am safe, I suppose. This unceasing step of the guard is as regular as the tick of a clock. It is kept up day and night. One man is on the beat for two hours: then he is relieved by another who paces two hours; and so on: being relieved

* Joint maintenance by the sections of the Monroe Doctrine in Mexico. — War Between the States, II, 589–626.

for four hours, when he must return and act as before for another two hours. One set detailed for guard duty goes through these rounds for twenty-four hours, then another set is detailed for twenty-four, the same set performing guard duty about two days in the week. The conduct of these men is often the subject of my attention; they not infrequently have my sympathy and commiseration. They are not allowed to sit or rest, but must walk to and fro, about fifteen paces, all the time. They often weary in their monotonous drudgery, and by night become sleepy, as I judge from their sighs and yawnings, and their inquiries of some passing corporal, "What time of night is it?" or, "Is it not 'most time for the relief to come?"

The relief is well known some distance off by footsteps on the stone pavement; when it is near enough, the guard on duty wheels about, faces the front with musket duly presented, crying out, "Who comes here?" The officer in charge of the relief replies, "Relief!" Whereupon the guard on duty says, "Advance, Relief!" Up comes the officer with the new guard, asks the one about to be relieved sundry questions, such as "What is the news?" or "Is there anything new?" Hereupon follows a colloquy, the tenor of which I have never heard. It is, perhaps, a report of my actings and doings during the last two hours. Then, the officer, in audible voice, gives the newcomer instructions, just as a solicitor in our courts swears in a bailiff to a jury. An observer would suppose that the bailiff was thus informed for the first time of his duties from the manner in which he looks at the solicitor while repeating the oath. So with the new guard; he listens as attentively and demurely to his orders as if he had never heard them before. He is to keep close watch; no one is to be suffered to pass in or speak to the prisoner, except Lieut. Woodman or by Woodman's command. He is not to speak to the prisoner unless spoken to by him and then only to know what he wants. Should prisoner speak to him, he will immediately call for Corporal of the guard for post No. 24, to whom prisoner will make known his wants. When the orderly goes into the prisoner's room by command of Lieut. Woodman or any officer, the guard is to go with him and hear all that passes. This and some other matters of like import, which for delicacy I omit, constitute the gist of the instructions, which no sooner than over, the officer with the fatigued, gaping guard moves off, while the new guard commences his pacings.

So the days pass, and so the nights roll around, with this sort of clockwork fooling for me to count time by, if I had no better method of noting its passage. What absurdity is all this! Who believes I would attempt to get away if my door was open and no guard about? How could I get over the walls of this fort? How get away from the island if I could scale the walls? Again, what need of any guns in the hands of those about my barred, iron-grated windows, with my door locked, bolted, and barred? It is sheer nonsense.

Much is said in the papers about "reconstruction"—the principles on which it should be based; and about Negro suffrage in the subjugated states. Much more will doubtless be said and written upon this subject before it is settled. Negro suffrage is a great and grave question, as great and grave if not greater and graver than its antecedent, abolition. It was unconsidered, and perhaps unthought of, by those whose acts in effecting abolition opened up this new problem which now presents towering proportions. This question deserves calm thought, mature reflection, wise deliberation and action. The condition of the black population of the South under their present freedmen's status, without some sort of representation, under judicious limitations, in government, will unquestionably be worse for them as a race than their former status. Their position will be anomalous. They will have neither the franchises of a citizen nor the protection of a master. Their condition will be worse than was that of the Moriscoes in Spain, and not much better than that of the Gypsies in England, or the unfortunate tribes of Israel in all countries of Europe during the Middle Ages.

There is evidently a disposition at Washington to put down discussion of this subject. The ground upon which the officials attempt to silence discussion is untenable as coming from them. They say the Constitution prevents the Government from taking cognizance or jurisdiction of the question. This position is in itself unquestionably true; but by the same rule of construction the Constitution prevents the Government from changing the former status of these people as fixed and regulated by the states themselves. The Government has assumed to do this in the teeth of the Constitution. If it has, as one of the results of the war, constitutional right and power to say to South Carolina and Georgia, "You shall not be represented in Congress unless you abolish slavery," it would be difficult, I think, to show why it may not say on the same principles to the same states, "You shall not be represented unless you extend the right of suffrage to the class thus made free." The Government has estopped itself, has closed its own mouth, against the force of this argument. The position, strong and impregnable in itself, has been surrendered to their adversaries. They cannot hold up long under the raking fires which will be poured upon them, and that soon, too, I think, by batteries planted upon grounds of their own creating in their flank and rear. The question has inherent intense interest of vast magnitude. It is going to become a much greater than it is now considered and treated by many; if, indeed, it does not become the absorbing one and, like Aaron's rod, swallow up all other political questions of the day. Now, taking things as I find them, and acting on the principle that it is the duty of a public man to do with existing facts the best he can without quarrelling with what he cannot change or control, I have some ideas which I wish it were in my power to make public, or, at least, present to whoever can deal with this matter. It is a question that ought to be taken up, discussed, considered, and properly settled if it can be. Can it be? That is, in itself, a great question. I am inclined to think it can if reason and justice govern deliberations. I would not now be prepared to go into detail, were I called on for my plan. I will only indicate the outline.

The view I entertain rests on the assumption that coloured people, holding the relation they now do to the whites, with distinct, separate, and antagonistic interests, if permitted to remain, ought to be represented in the Government to which they owe allegiance and with whose exactions in taxes and other requisitions they must comply. How can this be done with justice to both races and according to reason? I suggest one way. Let all the blacks in a state be put into a class, a sort of guild, corporation, or tribe, and let this guild or tribe have representation in legislation upon just, reasonable and equitable principles. Let the state be districted; let the basis of representation be first settled; let the blacks vote separately; let them choose their own representatives without restriction as to locality of the voter but with such restriction as to race as may be wise. Let the franchise be properly limited at first, with such conditions as will induce its enlargement. If it should be found best, postpone putting the system in operation for three, four, or five years, but go to work immediately and provide for it. Something of this kind ought to be adopted by the Southern States themselves, looking to their own future interest, safety, and advancement. The whole Negro population, under this system, would become a political power in the state. All commonwealths prosper best when there are adverse powers properly balanced. Whether a system can work when the adverse powers are two distinct races, time and experience would determine.

6.15. — Walked out with Lieut. W. Was in hopes of getting a good view of the new moon. Without being much of a believer in signs and auguries, yet I do like always to get a clear view of a new moon. Whether there is really any bad luck attending the first sight of her over the left shoulder as some contend, or through glass or bush or cloud as others maintain, I will not undertake to decide. Perhaps what Joshua Hill once advanced to me on this, and other like subjects, is true, "That all signs or omens are good to those who believe in them." I can see some reason for what most people would call a pure superstition even in that view of the subject, and perhaps that is the only view that can be defended on rational grounds. Without, however, committing myself to belief or disbelief in omens regarding a new moon, I say that I always like to get a first view of the crescent in a clear bright sky, without intervening obstruction. I was in hopes of such a view this evening, but was disappointed. It was cloudy, not even the sun, not yet set, was to be seen.

I handed Lieut. W. a note to Major Allen requesting the Major to make known to the Editor of the *Post* that the *Chronicle and Sentinel* statement about the Hampton Roads Conference was not at my instance, that I had never seen or heard of it until to-day when I saw it in the paper. I requested him, if he felt at liberty, to let them know that I wished this denial published; the statement presented several facts not before printed which were true, but in a connection calculated to work erroneous impression on several points. Whether the Major will feel at liberty to comply with my request, I do not know.

June 27.—A great rainfall last night, high wind and a storm. All the lights were blown out in the passages and there was quite a stir among the men on guard. This morning, spent several hours writing and copying letters to Linton and General Dix. These are copies:

My dear Brother: I see by the papers that a Provisional Governor has been appointed for Georgia: a Convention is to be called and a new Constitution formed under certain limitations and restrictions upon the right of suffrage in the choice of delegates to that Convention. Whether these limitations and restrictions will affect you except as to the terms of the general oath required of all the voters, I am not certain. How you stand under the 13th clause of the Proclamation of Amnesty, I do not know. I am inclined to think from my knowledge of your situation and past course that you do not come within the class of excepted cases therein set forth. How you feel upon the subject, whether you are inclined ever again to have anything to do with politics or public affairs, I do not know. These are matters I have had great desire to confer with you about. As for myself, I have no such desire. But with you, it may well be different. You are comparatively young and in the vigour of manhood. The men of each generation should act their part in their day and time. My part in the drama of life has been performed. Not so with you. In this crisis, my advice to you is not to stand aloof but to give your country the benefit of your counsels to the best of your ability, looking to the best attainable good under the circumstances, acting upon the principle that a wise man will always meet facts as he finds them, and do the best he can under them as they exist, without quarrelling with what is beyond his power to change or control.

Now, then, in our new Constitution, what ought to be done? Many great and grave questions will arise, questions affecting the structural organization of society and the proper distribution and limitation of the representative principle on which we have often so agreeably to ourselves — and profitably to myself, may I not add? — interchanged ideas. Does not the occasion present a fit opportunity for incorporating in our system some of those best features of the Constitution of Aragon on which you have been accustomed to expatiate with so much enthusiasm? It seems to me that it does. I will give you my ideas briefly: you can think over them, and make such use of them as you please in the Convention, if you be not excluded, or by giving them to those who may be in it, or to the press, as you think best. Of course the use you make will be in your own expanded form, and not in the crude state in which I thus hastily, and without order, present them. The outline is this:

Let representation in your State be on a different

principle from what it has been. Let the entire population be divided into classes according to professions, pursuits, interests, and conditions; and let representation be based on such classification. Let the universities be represented; the learned professions; the different religious sects; the large corporations; mechanical interests with proper classifications; so, with the agricultural; and other distinct and antagonistic interests: let the coloured population, with their present change of status, be represented; this is itself a great question, as great and grave as, if not greater and graver than, its antecedent, abolition. The right of suffrage to the freedmen of the South is now the "vexed question" at the North. It is true that under our system it is a question over which they have no rightful or Constitutional control. It belongs exclusively to the separate states. But the states owe it to themselves, their own safety, security, and prosperity for the present and the future, to take it up and settle it upon the immutable principles of reason and justice. Upon these principles, since this class of persons no longer hold the relationship of pupilage or wardship toward legal guardians and protectors through whom their rights and interests were represented under our old system, some sort of representation should be provided for them under that new system which is to be adopted. And on these principles of reason and justice upon which all governments should be founded and administered, what better plan could be devised for representation of this portion of society than the plan of their separate classification and organization as I suggest? To what extent the right of immediate suffrage should be limited, with what provisions as to qualifications so as to leave the door open for extension on attainment of requisite worth and merit, it is neither pertinent nor useful for me now to suggest. I barely throw out my ideas of a general scheme.

In this there would be no mingling of the races on the hustings: the rights and interests of the various classes, as they should be arranged on the fundamental law, would be attended to by themselves separately. This system would do much to prevent the rise and organization of those great parties, incident to republics based upon the principles of suffrage heretofore established, and from which our country has suffered so severely. The choice of representatives by the coloured race or by the other classes should not be restricted as to locality except as to residence in the state, nor should it be restricted to membership in this class: these matters should be left to those making the choice. Under the workings of the system, I have but little doubt that the ablest, most intelligent and virtuous men of the state, uninfluenced by party, would be chosen to fill office. Even the coloured people most probably for years to come would choose white men who would faithfully watch over, guard, and represent their rights and interests; or, if thought best, their right of choice might at first be confined to white men. By arrangements in the classification, all the elements of society could be wisely provided for. A proper representation of the virtue and intelligence of the country would be secured; so, of the moral and religious sentiments; so of all the distinct and antagonistic interests. But I can enlarge no further. You have the outline. If you can make or work out of it anything practical, and are so inclined, do it. Don't, without thought or reflection, pronounce it Utopian. My best wishes attend you and our beloved state.

Yours most affectionately,

ALEXANDER H. STEPHENS.

P. S. My health continues about as usual. I have not yet received a line from you since you left my house, the 9th of May.

MAJ-GENERAL JOHN A. DIX, NEW YORK.

Dear Sir: Enclosed I send for your inspection a letter I wish forwarded to my brother. It is upon matters that may be beyond the limits of the license granted me in making communications to friends at home. On this point I am not certain, and therefore submit it to your special notice and review. Should you feel at liberty to let it pass, I should be obliged: if not, I shall take it as a favour if you will have it returned immediately to me.

Yours respectfully,
ALEXANDER H. STEPHENS.

Read the daily papers. I see that the test oath prescribed by Congress for all officers of the United States Government, excludes, in the reconstruction process going on, all who ever accepted office under the Confederate Government, or aided that cause.

The *Tribune* republishes the *Chronicle and Sentinel* article. The more I reflect on that article, the more I am annoyed at its purporting to come from me. How any one with any knowledge of my character could attribute to me such sentiments as it expresses, I cannot conceive. I have lived to little purpose if a friend could ever think them mine, much less discredit me with such an expression as this: "I would not have gotten out of the way of a raid but for appearance's sake, holding the office I did." Such a sentiment I never entertained or uttered; I scorn it! I often said I would not get out of the way of a raid but for the office I held; this I said, not for the reason assigned, but because I believed I would be arrested and imprisoned in consequence of that office. Others not so connected with the Government, I advised to remain. I never said that I had no fear of Mr. Lincoln if I should fall into his hands. When asked, as I often was, what I thought would be the result in such a case, I invariably said — what was the truth —

that I did not know, had no idea. I knew Mr. Lincoln, thought well of him personally, believed him to be a kind-hearted man; but as to what he should feel it his duty to do under such circumstances, I could form no opinion.

I am in a quandary on a question of duty. What ought I to do in reference to my application to the President? Plenty of time for answer has passed, if he had been disposed to reply favourably even to its smaller requests. Is not his silence sufficient reason for my withdrawal of that application? I made it under embarrassment, from a sense of duty in doubt. Has not his silence settled that point of doubt? I am no supplicant for mercy at his hands; I only meant to make known my willingness to accept his offer of amnesty without inquiry as to guilt, as cordially as he had liberally tended it. He made me no response. My resolution is to wait not much longer without letting him hear further from me. When he does, it will be in the withdrawal of that application and a demand for my legal and constitutional rights; by them I shall abide.

Spent the evening on a draft of a letter to the President, withdrawing application. When I got through with it, saw by the evening paper that he is sick. Lieut. W. informed me that he had seen it stated that Mr. Seward was not to return in ten days. Shall I send the letter or hold it awhile?

6.15. — Walked out with Lieut. W. Had a beautiful first view of the new moon. Whether this is an omen of good luck for me during this lunation or not, I cannot say. I have met with few lucky moons in my life. Luck, after all, is a strange thing. Some persons seem lucky by nature, while others seem doomed to be unlucky.

I belong to the latter class. I never could compete successfully in any game or enterprise depending on chance, such as drawing lots or throwing dice; the result was almost always against me.

I never had but one streak of real good luck in my life. That was in examination for college and the sentence in Latin that it fell to me to construe. I had prepared at the Academy in Washington, Ga., and at home. I was told at the Academy that for admission into the freshman class, I must read the Eclogues and Bucolics and the first six books of the Æneid of Virgil, besides Cæsar's Commentaries and Cicero's four orations against Catiline, this being the Latin Course; but that I would be examined on Virgil. I had but nine months at the Academy for this and for the Greek course. I finished at the Academy in something like six weeks before Commencement; then went home, or to my uncle and guardian's which I called home — I had no other; and there set about reviewing my Virgil; I did not review one word of Cicero. The four orations against Catiline I had read rapidly at the Academy, frequently as many as 500 lines at a lesson.

I saw announcement that candidates for the freshman class at Athens must present themselves for examination in the college Chapel on Saturday preceeding Commencement, which was to be on Wednesday. I was young, green, and raw. Without consulting anybody, I went into the Chapel at nine, the hour named. I found twenty-five candidates, all seated on benches. The faculty was present. I took my seat at the end of the hindmost bench. I had my Virgil and Greek Testament, supposing as a matter of course that I should be examined on these as my teacher had told me; but to my great surprise, Dr. Waddell [College President] opened with Cicero, and the first oration, which I had never looked into at all. What to do I did not know. Luckily, examination began at the front bench. A copy of Cicero was handed me. I glanced over parts of the oration to see if I could make any out at reading it. The out was a very bad one. Another oration was reached; I made as bad an out at this. One oration after another was taken up or passed over, until those against Catiline were reached. I thought I might stammer and blunder along in almost any part of these as well as a majority of the boys were doing in parts assigned them. This hope was soon somewhat dashed. The first, second, third oration were over — for skips were wide — and I was not reached; several boys were still ahead of me. The fourth oration was entered.

I began to tremble and sweat. I was the last candidate, and might not the Doctor turn to the next oration before my time? I tried an experiment on the next to see if I could read anything in that. The boy beside me was assigned a paragraph still in the fourth, but in the latter part. He took his seat, and Dr. Waddell said "Next!" It was an awful moment of suspense, but as good luck would have it, he assigned me the only paragraph in the whole book with which I was perfectly familiar! Was that luck or what was it? In this paragraph, Cicero alludes to the views of the senators as to what punishment should be inflicted upon the conspirators, and quotes Cæsar's opinion that capital punishment should never be inflicted, that as life is the gift of the gods, it ought only to be taken away by the gods. The idea, a new one to me when I read it at school, had deeply impressed me, and I was almost as familiar with that sentence as with any rule in my grammar; I read it off without the slightest pause or hesitation.

The Doctor raised his spectacles, looked at me, gave me a few words to parse. These, luckily for me, as I afterward found out, called for his pet rules. I gave them readily. Again he raised his spectacles, expressed satisfaction and asked if he remembered correctly where I was prepared or under whose tuition, doubtless believing me much better prepared than I was. He had given me the one paragraph in the book that I could read without a balk. This, then, was the streak of good luck which got me into college when my own blunder in presenting myself as I had for examination came so near exposing me and perhaps causing my rejection. Mr. Dobbins's boys were those I found in the chapel; they had been prepared in his grammar school connected with the college, and were ready on Cicero. I ought to have waited and been examined separately.

How strange this little streak of luck considered in connection with my destiny! The whole world is discussing what punishment shall be inflicted upon me and other officers of the Confederacy charged with being conspirators against the United States, whether death, exile, or lighter punishment, even as the Roman Senate was discussing the punishment due Catiline and his infamous crowd when Cicero uttered the sentence it fell to my lot to construe. Little did I think, when pondering, in my attic room at Mr. Adam L. Alexander's the views of that debate, that I should ever be held in the estimation of anybody upon a par with such characters.

CHAPTER X

JUNE 28. — The sun shines brightly in at my windows, the guard moves with elastic tread; all nature without seems to wear a gay and joyous aspect, while within, I am left, solitary and alone, with nothing to sooth my reflections but my ever-at-hand good old meerschaum. Heaven's blessing rest upon Girardey! How much I am indebted to his gift for my quantum of comfort in this place!

ANOTHER FANCY SKETCH AND NOT ALTOGETHER FANCY:

[*R. M. Johnston* entering prison by window of imagination.]

Johnston. Well, how are you to-day?

Prisoner. So-so, only so-so. In mind much harassed.

Johnston. By what in particular?

Prisoner. That *Chronicle and Sentinel* publication.

Johnston. What point in it annoys you? I thought upon the whole that you, perhaps, would approve the publication. I saw in it many things I had heard you say which I thought the public ought to know.

Prisoner. The whole tone and temper of the article is wrong. Facts are not stated in proper connection; and this distorts truths which proper connection would present. Then, some things are stated which are not facts, as my remark to Campbell concerning the cat's-paw which is not given as made by me. Campbell, not Hunter, said he felt no uneasiness about his neck so long as

Mr. Lincoln was at the head of affairs at Washington; the remark itself is not correctly quoted nor is Mr. Lincoln's reply. The article, as intermixed with the official report and put over the signatures of the Commissioners, comprises a downright forgery. The reason I am reported to have assigned, for not making public what Mr. Lincoln said about compensation for emancipated slaves is not accurately put; nor is what Mr. Lincoln said on that subject. My reason for not getting out of the way of a raid is misstated; I am exhibited in a light which excites in me nothing short of indignation, contempt, and scorn.

Johnston. Why don't you correct it? Why not publish a statement under your own hand? I requested you to do this soon after your return from Fortress Monroe. Had you done so, there would have been none of this.

Prisoner. Why don't I correct it? Why don't I publish a statement under my own hand? That is one of the horrors of my confinement! I am suffered to speak to no one except a few officers here. I am prohibited from holding any communication with the outside world except on matters of exclusively private, personal, and business nature. As for my having made a statement when I could have done so, I did not think it proper then. The effect of such disclosure as I should have felt it my duty to make, if I had gone into the matter at all, would have been to divide our people.

Johnston. But when, as you say, you saw that collapse was inevitable, that your silence could not prevent it, was it not duty to yourself to put yourself right before the country? Might you not have thus avoided the evils you suffer?

Prisoner. Perhaps I might, but no personal immunity

or security could ever sway my sense of duty to myself or to my country. This sense would prompt me to meet death rather than give any just ground in the estimation of my people, erroneous though their opinions might be, that I was untrue to the great cause of States Rights and State Sovereignty in the maintenance of which we were engaged. A man, to be useful, must not be disregardful of the effect of his acts upon the minds of his comrades; in this view he must often omit to do what he knows would be wise and proper in itself. I saw clearly the ruin coming, and deliberately made up my mind to meet and bear it with all its misfortunes and penalties, so far as I was personally concerned, rather than give any grounds whatever for the suspicion that I was untrue to the cause in which I had embarked. A public man, to be useful, must be as Cæsar's wife, above the breath of suspicion as to his integrity of purpose or resolve. Events I could not control; my fate, through the mercy and grace of God, I could meet and endure.

Johnston. Don't you think now it would have been better for you, and perhaps for the country, if you had never countenanced the new organization, or Confederacy; if you had stood aloof, held your original ground on the impolicy of the measure: in short, if you had had nothing to do with the war, giving it no countenance, aid or support?

Prisoner. My mind in the beginning and before the beginning, when in 1860 I saw the ruin coming, was made up to go with my state, let consequences be what they might. Her people were my people, her cause mine; and though I believed her destiny and my own controlled by unwise counsels, I preferred to die, even on the scaffold or under the gallows if such must be, rather than raise my arm against her sovereignty or be in sympathy with those who might strike her, even though by the reverse course I might be clothed with all the honours this world could bestow. What effect my standing aloof from the strife might have had upon the state and the war, must be a matter of conjecture only. My opinion is that it would only have intensified troubles. Had I thus acted, we might have had war among ourselves — the greatest calamity and curse that can befall any people. Foreign war is a great curse, but intestine war is a greater. My act, I think, prevented this amongst our people. As for stopping the war between North and South, that was out of the question. The political atmosphere was charged to the bursting point, the storm had come. The moral epidemic, as I t' en styled it, was abroad; it was infectious and contagious as well as malignant. Statesmanship could do no more in arresting its progress than can medical skill and science in arresting plague, cholera, or yellow fever. As good physicians do not desert their fellows when afflicted with these dreadful calamities, neither should good and true statesmen desert their countrymen when afflicted with a no less relentless scourge of moral or political epidemic. They should remain with them and do all in their power to assuage what they cannot control or prevent even though they themselves become victims thereby. So I thought, so I acted. So Lafayette in France thought; so he acted. He became a victim, not unto death, it is true; and so it is with me. Whether I shall ultimately escape as well as he, God only knows. No man ever bore a conscience more void of offence toward God or man in all that he did than I in all that I have done in these troubles. I, therefore, in full review of the entire past, have no regrets for anything I have done. If the whole were to go over again I do not see wherein I could act differently.

[Enter, not at the window, but at the unlocked and unbarred door of the room, *Major Seaverns*, accompanied by another person. *Johnston* steps out through the window of his entrance. *Prisoner* rises.]

Surgeon Seaverns. This is Colonel Lyman, Medical Inspector. In discharge of his duty he is visiting the prisoners to see their condition, etc.

Prisoner. Good morning, Major. Good morning, Colonel.

Colonel Lyman. How is your health, sir?

Prisoner. Tolerably good, I thank you, sir.

Colonel Lyman. Good as usual, good as when you came here?

Prisoner. Yes, sir; on the whole, about as usual. I am not so strong as when I came, which, perhaps, is owing to the want of my usual outdoor exercise.

Colonel Lyman. [Looking about the room and at the bunk, which wears clean sheets and pillow-cases at *Prisoner's* cost so far as washing is concerned, and is decorated with his afghan brought from home.] Very comfortable quarters.

[*Prisoner* mum, but if looks ever had a language, his said plainly, Silence does not always give consent.]

Colonel Lyman. [Note-book in hand, bowing out.] Good morning, sir.

Prisoner. Good morning. Good morning, Major.

[Exeunt new parties, door again locked and barred. *Prisoner* fills his meerschaum, lights it, and seats himself, thinking of his friend, *Johnston.* Enter *Lieut. W.*, letters in hand.]

Prisoner. Good morning, Lieutenant. I see you have letters. Who from? Any from home?

Lieutenant. There are only two, both from Savannah, from Dr. Willis. There is a blank check in one.

One letter is of the 17th and the other of the 20th inst. There is nothing direct from Linton, yet the Doctor writes that he had learned of Ed Soullard Alfriend, who had come from Sparta, that Linton had been quite sick but was then up and on the streets though not well; Alfriend had seen in Sparta a few days before, one of the *Prisoner's* servants, Adam (Harry most probably), who told him all were well at *Prisoner's* home and getting on as usual. This was of great relief to *Prisoner*, and as he puffed his meerschaum, he ejaculated many silent thanks to Dr. Willis for these welcome and kind letters. *Geary* appears at the window: "Here are the morning papers, sir." *Prisoner* rises, goes and gets them through the bars with, "Thank you." Then takes his seat, and picks up the papers.

Dinner: meats, vegetables, and real Yankee pumpkin pie. That pie was indeed excellent. The snap-beans here are not such as Harry grows.

6.15. — Walked out as usual. Geary brought tea, bread, pound-cake and strawberries. I took nearly all the berries, and a "right smart piece" of the pound cake. Read Cicero on Oratory this evening.

I intended to note yesterday a present from Lieutenant Woodman of a bottle of gin. I asked the surgeon to endorse an order from me for some gin; Lieut. W. got a bottle and presented me with it.

June 29. — Job, Chapter xxviii, is on the text, "But where shall wisdom be found? and where is the place of understanding?" The imagery, poetry, and philosophy with which this inquiry is treated are of high order. After breakfast took up my letter to the President, revised it, and put it finally in these words:

Mr. President: Again, I ask to be excused for presenting myself to your notice. On the 8th, just three weeks ago, I addressed to you a communication which I presume you received shortly after, as I saw by the newspapers that it was in the hands of subordinate officers in Washington. The embarrassment under which that communication was made, with the causes of it, were set forth with sufficient clearness to make myself fully understood, I thought. I had doubts as how such an application as was therein made would be received and considered by you, coming from me. I did not wish to be obtrusive in seeking the benefit of favours pronounced under a general offer which were not intended for me in particular, nor did I wish from over-sensitiveness to be remiss in doing what I thought a proper act on my part under the circumstances, admitting doubt as they did. I wished only, frankly and promptly, to state that if my case, which was given quite at large, came within your proffered tender of amnesty without inquiry as to guilt, on which point I was uncertain, it would be as cordially accepted by me as it had been liberally tendered to me.

Your long silence *even upon the other and minor points* of that communication, touching a parole, or a mitigation of the rigour of my present imprisonment, leads me to the conclusion that my case does not come within the proffered tender of Executive clemency. The doubts and uncertainty on this point resting on my mind being thus removed, I now, therefore, address you for the purpose of withdrawing that special application for Amnesty in my behalf, which would not have been made but for the uncertainty on the point stated. I did not, and do not, wish to be considered as a bare suppliant for mercy. I have not the slightest sense of being a criminal before God or man for anything that I have done in the late most lamentable war between the states. I should but act the hypocrite if I pretended to have any such feelings. I was, however, perfectly willing (and not without a due sense of proper obligation) to accept in my own behalf, and under like conditions, the Executive clemency extended to others, waiving legal investigation, had it been your pleasure to grant it.

That not being the case, as I am constrained to believe from the facts stated, I now address you, not as a suitor for a probable tendered favour, but as a claimant for my clear legal rights. What I now ask is not *ex gratia* but *ex debito justitia*. If I have offended against the laws or Constitution of my country, to these laws and their proper administration under the Constitution, I most respectfully and earnestly appeal. I have been under arrest and in close custody for seven weeks, without any charge or notification of the cause of my arrest. How long is this to continue? In your late interview with a delegation from South Carolina you are reported to have referred to England's Magna Charta as the source from which you had imbibed some of your political principles. That Charta secures to all British subjects essential rights thus far denied to me. It declares that "no freeman shall be seized, or imprisoned, or fined or otherwise injured but by the judgment of his peers and the laws of the land." But a higher authority in this country than the British Magna Charta, and one not less regardful of personal rights, the Constitution of the United States, declares that "no person shall be deprived of life, liberty, or property without due process of law."

I was seized at my home in Georgia and brought to this distant point, and am imprisoned and deprived of my liberty without any judicial process, warrant, or legal authority whatever. Whether this was done at your instance or by your order or without your knowledge, I do not know, but such are the facts of the case. Were I able without risk to my health and life to bear the unaccustomed privations of my present situation, which I am not (especially if prolonged), the outrage upon my rights would be the same, though the consequences to me personally might not be so serious. If the Government has any charge to prefer against me, and is not ready for any cause to proceed with it before the regularly constituted tribunals having jurisdiction of it, and I cannot be trusted on parole as others have been, then let any required amount of bail be stated for my appearance to answer such charge whenever or wherever it may be instituted. The Government, or those charged with its administration, may be assured that the bail will be forthcoming, that the appearance and answer of the accused will be punctual, *Deo volente.* The charge will be met; and the result will be abided by, whatever it may be.

I, therefore, again most respectfully and earnestly approach you, the Chief Magistrate, under a high and sacred obligation, as you are, to see to the faithful execution of the laws: and I thus submit to your serious consideration whether the Constitution you are sworn to support can be rightfully or righteously upheld, even in putting down a rebellion or insurrection organized for its overthrow, by denying its plainly guaranteed rights to the humblest offenders even in a crime so heinous, atrocious, and monstrous. That justice according to the laws under the Constitution may be meted out to him without any unnecessary privations, suffering, or cruelty, is what is now claimed as a matter of right by your prisoner,

ALEXANDER H. STEPHENS.

Lieut. W. brought two letters, one from Hidell, of the 21st, Louisville, Ky., the other from Raymond W. Burch, near Washington City. Hidell left Crawfordville on the 7th; all were well then. He was at Sparta the week before and left all well there; Linton had returned. He gives no particulars about home, where John was, whether the boys were at school or not, nothing about the weather, prospects of crops, etc.; so, on the whole, while the letter is welcome, it is too indefinite on important matters to be hailed as at all satisfactory. The other letter is from an old friend, though not an old man. I did him some favours while in Congress. He has ever since manifested much esteem for me. He used to visit me when sick. He named his first daughter for my mother, Margaret. This letter is comforting. It shows that I have some friends in the world who sympathize with me. Mrs. Burch adds a line. This is very gratifying to me.

Neither say anything of John C. Burch, a brother, who used to be a clerk at the desk in the House. He was a true man and a true friend of mine. He it was who gave me the famous and devoted dog, Rio. He had hemorrhages from the lungs. I fear he is dead. These Burch boys are sons of the Burch who was Chief Assistant Clerk of the House of Representatives for a great many years; he was there in the days of William H. Crawford; was turned out by McNulty in 1843.

Geary brought daily papers. Dinner at 2.45: Roast beef, chicken, beans, turnips, potatoes, currant pie, huckleberries and milk. I asked G. if there was no pumpkin pie; he went and brought me a piece. It was cold but very good. I left the other pastry for that and told Geary always to bring me pumpkin pie if it was to be had.

6.15. — Walked out with Lieut. W. Handed him my letters. I have felt very weak in the hips and loins to-day. I got quite tired in the walk; rested twice.

This day seven weeks ago I was arrested; five weeks ago, I entered these walls. Sometimes months seem as days and at others, days as months or even years.

June 30. — Very warm. Flies very annoying before I got up. Until the last few days, there have been none. This morning they are in swarms. Thermometer, when I rose at 7.30, was 80. These words in Job in my morning reading touched every chord and fibre of my heart:

Oh that I were as in months past, as in the days when God preserved me; When his candle shined upon my head, and when by his light I walked through darkness; As I was in the days of my youth, when the secret of God was upon my tabernacle. When the ear heard me, then it blessed me; and when the eye saw me, it gave witness to me: Because I delivered the poor that cried, and the fatherless, and him that had none to help him. The blessing of him that was ready to perish came upon me: and I caused the widow's heart to sing for joy. I put on righteousness, and it clothed me: my judgment was as a robe and a diadem. I was eyes to the blind, and feet was I to the lame. I was a father to the poor: and the cause which I knew not I searched out. And I brake the jaws of the wicked, and plucked the spoil out of his teeth.

Memory recalled the first time the substance of these verses came to my notice. It was in an address by Blair, I believe [Scotch author and divine], on charity. An extract from this address was in a book which fell into my hands while going to school in the little log cabin that stood in what is now my field. This was in 1820. The book was not mine, but I took great delight in reading in it at playtime and during other hours when not engaged on my regular lessons. The school was taught by my father. He was arranging for the "Exhibition," as it was called. At exhibitions, in those days, select speeches were declaimed by the boys, and plays and dialogues were acted on a stage erected in front of the schoolhouse. Large audiences attended. Though a small boy, I was required to take part. My father permitted me, as he did most of the boys, to select my piece. I was to appear twice. I chose one piece of gravity and one of humour, the latter a short poem, "The Cuckoo." For the grave piece, I selected Blair's address on charity which contained these sentiments of Job. They had made a deep impression on my boyish mind, and have followed me through life. As I read them this morning, and my mind went back through all the shifting scenes of my strange life, I felt that I could make the same outcry with Job.

When did the voice of distress reach me and I did not relieve if I could? Was I not willingly eyes to the blind and feet to the lame? Did I not at all times act the part of a father to the poor? And have I not often searched out cases of distress? It is a consolation to remember these things in the midst of my present troubles.

Geary brought breakfast before making up my bunk. He was in a new attire. Upon my asking him how this was, he said he had to go to muster; these were his mustering or military clothes.

Read Judge Advocate Bingham's argument before the Military Commission in Washington in reply to Hon. Reverdy Johnson. It is rhetorical sophistry, specious and plausible to the careless or uninformed reader: but it is utterly fallacious. It affects me in nothing so much as in the sadness it produces when I view it as but an additional evidence that Power, in its incipient and dangerous strides in trampling on the liberties of a country, is never wanting in able and brilliant advocates and defenders. I have not access to the authorities by which to expose its many radical errors. It is no answer to Mr. Johnson. It does not graze a single position assumed by him. Its main ground, that the Constitution, with its guarantees as to rights of persons and property, is intended and was made for peace only and not for war, is fundamentally wrong. The Constitution was made for war as well as peace. To the various questions put by the Judge Advocate: Whether in war, men are not slain, prisoners captured, property taken, all without due process of law; the answer is, that they are not; no more than a man who, in peace, puts himself in defiance of the law officers, and is shot down by the sheriff or his posse: that is due process of law in such case. So in war. In the cases of rebellion and insurrection, the only military forces known to the Constitution are such as are called out in the nature and character of the *posse comitatus*. For their government, when so called out, laws are made, as well as for the government of such permanent force as may be kept on hand.

What a soldier rightfully does in taking life in battle he does according to law prescribed, and orders given in accordance with that law. All seizures of property are wrongful and the injured party is entitled to redress before the courts unless the seizure be in pursuance of law allowing just compensation. No soldiers, even in war, can be rightfully quartered on any man's premises except in accordance with law previously prescribed.

This is an express provision of the Constitution. The idea that the Constitutional guarantees are all suspended in war and that during war martial law takes the place of the Constitution is monstrous. The Judge Advocate's remark about the natural principles of self-defence, and that the nation, as a man, may resort to any means to save its life, is rhetoric and not argument; its sentiment is ruinous to liberty. The life and soul of the United States Government is the Constitution and the principles with all the rights therein guaranteed. Whoever strikes at them, or at one of the least of them, strikes a deadly blow at the life of the Republic. Nothing can be more absurd than that the life of a man can be preserved by an extinction or suspension of all the vital functions of his organism; and yet this is no more absurd than is the argument of those who speak of warding off a blow at the life of the nation, by a suspension or violation of the guarantees of the Constitution.

Geary has brought the daily papers. I see an article in the *Tribune* on Negro franchise at the South; with its general tone I am pleased. The *World* has an impressive editorial on the question of the extinction of the Negro race. To return to my thoughts, which Geary interrupted: With the persons on trial at Washington I have no sympathy other than such as I have ever had for fellow-beings in suffering. But I think they ought to be tried by the Constitutional tribunals and that justice should be meted out according to law under the Constitution. In trying them there is less necessity for creating dangerous precedent than in almost any other case that could arise. The crime charged, and nearly proved (as far as I have seen), against several is so atrocious and appalling that no fear need have been entertained in leaving disposition to the regular courts of the District.

2.30.—Dinner: as good as epicure could desire. The salmon (by the by, the best fish for constant diet I have ever seen) was as good as could be. Took a little of all the good things except the pumpkin pie; I did not take a little of that barely, but ate all of it except the pastry. Read Cicero. Walked my room. Saw in Boston *Journal* one of the best and most sensible of Mr. Lincoln's friendly, good illustrations by jokes. General Sherman tells it.*

6.15.—Walked out with Lieut. W. Paid board bill, $22.75 and $5.00 making $27.75. All up to date $95.98. Tea as usual. Geary would not accept the draft I drew in his favour for $5.00; so my expenses are really but $90.98.

* Sherman asked Lincoln if he must capture Jeff Davis or let him escape. Lincoln replied with an anecdote in which a temperance lecturer, refusing liquor in his lemonade, suggested that a drop might be put in "unbeknownst" to him. "You might let Jeff escape unbeknownst to me," Lincoln concluded.

CHAPTER XI

JULY 1. — Wrote to Linton. This is his birthday. Inclosed letter to Dr. Willis, of Savannah, requesting him to forward. Would like to copy it, but have not space. I have ordered another blank book. I am compelled to shorten entries. Read papers. Read Cicero. Dinner at 2:30. Better appetite than for several days. The lamb was a choice bit. Geary usually brings the most select parts of whatever he has to choose from.

6:15. — The rain cut my walk short. Geary brought a clothes-brush, 62½ cents, the blank book, $2, and a cane-bottom chair, $3.50. All expenses up to date, $97.10½.

Sunday. — Cloudy and raining. Read eleven chapters in Job before breakfast. Finished Cicero on "Oratory," and commenced his conversations on orators. Felt greatly the need of cyclopedias which are ever at my elbow at home. I want to give locality, dates, and proper position to his characters, and to take views from these various standpoints of the prominent men who figure in his pictures. Otherwise, I see only profiles; I wish to examine them in front and rear as well. In this way only am I accustomed to form my own estimate of character, and of the true position all celebrities, ancient and modern, should occupy in history.

This treatise of Cicero upon "Orators" falls in style

below everything else I have read from him. In some parts it is but slipshod narrative that drags limpingly along. How much of this may be due to the translation I do not know. His "Oratory" I had not read before since I read it in the original at college. I was highly pleased with it then, and am much more so now. I only regret that I did not make it my study when first admitted to the bar. With all its gloss and tinsel of rhetoric, I find it abounding in practical good sense and the highest principles of wisdom.

At the usual hour for walking, rain came down in floods. Just before expiration of hour, I ascended the steps and looked out, but was driven back by rain. Tea as usual. This volume closes with the record of a gloomy day.

July 3. — The sun shines and all nature seems cheerful. Still reading Job. I was more struck this morning with the character of Elihu than ever before. He is certainly a representative man; more so than Job. Thousands of Elihus are to be met with to one Job. I have encountered many. Finished Cicero's "Letters." The reading of these fragments tends to produce nothing so much as a sadness — not at all lessened by suspicion of their authenticity thrown out by the editor. This suspicion but gives them the character, to some extent, of vague and indistinct whispers, overheard in the dark, passing between uncertain and unknown parties, concerning the fortunes and fate of those in whom we feel deep interest. With some of these letters, whether genuine or spurious, I was impressed. This first from Cicero to his brother Quintus, written at Thessalonica, after his first exile, touched my profoundest sympathy.

Whose heart is so dead that he can read without a sign, if not without a tear, this:

Could I be unwilling to see you? Nay, I was rather unwilling to be seen by you. For you would not have seen your brother. You would not have seen him whom you had left, him whom you had known, him who had attended you some way on your journey: him to whom weeping, you had bidden farewell, yourself weeping—of whom you when departing had taken leave after he had attended you some way on your journey: you would have seen not even a trace or image of him but a sort of effigy, a breathing corpse. And I wish that you had seen or heard that I was dead. I wish that I had left you surviving not only my life but my dignity.

These letters, as well as other writings acknowledged to be Cicero's, show for Quintus an unusual affection. These brothers seem to have been knit together by closest and tenderest ties, their several beings almost blended into one. Bearing somewhat similar relation to my only surviving brother as Cicero bore to Quintus, causes me, perhaps, to appreciate his fraternal affection more keenly than others differently situated may do. One of Cicero's letters to Quintus interests me in its delicate allusion to some family matters; he refers to the marriage of his daughter, Tullia, to Crassipes, and remarks:

On the 6th of April, I gave the wedding feast to Crassipes, but at this banquet that excellent boy, your and my Quintus [his nephew, son of Quintus], was not present because he had taken some offence; and therefore, two days afterward, I went to Quintus, and found him quite candid; and he held a long conversation with me, full of good feeling about the quarrels of our enemies—what would you have more? Nothing could be in better taste than was his language. Pomponia, however, made some complaints of you; but these matters we will discuss when we meet.

So, it seems that men and women then were subject to like passions, whims, caprices, and gossip, even in the best-regulated families, as they are now. But what could have been more brotherly than this little communication, and how could the matter have been put more delicately?

ANOTHER FANCY SKETCH, YET NOT ALTOGETHER FANCY:

[*R. M. Johnston* entering prison by window of imagination.]

Johnston. How are you to-day, my good friend? We are all very anxious about you. Linton and I, and Jack Lane, Simpson, Ben Harris, and Ben Hunt had a long talk about you the other day. Indeed, I see nobody but inquires if I have any news from you.

Prisoner. I am truly glad to see you, and just as truly wish it were under different circumstances. I wish it were even just as it was at Liberty Hall, when you and Jack came over there last February, arriving at night, dripping wet after a long ride on horseback through mud and rain. I am, in bodily health, quite as well if not better than then, and as to my mental anxiety, etc., I believe I am as well off. I have new troubles, but am greatly relieved of others which pressed heavily then. War is over; the issues are known; there is to be no more bloodshed — at least, in the field; anxieties for friends are removed.

Though I was prepared for it — nerved for it as you

would be for the extraction of a tooth — my arrest and close confinement, privations, discomforts, and being cut off from the world and all communication with friends, was a great shock — crashing, and crushing.

You know how I was welded by strongest and tenderest ties to the dear ones at home; how I was linked in sympathy and soul with Linton; how strongly I was attached to the persons and scenes about my home, and to the old homestead with its cherished associations; attached not only to my relatives, those near in blood to me there, but to my servants, my dogs — my ever-faithful daily companions — my gardens, my trees, my orchard, my vineyards. To all these I was bound by such cords as you know bind few mortals. But that shock has, to some extent, passed off. I am almost as cheerful in my solitude here as I was at home; not that my home attachments grow less strong (the very thought of that result would almost kill me!). I have become more master of myself; better able to discipline emotions according to dictates of reason. But even yet — as was the case this morning, when my thoughts in their wanderings embraced Linton, yourself, and other dear ones, and dear spots at home — suddenly my eyes fill with the rising flood-tide of the heart.

I make it my business, under a system I have instituted, to occupy my thoughts as much as possible with subjects entertaining, useful, instructive, and amusing. I have access to a good Post library; I get the daily papers. I read a good deal, write a good deal; so, time passes off on the whole much more pleasantly than when I was first locked in these walls.

Johnston. I am glad to hear this. Really, I cannot see anything here that could amuse me, though, as you know,

I like to laugh, and am as fond of fun as anybody. What can you find to amuse you?

Prisoner. Oh, plenty. Humour can be found in almost anything, in men's actions, looks, voices, attitudes. I have a guard pacing by my window, night and day. Great variety of countenance and manner is exhibited by the different men on the beat; divers little conversations are heard, which present elements of humour. There is a family living in the rooms over me; there is a pianoforte up there; there are children; and there is a cat; of all of which I have become apprised by divers sounds which, if I were to take off as I could, would make you laugh; but I can't do it because there is no knowing who might hear me nor what would be the consequence. I am a prisoner, you see; and nothing in the world do people more dislike than to be made the subject of fun or jest. Amusement, however, may be drawn from people and their doings without the least detriment to their characters or dignity, just as honey is extracted from the flower without an injury to it: but this they do not understand. I used to think that even Rio [his dog] did not like to be laughed at; nor even yet Frank — that little black dog of mine to which you once applied harsh terms because he gave you decided demonstrations that he did not like to be made sport of. Do you remember your letter to me afterward?

Johnston. Ha! ha! ha! You've made me laugh, though I little expected it when I came in. I had forgotten my row with Frank. I am relieved to find you in such spirits. I know Linton and Lane and all the rest will be glad to hear it, but really I don't understand how you can be thus in your situation.

Prisoner. My situation gives me no uneasiness except

as it affects others and subjects me to personal inconvenience and discomforts; and except, of course, as to the great outrage on my rights and my indignation on that score — there is no bounds to that; I have no disquietude as to the result as it may affect me personally, if it does not bring on disease. As for my character or reputation, or the agonies of the extreme penalty of a conviction for treason, such reflections disturb me little; not half so much as the smartings I feel from a sense of the injustice done me.

Johnston. What do you mean?

Prisoner. I mean this: that while others quite as much or more implicated than I in the late troubles, are at large on parole — some honoured with high official position — I am confined in this cell. Take even Johnson, of our State — for whom I entertain a high personal regard — did not he advocate and vote for secession candidates when I was opposing secession with all my might? Look at Perry, just appointed Provisional Governor of South Carolina. Did he not accept and hold the office of District Judge under the Confederate Government, filling the vacancy arising by the resignation of McGrath when elected Governor? Look at the conduct of the officials at Washington toward Governor Brown of Georgia, Governor Smith of Virginia, General Cobb of Georgia, and thousands besides, in granting them pardons or paroles, while I am held here. I am gratified that these gentlemen have received favours; but my sense of the injustice done me is intensified by the discrimination against me.

Johnston. Have you any reasons for the Government's course? What do you think they really intend to do?

Prisoner. I have no idea. Perhaps they have no definite idea. They may want to distress, worry, wear me out, and impoverish me under this mode of imprisonment; or they may, so soon as the Federal courts in the Southern States are again regularly established, transfer me for trial, conviction, and execution as an example, I being a leader in the "rebellion," as they term it.

Johnston. What has become of your special application for amnesty? Have you received any answer?

Prisoner. No. But this is what I have done. [Shows his letters to the President as entered in this Journal.]

Johnston. [Reads both.] Don't you think you acted too soon in making your withdrawal?

Prisoner. No; my greater doubt has been as to the making of the application.

Johnston. By withdrawal of your case you take it from their consideration.

Prisoner. That cannot blot the facts from their memory. I was and am willing to accept the fate of war and to abide by it, but to supplicate them for mercy I never shall.

Johnston. You are getting too serious again. I would rather have your humorous vein.

[Enter *Geary* with *Prisoner's* dinner. *Johnston* exits through window of imagination, causing *Prisoner* to laugh at the anxiety depicted on his countenance in his hasty retreat lest he should be seen by *Geary*.]

The papers were brought; nothing of interest except a letter from General Ewell, a prisoner here. About 5, there was great shouting and "huzzaing" by soldiers on the parade ground. Something must be in the wind.

6:15. — Usual walk. On the western bastion, took a survey of Boston, and gazed toward Cambridge, thinking of Linton and his law-school days there; wheeled about and kept on the tramp for the full hour. Lieut. W. informed me that the "huzzaing" I heard was a demonstration upon the departure of two companies of his Volunteer Battalion which have been mustered out of service. The boys were going home, and there was jollification generally. Geary brought tea at the usual hour, that is, soon after my return from evening walk; with it, a saucer of raspberries. Made my supper mostly of raspberry tea. I have heard of raspberry tea in Confederate times; I never drank any before; and as Judge Berrien said to Cable about the Hock wine, perhaps the raspberry tea which I heard of was not of the "Hock" kind which I partook of to-night. That, perhaps, was a concoction of the leaves; mine was juice of the berries "straight" with a little sugar and milk.

CHAPTER XII

JULY 4.—The ever-memorable Independence Day, an anniversary which should be hailed with profoundest emotions of gratitude and patriotism by every friend of Constitutional liberty and representative government the world over. Great celebration will doubtless be made throughout the North. As an indication of its spirit, I clip an editorial from the Boston *Journal*, which is a fair sample of the genius of the times now rampant in this section. Would I could see in past or future so much to exult over, to look to with assurance, as this editor seems to see! The war, which every true friend of liberty has deeply regretted, has been terminated, it is true. But how? By maintenance of the principles set forth in Independence Hall on this day, 1776, that governments derive their just powers from the consent of the governed? Has it not been terminated rather upon the principle that might gives right? that the weak must yield to the strong? Have not the States South, which joined those of the North in a pledge of their "lives, fortunes, and sacred honour" in the achievement of their separate Independence and Sovereignty from King George of England, been completely overrun, and subjugated to the rule of a Ring at the North? Where is the boasted liberty that makes the people of the United States the freest on earth? Why am I here without warrant, or charge of crime? Why are the forts, prisons, and bastilles all over the land, this day filled with thousands, imprisoned as I am? How is it that no man is safe in the utterance of his sentiments unless they be in accordance with the views of those who rule in almost absolute sway from the Canadian to the Mexican borders?

This liberty and freedom, over which this Boston editor so exults, is like the freedom of which a Kentuckian once boasted in Lexington, according to a story Judge McKinley, of the United States Supreme Court, used to tell: a Congressman from the District had said something or had cast some vote offensive to parties in the city; they got up an indignation meeting. The demonstration was at night; a long procession with torches and drums, tin pans, and like accompaniments, marched through town bearing the delinquent in effigy, to be hanged in the suburbs with all possible marks of obloquy. Some one on the sidewalk said in undertone to his neighbour: "This is a d—— shame!" Whereupon, one in the crowd, overhearing the remark, stepped up to him who made it and, seizing him by the collar, exclaimed: "What is that you said, sir? I'll let you know this is a free country, and we will do what we d—— please, and you shan't say anything about it!" This is the sort of freedom the Boston editor exults in.

My morning Bible-reading on this ever-memorable anniversary of constitutional law and liberty brought to mind a case analogous in some respects to mine. "Paul [a prisoner] earnestly beholding the council, said, "Men and brethren, I have lived in all good conscience before God until this day. And the high priest Ananias commanded them that stood by him to smite him on the mouth. Then said Paul unto him, God shall smite thee, thou whited wall: for sittest thou to judge me after the law, and commandest me to be smitten contrary to the law?"

Those in Washington and elsewhere who make such an ado about preserving the life of the Nation, should be brought to know that no more fatal blow could be struck to the vitals of the Republic than one against the principles and guaranteed rights of the Constitution. These constitute its life and soul. So long as these are maintained, we shall have a free country, whether divided into one or more confederations, of which we may well be proud, but without maintenance of these, the boast of freedom is but mockery. We may in name be free, but in fact we shall be nothing but serfs and slaves.

Daily papers at usual hour, 10:30. Wrote Linton; enclosed letter to Dr. Willis, of Savannah. Firing of guns shows that the day is being observed here. I have been perplexed last night and to-day over the following charade; cannot find the key to the answer:

My first's the last destructive foe
Of nature's fairest form below;
My second is Albion's boast,
And both defends and decks her coast;
My whole (such change from union flows)
The bitterest boon the earth bestows.

Dinner: an elegant one. Geary brought the volume requested of "American Cyclopedia." I read the article on Cicero, but did not get the information desired. I fell into my second daytime nap here. Thermometer to-day ranged from 78 to 80. I never before was in such a uniform temperature, day and night. The variation is seldom more than four or five degrees in any twenty-four hours; the greatest since I have been here has not been more than thirteen. This uniformity is maintained by constant fire. The grate has not been without fire since I came. By raising or lowering the windows,

I preserve uniformity; this can be done until the external heat shall tell upon the room, or until it penetrates as low down as I am — in a sort of Mammoth Cave.

6:15. — Took usual walk with Lieut. W. We looked for the advertised balloon ascension at Boston, but it did not come off. To south and southeast there was a magnificent rain-cloud in full view.

July 5. — My circulation is too sluggish; I do not like my symptoms. My morning reading included Paul's defense before Festus and Agrippa, an ingenious and strong speech. What fixed itself most deeply on my mind this morning was the reason Festus gave Agrippa for bringing Paul before him. His own investigation had found no legal charge against Paul. He brought Paul before Agrippa, his superior, that after examination by Agrippa he, Festus, might have somewhat to write in sending Paul to Rome: "For it seemeth to me unreasonable to send a prisoner, and not withal to signify the crimes laid against him." There is good sense in this and some regard to human rights and liberty that the screaming-eagle orators of yesterday might have done well to consider. There is something in it that the rulers at Washington might profit by.

This morning, after breakfast, Geary brought me a lump of ice and put it in my pitcher.

Daily papers. A long account in the *Herald* of Mr. Davis's flight and capture; well written and graphic. One thing it would imply, that the writer had remained with Mr. Davis until his capture, and had then escaped. Still, how could such a party know what occurred in Mr. Davis's tent? None of his staff were in the tent with him, as Reagan told me. Reagan told me he knew nothing of what occurred in Mr. Davis's tent. Is it not strange that the *Herald* does not give the writer's name?

3 P. M. — The firing of a salute on the parapet and a band of music playing indicate that the Post is honoured by some notable visitor, an officer of rank. A crowd passed in front of my cell; this walk is much higher than my windows, though there is a space of some eight or ten feet between the prison wall and the wall on which it runs; in this space the guard keeps up his constant beat. I was walking my room, smoking my after-dinner pipe, my meerschaum. Two officers, judging from swords and other insignia, stopped opposite one of my windows and looked down upon me. I paid no attention, but walked on. After a while other crowds came and stared down. I did not again glance up to see who they were or what they looked like. I got a glimpse of the first party only as I, Diogenes-like, looked up to see what obstructed my light. When I was tired of walking, I resumed my seat and my reading. Again a crowd darkened the window. I then took up this Journal and commenced this entry; during its writing, the window has been repeatedly darkened. Once, I threw up my eyes and saw quite a crowd of boys squatted down to get, I suppose, a good view of, or a peep at, the rebel ex-Vice-President.

Have again been thinking of the charade that puzzled me. An answer occurs which fits, but I should hesitate to offer it in a company in which there were ladies, because it might be thought ungallant in such a presence. I will, however, venture to put down here what I think was in the head of the churly propounder when, in his poetic ravings, smarting perhaps under rebuffs from a certain quarter, he produced this enigma: "Woman."

6:15. — Took usual walk. Lieut. W. informed me that the salute was in honour of General Robert Anderson and Rear-Admiral Farragut who visited the fort with a party. He asked me if I knew Elder Harmon Lincoln, of Boston. Upon my saying I did, he asked if I would be willing to see the elder, who had gotten permission from the Secretary of War to visit me, but not knowing whether I would recollect him, or be willing to receive him, had requested the Lieutenant to make inquiry. I told the Lieutenant to say to Mr. Lincoln that I remembered him very well; he boarded for a while in our mess at Mrs. Carter's in Washington, D. C., Mrs. Lincoln with him; I should be glad to see him, and Mrs. Lincoln also, if she is living. If living, she must be very old; he must be aged; he was an old man when I knew him sixteen years ago. Lieut. W. said he is over eighty. I had sciatic pain in hip, and did not walk much. Rested under the arbour. Geary brought tea.

July 6. — Have been quite sick since breakfast; on my bunk a good part of the time. Read Rev. Jacob M. Manning's speech on the Fourth before the City Government of Boston. It is a fair specimen of clerical rhetoric and political sentiments in this section, I suppose. As far as my observation goes, preachers have less charity and magnanimity than any other class of men. These are qualities for which, as a class, they are not distinguished. There are many exceptions, such as Henry Ward Beecher and others of much less note. Still, what I have said is true of the average in all sects. So much have I been impressed with this, that I would seldom permit a preacher to sit on a jury for the trial of any person accused of crime, when I was counsel for the defense, if

I could prevent it. It has been my usual course promptly to challenge for cause, and for no other cause than that the juror presented was a preacher. In some instances, when I knew the preacher personally and knew him to be imbued with the spirit of his Master, and a liberal, unprejudiced mind, capable of arguing facts and of acting justly, I announced, "Content." Such was the case with old Uncle Bird, Carlos W. Stevens, and others I could name.

I once had a pointed talk with a reverend gentleman of my own church, who undertook in a pious way to lecture me on the sin of defending criminals. I was engaged in Richmond Court in the defense of Keener, charged with murder of Reese, one of the most important criminal cases in which I ever appeared. Excitement against Keener was intense. The homicide had been committed at a house of ill-fame. Little or no sympathy was felt for him in any quarter, and least of all among those professing to follow the teachings of Him, who, in the case of the Syrophenician woman, said to those demanding condemnation: "Let him who is without sin cast the first stone." Facts clearly showed that the homicide was not murder under the law; that, at most, it was manslaughter, if not a perfectly justifiable act under the State Code. But the reverend doctor of divinity, wholly incapable of weighing these facts, with the usual bloodthirsty propensity of his calling, demanded to know if I did not think I was committing a sin in preventing the execution of "justice?" I replied: "No. In the first place I do not consider Keener guilty of murder under the law; the law requires that he should not be so convicted or punished. In the second place, if the facts were different and he were guilty, I should not feel myself a sinner in endeavouring to procure his release. If we all had justice done us, that justice which with your view of the facts and the law you are so anxious should be meted out to Keener, we should, according to your own teaching, have been in hell long ago. If Christ died to save the guilty from damnation, I do not think I sin in trying to prolong their lives that through grace they may escape hell. Much less do I feel that I commit a sin in trying to save one who is not guilty, even though I oppose a multitude." This closed our conference. He gave me up, perhaps, as a reprobate.

But I did not abate my exertions for Keener. Such was the feeling against him inspired by clerical advocates of justice, and others imbued with like ideas, that he was convicted on the first trial; convicted in part by judicial wrong rulings to which I took exceptions: the case went to the Supreme Court; a new trial was granted; and Keener was acquitted. The judge and the preachers, as well as the whole tribe of Javerts, were scandalized at the escape of their victim. The old Aztec Priests could not have felt more rage at the escape of one stript and bound for their sacrificial altars, than did these fanatical devotees who wanted human offering made to their idol of human justice. But I rejoiced in the successful performance of much labour and in a result that was a nearer approximation than that of their desire to the standard of Divine Justice. If I am ever to be tried for anything, may Heaven deliver me from a jury of preachers! I do mean to express disrespect to ministers of the Gospel. They are but mortals with the rest of us. They have their weaknesses and faults; and their most striking defect is a want of that charity which they, above all men, should not only preach but practise. They are too impressed with the idea that they are God's vice-gerents here below, especially commissioned to deal out His wrath and vengeance.

Eight weeks to-day have I been a prisoner; six weeks in this place; all without the slightest intimation of the cause. Seized by an armed force, sent here by an armed force, kept in close confinement, guarded by an armed force, deprived of all means of appealing to judicial power for redress; and yet Eagle-orators and reverend rhetoricians scream and shout about the glorious freedom we enjoy.

P. M. — The article on naturalization in the cyclopedia attracted my attention. It is strange what errors have crept into vogue and pass without scrutiny or question; especially on naturalization and its sequence, citizenship of the United States. The subject is treated as if Congress were empowered by the Constitution to confer upon aliens citizenship of the United States distinct from citizenship of particular States and Territories. The truth is, Congress has no power to naturalize or to confer citizenship of the United States. Its only power is to establish a uniform rule to be pursued by the respective States and Territories on admitting aliens to their own citizenship. Before the Constitution was adopted, each State possessed the right as an Independent Sovereign Power to admit to citizenship whom she pleased, and on such terms as she pleased. All that the States did on this point in accepting the Constitution, was to delegate to Congress the power to establish a uniform rule so that an alien might not be permitted to become a citizen of one State on different terms from what might be required in another; especially, as in one part of the Constitution it is stipulated that the citizens of each State shall be entitled in all the rest to the rights and privileges of their citizens. But no clause of the Constitution provides for or contemplates citizenship of the United States as distinct from citizenship of some particular State or Territory. When any person is a citizen of any one of the States united, he thereby, and thereby only, becomes and can be considered a citizen of the United States. Errors in the public mind on this question are radical and fundamental, and have the same source as many others equally striking.

I was first struck with these on the annexation of Texas. How could her representatives, it was asked, take their seats in Congress, not having been citizens of the United States for the term of years required by the Constitution? The answer, upon the true principles of the Constitution and the only citizenship it contemplates, was plain: members and senators could not present themselves until the State was itself one of the United States; then, whoever might present himself as a member, having been seven years a citizen of Texas, would, in the terms and meaning of the Constitution, have been seven years a citizen of the United States then constituted; so, of the senators for nine years. Just as was the case of the North Carolina and Rhode Island members and senators; these States having come in some time after the eleven others had put the Government in operation, their members and senators were in no sense citizens of the United States until their States ratified and adopted the Constitution; and in no other view of the subject could they have been properly admitted.

July 7. — When I woke it was raining. I had a severe pain in my foot; could hardly walk. Rheumatism, I suppose. Read II Timothy. This letter of Paul's is written with spirit and energy. Breakfast; the coffee was cold. Geary went at my request and brought me another cup, hot and smoking.

9:30. — The sun breaks forth. I have a premonition that I shall get news from home to-day.

Morning papers. Telegram from Philadelphia, published in all, is important if the country were in condition to hear and defend the truth. It is that "In the Cozzens habeas corpus case, Judge Thompson, of the Supreme Court of Pennsylvania, ordered the release of Cozzens and delivered an opinion that the right of the President to suspend the writ of habeas corpus is only given him by Congress during the continuance of war." This little item, as the chronicled cloud, no bigger than a man's hand, would soon spread over this land if the political atmosphere were only in proper meteorological condition. As things are, perhaps we shall hear nothing more of it.

1 P. M. — No letters. My fire is nearer out than on any day since I have been here, yet the thermometer stands at 79. My foot still pains; I can limp about, but my system seems out of order; shooting pains in left wrist; had them in right hand this morning; I fear a general attack of rheumatism. Read Aristotle's "Politics." Dinner: turtle soup, etc.; good but I could not indulge.

6:15. — Lieut. W. called for the walk. I doubted if my foot would bear me, but concluded to try; I would have an airing, if nothing more. I got along in a limping way until on the terreplein; rested under the arbour; took a turn, but made so bad an out of it that I returned to the arbour. Lieut. W. informed me that his full name is Wm. H. Woodman. I asked, as I wanted to write for some tobacco to be sent me in his care. He told me that Reagan says a man of their party, named Stewart, escaped with Colonel Wood from the Davis camp when Mr. Davis was captured. He must be the writer of the *Herald* article. Geary brought tea. Darkness is approaching. I had looked almost confidently for some news to-day. I will betake myself to my pipe and Aristotle until bedtime.

July 8. — Had a quiet and pleasant sleep. Woke at dawn in a dream, my eyes streaming with tears. I was at home, down at the Homestead, at one time in Bob's house [his Negro servant] where he had a sumptuous dinner prepared for me; then I was in the field in the midst of high corn loaded with large ears — numbers on each stalk, and the like of which I had never seen before. Here were Bob, Fountain, George, and Harry, and Charlton, Bob's little son. I was seated, talking to them about their new condition, contrasting it with their former; pointing out some of the evils they would most probably encounter, advising and instructing them how to act so as best to guard against these when I should be gone; impressing upon them the importance of industry, honesty, economy, obedience to the laws, with as few dealings with the vicious of their own and the like class of the white race as possible. I was telling Bob and Harry how to bring up their children. It seemed as if I was about to leave them forever, never to see them again, and was giving them my last parting words. In this valedictory, the fountains of the heart were broken up, and I was lecturing and weeping at once.

Read I Timothy; not so connected, clear, or able as II Timothy. Some parts seem to have suffered in translation; for instance:

But refuse profane and old wives' fables, and exercise thyself rather unto godliness. For bodily exercise profiteth little: but godliness is profitable unto all things, having promise of the life that now is, and of that which is to come.

This gives the impression that Paul placed little estimate on benefits of bodily exercise. I am inclined to think otherwise, that the great advantage of exercise in the development of the physical part of man was taken by him as an admitted fact; and that he designed to show that like exercise of the moral or spiritual part is of as much higher importance as the soul is greater than the body. His idea, it seems to me, was that bodily exercise profits only in a limited degree and for a limited time while exercise of the spiritual part of man, leading to "godliness," is profitable to the entire man in all things present and to come. Paul was a close reasoner, and I cannot see why he should have said, "For bodily exercise profiteth little," as an illustration of anything he had said before.

Wrote Raymond Burch to express me Savage's book, "Representative Men"; wrote Travis, at Richmond, to send me by express 5 lbs. of smoking tobacco. Geary brought papers. Read account of the execution yesterday of those condemned in the assassination trial.

While I was lying on my bunk, still glancing over the papers to see if I could, in any corner or nook, find anything of interest, Lieut. W. entered, bringing me a letter, stating as he handed it to me, that it was from my brother but looked as if it had gone through the wars. I reached for it with great eagerness. The envelope was worn and torn; it bore no marks of approval from General Dix or anybody else. The letter was dated May 24th, the day before my arrival here, the day on which Myers wrote me. This seems the first letter Linton has written me. Where it has been this long time I can't imagine. I have an idea that it reached here yesterday, but was kept back by Major Allen because of its having no endorsement of approval. When I opened it, and recognized the well-known hand, my eyes filled with tears. The reading did me great good, gave me great satisfaction. Where could this letter have been kept so long? And why has it been withheld? May not the same parties have other letters still held back for the purpose of torturing me?

6:15. — Walked out with Lieut. W. My foot well enough to allow me to limp. Saw the two balloons that were advertised to ascend from Boston this evening. Both had been up some time, and both aeronauts were visible. One airship was off to the southeast in which direction it finally went out of sight; the other flew over the harbour up toward the city; it was still in view when I came down, had shifted position and seemed to be going somewhere north of Cambridge. Lieut. W. told me General Jackson was released from this place to-day — the order came this morning, and he left this evening. I am truly glad of his good fortune. But why he should be discharged and other officers kept, I do not understand; nor do I understand why he should be discharged and I held. He bent his energies to bring about secession; I strove with all my power to prevent it. I addressed the legislature against it; he opposed me in speech there and then; and afterward in a series of letters published in pamphlet form. I doubt not his patriotism and honesty in it all; but I don't see why justice that lets him go at large keeps me here. I have a high personal regard for Jackson, and rejoice at his liberation. Geary brought tea.

CHAPTER XIII

SUNDAY, July 9.—The fife, the drum, and the drill go on as on all other days. No more regard is paid to Sunday here than in Siam, Timbuctoo, China, or the Fiji Islands, and yet the Fourth of July Eagle-screaming preacher-orators rant lustily about this being a land of Christianity as well as liberty. It is as much one as the other. It is, very much mixed. There are in it many devout worshippers of the true God; there are many who enjoy liberty. Who, however, has any security for that liberty he enjoys? Rights without securities or the power to enforce them are little less than mockeries. Who can read without deepest indignation the daily accounts of tortures inflicted by high officials, and that, too, upon the poor unfortunate race to whom they are proclaimed to be, under God and our Christian Government, the ministering angels of deliverance and liberty? Such, for instance, as the thumbscrew operation the other day at Raleigh, upon the poor Negro who died from it; and that other infamous outrage at Fortress Monroe upon another poor son of Africa who sought and obtained relief by drowning. Mrs. Stowe ought to write another book. The Legrees are multiplying fast all around.

Finished Hebrews. Reviewed simply as an off-hand letter, hastily penned to be sent by Timothy, as it seems to have been, it is a wonderful production; in learning, style, vigour of thought, and form of illustration, far above the class of like character in that day even in Greece or Rome.

Geary brought the Sunday Boston *Herald*. No news. This is a racy paper. The column devoted to "Fact and Fancies" is generally rich. A good thing in it to-day is a pass of some years ago between Saxe, the poet, and Chief Justice Redfield, of Vermont. Saxe was running for Governor of Vermont and, being a Democrat, had little prospect of election, as his party was largely in the minority. The Chief Justice, on meeting him, said jocosely, "So, Saxe, you expect to be Governor?" "Yes," said the latter, "I expect to govern myself under the misfortune of a defeat." "Ah?" said the Judge; "it is a great man that is governor of himself." "True," said Saxe, "but he is greater who is judge of himself." Another good thing done up as original, is this: "When lenity and cruelty play for power, the gentler gamester is soonest winner." This is by no means original with Messrs. Baily & Co., the publishers of this spicy journal. It was said by Shakespere, and there is a philosophy in it that some high officials, now playing for power in this country, might profit by.

Gleaned everything from the *Herald*; read it to the advertisements, and even some of them. Walked my room. Got a good view of Reagan as he returned from his evening walk. He saw me, and we exchanged bows for the first time since we parted on the *Tuscarora*. Whether such salutations are against prison rules or no, I do not know. I shall inquire; I do not wish to violate any of the rules, though I am clearly convinced that my confinement and everything pertaining to it is illegal, wrongful, and an outrage on my personal rights.

6.15 — Took usual walk. Soon after I mounted the

parapet my hat blew over the wall. Lieut. W. called to a soldier to go over and get it. Meanwhile, I stood bareheaded in wind and sun. On the soldier's coming to me with the hat, I said "Thank you"; he replied in the old vernacular, "You are welcome, sir." I told Lieut. W. of my having bowed to Reagan as he passed my window, and asked if it was against rules. He replied that it was against his orders to allow any communications. I considered this equivalent to a prohibition. Twinges of toothache; threatened with neuralgic headache. Came in from walk before expiration of hour. Saw, as I returned, two Confederate prisoners carrying buckets of water. One bowed to me. I did not recognize either. They were under guard. They must rank as high as major, for all prisoners under that grade have been released. Wish I knew who they were.

July 10th — Did not sleep well; suffered a good deal. As Geary was late bringing breakfast, I read both Epistles to the Thessalonians, written in the names of Paul, Silvanus, and Timothy. Evidence from style is strong to my mind that Paul did not write either. They were joint letters, perhaps penned by Timothy; and Paul signed them as did the others. In the conclusion of the second, he says, "The salutation of Paul with mine own hand," which is the token in every epistle. From this it would seem that he actually wrote with his own hand nothing but this salutation at the end, which was token that he endorsed what had been drawn up by others.

8.30 — Answered Linton's letter. On the subject of his visit to me, wrote I would be glad to have him come if he should be permitted: how to advise in this matter, I hardly knew; I supposed that special application would have to be made to the Secretary of War; if he were to make an application stating the facts, and get it approved by Governor Johnson, it might have weight with Secretary Stanton. I added:

> In no event do I wish anything in such application but a simple statement of the facts of the case, with the reason assigned for the interview. I wish nothing like entreaty or adventitious influence brought to bear in my behalf. You understand me. I wish no favours and I shrink from no responsibility. I would sooner die, be hanged, quartered, and gibbeted than to beg for kindness from any mortal on earth, though I am as grateful as any one ought to be for favours given with that dignity which becomes the bestower and the receiver.

Took up Aristotle on "Economics." His views on family government and economy, the marriage relation, the duties of man and wife, are admirable. His treatise on politics, I consider of little value; but there are some good ideas in it, such as that of "quality and quantity" in the composition of States; and that property, population, and virtue, or "riches, number, and merit," are the three great elements to be looked for in forming a government for society. But the true idea of representation in the administration of the supreme power residing in all commonwealths, does not seem to have entered his head. He saw clearly the evils attending all kinds of governments — monarchies, oligarchies, aristocracies, and democracies — and clearly shows preference for a mixed government partaking in some measure of each of these forms. His opinion that the ends of all government should be the general good, or the happiness and prosperity of all the individuals of the state without injury to any, is also apparent. This is a correct and great idea in itself.

But he excludes slaves from this consideration. As persons they do not, in his view, form any part of society. This is a very great error. Much that he says upon slavery has the sanction of reason and justice, but a great deal has not. Though slavery be justified on grounds stated by him, slaves enter nevertheless into the composition of society as constituent elements, and the interest and rights of that portion of society should be looked to and guarded in its laws as well as those of any other part. What he says of emancipation being held out to slaves upon their proving themselves worthy, meets my full endorsement.

July 2. — Not well. Read Colossians; written in better style than either Thessalonians. I think Paul wrote this himself.

9.15 — Breakfast. Took little of anything.

2 P. M. — It has been raining all day. I have felt worse physically than at any other time since I have been here. At eleven the surgeon called. My pulse was then about eighty; it had been as high as one hundred. My head still ached. He sent me some pills and a small bottle of buchu.

Daily papers; nothing to interest me, but I whiled away the time the best way I could, reading and gleaning. Had hoped for a letter. It cannot be that my friends have forgotten me. Is it possible that my letters are withheld by the authorities? I am slow to believe this. The reason I receive no letters from home is probably due to the lack of mail facilities in the South.

6.15 — Lieut. W. called for the walk, but I did not

venture out. I was too weak. I have been reading Bacon's "Essays" and looking over some numbers of *Harper's Weekly* Lieut. W. sent me last night. The thought of being seriously ill here preys heavily on my soul.

July 12. — Didn't get to sleep until late. Suffered much pain. Feel better this morning, but prostrated. Read Philippians; another of Paul's earnest, clear, and powerful exhortations. While I was making this entry Lieut. W. and Dr. Seaverns called.

If any mortal ever existed with more cause than I have for disquietude of mind and bodily suffering, I sincerely pity him. Weak and frail from my cradle, my whole life has been one of constant physical pain. Health I have never known. Yet my exertions, from the time I have been able to make any, have been directed more to the benefit of others than to my own. I have thought more of the sufferings of others than of my own, and have done more for the relief of others than I have ever done for my own relief; yet, strangely, misfortunes multiply and intensify upon me. Here am I, bereft of friends, cut off from communication with them, deprived of those needful attentions and comforts which even such means as I have been able to procure by my own labour might command were I permitted to use them in paying some one to stay with and wait on me, doing such things for me as I am unable to do myself and which my necessities require. And all for what? What have I done that I should receive such treatment? Did I bring on the war? Did I stir up men's blood to strife? Did not I do everything in my power to prevent it? Are not thousands who did exert themselves to bring it on now at large? Whatever be my fortitude to bear,

I am far from being insensible to injustice. I feel that I am wronged deeply, grievously. I, who never intentionally wronged man or brute, feel myself the helpless victim of the most cruel and wanton wrongs. Against them whatever of spirit there is in me, so far from being humbled or overwhelmed by such treatment, only rises with new energies in protest. Unable, as I am in this cell, to do anything else, I can, at least, and do, therefore, here enter my protest against such gross injustice and inhumanity.

I was walking my room when Lieut. W. brought me two letters, saying one contained news from my brother. With great anxiety, I read them. One from Dr. Willis, of Savannah, of the 6th, stated that he had received a letter from Linton, of 29th June, saying all were well, but that he had heard nothing from me. The other, from Joe Myers, Augusta, 28th June, reports all well, rains plentiful, crops good; he has written me three letters; Dr. Paterson got the one I wrote him, and took two out of the office for Linton from me. Both letters did me a great deal of good, but somehow before I was aware of it, tears were dropping on the pages.

Geary brought papers. In the New York *Times* is an interesting article in the form of a circular from G. W. L. Bickley, President of the Order of the Golden Circle.* It is dated from this Fort, 28th June, 1865. He is a prisoner here; and, bad as my condition is, his seems to have been greatly worse. In weighing this difference, his physical ability to stand more than I can must be taken into account. I could not have stood what he has. I should have died. The other evening, I men-

* According to the circular, it comprised men, of all sections and creeds, opposed to cruelty in warfare, and radicalism Northern or Southern; Bickley had been kept in close confinement from July, 1863, and carried from prison to prison as his friends would discover his whereabouts and seek to secure his release or trial.

tioned that on returning from my walk I saw persons whom I took to be Confederate prisoners going, under guard, with buckets for water; and that one of them bowed to me. I inquired next day of Lieut. W. who they were. He said one was a Captain Hunter of the Navy, and the other Dr. Bickley of the Golden Circle. Bickley's circular is an able paper. Men are not to be judged by appearances. Little idea had I that either of the bucket-bearers was master of such thoughts as are found in this circular.

6 P. M. — I ventured out. My main object was to let my room have an airing while I got one myself. I did not feel able to walk. We ascended to the music arbour; there I rested; a sprinkle of rain kept us under the shed until I thought it best to return. Lieut. W. brought to my notice what purports to be an extract from my speech, in the Georgia Secession Convention. He said he had been requested to ask me if it was genuine. It is the same as that in the John M. Botts letter, which I have mentioned. I told him it was not correct; when or how it ever got started, I did not know. He said there was lately published another extract, purporting to be from a speech of mine in Congress, in 1859, about which there is some question, and he should like to know if that was genuine. Upon our return he went and got it. This "extract" is utterly false and was probably fabricated to prejudice the public against me. Lieut. W. expressed himself as highly gratified at hearing what I said about it. The "extract" represents me as indulging in a tirade of abuse of the North generally. The heading introduces it as a specimen of what Mr. Giddings* used to call "plantation manners."

*Joshua Giddings anti-slavery leader and author.

CHAPTER XIV

JULY 13. — I clipped from the Boston *Journal* a piece headed "The Hero of the British Tories," copied from the London *Herald*. The *Herald's* appreciation of Mr. Davis is as much over the true mark as the *Journal's* is under it. Mr. Davis is neither the greatest nor the worst man in America, in the United States, nor in the late Confederate States. How he will tower in history or be estimated by posterity, I do not know. It certainly is not my object to detract from Mr. Davis, but the truth is that as a statesman he was not colossal. If he had been a statesman of great stature the condition of this country, or of those States which put him at the head of their affairs, would be far different from what it is. After the Government was organized at Montgomery, it was reported that he said it was "now a question of brains." The remark I thought a good one.

If the real truth of history in relation to the Southern Cause shall ever be written, it will be to this effect: The Southern mind was influenced and misguided by a class of public men, politicians not statesmen, newspaper editors, and preachers, who possessed far more ambition and zeal than wisdom and knowledge. By their power over the passions and prejudices of the multitude, they precipitated the Southern people into reassumption of their independence as States, more as an escape from anticipated wrongs than from actual grievance. These people were as patriotic, as true and loyal to the principles of the Constitution as were their fathers, in 1776, by whose acts and sacrifices these principles had been established. They were led to believe that the only way to maintain and preserve these principles was to take the course they did. Independence was resorted to by them, the resumption of the reserved sovereignty of each State separately, and the formation of a new confederation, as the only means left for the security and perpetuation of the great principles of self-government established by their ancestors in common with the ancestors of their former brethren of the North, and which were set forth and guaranteed in the Constitution of the United States. It was through their devotion to these principles that the Southern masses were precipitated into the fatal step they took. If the statesmanship of the leaders had been equal to their ambition and zeal, the results would have been vastly different.

The people, the masses, even those who opposed secession as long as that was an open question, did more than their part. Never did a people exhibit higher virtues in patriotism, in courage, in fortitude, and in patience under the severest trials and sacrifices. The disasters attending the conflict are chargeable to their leaders, to the men in authority, to those to whom the control of public destiny was confided, and to no one is it more duly attributable than to Mr. Davis himself. He proved himself deficient in developing and directing the resources of the country, in finance and in diplomacy, as well as in military affairs. To specify and establish his deficiencies and errors in each of these particulars would require more time and space than I now have, even if I had inclination. His greatest failure in statesmanship was either in not understanding the popular aim and impulses, or in attempting to direct the movement to different ends from those contemplated by the people who had intrusted him with power. If he did not understand the purpose of the people, he is certainly not entitled to any high rank as a statesman. If he did understand them, and used position to abuse confidence, then he equally forfeits the title to honest statesmanship.

Now the leading object of the Southern masses was the security and perpetuation of Constitutional Liberty. They had no hostility to the Union *per se*; on the contrary, their attachment to it was strong; had grown with their growth and strengthened with their strength. It was only when their leaders had taught them that they should no longer remain in the Union and preserve their rights and liberties that they, in an evil hour, resolved to quit it. It was not that they loved the Union less but that they loved Constitutional Liberty more. This was the spirit that animated and moved the masses, improvised armies, and rendered the South so united, so enthusiastic and successful during the first years of the war. It owed its origin to the apprehension and belief impressed upon them by their leaders, that their liberties were endangered from disregard for constitutional barriers by the authorities at Washington. This was greatly increased by President Lincoln's proclamations and orders blockading the ports, calling out the militia without authority of law, and assuming the royal prerogative of suspending the writ of habeas corpus, a prerogative no sovereign in England in this day would dare assume; these acts brought the border States to the side of the Confederacy; and it was these acts and others of like character that rendered the Southern people, however before divided, almost a unit in the cause, as they supposed, of the maintenance of their liberties. These acts were heralded as confirmation of the wisdom of their leaders who had forewarned them. Those who had opposed, not only now ceased opposition, but in many instances rushed with zeal to the front ranks of the defenders of the Constitution. The Union they considered gone, but the Constitution must be saved.

This was the state of things when Mr. Davis went to Richmond. This was the state of things at and after the first battle of Bull Run. This was the state of things up to his inauguration as President under the Constitution for the permanent government. At that time he was at the head of a more united people than ever man was before in a war of such magnitude; nay more, he not only had the cordial support of his own people, but he and they had the sympathy of at least seven-tenths of their nominal enemies. More than half the North were politically hostile to the dominant party at Washington, while at least two-tenths of the Republicans were ominously alarmed for their own liberties because of what they considered usurpations at Washington. Under these circumstances, if Mr. Davis had had those high qualities that mark the great statesman, how easily he could have controlled events for the safety, honour, dignity, and glory of his country, instead of taking that course which has brought disaster, desolation, and ruin, not only on that country but upon himself. He utterly ignored, or did not understand, the popular sentiment which was not directed so much to disunion as to security of right. The Southern masses would have been satisfied with a settlement of the strife upon any terms giving security to their rights under the Constitution; they had no desire for separate independence except as a last resort. Had Mr. Davis possessed any statesmanship, can anybody doubt that, under the circumstances, he could have shaped events so as to effect a settlement that would have been satisfactory to the great majority of the people of both sections, making more secure, as it might have done, the liberties of both sections or the entire country?

But he was no sooner established in office under the permanent Constitution, than he began to exhibit total disregard for the principles, aims, objects, and views of the masses of his own people. One of the first things he asked of Congress was suspension of the writ of habeas corpus. He asked that he might be permitted to do the very thing the doing of which by Mr. Lincoln had brought thousands and thousands to the Southern armies. Then came his demand for conscription, the first great fatal step he took. That act by Congress struck the Confederate cause a stunning blow upon the brain-cap from which it never recovered. Had Mr. Davis been a statesman he would have understood the people. They were fighting for rights, not for dynasty. Every indication of a sympathizing movement on the part of the Northwest or the North toward making a common cause for the maintenance of a common liberty for a common country he repelled. He looked to nothing but independence or separate nationality. His internal policy thoroughly impressed many people with the conviction that the only independence he was looking for was the establishment of an irresponsible despotism of which he was to be the head. Whether such was his real object or not, such at least many at first feared;

and the people very generally toward the close believed such to be his object. Hence, that sudden letting down, that wonderful collapse, that unexpected "falling out of the bottom of the bucket" of the Confederate Cause, which has been the subject of so much surprise. I cannot extend these remarks. I only wish here to say that whatever else may be said of Mr. Davis it cannot be correctly said that he was, or is, a statesman in any exalted sense of that term. It would be difficult to find in the history of the world a man with such resources at his command who made such poor use of them.

Never was there such a body of people as those of the Southern States, possessed as they were of so many high qualities of mind and soul, to say nothing of material powers and resources, so miserably misled, misdirected, and misgoverned as they were. It would be hardly less just to claim statesmanship for him of a high order when the case was as it was, he holding the position he did. It is with no ill will to him I thus express myself. It is from a profound conviction that if he had been a man equal to the crisis, a man with the right head and heart for the occasion, a man of real ability, patriotism and wisdom, we should now have peace and liberty on a much better basis and securer footing than the country now has, ever had, or will have. Whether the old Union would have been restored under the Confederate States Constitution, or whether some, or what, modifications might have been made in it, looking to the best interests of all parties concerned, it is useless now to speculate.

The above remarks are penned as if I were a disinterested spectator, a bare "looker-on in Vienna," one simply conversant with all the facts without taking any active part in making them. Indeed, such chiefly has been my situation. I have been a close observer, but in no way, not to the least extent, a controller of events. The lack of wisdom on the part of the leaders who brought about the "precipitation," I saw from the first, or thought I saw. My opinion then was, and was expressed, that some of them were influenced more by passion, impulse, and ambition than from any strong motive of patriotism.

Should Mr. Davis be executed, this will also go a long way in giving him name and place high on the roll of martyred heroes and statesmen. His present imprisonment has made him thousands of friends and sympathizers where there were few. This, too, is the way history is made up. All this I know; but it does not change my opinion, nor modify its expression to the extent herein made. Men's acts and policies often tend to produce, and are efficient in producing, just what they profess to desire to prevent. So it was in his case. A desire to maintain Southern institutions was the object professed, but these institutions were safe enough for all practical purposes. There had been no positive aggression on them, or violation of the Constitution in respect to them by the Federal Government, though there had been breach of faith by several Northern States. It was, however, apprehended that some such violation would be made, and to guard and provide against apprehended danger, the counsel of these leaders was instantly to abandon the Union and take position outside of the Constitution, not trusting to its proper barriers. This was done while there were decided majorities in both Houses of Congress in favour of sustaining all the guarantees of the Constitution. The people followed this advice and in their new position lost everything. The advice and the result are as if the commander of a fort should counsel its inmates to leave their position behind its walls and sally forth to repel an approaching attacking party, lest if they should remain where they are, to receive the assault, they may all be cut to pieces.

Apprehensions may have been well founded; Southern institutions may have been doomed anyhow; but in no possible event could the people of the South have suffered worse than they have; in no probable event could they have suffered one-tenth what they have, even if their peculiar institution had been swept away by an open and palpable breach of the Constitution. But the truth is this: by following the advice of their leaders, they put the whole machinery of the Federal Government, with all its claims and powers, in the hands of a small party at the North, comparatively a very small portion of the population of that section. What wise man, now looking at the past, can doubt that if the Southern people had remained in their strong position behind the ramparts of the Constitution, the assaults of that party would have been harmless; and that long before this, it would have been impotent to do any injury to those thus fortified? Their leaders suggested and they followed the very course above all others their enemies would have had them take.

It is one thing to look at matters after they have occurred and a very different thing to judge of what would have happened under a different line of policy. With politicians it is as it is with quacks in medicine: if the patient survives, the great work of cure is claimed to the credit, honour, and skill of the doctor who almost killed him in spite of nature: while if the patient dies from the prescription of the quack, it is all, with due submission and resignation, turned over to the score of Providence. So, I suppose, it will be with the Southern States, their cause, their institutions, their ruin, and their leaders. These Southern leaders were certainly short-sighted; they evinced no wise forecast of statesmanship. Mr. Davis, in my opinion, ranks with the rest of them. If he had been a real statesman, he would have opposed secession.

With several of these leaders, whose names I need not mention, I was intimate. A few were, and are, men of great ability, equal to any of their generation on the continent, with native genius of a high order, thoroughly cultivated; practised on the hustings, in the forum, and in the public councils. In eloquence and the power of swaying the passions of the masses, they had no superiors in any age or country. Some, I believe, wrought themselves up into a misguided patriotic fervour; like some religious enthusiasts, they exhibited zeal without knowledge; yet I believed them to be honest in it. Of others I had, and have, a different opinion. These latter were influenced more by ambition than by impulses of patriotism. Still, I believe even these mistook their ambition for patriotism. They aimed at nothing but good government under their own administration. All were more or less blinded by passions, prejudices, or zeal. They had but little of that cool calculating wisdom that marks the true and generous statesman. Such will be the language of history if the record is ever rightly made. Mr. Davis belonged to neither of these classes. I doubt if he really favoured secession. He simply went with the crowd. He made no secession speeches that I ever heard of. He is a man of good character, well educated, of more than fair ability, and of agreeable manners, but, in my judgment, far from being a statesman.

Lieut. Woodman brought me a letter from Dr. Berckmans, Augusta, July 1. This was a real treat, and I feel greatly obliged to the doctor. Wish I could feel as sanguine of my early release as he expresses himself to be. He sends me a photograph of Marshall P. Wilder, of Boston, President of the American Horticultural* Society of 1857. I should like to make the acquaintance of Mr. Wilder on the doctor's account.

This day completes the ninth week since my arrest, the seventh of my incarceration here without accusation, warrant, or notification of the cause, and yet it is claimed that this is a free country.

I see in the Boston *Journal* an editorial on a speech by Wendell Phillips; † and the report of an interview between President Johnson and a Richmond delegation.‡ Such pieces cause me deep pain and mortification from the clear, vivid view they present of the complete subjugation and degradation of my country. How more abject could any people be, and dependent on the mercy of another than are now the people of the South on the people of the North. The evening paper says it was decided in Cabinet meeting to keep in abeyance for the present the question of pardon of the Confederate generals and others of high official station.

6.15 — Walked out with Lieut. W. I was too weak

* Perhaps The American Pomological Society is meant. The encyclopædias give no account of any horticultural society of this date of which Mr. Wilder was president.

† Urging measures to protect Congress against the seating of Southerners in that body.

‡ Leading citizens asking Johnson to amend the "$20,000 Clause" in the Amnesty Proclamation (excluding owners of this much), as it tied up capital and so worked hardship on the poor. Johnson replied insultingly that the rich men at the South had brought on the war, etc.

to walk much. I rested twice, and returned before time was up. Lieut. W. has just come and handed me a book, entitled the "Rebellion Record." I expect to find much in it to entertain me. I am truly obliged to him for it, and so told him.

Geary brought tea as usual. I took a few sips and asked what would be the prospect of my getting milk instead. He said I could have as much milk as I wanted, and proposed to go and get some. I replied, if it would not be too much trouble to him, I wished he would. He brought me a glass of rich, cool milk.

Until lights were extinguished, looked over the "Rebellion Record." I see my letter on Martial Law to Mayor Calhoun of Atlanta.

July 14. — Read Galatians, a letter written by Paul's "own hand." It is firm, earnest, and zealous, of great power and clearness. One expression in it has given rise to a great misconception concerning the doctrine of "falling from grace," that is, the possibility of one who has once been regenerated, or "born again" of the spirit, falling back into his original condition, and becoming a reprobate. Now, without saying anything on this point of controversy, I mean only to give my opinion that the text has nothing to do with that doctrine. The words are, "Ye have fallen from grace," but the whole verse reads: "Christ is become of no effect unto you, whosoever of you are justified by the law; ye are fallen from grace." The meaning, taken with the context, is, as it appears to me, simply this: those who look to the law for justification and not to Christ through faith, rely on themselves, on works alone and not on grace, for their salvation. You who do this, says Paul, rely on something other than grace; you abandon grace. The whole epistle seems to have been written to eradicate a certain misconception amongst the Galatians, who seemed to think that the Mosaic ceremonies were not done away with in Christ's dispensation. Some amongst them taught that circumcision was to be continued. What Paul says of his interview with Peter is worthy of note as it exhibits the characters of the two men in striking contrast and shows the spirit and temper in which Paul dealt with a co-labourer.

Read in "Rebellion Record" Toombs's speech before the Georgia Legislature in November, 1860. This is an able speech; but it is not exactly as delivered; he wrote this out after my speech in reply to his was reported. I never wrote mine save to the extent of correcting the notes of Mr. Marshall's report. Mr. Toombs's written speech contains replies to views presented by me in answer to portions of his delivered speech. The speech as delivered by him was much more eloquent, animated, and soul-stirring than this, prepared for the press after the ardour and fire of the occasion had passed off. The ideas in the main are the same, save on the few points excepted, but the language, strong and powerful as it is, is not equal to that he used in delivery. It is not so concentrated, does not hurl his thoughts in such burning, blazing, irresistible, Jove-like bolts as did his words when prompted by his huge brain all aglow.

Geary brought the morning Boston paper, and New York *Tribune*, *Times*, and *Herald* of yesterday. I see confirmation of yesterday's telegram that the Cabinet does not intend to make decision on special appeals for amnesty in the case of Confederate generals or other high officials for the present; these cases are to be held in abeyance. The *Times* has an editorial to the effect that Mr. Davis, and the other high civil officials now in custody, will before long be put on trial before a civil tribunal. Boston *Post* gives definition of "Amnesty," as accepted by all writers of authority: "A sovereign act of clemency by virtue of which the past is consigned to oblivion and the victor and the vanquished are placed on an equal social and political footing." Would it not be better to say "placed on their former (ante-bellum) social and political footing?"

11 a. m. — Lieut. W. and Dr. Seaverns called to see how I am getting along. Told the doctor I was free from pain and doing well, After a short stay they left. When they came in, they found me spreading out my silk underwear before the fire to dry thoroughly. Ever since I have been here, my clothes have been sent in rather damp, particularly silks. I find that silk is the most difficult of all cloth to dry; it seems to have a stronger affinity than any other for water.

Have nearly finished Bacon's "Essays." Am disappointed in them. They are nothing but loose sayings on divers subjects. They are, in some respects, not unlike Solomon's Proverbs. The best is on "Friendship"; there is much worth reading in that.

6.15 — Did not walk much. Felt weak. Had but little conversation. Stopped once at the eastern bastion and looked over the parapet upon the sea — the quiet, deep, mysterious ocean, emblem of time, of eternity, of the soul, and of God. My eyes filled with tears; why, I could not tell. A deep, sad voice seemed to come up from its silence, responsive to the melancholy brooding in my heart. To me all things in nature looked sad. The ships out at sea, with their flapping canvas, looked sad. The prisoners on the opposite bastion, walking to and fro in pairs, looked sad. The soldiers, sitting about their quarters in the fort below, looked sad. The very chirping of the swallows held a note of sadness. Indeed, all nature — earth, sea, sun, and sky — looked sad.

Geary has just brought me a glass of milk, which, with some bread, made my supper. Lieut. W. has just brought me another "Rebellion Record."

July 15. — Rose as usual at 7.30. Read in Corinthians. Geary brought breakfast at 8.30. Lieut. W. and Dr. Seaverns called while I was eating. No new directions. Wrote to Governor Johnson of Georgia:

Governor: Please excuse me for addressing you officially a few words in my own behalf. I am now a prisoner, as you may know, in this place. I have been here upward of seven weeks. My health is far from good. My privations are telling upon the energies of a constitution at all times weak. I am becoming more enfeebled. On this account I wish for release on parole, or for a mitigation of the rigour of my present confinement, so as to be allowed to take such moderate out-door exercise as I am able, in walking at pleasure on the grounds during the day, and to be allowed to procure the services of some one to be with me at all times to render such attention as my condition requires. Besides, I am anxious for release on parole for other considerations. Much business in my hands at home requires immediate and prompt attention; business affecting not my private interests alone but the interests of others; of a professional character as well as of a more fiduciary nature. I have the management of several estates, and am guardian of a number of minors, as well as of persons of colour, under our late laws. It is important for the interests and welfare of others, therefore, that I be permitted to explain, arrange, adjust, and turn over these trusts. I have asked the President for release on parole in consideration of these things. It has not been granted. From what I have keen able to hear in my present situation, I am induced to believe that perhaps such matters depend to some extent upon the recommendation of the Provisional Governors of the States, who are presumed to be better acquainted than others with the facts of each case. In this view of the subject I now address you. You have known me from our college and classmate days. My whole life, or my public acts, at least, are known to you; therefore, upon them I make no comment, further than to state what you yourself know, that my utmost exertions to prevent the troubles that have come upon the country, were put forth at the critical time when like exertions to bring them on were made by many who are now at large, some on parole and some with amnesty fully granted. I think I may be excused in alluding to this as a reason why, upon the principles of equal justice, release on parole, under the peculiar circumstances of my case, should be granted to me.

Now, if, in view of these matters, and from your own sense of what is right and proper and not prejudicial to the public interest in the premises, you feel at perfect liberty to call the attention of the authorities at Washington, the Secretary of War, or the Secretary of State, or the President, or whoever may be the proper one to address, to the facts as you know them, with a recommendation for release on parole, etc., I need not state that I should consider it a great personal favour and should appreciate it exceedingly. I simply present my case to your notice and ask that you act upon it according to your sense of public duty. I ask for myself individually nothing that may not be approved fully, cordially, and cheerfully by the dictates of your own judgment, looking as well to public interest as to the accommodation of private individuals. I should like very much to hear from you and to know, at least, that this communication is received by you.

Yours most respectfully,
ALEXANDER H. STEPHENS.

After sending this to Lieut. W. to be mailed, I wrote:

Governor: It is but proper to state for your information, that in case I should be released on parole I would say or do nothing tending to thwart, obstruct, or oppose the policy of the Administration in restoring and readjusting the relations between the States and the Federal Government; on the contrary, if permitted, I would do all in my power in aid of the speediest restoration of harmony and prosperity on that line of policy. But I have no desire to take any part in public affairs. What I earnestly wish, and all I ask for, is to be permitted to look after my health and private matters. I am perfectly willing to abide by any terms or conditions restricting my intercourse with the people, that may be imposed. My word of honour may be relied upon in any pledge that I may give upon this or any other subject.

Yours most respectfully,
ALEXANDER H. STEPHENS.

In the papers I see an account of Governor Brown's arrival in Macon on his return home. He was arrested two days before I was, and has been released on parole. Looking over the "Rebellion Record" I see reports of my speeches in Richmond on the 23d April, 1861, and in Atlanta on the 30th June and the 23d May, which do me great injustice, especially that of the Richmond speech. I used no such language at Richmond; I spoke strongly against unconstitutional use of power in blockading Southern ports, calling out the militia without authority of law, and other stretches of authority by the Administration at Washington, as foreshadowing the breaking down of all the safeguards of liberty under the Constitution, and the ulitmate consolidation of the Government into an absolute despotism; and I urged union of effort by all friends of Constitutional liberty everywhere, as the surest hope for the present and the future; the ark of the covenant of our fathers was with us; the fate of American Constitutional liberty, the light and hope of mankind, was with us. But I used no epithet or term of personal disrespect toward Mr. Lincoln then or on any other occasion. The reporter wrote out such an account as suited his purpose. I have often been provoked by similar liberties. So much so, that for the last two years I have almost invariably refused to make a speech unless I could revise the report. There seemed to me from the beginning a fixed design on the part of the Richmond press to keep me in a false position before the public. My general views and feelings in 1861 can be known by reference to my speech in the Virginia Secession Convention. It was in a secret session; it was off-hand, but it set forth clearly the views I entertained; it was published with the proceedings of the Convention. The Convention had a reporter in their secret sessions, but of this, I knew nothing at the time.

Reports of the Atlanta speeches are such sketches of my remarks as it suited the reporters to make. I have no idea that there was intention to misrepresent, but any writer who undertakes to reproduce from memory what he hears another, and particularly a public man, say, will be apt to give to it the colouring of his own thoughts. There was, for instance, no *boasting* in my speech. My heart was filled with sadness. My apprehension was that what I had to say, when I was called out and almost forced to speak against my will, would disappoint the people. I did not say, "Well, let them come on; we are prepared for them." After speaking of the threatening prospects, I said, "We must prepare to meet the crisis. Argument is exhausted and, if needs be, we must now stand upon our arms." This, I know, was the form of expression used; for I was called on for a speech at almost every depot on the road, and I have reason to remember this expression from repetition, if nothing more. I used no gasconade. Nor did I say that Mr. Davis would head our armies. All this colouring was added by the reporter, either from what others said, or from a misconception of what I really did say about the removal of the Government and Mr. Davis to Richmond. The idea that we "could call out a million of people, and then another million when these were cut down" never entered my head.

The Milledgeville speech against secession, November, 1860, as in the "Record," is in the main correct. It was an off-hand address. Mr. Marshall's report, taken from the Georgia papers doubtless, was copied in the New York *Times* from which the "Record" got it. The "Corner-stone" speech, which I made in Savannah, appears in the "Record." The report was taken from the Savannah *Republican*; how it was made I have before stated; I see in this report several errors; for instance, in the estimate of the property of the Southern States. But in the main it is correct. The item, in the "Diary" part of the "Record" from the New York *Post*, of my having been tendered a place in Mr. Lincoln's Cabinet, is without foundation in fact.

The item about Linton's approval of the Ordinance

of Secession in Georgia is also without foundation. He greatly disapproved it. Thus it is that records, histories, and biographies, in most instances, are made up. Some truths with more fictions strangely interwoven, and all so transcribed as to make such a figure of a man that he could never recognize it as intended for him if it were not duly labelled, marked, and laid away with his name superscribed.

6.15 — Took usual walk with Lieut. W. He was up to Boston to-day and my letters did not get off. On request, he has returned them; and I have copied them into one, making a postscript of the second. It is now nearly the hour to extinguish lights.

CHAPTER XV

SUNDAY, July 16. — Dreamed of Dick Johnston, his wife, and daughter, Mary Walton; of the whole family; I was at his house. It would be as impossible by language to convey an idea of the effect of this dream as it would be for me to reproduce in symbols strains of music which had just swept by, producing the sweetest harmony and the most soothing melody. Read both Corinthians. Became absorbed in study of these letters by Paul; new ideas, new views, latent force and beauty disclosed themselves, as the outlines and just perspective of a picture by a master hand opens up on close and studied gaze. Adversity has compensations. But for my present confinement, I might never have enjoyed as I do these masterly productions. And perhaps Paul spake not of himself but by commandment when he said, "For our light affliction, which is but for a moment, worketh for us a far more exceeding and eternal weight of glory."

I think that if many of the ministers of the Gospel would, on the Sabbath, read to their congregations one of Paul's Epistles, instead of giving their own comments on particular texts, such exercise would be attended with infinitely more good than the sermons usually preached. Few people read connectedly these Epistles, the best sermons ever produced except the Sermon on the Mount. The real doctrine presented in the whole argument is lost by looking only at fragmentary scraps. Much of the preaching of these days, to say nothing of the manner of reading the Scripture in families, or by individuals, is of the same kind as the dilating upon, or the reading of, "garbled extracts" from speeches.

Read Sunday *Herald*. See that Mr. Orr, late Member of Confederate Congress from Mississippi, has been pardoned. Walked out with Lieut. W. Saw ship coming in and going out of the harbour. The tide, that emblem of fortune and of the fluctuations of the soul, was at full flow. Lieut. W. told me that General DuBose is becoming homesick. Another prisoner was pardoned to-day, Postell, of Savannah, Ga; a blockade runner; would have been discharged some time ago, but refused to take the oath.

July 17. — Dreamed of being at my sister Catherine's. It did not occur to me that she was dead. The dream was like my visits to her years ago, when most of her children were small. It was an exceedingly pleasant dream, notwithstanding I was weeping while talking to little Mollie in my lap. My tears were of pleasure, or at least, not of grief, when I woke. The time of my dream was when Mollie was about seven years old. She is grown. So far back on the dial-plate of time was my spirit in its rovings. To give another an idea of my dream would, as I said yesterday, be as impossible as to reproduce in symbols the strains of a melody which had refreshed the spirit. Let none who may read these jottings suppose that when I note dreams, now and then, these are my only dreams. I seldom sleep without dreaming. For the most part my dreams seem nothing but the aberrations of my own mind. Again, they seem special visitations; visitations of two kinds: social or every-day visits, and visits portending something that impress as presentiments.

It was raining torrents when I got up. Geary was late coming in. He usually makes the fire a little after 6; I was up before he had it going.

Much has been said on friendship. Goldsmith asks, What is it? And, in poetic reverie, answers, "A phantom, a shade that follows wealth and fame." Burns, in like strain, makes a better suggestion. Cicero has written a book on it. But Bacon's short essay, which I have again read, embodies in a nutshell more true philosophy than all else I have seen upon this subject. Intercourse with his kind is almost essential to man's existence. The ties that bind him to his fellows, the cords of friendship, are the sympathetic nerves through which communication is kept up between himself and outside humanity. According to Bacon, the cultivation of friendship is essential to the development of the affections and the understanding; and these are necessary to all success. Every one needs some congenial spirit to whom he can unbosom himself; the stoutest of hearts requires such relief. This "communicating of a man's self to his friends" does indeed work "two contrary effects." "It redoubleth joys and cutteth griefs in halves, for there is no man that imparteth his joys to his friend but he joyeth the more, and no man that imparteth his griefs to his friend but he grieveth the less." What Bacon says of the effect of conversation in the development of the understanding is true. As well said is this: "A man were better reciting himself to a statue or a picture than to suffer his thoughts to pass in a smother."

Judge Collamer, of Vermont, now in the U. S. Senate, then member of the House, used to tell an anecdote of a man who was in the habit of talking to himself, which anecdote greatly amused Judge Story, one of our mess at Mrs. Carter's in Washington in the winter of 1844–45. Judge Story had quite a taste for humour; it was a common saying with him that a man should spend one hour every day in laughing. In Collamer's anecdote, a man caught in the awkward predicament of talking aloud to himself and asked why he did it, replied that he had two good reasons: "First, he always liked to talk to a sensible man; and second, he always like to hear a sensible man talk." According to Bacon he might have given one reason better than the two assigned.

The *Tribune* has a good article against military usurpation and a strong appeal for restoration of the writ of habeas corpus; but arguments on such subjects before the people or their rulers is much like casting pearls before swine.

Walked out with Lieut. W. He informed me that his battalion will be mustered out of service in about two weeks. This was disagreeable news. I doubt if anybody will fill his place who will be so kind to me. He expressed a desire that all prisoners here might be discharged before he left; in which I cordially united. I rather think all the military prisoners will be, but not Reagan and myself. He brought the six other volumes of the "Rebellion Record."

July 18. — Soon after breakfast, had a severe paroxysm of pain. It grew worse. Saw Lieut. W. pass the window, called to him, and asked him to send Dr. Seaverns. I was apprehensive of an attack of calculus. The pulse was 100. The Doctor came, and returned to his office to bring something, which he applied externally. I remained for some time quiet on my bunk and the paroxysm passed off.

Last night, before extinction of lights, now at ten, I looked over the volumes that Lieut. W. brought me. The little in them relating directly to myself is of the same sort as that before referred to: for instance, my Charlotte, N. C., speech of 1863, as reported in a Charlotte paper, is a complete distortion of my tone, temper, and sentiment. I complained of the misrepresentation soon after I saw it. This report in conjunction with that in a Columbia, S. C., paper of a speech I made soon after, caused me to decline further to address the people. I could not get what I said truthfully published. The leading idea of my Charlotte address was to arouse the public to a proper appreciation of Constitutional liberty and a determination to direct all their energies to its maintenance. I called attention to the popular tendency, under the guidance of the Richmond press, to give up all liberties in the delusive hope of thereby being the better enabled to preserve them. I had become alarmed, at the tone of our press at the seat of government and under the eye, if not the direction, of the President and his Cabinet. I knew that our people had gone into the struggle with no other view than to maintain and preserve the principles of the Constitution as established by their fathers, and if this great object should be abandoned by the Government, our cause would be hopeless. If, however, Government and people should prove true to this cause, I doubted not that, finally, after great sacrifices, much tribulation and suffering, war would be brought to a close upon some settlement securing the rights and sovereignty of the States and perpetuating the principles of self-government.

I held out no prospect of early termination of war; made no appeal to the country to sustain the authorities at Richmond and put down croakers. "Croakers" were not named by me. I rather endeavoured to impress the people with the importance of bringing public sentiment to bear upon the authorities, thus keeping them upon the only line in which I saw how success, even after the severest and most prolonged suffering, could be won. I thought the movement of General Lee into Pennsylvania a most ill-advised measure. I did not openly arraign or condemn it; no good could be thus accomplished. But by pointing out the course we should pursue, I must have left the impression on all thinking minds that I did not approve that expedition and much less Morgan's expedition into Ohio. Our policy was to husband our resources, act on the defensive, keep the people alive to the real cause, and zealous in its maintenance. If this should be done, I doubted not that, sooner or later, a reaction would take place at the North (perhaps in the change of administration if not before), and in that way, the true friends of Constitutional liberty, North and South, could and would adjust the questions at issue upon the basis looking to the real interest of all parts of the once prosperous and happy country.

"Reconstruction," that is, abandonment of our cause and return to the Union in hopes, or with the expectation by the States, of being received and treated as before secession (this was the idea of reconstruction as the term was then used), I looked upon as utterly delusive. The idea that the old Union and the old Constitution (as it had been) with all its comeliness of proportions, its government of united and delegated powers with the reserved rights of the States, could ever in that way be restored I regarded as vain and hopeless. But I at no time had any opposition to any such Union or Unions as might be effected by reason upon the same principles as those upon which the old Union had been formed. My whole soul was enlisted in the establishment of the principles of self-government as we had received them from our fathers, both of the South and the North. The only object I earnestly looked to as the final result of the deplorable struggle was the recognition and establishment of these principles throughout the continent.

The Richmond letter, in the "Record," to the *Tribune*, pretending to state the objects of the mission to Washington which I proposed in July, 1863, is without foundation in this respect. These objects were set forth in my letter to Mr. Davis, proposing the mission. My note to Rear Admiral Lee, as published in the *Record*, is incorrect; the true sense is marred by punctuation. The report of my speech in Augusta, July 11, 1861, is in the main correct, though there are several egregious errors in it: as, for instance, the amount of taxable property in New York; and my stating that I was not particular in my statistics. The truth is, I was exact. I had prepared them. Here, they are given correctly in hardly a single instance. I never saw the report of this speech until after it was printed, when too late to correct it. I never spoke of myself as a "Southern orator"; "chronicler" was the word I used. I resented this report the more from the fact that I had requested the reporter to submit it to me before giving it to the press. When I saw him on the stage, I regretted his presence there. It caused me to omit one topic I fully discussed in all my speeches about the produce loan: that was the point on which I differed with the Government about the cotton loan; and my policy for raising the blockade with cotton.

The Government plan was to receive the product of the sale of cotton as a loan; mine was for the Government to buy cotton with bonds; and then with the cotton, as an element of power greater than money, to raise the blockade. I did not wish these views to reach the enemy, and as I saw a reporter present, I did not give them. These views I later presented at Crawfordville in vindication of myself, when my plan had been ignored and rejected, myself unjustly assailed and my views misrepresented. When I was in Augusta, on this cotton loan agency in the summer of 1861, I was in strong hopes, as I stated on all occasions, that after the assembling of Congress in Richmond, the Government would change its policy on this subject, and adopt some such scheme as I was in the habit of presenting to the people. If I had not had such hopes I should never have raised my voice in behalf of the Cotton Loan; there is hardly anything in my past life that I have looked upon with so much chagrin and regret as my hopes connected with that matter. When I spoke in Augusta, I was, as I afterward found, influenced by illusive hopes, not only as to the cotton business but as to the general views of our Government officials on the war, both as to the manner of conducting it and the ends aimed at. I thought I was speaking for them in giving my own views on these subjects. In this, I later found out, or thought I did, by their acts and policy, that I was sadly mistaken.

Daily papers. In the *Herald*, an address by Governor Brown to the people of Georgia. I like its general tone, style, and views as I do most that comes from him. I have differed with him on many important matters, and on none other so important as secession; yet I have ever regarded him as a man of unquestionable ability and patriotism. In his address, I see he has been released upon the ground of his being at the head of the State forces, and entitled to a parole on surrendering them, under the same conditions as generals in command. Rather a fictitious ground, I think; but I am glad of his release. There is much in luck. Some seem to have been born under propitious stars, and by nature to be lucky. He is of this class. I have often remarked it. In the greatest difficulties that threaten him, when one sees hardly any chance for his escape or for his surmounting them, some little lucky incident turns up in his behalf. With me, the contrary has been true. Luck never was my forte. I am curious now to know on what grounds, fictitious or real, Governor Letcher [of Va.] has been released.

Read in the *Record* Andrew Johnson's speech in the U. S. Senate, July 1861. It is the ablest paper I have seen from any quarter against the Confederacy. Johnson does not argue the right of secession, the constitutionality of the suspension of habeas corpus, etc.; he reviews the objects aimed at by many leading men in the secession movement in terms able, eloquent, and true. This country's great misfortune is that it was thrown into the ridges or waves of party like a ship between two seas. The controlling parties were only a small portion of the people on either side — the extremists, North and South; but these few held the lever and shaped destiny. Johnson did not belong to either. In political association, he was connected with the extremists of the South; in sentiment and sympathy, with the great mass in both sections who were devoted to the Union as the embodiment of the principles of good government, and who believed that good government depended on its preservation. This address, I have no doubt, did more to arouse the North and excite the war spirit than any other one speech.

Delivered when and where it was and by whom, a Senator from Tennessee and a Breckinridge Democrat, it struck a tremendous, a terrible, if not a fatal blow, to the Confederate cause, in allaying inquiry into usurpations at Washington and exciting indignation and resolute determination to put down at the South what is described as unprovoked, actrocious rebellion prompted by disappointed ambition without pretext of justifying cause. Such was doubtless the impression made upon the Northern masses by this speech: no doubt it was spread broadcast. Thousands rushed to war, animated by the most patriotic motives; just as thousands at the South, so animated, rushed to the same bloody fields. What a strange spectacle! brother not only fighting brother, but for the same object — to perpetuate their liberties achieved by their common fathers. Is there a parallel in the history of the world? Yet such is the truth, the truth as to the great majority in the armies on both sides. The extremists North, the few that held the lever, were, it is true, looking to other and ulterior objects; they availed themselves of the powerful aid of Johnson and a few others over the South of like sentiments though of less ability; and of the high and generous patriotic sentiments of their own people to effect their sinister object, which the extremists at the South had given them opportunity to effect: that is, to break down State institutions by the war power.

CHAPTER XVI

JULY 19. — Sun shining in my room. I feel very weak. I lay down on my bunk, and took up the Bible. Just as I had finished Revelations, Geary brought the daily papers. I read General Dix's order retiring from command of the District of the East, and Gen. Hooker's assuming command. While I was looking over the papers, Lieut. W. brought me Linton's letter of the 6th. This letter did me a great deal of good, but not so much as it might have done if he had gone more into particulars: if he had told me how my crop was, how much wheat had been made, how the oats had turned out, how the corn had held out; and such information as I think he might have got from John A. Stephens and Mary Reid, who were with him. He speaks of two previous letters; that of the 24th of May, and another that has not arrived. I hope I will soon receive it.

Have been resting, reading nothing in particular. The newspapers I glanced over, then walked the room a while, then took the bunk; alternating repeatedly, allowing the mind as much relaxation as possible. If I had some friend to join me in a game of piquet, or something of the kind, to divert the mind from cares that oppress it, how much good it would do me! Much is said in the papers about the treatment of prisoners at Andersonville and other places, where I doubt not conditions were bad enough, but my opinion is that the severest, most cruel punishment that can be inflicted upon a rational, intelligent being is solitary confinement. If it was an act of inhumanity in the Confederate authorities to keep prisoners at Andersonville, where there was so much bodily suffering from necessity, what sort of act is it in the U. S. authorities to keep me here? Punishment was not intentional at Andersonville; the sufferings there necessarily attended the situation. No better provision could be made, and it was not the fault of the Confederate authorities that prisoners were held, but of the authorities at Washington who refused to let them be exchanged though fully apprised of their condition. But in my case and that of a number similarly situated, the suffering is inflicted intentionally as a punishment, and that, too, without any conviction of offense.

Walked out as usual. Lieut. W. told me he had sent off General Ewell and Major Brown, of Ewell's staff, to-day. Right glad am I that the General, lame as he is, has been discharged. Major Brown is related to Mrs. Ewell. Saw notice in evening's paper of Mr. Davis's ill health. Also, a remark that Mr. Seward is reported,* by some Georgia persons, to have made about me. I see it stated that G. B. Lamar has been released from the Old Capitol Prison.

July 20. — Thor's Day, as our ancestors called it, the Day of Thor. I am not so versed in their mythology as to know if they looked to Thor as a good and propitious deity or the genius of bad luck. On Thursday I was arrested, ten weeks ago to-day; Thursday, I was

* An Atlanta paper of July 8 publishes this: "Two gentlemen from Georgia made an appeal to Mr. Seward, Secretary of State, to the effect that some privileges promotive of his comfort should be bestowed upon the Hon. A. H. Stephens. The Secretary kindly assured them that he would investigate, and if it could be done, the privileges solicited would not be withheld."

imprisoned in these walls eight weeks ago. It is a day of the week which will not be forgotten by me while memory lasts.

Lieut. W. has just called to see me and to say that he is going to Boston to-day if he can get off, and that Lieut. Newton will attend me in his absence. I requested him to see what a single bedstead and mattress and a large feather pillow could be got for in Boston. My bunk is uncomfortable; I must get some other sort of bedding if I can. Also requested him to ascertain if I may be allowed a screen; and, if so, the probable cost. I want a folding paper-screen to protect me, when stript and bathing, from the gaze of passers-by.

Lieut. W. brought in Lieut. Newton and gave him an introduction. Lieut. Newton approached me and shook hands. This was the first civility of the sort extended to me since I have been in this cell. When I saw him approaching with the evident intention of offering his hand, I arose and met him, cordially responding to the courtesy. I permitted the advance, however, to come from his side. My first introduction to any one here was to the surgeon, I believe, when there was no offer of this sort, or anything indicating a disposition to entertain such civilities. I have felt here at times much as I have often imagined a well-bred Negro in our country felt toward those who set themselves, in their own estimation, above him. I stood quite as much upon my dignity as those who seemed to think that it would be a condescension on their part to take my hand or offer theirs. The first advance, I thought it proper, should come from the other side. I had no idea of subjecting myself to the mortification of having my offered hand rejected or reluctantly taken. My habit was always to shake hands with persons of all colours, races and conditions whose actions displayed modesty, respect and good bearing; my instructions to my servants on this point of manners, so far as concerned white people, was to be always ready to shake hands when the offer was made by the white person, but never to make the advance in that form of salutation. This I thought the best rule to be governed by: the superior, or whoso considers himself such, whether in bare position or otherwise, should always make the advance. Officers never shake hands with men of the line, and I suppose they look upon a prisoner as no better than one of their men of the line. This was not the case with Lieut. Newton.

Another Fancy Sketch, yet not Altogether Fancy:

Visitant. [Entering through the window of imagination.] Well, how are you to-day?

Prisoner. Not so well as when you were last here.

Visitant. What is the matter? anything special?

Prisoner. This cold stone floor and damp atmosphere do not agree with me. I am growing weak — losing flesh — can't balance myself in walking — haven't the right use of my legs. I have sat here in this chair until the hip-bones are sore, and it seems as if the hips themselves have become weak. There is exceeding weakness in the region of the loins when I go to walk. Sometimes I almost stagger. From some cause, I know not what, I am not so well by far as when you were here last.

Visitant. Maybe your mind — your confinement and brooding — has something to do with it.

Prisoner. If I could but have the free use of myself as I please, go in and out when I please, take exercise in walking or driving when and as I might please, and confer with friends here and elsewhere without restraint, I think my mind would be as much at ease as it has been for many long years.

Visitant. Do you feel no anxiety as to your fate? When I was last here, I thought you would have been discharged before now. I must confess that I, and your friends generally, have become much more uneasy than we were. What is your idea as to the intention of the authorities?

Prisoner. In my judgment, the authorities have no settled purpose. I and others are held only as political capital out of which they will make the most they can. They have probably not reached any conclusion as to the best market to operate on. We are kept as hostages for the good conduct of our friends and sympathizers at large, and as an example *in terrorem* over them. That is the present political market in which we are speculated upon. When that closes, what new enterprises may open up for bold strokes, time must determine. All that is certain is that we are political capital to be made the most of according to times, circumstances, and exigencies. We are held, as captives were by the old Aztec tribes, to be disposed of in such way as will most promote the interest of the captors. The main thing is the ransom, the political advantage to follow the disposition determined upon. Little thought or care about the captives is indulged in. Whether they shall be graciously set at large, or be piously delivered over as victims to the eager priest at the public sacrificial altar, is a matter which depends upon which course will pay best. I feel intensely the wrong of my confinement as well as its privations and discomforts, but I trust my fortitude will not fail to sustain me throughout; and even to the end, let that be what it may. It is my earnest wish that no friend of mine shall be influenced in any degree in his course by my treatment or fate, but that all will act from their own conscientious sense of duty to themselves and the country. What in my opinion that duty is, I have told you.

[Enter *Lieut. Newton*. Exit *Visitant*.]

Lieutenant. Here is a letter just come by the mail.

Prisoner. [Rising and receiving it.] Thank you, sir. [Lieut. N. exit.]

Letter from Hidell, Memphis, Tenn. Dinner at usual hour. The syrup is excellent. At first, I thought from its thinness, it had been watered. It is maple syrup, quite thin but well prepared. It stays in my room and I use it when I please, and I have a fancy for it.

Lieut. Newton called at 6.30 to walk with me; said he could not find the key to my room and was detained thereby. I was not able to walk much. Staid out only a short time.

July 21.—Had a bad dream last night; it was about Eliza at home: she was badly hurt, the hurt inflicted by Harry, not intentionally. Judge Cone figured; it did not occur to me in my dream that he was dead.

Before breakfast I glanced over Romans. I is written with great ability, but there are parts, as Peter says, "hard to be understood." The letter, it seems, was not written by Paul; this occurs in the conclusion: "I, Tertius, who wrote this epistle, salute you in the Lord." Did Tertius copy, or write at Paul's dictation? The argumentative strain is characteristic of Paul, but the style in some particulars is not his. The repeated questions with the answer, "God forbid," is not seen in his other letters. One thing remarkable in all his writings is that they say so little about the life and teachings of Jesus while in the body. They embody the Christian teachings, yet seldom refer to anything Christ did or said while on earth. Paul alludes to the Lord's Supper, the resurrection, and to the persons by whom Christ was seen; but he makes no mention of the miracles, parables, Sermon on the Mount, or any of the general principles inculcated by Christ. The same is true of the other apostolic letters. Peter makes a brief reference to the transfiguration. It is singular that all the apostolic letters say so little about the sublime and divine teachings of Christ himself. Paul seems to rest all his superstructure of Christian principles upon his own miraculous conversion and the teachings of the Divine Spirit in his own breast together with the precepts of the Prophets. He seems to have been thoroughly familiar with the Old Testament; he often quotes from it. But he seems not to have known much of the actions and sayings of Christ when in the flesh except what was imparted to him in his own spiritual development and through the agency of the Spirit.

Lieut. W. brought letters from Joe Myers, Gip Grier, and my old friend, J. A. Stewart. I answered all, and wrote to John A. Stephens. I was right glad to see Lieut. W. I was not expecting him before Monday. He has got to be a sort of familiar acquaintance, the only one I have here. Reread all my letters. Spent the evening on my bunk in silent meditation. Walked at usual hour. Was weak but better than yesterday. Lieut. W. with me. This has been the closest and sultriest day since I have been here. The thermometer has not been higher, not above 82, but there has been no breeze, no draught in my room except that produced by the fire, which is the only way the smoke from my pipe escapes. For supper, bread and milk. Opened the Bible and the eye fell on Job x. — its every line applicable to me!

Saturday, July 22. — This day, thirty-one years ago, I rose at dawn. I had slept but little. It was the 22d of July, 1834; a day of intense interest to me. I was to be examined for admission to the bar in Crawfordville. I had been reading law for a short time only, not much over six weeks in all. I had had no instructor; had bought and applied myself to such books as I had been informed were necessary: Blackstone's Commentaries, Chitty's Pleadings, Starkie on Evidence, Maddox's Chancery, the Statutes of the State, and the Rules of the Court. All these I had read and reread, and had got the general principles well fixed in my head. But how I should be able to stand the ordeal of a legal examination, I did not know. I had never witnessed one. All I knew about it was what my friend, Swepston C. Jeffries, a lawyer in the village, had told me. Should I be rejected, my prospects and fortunes would be blasted. My anxiety and agitation as the time grew near were great. The night before examination was spent in reviewing, in systematizing and arranging in my mind the principles of each text-book, under the various heads, in the best order and method I could. It was nearly day when I got through and lay down to rest. I am not certain that I slept any. When it was light enough to see how to read, I was up and at my books again. Examination was to be at eight in the court-room. I was in my place at the appointed time. I remembered my examination for college and how I had been mistaken in all my special preparations.

The examining committee were: Joseph Henry Lumpkin, one of the most eloquent men in the State as well as one of the best lawyers. He has been a Justice of the Supreme Court of the State since the organization of that tribunal in 1846. He was to examine me on the Common Law. Wm. C. Dawson, then one of the most prominent members of the bar, was to examine me on the Statutes of the State, the Rules of the Court, etc. He was afterward in Congress and the Senate; he was a man of great amenity of manners, a wit and humourist; his personal popularity for several years was greater than that of any other man in the State. Daniel Chandler, then Solicitor General, was to examine me on the Criminal Law. He was considered the most eloquent and promising of the rising young men of the State. Two years later he moved from Washington, Ga., where he then resided, to Mobile, Ala., where in connection with the Hon. John A. Campbell, his brother-in-law, he attained great eminence but not so great as was expected. He still resides in Mobile. In grace and beauty of declamation, flow of language and energy of expression, he had few superiors. The presiding judge was the famous Wm. H. Crawford. Jeffries had informed me of a remark reported of the Judge upon some similar occasion, which gave me about my only consolation. It tended to show that he was not very exacting. Jeffries said that the Judge, after an examination to which he paid little attention, ordered: "Swear him, Mr. Clerk; if he knows nothing he will do nothing." I thought if he would take but the same course and do the same by me, I would be satisfied!

Examination began, Judge Lumpkin leading off on Blackstone, with which four books I was perfectly familiar; I had in my mind an analysis of every chapter. He also had in his a distinct outline of the whole method and system of these Commentaries. With the first question, "What is law in its most general sense and application of the term?" promptly answered, he went on in the regular order, which suited me exactly. He had but to name the subject of a chapter, and I gave the whole substance without a balk. He seemed surprised and pleased. Only one question I missed: "What is necessary for the validity of a plea in abatement?" I paused. He stated, "It must be sworn to." This I knew well, but it had not occurred to me that it would answer his question. When through, he turned to Judge Crawford and said he was perfectly satisfied with the examination, had never heard better. That was very gratifying to me. Mr. Dawson followed with questions in his department. So with Mr. Chandler. Both used complimentary terms of me in reporting to the Judge. The Judge, I noticed, was paying attention all the time to the examination. When the last report was made, he said: "Take an order for the admission, Mr. Solicitor, and have the oath administered. I, too, am perfectly satisfied." Thus, the ordeal was over.

Several members of the bar, the Examining Committee first, came up, giving me a congratulatory welcome into the fraternity; then others, particularly my old friend, Jeffries, who had taken deep interest in the examination, and was profuse in commendation. After these, while the clerk was preparing to issue the license and the oath, and I was still on the outer circular bench where I had sat during the examination, other manifestations were made which were equally gratifying. These were by old rustic acquaintances, some of my schoolmates in early days, and some old farmers in the vicinity, neighbours and friends of my father, who, from the interest they took in me, had come that morning to see how I would acquit myself. While the examination was progressing, they had been silent but deeply agitated spectators, equally moved and agitated with myself. When it was over, and they could do so without attracting attention, they came up, one after another, to where I was sitting, and leaning over the railing, with smiling countenances, expressed profound gratification in their own homely way. For from what they saw and heard, though they knew no law, they knew that all had passed off well.

Such were incidents and scenes of my life on this day, thirty-one years ago. How different from my present surroundings! Judge Crawford held but one court after that at which I was admitted. Next week he went to Wilkes; and on his way to Madison court, was taken ill and died. Mine was the last lawyer's license he ever signed. Jeffries died three years later in the prime of manhood. Dawson rose to great eminence; he died in 1855. Chesley Bristow, the old clerk who made out my license and who was one of my best friends, lived until 1845, when he too passed away. Quinia O'Neal, then Clerk of the Inferior Court, who took great interest in my success, and had spent much time in my room during my studies, witnessed the examination with great pleasure. He is still living, or was when last I heard from him. His head is white with age; he is near seventy. For thirty years he held some of the clerkships of our courts, and for several years, all of them. He lived with me for some time after his wife died. Two years ago, he resigned all his offices in consequence of the infirmities of age, and moved to Dougherty County to reside with his daughter. Last summer, he came up to Liberty Hall and spent the hot months with me. He is a most remarkable man. Few excel him in propriety and virtue. He was known for years in our village by the sobriquet of "The Parson."

Did not rise this morning till eight. Found the Bible open as I left it last night. Again read Job x. Took a cup of coffee. At eleven Lieut. W. called. I was reading the daily papers. He sat down and talked with me for some time — the first time he has sat down and talked with me since I have been here. He talked about my health, and asked about such modifications of confinement as I thought would be more conducive to it. I told him the privilege of going out and in when I pleased and taking exercise at will would be an advantage; also having the locked door of my room open so as to allow free passage of air through my quarters. The main thing was to be released from close custody and to have the privilege of getting some one to stay with me and attend to my wants. If I had some one to rub me when I bathe, it would strengthen me. I am not able to rub myself. At this point, recollections of home, and remembrance of kind attentions I have ever had when sick, rushed upon me so suddenly and with such force that before I was aware of it, I was weeping. I bowed my head and wept in anguish, the more from the fact that I could not restrain myself in his presence.

He retired, and, after awhile, brought Dr. Seaverns. They found me walking my room, smoking my meerschaum, and trying to allay disquietude. The Doctor took a seat; so did I. He talked for some time on the same subject that Lieut. W. had conversed on. But I was not in condition to converse. I could not talk without betrayal of emotion. He did not talk to me as if he had any sympathy with me in my condition, bodily or mental; made no examination of the pulse, and asked no such questions as physicians usually do who have any inclination to inquire into or prescribe for disorders. He seemed to act as if he thought that all that was the matter with me was lowness of spirits. Perhaps in this he was partly right, yet lowness of spirits is a formidable disease when its effects are telling upon all bodily functions. I do myself think my present debility is attributable in part to mental causes, to the mind's being deprived of its accustomed stimulants of social and friendly intercourse. I greatly need that recreation which an hour or two of social conversation daily with some friend or acquaintance would furnish. This natural nourishment which the mind requires and for which mine is famished, would add nourishment and strength to my body.

The Doctor, in a light and agreeable manner, advised stimulants: asked about my whisky and recommended it. I told him I had some yet (all of Harry's bottle is not gone; I have besides the gin Lieut. W. gave me), but that I do not like alcoholic stimulants; I did not feel that they would do me any good in my present condition, though ale or lager or some such drink, tonic as well as slightly stimulating, might possibly benefit me. The conversation lasted ten minutes, when he and Lieut. W. retired, the Doctor saying he would recommend to the commanding officer some modification of my confinement; what, I do not know.

I stretched myself on my bunk with Cicero on "Moral Duties." I commenced reading, but soon found myself weeping. Read I could not. The crevasse was broken and the current continued to flow in spite of all my efforts to stop it. I walked the room, and the tears still came. I washed my face again and again, and still the tears would not cease. Everything around seemed sad. I looked out upon the far-off sky; the fogs and clouds are now gone; but the sky looked as sad as all things else.

Dinner at usual hour. I had no appetite. I did not seem sick or in any pain, but I felt that heavy load upon the mind that we feel when some dear one is dead in the house. My soul is sick, and I have no one to whom I can impart my griefs. I took a few mouthfuls of food — the tears rolled down upon my plate. I set the things aside, and resumed my walk about the room.

Walked out at usual hour with Lieut. W. Rested in the shade of the wall. Saw a curious seashell. Picked it up. Lieut. W. said it was a sea-snail's. Supper was brought by a new orderly; Geary has gone to town to be absent until Monday. The new hand at the bellows does not do as well as Geary. My fire was nearly out. He did not know how to manage it. Before it was started, all the coals had to be taken out of the grate and wood added. I fear I shall greatly miss Geary.

As I returned from the evening walk, a little girl handed me a bunch of flowers. They were sweet and pretty. I have put them in a tumbler of water on my table.

July 23. — Read in Psalms. Breakfast 8.15, before fire was made. New orderly does not know how to get the fire going. Lay on my bunk. Lieut. W. brought *Harper's Weekly*. The Boston *Herald* says order has been issued for release on parole of all Confederate officers on their taking the oath of allegiance. Good news to DuBose and all officers confined here and elsewhere. I requested Lieut. W. to send the Surgeon to see me. He said Dr. Seaverns was away but would call on his return. He brought letters from John A. Stephens and F. T. Bristow, both dated July 10. Their perusal did me much good.

Lieut. W. and the Surgeon called. I submitted to the latter a paper in writing touching my case, as I did not feel able to talk about it. Spent the evening reading Cicero on Moral Duties. At 6.30 walked out with Lieut. W. It was so hot we kept in the shade of the wall below. As we passed Dr. Seaverns's quarters, he came out and offered me a chair to rest a while. I accepted. Mrs. Seaverns soon appeared, and he gave me an introduction to her. This was unexpected; she remained, and talked with me some time. She seemed to be an exceedingly agreeable lady, easy to become acquainted with. I saw the little girl who handed me the flowers yesterday. It was Mrs. Seaverns's little daughter, Annie, a pleasant-looking, kind-hearted little girl. After spending about twenty minutes in conversation with Mrs. Seaverns, which really did me a great deal of good, I walked on with Lieut. W. We went upon the terreplein and looked over the parapet. The tide was low. We saw a good deal of shipping. The Lieutenant said they had had quite a sight a few hours before in the passing of the *Vanderbilt* and the *Dictator*; if he had seen them in time, he would have brought me out to get a view. I told him I should have liked to see the *Dictator* though I did not like her name. If there is anything in the world I detest, it is the idea of a dictator; the ship I might have admired, but her name I never could. We remained until sundown. I looked for the new moon in the clear sky but she was not visible; too young and new, changed only yesterday.

Baily, the new attendant, brought tea and bread. I feel much better than for several days. The letters from home did me good, and the conduct of the Doctor this evening, and the conversation with Mrs. Seaverns, small as that little incident was, did me good. I feel the effects yet.

July 24th. — Did not sleep much. Was quite ill in the night. Soon after breakfast, Dr. Seaverns and Lieut. W. called. I was writing to Linton and John A. Stephens.

Lieut. W. called again and brought me a bouquet of flowers, from Mrs. Captain Livermore, I believe he said.

At the usual hour for walking, Lieut. Newton called for me. While memory lasts I can never forget the unutterable pang that struck my heart when I saw him instead of Lieut. Woodman. Lieut. W. had gone to Boston with the released officers. We walked out but, oh how badly, badly, badly did I feel, and do now — sick in body and sick in heart. I expected to see Lieut. W. before he went off with the officers. I was sadly disappointed in this. I did not think they would get off before to-morrow.

July 25. — Slept more last night. This is the beginning of dog days, The sun rose very hot. Read several Psalms; these verses did me good: "I had fainted, unless I had believed to see the goodness of God in the land of the living. Wait on the Lord: be of good courage, and he shall strengthen thine heart: wait I say, on the Lord." Wrote Secretary Seward as follows:

Dear Sir: I take the liberty of addressing you a few lines in my behalf. This, I have intended to do for several days but have not been in that condition physically or mentally to do it as I wished. In both respects I have been almost completely prostrated. I have been induced to address you partly because you are the only member of the Cabinet with whom I have any personal acquaintance, but mainly because I suppose the subject matter relates properly to your Department. One thing especially that I wish to say to you is in reference to the Hampton Roads Conference.

But in the first place, allow me to say that I have lately seen a circular from the Attorney General, dated 12th June, requiring all special applications for amnesty to be accompanied with the prescribed oath of allegiance. It has occurred to me that perhaps the absence of that oath, or the omission of it, in my application is the reason I have heard nothing from it, or on the minor requests in it anterior to my second letter to the President. Will you be kind enough to have me informed if this is the case? Is this asking too much? I did not know at the time mine was sent on that such was the requirement before any such application would be considered. My attention has been called to it only within the last few days. If this be a defect in my application, you may assure the President, as I hope you will, that the omission arose entirely from my not knowing of any such requirement, and if the paper shall be returned to me, I will most cheerfully and in the most perfect "good faith," as I stated in my first letter to the President, supply the omission: or without its being returned, will, upon being notified that that is lacking for its consideration, take the oath before any officer who may be directed to administer it. Due allowance, I trust, will be made for one situated as I am, being cut off, as I am, from communication with the world to a great extent, and being, moreover, so much enfeebled by disease as I am.

I take this occasion, also, to state to you my earnest

desire to be at least released on parole, or on bond in any amount that may be thought sufficient. There are reasons of very great importance why I should be thus released, relating not only to myself, to the preservation of my health and perhaps of my life, but to the interest of others. On this point, I refer you to my letter to the President. You will allow me to say, moreover, that I do not think if I were permitted to see the President and to confer with him face to face, as others equally complicated with myself, if not more so from the positions they held, in the late Confederate organization, have been permitted to do, I would quickly satisfy him that, upon public consideration alone, without reference to those of a private nature, I am equally entitled to such release. I know that no man more true, more loyal, or ardently devoted to the Constitution of the United States and the principles of civil and religious liberty it embodies than I am, ever breathed the vital air of Heaven; and no one can rejoice more heartily than I do at the prospect of seeing peace, harmony, and prosperity once more restored to this whole country under its benign influences.

On the question of restoration, I have some views that I would take pleasure in communicating to you and the President, particularly on the subject of suffrage so far as that relates to the coloured race. This I regard as a question of not less importance than that of emancipation itself. Upon its wise and proper solution depend the future interests of both races. I have thought a great deal upon this subject, and may be excused in saying that I think the question can be adjusted upon the principles on which all representative governments should be based. These principles require such a structure of society as will secure the rights of all without injury to any. While I have no desire ever to mingle in public affairs again, yet I should take pleasure in giving these views to the President and the people of my State. You and the President may be assured that these counsels, if I were permitted to give them, would tend to nothing but the speedy restoration of harmony and prosperity upon a permanent and lasting basis.

My object in making these remarks, I trust will not be misconstrued. I wish only to make myself better understood. It is far from my intention thereby to propitiate favour. I know, in the extraordinary and wonderful events through which we have passed, I, with the wisest and best men, may have committed errors in judgment as to the best means to be used, or the best course to be taken, for the preservation and perpetuation of the liberties of our fathers. But I do know, whatever error I may have committed in this respect was of the head and not of the heart. And if to err in the wisest and the best is but human, it is some consolation to know that to excuse and forgive is divine. On the point of amnesty and pardon, therefore, in my own case, I have no further argument or appeal to make. I wish the President to act upon it, if he be pleased to consider it, as he may think best under his own sense of duty to me and the country. But what I do ask and entreat upon the subject of release on parole or bail is, at least, a mitigation of the rigour of my present confinement. I consider it as due to humanity. For I assure you that continued close confinement with its necessary privations, is, in the complication of disorders with which I am afflicted, equivalent to death. I cannot believe that such a result is the object of my imprisonment. But it is due to you and the President to let you know that in my belief such will be the effect.

What I wish to say to you upon the subject of the Hampton Roads Conference is this: I have lately seen a publication taken from the *Chronicle and Sentinel*, Augusta, Ga., purporting to be my version of the Conference and what transpired at it. You may have seen this publication. Be assured that I authorized no such. Where the editor got his materials from, I know not. I have not seen him since the Conference and have had no communication with him. Some things in the publication are true, but in it are many errors, and even the truths are so stated as to make a very erroneous impression on several points. I felt much annoyed at the publication, and I desired to have it denied in the papers that I had any knowledge of it. This, however, I could not have done. I, therefore, avail myself of this opportunity to make denial as I thus do to you. It is, perhaps, a matter of but little consequence any way, but I wish you to know that that publication was without my knowledge or sanction. Upon the subject of that Conference, I made no report for the public but that which was joint with the other Commissioners and which was published in the Richmond papers. Upon the main points in that Conference, those upon which it was sought, I have never even in private made any statement that could reach the public. For great public reasons, I abstained from it.

To you in this communication it is also proper to state that this Hampton Roads Conference was not such a one as I desired at that time and was striving to obtain. I consented to it from the hope that, from what *I had heard*, an armistice might possibly be effected upon the "exterior" question to which you referred in your letter to Mr. Adams.* To the extent of an *armistice* only did that policy meet my approbation. Under an armistice I was strongly in hopes that such a Conference as I desired would take place, and that a restoration of peace upon some satisfactory basis, without the further effusion of blood, would speedily follow. From the beginning, I had been of the opinion that if reason should once be permitted to get control of the questions, peace and harmony would soon be restored. It was with these views only, looking to objects not embraced in any power or instructions given to the Commissioners, that I consented to be a party to the Conference. Hence, the free interchange of views we had upon the whole subject of

* Reference, perhaps, to Seward's idea, expressed before the war, to Charles Francis Adams, that prospect of a foreign war would unite the sections.

the war. I was in strong hopes that good would result from that interchange of views, as I assured Gen. Grant on our return; that while nothing definite or satisfactory had been effected, yet I was in strong hopes that good would result and that peace might be the consequence. While it is far from my wish or intention to cast blame or censure upon any person whatever, it is but due to myself to say that no one could have been more chagrined and mortified than I was at the course adopted at Richmond after the report of the Conference was made. This much, by way of explanation on this subject, I have thought it due to you and myself to state.

All of which, without any regard to method or order, but with much feebleness, is submitted to your consideration. Yours most respectfully,

Alexander H. Stephens.

I requested Corporal Geary to give the letter to Lieut. Newton to be mailed. I was much exhausted after copying it. It was not to my liking but I was too weak and feeble to better it. I sent it as it was. It thus throws out something upon which the mind can look and hope for a week, perhaps, at least. This may keep me from sinking, as I feel I should do without something on which to hang hope. To such extremity am I reduced. After getting through with the copy, I got up to walk but it was with difficulty. The legs seem to have lost their proper use.

While I was writing above entry, Lieut. Newton brought me three letters: from S. J. Anderson,* of 18th July, and Raymond W. Burch, 16th July, and Miss Elizabeth R. Nichols, 19th July, Washington, D. C.; she is sister of J. Nichols.† All these letters had been sent here, and then

* S. J. Anderson was a clerk in the House when Mr. Stephens was a Member.

† The name rendered Nichols may be "Echols."

back to General Hooker for inspection. Hence my delay in getting them. Their perusal did me good. It shows me that I am not forgotten. Yesterday and to-day have been two of the most miserable days I have passed. Why, I do not know. But with weakness and pains of the body, the mind seems to have sunk under the apprehension that if I remain here much longer I shall be bedridden, and that thought is harrowing. I do my best to drive it off.

The doctor called while I was writing to Mr. Seward. He asked if I had been able to use the catheter he sent. I told him I could not give it such bend as was necessary for introduction without much pain. If I had something that was round and smooth, I might give it such bend. He suggested a glass tumbler. That I shall try.

If any one shall ever see these pages and feel surprise at such an entry, or curious to know why I make it, let this explanation suffice: I am writing now simply to stamp here as far as I can, the full impression of my present situation and surroundings, and also to occupy the mind, to give it any other direction rather than let it brood over matters that it can neither change nor control. There is nothing so essential in keeping the spirits up, or, if that is impossible, to keep them from utter collapse, as to keep the mind employed at something, and to draw it away from reflections on its cares, anxieties, and disquietudes. This journal thus far has been of great service to me in this particular. Had I not had access to books and stationery, and something thus to divert the mind, I believe I should have died or gone crazy before now.

6.15.—I was unusually weak this evening: more

so than in my previous walk. Geary brought me tea and toast. I took some of each.

I omitted to state in its right place a little incident of to-day. A little girl brought me some flowers: she got the guard to hold her up, and gave them to me between the bars.

[The impression made upon Mr. Stephens by small acts of kindness is indicated in his "War Between the States" by the following reference to this flower-giver, the child of Major and Mrs. Appleton:

"Their charming little daughter, Mabel (not four years old), brought me flowers almost daily. She would get the guard to raise her up, and would put them herself, with her little tiny hand, between the bars of the iron grate of the window, where was placed a vase to receive them when I was unable to take them myself."—*Editor.*]

CHAPTER XVII

JULY 26. — A clear, bright morning. I slept little last night, not an hour of good sleep. Waited anxiously for Geary. He came at 7.20. I soon got up, weak, weary, and unrefreshed. Read Hosea. Took cup of coffee. Succeeded in using catheter; it was painful and weakened me very much.

Had a sort of row with bedbugs. Was certain last night I felt one. Examined my bed to-day and found several. What I am to do to get rid of them, I do not know.

1 p. m. — Feel better. Read the daily papers. Saw Governor Johnson's address in Macon, Ga., and his proclamation for an election in October. See announcement of prisoners released from this fort. It is not correct, I think, in the statement that Judge Reagan and myself are the only ones left. Lieut. Newton told me yesterday that there are two others. These, I think, are Dr. Bickley, of the Golden Circle, and Captain Hunter,* the two I saw going for water. The most important item to me is that Mr. Seward leaves Washington to-day for Cape May. If so, he will not get my letter. Another instance of the bad luck that attends me. It so happened that when my application was sent on, it was, according to report, turned over to him; and just

* Whether this prisoner is the same as "Vernon," hereafter named in connection with Bickley, the Journal does not indicate. Inquiries to the War Department as to whether there were a Hunter and a Vernon in prison at Fort Warren with Bickley, or as to Bickley, have been returned with the statement that it would be a violation of the rules of the Department to answer.

about that time, Mrs. Seward died; he was called away, and perhaps has never given any consideration to it. And now, just as I send him a special letter, he leaves before it reaches him. Surely I am *unlucky!*

Dinner at the usual hour. I felt better than for five days past. For the first time in that period, I was hungry. The heavy gloom that has rested over me for several days seems to be lifting from the soul as a fog rises from the bottom of a lake.

Dr. Seaverns and Lieut. Newton called to see how I was. Lieut. Newton took some of my Chanticleer brand of smoking tobacco as a sample for Lieut. [Captain?] Livermore. It is the best I ever used. I gave him a pipeful yesterday while he was sitting with me after our early return from walk. He liked it very much and so to-day took some for his friend to try. The doctor sat some minutes after the Lieutenant left.

Finished the first book of Cicero on "Moral Duties." I can hardly believe the translation does Cicero justice in this: "All who follow mechanical pursuits are mean." I cannot think his idea was that there was any moral deficiency in this class; their pursuits were simply not those of high ambition: that he meant to speak of themselves as viciously low or to be regarded with scorn is inconsistent with what he says elsewhere of the estimate in which even slaves should be held, and how they should be treated.

I see in the evening paper that the Macon *Telegraph* has an article expressing apprehension, endorsed by the Atlanta *Intelligencer*, of a Negro insurrection. I cannot think there is any real foundation for this.

6.15 — I was truly glad to see Lieut. Woodman enter my room for the evening walk. He is the only man I have met here who begins to fill the place of an acquaintance. He even begins to fill that of a friend, or I begin to give him such a place in my feelings. Walked on the terreplein. Was weak, but stronger than I have been. I rested a while; as the sun was sinking, I got a view of the new moon in perfect crescent form. If there is anything in signs, I shall certainly have *good luck* this moon; for I got, directly over the right shoulder, a clear view of her in an unclouded sky. So we shall see how it will turn out. Perhaps I may be as unfortunate in this sign as Dave Holt was in his sign of a wet moon. The story Dave told of himself was, that after losing all his money gambling in Kentucky, he had to foot it home to Georgia. In Tennessee he could go no further without money and had no way of raising it except by work. A farmer offered him ten dollars and board for a month's work at splitting rails; it was about dark; Dave had no other hope for lodging. He happened to glance at the new moon; all signs portended much rain. He said he would accept if he should not be required to work in the rain. The farmer agreed. Dave expected he would not have to work half his time, for, he said, it was a "perfectly dripping new moon." To his mortification, twenty-six of the driest days he ever saw succeeded.

This Dave Holt was author of the letters signed "Ned Bucket," and published by papers all over the country. Who "Ned Bucket" was, nobody for a long time knew. The letters were humorous, witty, and sometimes scurrilous. Anonymous letters came to be called "Bucket letters." This is the Dave Holt who made the celebrated speech at Montgomery, Ala., on the departure of volunteers to aid Texas in 1834 or '35; Dave, again broken in fortune, was one of that band of patriots. Funds had been raised to equip the volunteers; a boat chartered to take them: a flag with a lone star was to be presented, an orator was appointed. A crowd assembled to bid the soldiers adieu. The presentation speech was made on the banks of the river. To this Dave responded, from the deck, in behalf of his comrades. His speech was short and pithy:

> Fellow citizens, ladies and gentlemen:
> This great cause is little understood:
> We patriots here form a noble band
> Who quit our country for our country's good.

He was at the Alamo, but escaped from the massacre. When asked how he got away, and if he did not run he said, he did "some tall walking." Dave was a character.

After my sight of the new moon, I descended with Lieut. W. to the plane below, and paid a visit to Dr. Seaverns's office; sat with him a while, and made the acquaintance of the hospital steward, a curious character. He keeps a register of the weather. Told me that he used to be at Old Point. Knew my friend, Judge Wayne, and his son-in-law, Dr. Cuyler. Returned at sundown to my cell. For supper, took a glass of milk, and some blackberries, the first I have seen this year. I ate more for supper than for several days. I feel a great deal better than for a week. Oh, if I could only keep my health.

Thursday — Did not rest well in the night. I was still feverish. The flies, which have become numerous in my room and very annoying, prevented me from sleeping after daylight. Read in Job. My spirits underwent the changes of the tide. At low ebb, they chimed in with the sentiments of the third chapter; and they rose to the point of fortitude, patience, hope and faith as I reached the close of the fifth. Breakfast: Geary brought plain cornbread for the first time. I have asked for this but the cook did not know how to prepare it. I gave directions and she has succeeded pretty well.

I am sitting in a quiet meditation, smoking my second pipe, free from pain except the uneasiness that accompanies weakness. This is the ninth round of seven days since I have been in this prison. This too is the 27th of July, a day ever memorable to me as the anniversary of important epochs in my life. On this day in 1827, a boy, I quit my then home at my uncle and guardian's, and started to school at Washington, Ga. That was a great turning point in my life. Thursday, 27th July, 1843, when 32 years old, I started from home on my first electioneering tour in a canvass for Congress. That, too, was another great turning point. These points, their turns, and the roads taken in both cases, led me here. Perhaps it is best for me that I am here. Believing in the providence of God, I so accept it.

I delivered to Geary four short letters for mailing. One was to Linton by way of Augusta, one to Raymond Burch, one to Miss Nichols, Washington, D. C., and one to S. J. Anderson, New York. This is a sultry morning. The sun shines hotly in my room. There is no air stirring. From appearances, it will be one of the hottest days of the season. It is now only 9 a. m. My room, however, is always warmest in the forenoon; it fronts southeast.

Have been reading Cicero's second book on "Moral Duties." His standard of morality, honour, and virtue was very high. I know of none higher taken by Christian philosopher. Paley's [English divine and moralist] is not so high. If writings can be taken as index of the mind, I should think Cicero a better man than Paley. I feel disposed, however, to condemn one point he makes speaking of advocates: "The duty of a judge in all trials to follow truth; that of a pleader sometimes to maintain the plausible though it may not be the truth." But he is not so objectionable as Dr. Paley on the same point. Paley says, "There are falsehoods which are not lies; that is, which are not criminal, as when no one is deceived, as is the case in parables, fables, novels, jests, compliments in the subscription of a letter; or a servant's denying his master; or a prisoner's pleading not guilty; or an advocate asserting the justice of, or his belief in the justice of, his client's cause. In such instances, no confidence is destroyed because none was reposed; no promise to speak the truth is violated because none was understood to be given." Now, in some of these instances, the doctrine laid down is monstrous. It so seemed to me when a boy at college and it has so seemed to me through life.

I could never justify the practice of having a servant say his master or mistress is not at home when the reverse is true. Such practice lessens the regard of servants for the truth for the truth's sake; it instills the principles of prevarication. They cannot discriminate between a lie of this sort and any other told to answer convenience; if, indeed, there can be any discrimination, which I doubt. How much more conducive to good morals, to let the servant say that the master or mistress is engaged, or cannot receive company. Cicero tells a good story illustrating the absurdity of this polite custom of "denying." Some Roman of distinction, calling to see his friend, was told by the servant that the master was not at home, when the visitor knew otherwise. Soon after, this friend called on him. Hearing inquiry made of his servant, he spoke out, telling the visitor he was "not at home." "But," said the visitor, "don't I see you and know that you are at home?" The other replied, "Why, I had to believe your servant the other day, and can't you believe me?"

What Paley says of a pleader being justified in asserting the justice, or his belief in the justice, of his client's cause, leaving inference that he may rightfully do this when he does not believe as he asserts, seems wrong in principle and highly immoral. It goes further wrong than Cicero, who says only that the pleader may maintain the plausible, that is, I suppose, present the plausible view to judge and jury without declaration of belief in its truth. Even to that extent, the rule cannot receive my sanction, if the advocate knows the fact to be contrary to his view. When he is in doubt as to how the fact really is, then I hold that he is not only justified in presenting the case of his client in as fair and plausible light as possible, but that it is his duty to do so. When he is convinced of the truth or justice of his client's case, his whole soul should be thrown into its defense; but in all that is said or done by him in this, the strictest regard to truth, propriety, and decorum, should be maintained. All cases involving the principles here discussed depend on matters of fact, or questions of law, or both combined: that is upon conclusion of law from matters of fact. No advocate should ever assert as matter of fact in his client's case what he knows is not such; any code of morals justifying him in this does not deserve the name. The same is true as to any assertions he may make touching the law of the case. Lawyers should be bound, in all they do and say, by the same strict and pure principles of morality that should bind other persons. By this rule I have ever held myself governed.

My rule from the time I was admitted to the bar was: first, to investigate a case submitted to me, to inquire into the facts and the law applicable to it; then, if I did not believe the party entitled to success before the court, I told him so and declined to appear or prosecute the case. Cases are often very complicated, presenting great variety of facts as well as involving many points of law; such, I have never hesitated to take and to do with them the best I could, if on any points there seemed to be right or justice with my client, or if what was right and just in the premises was unsettled and a matter of doubt. These remarks apply particularly to civil and equity cases. My rule in criminal cases has been never to appear in capital cases for the prosecution of any one whom I did not fully believe guilty as charged, and not always then. When I have appeared for the prosecution, it has been only when the nature of the offense was such as made it my duty, apart from all pecuniary considerations, to aid in bringing the offender to justice. In defense of persons charged with homicide, I have seldom declined to appear; I have never failed to appear when there was the least doubt as to the fact, the motive, or the criminal intent; or the proper conclusion from the facts, the intent, and the law. I know how readily from sympathy we may be misled in judgment concerning the actions of those in whose cause we are enlisted. I am prone from constitutional tendency to sympathize with unfortunates in distress from any cause whatever. Hence, I am fully conscious of how my judgment, touching the real guilt of those I have defended, may have been misled. But I can say that I never defended any person charged with crime when I did not fully believe every position as to fact, motive, and law, assumed by me before judge and jury.

I never appeared in the prosecution of a person charged with murder who was not condemned, and no client of mine, white or black, was ever hung. One that I appeared against died before the time set for execution; the other (there were but two) was hung. I engaged in the prosecution of another case but gave it up before trial, on my election to the vice-presidency. I have had clients who on first trial were found guilty and sentenced to be hung, but new trials were granted for error in the rulings of the judge; and final acquittal, or a modification of the verdict, reducing the grade of offense from murder to manslaughter, which I insisted was the right finding, has been the result in all. I have not, in every case, fully believed in the innocence of the accused whom I defended. For instance, in the case of a woman charged with poisoning her husband: there was no latitude for motive, no grade in the offense, most foul was the crime; all the evidence was circumstantial; the links in the chain were incomplete: it was far from being conclusive either way. I did not hesitate to throw my energies before judge and jury in presenting the inconclusiveness of the testimony, and insisted that under the law, when there was doubt, there should be acquittal. There was an acquittal. This was nearly twenty years ago. The woman is still living, or was lately. No further discovery has ever been made.

On Paley's idea, lawyers, as a class, are nothing but a set of mental prostitutes whose calling is to make a living by lying, and who are excused from all responsibility to the moral law in this respect from the fact that their infamy is so notorious that nobody is expected to believe them, and upon the principle that where there is no deception there is no falsehood, and no crime or turpitude in telling a lie. In vindication of that profession to which I belong and which has been the pride and glory of my life, I propose to say a few things.

No pursuit in life is more honourable or useful than that of the law, when followed as it should be. None requires more rigidly a stout adherence to all the precepts and principles of morality, or the possession and practice of the highest and noblest virtues that elevate and adorn human nature. Not even the office of the holy minister opens up such a wide field for simply doing good to one's fellow man. The lawyer's province is to aid in the administration of justice, to assist the oppressed, to uphold the weak, to contend against the strong, to defend the right, to expose the wrong, to find out deceit, and to run down vice and crimes of all grades, shades, and characters. What a field is his for calming passions, allaying strife, composing disputes, settling quarrels, and quieting contentions.

A good lawyer is ever a peacemaker. Pettifoggers there may be whose sole object is to stir up litigation that they may profit by it. The man who enters the bar with soul fired by aspirations fitting his high vocation, looks to nothing but the advancement of justice. The tangled web of most private controversies can be better unravelled and straightened by bringing the parties together in private conference than by carrying them into court. This the lawyer, properly imbued with the spirit of his calling, will always strive to effect. Contentions that originate in impulse, passion, or misunderstanding can often in this way be speedily adjusted and reconciliations brought about. In controversies involving doubtful questions of law in the settlement of estates, the descent of property, construction of wills and conveyances, the judicial forum must be the resort. But with what intense regard for truth, for right and justice, does the lawyer investigate facts and pore over his books, preparing himself for such occasions. In the Temple of Justice he glories in the fact that everything is weighed in her scales. Reason and wisdom are his necessary weapons. The materials to be handled are human acts coloured with human passions, prejudices, and infirmities. What a field here for exhibition of the noblest virtues in exposing knavery, fraud, villainy, and falsehood of every sort, and of securing to honesty, right, and truth, their just reward.

The lawyer is brought in contact with men of all characters, the lowest and the vilest as well as the highest and purest. Hence, his means of acquiring thorough knowledge of human nature are superior to those of all other classes combined. His opportunities, not only for allaying strife, settling quarrels, and bringing about reconciliations, but for giving proper rebuke to crime and iniquity, are better and far more numerous than those of the minister of the Gospel. He sits, as it were, in the marketplace and on the highways; not a day passes in which he may not and should not dispense with a liberal hand the Christian charities of his counsel in the succour of the needy, the destitute, the wronged, the widow, and the orphan. There should be nothing mean or low about him. He should understand the shifts of fraud, deceit, and cunning, in order to be able to circumvent those who deal in these, without ever practising or countenancing them himself; but, on the contrary, ever exposing and holding them up to condemnation. He should have no ambition but to serve his fellow men and to do good. In doing the greatest possible good to others, he achieves the greatest good for himself.

The doctor has not called to-day: it is now near six. I looked anxiously for letters by morning mail, and by the evening, but none came. I grow anxious to hear from Linton. Why do I not get that other letter he wrote? or the letters written by him since? Only greatest efforts prevent me from falling into deepest melancholy while thinking of him. Tears start when my thoughts turn toward him. O my brother! how I pray my God for you! that He may protect, guide, and direct you! I felt much better the forepart of the day. Now, gloom seems creeping over me like the twilight which foreruns the night.

Lieut. Newton did not come for the walk until 6.30. I was impatient, fearing something had happened. Lieut. Woodman has gone to Boston again. I fear I shall see little more of him. His main duties here have been to look after prisoners. All of these are gone except Reagan, myself, Vernon, and Binckley. I do not know if I have before stated that Vernon is an Englishman, or claims to be such. He was captured on a blockade-running expedition, and will not take the oath; if he would, he would be discharged. Lieut. W. will spend, I expect, but little time at the fort between this and the mustering out of his company, which he looks for the first of August. In my walk, I called and sat a while with Dr. Seaverns. Then went on the terreplein to where I used to see the Confederate officers. It made me sad.

I saw quarters where DuBose and Jackson lodged so lately. Oh, if I could then have gone where I was this evening and talked with them, what relief it would have been to me! Geary brought tea and bread for supper. No milk.

July 28.—Did not sleep well. Cause, general weakness, perhaps. I lay on my bunk quietly but sleeplessly. After the relief guard at 12.30, went into slumber which lasted until day. Rose at 6.45. "Truly the light is sweet and a pleasant thing it is for the eyes to behold the sun." Read Ecclesiastes. In this book is practical wisdom for everyday life. It is a matter of doubt to me whether Solomon believed in the immortality of the soul. Some portions of his treatise indicate that he did; others that he did not. For instance:

> For that which befalleth the sons of men befalleth beasts: . . . as the one dieth, so dieth the other; yea, they have all one breath; so that a man hath no preëminence above a beast; for all is vanity. All go unto one place; all are of the dust, and all turn to dust again. Who knoweth the spirit of man that goeth upward, and the spirit of the beast that goeth downward to the earth?

His standard of morals in these writings is high; uprightness of conduct in all things, and in all conditions in life, from subject to ruler, with purity of heart, and reverence and devotion to God, is strongly enjoined. This, he teaches, is best for man and society without regard to a future state, or without any argument drawn from that view. "Sorrow [even without looking further than this life] is better than laughter: for by the sadness of the countenance the heart is made better." My opinion, founded upon observation, is that adversity makes men better or worse. It is never negative. It is a terrible crucible.

Daily papers. I see another letter from Fortress Monroe about the health of Mr. Davis. He is permitted to walk out. I am truly glad to know this. I was very anxious to get letters. I do not understand why I hear nothing further from Dr. Willis or Linton. I was also expecting to hear from the application sent on for mitigation of my confinement, but it is now near noon. As no announcement has been made to me of any reply, I take it for granted that if any has come, it is unfavourable. I rejoice that I am so much better than when the application was made, that I can, I trust, now stand an unfavourable reply. Then, I do not know how it would have been. Dr Seaverns called, while I was reading Ecclesiastes. It is the earliest call he has ever made me.

The drum is beating the hour of noon. It is a clear hot day. Finished Cicero's third book on "Duties." I like his doctrine against concealment of defects, quality, etc., in matters of trade. Open, fair, honest dealing alone is honourable. It marks the upright man. Walked the room until mail hour. Lieut. Newton brought me the book Burch sent, Savage's "Representative Men."

6.15 — Walked out with Lieut. N. Called at Dr. Seaverns's. We walked around the parapet, three-quarters of a mile, I think. Find Lieut. N. agreeable, and disposed to talk. He gave it as his opinion that it would be windy to-morrow; said he had signs for wind and rain. His sign for wind were clouds which he pointed out: one of his signs for rain is when swallows and seagulls fly low, near the ground or water. For supper, I took bread and water.

July 29. — Geary, by direction, put on no coal this morning. He kindled a wood fire; this was to make sufficient draft to clear the room of tobacco smoke and other impurities. The morning clear and hot.

Read the Song of Solomon. How this book came amongst the inspired writings, I cannot imagine. Who gave the headings of the chapters, as, for instance: "The church's love for Christ. 5. She confesseth her deformity. 7. and prayeth to be directed to his flock. 8. Christ directeth her to the shepherds' tents," etc. I should like to know upon what authority or principle it was done. To me it is inexplicable. From nothing in this composition can I perceive that any such allegory was in the mind of the writer. It seems only such love-songs as Solomon may be supposed to have indulged himself in writing. Nothing in it is of a debasing character; in this it is far above the standard of many such productions. But that Solomon had any idea of Christ, or the Christian Church in his mind in writing these love ditties, if they be so termed, I see no grounds for conception. This interpretation of the text seems to me not only a forced construction but not much short of impious.

Wrote to Sheppard Knapp, President of Merchants' Bank, New York, asking to be informed if Dr. Willis had reached New York and had got the letter I addressed him, care of Knapp.

9.30 — Dr. Seaverns called. Sat and talked some time. He told me that Major Allen, who commands here, has been ordered to take command of his Regiment, the 2d U. S. Artillery; is to go to San Francisco. Major

Appleton, of the 1st. Mass. Vol. Art. Reg., now stationed here, is to command for the present. This regiment, it is expected, will soon be mustered out. The doctor remains, but does not know how long. He expects to have other duties assigned him soon. Into whose hands I am ultimately to fall, I do not know. I was introduced to Major Appleton several evenings ago in my walk with Lieut. W. He seemed kind and agreeable. I met him again yesterday at Dr. Seaverns's. I don't know that my situation will be worse under him than it has been. I asked the doctor if he had heard anything from his recommendation in my behalf. He said, "Not a word."

CHAPTER XVIII

JULY 29. — Oh, what a change has come to me since the last sentence was penned! As I was finishing the last word, Dr. Seaverns entered my room, and announced that he had just got an order authorizing my release from close confinement. The boat had come while I was writing, bringing the mail and with it the order. He took it out and read it to me. By it, I am allowed to go in and out at pleasure, and walk the grounds when I choose, between sunrise and sunset; see any member of my family or any of my personal friends; and converse with officers and persons in the fort besides those having special charge of me. In other words, I am simply put on parole in the fort. This was elating and joyous news. At least, one might so imagine and I should have thought so ten minutes before; but it brought from me a flood of tears, an outburst of weeping. The doctor instantly retired.

Lieut. Newton soon came and read me a duplicate that Major Allen had received; and immediately took the lock off my door. No language can express the relief that sound gave me — the sound of the clanking iron as it fell upon my ears. Jean Valjean could not have felt greater relief when the lid of his coffin was lifted and he was saved from being buried alive. The clanking of that same iron when I was for the first time locked up in a prison had penetrated to my very soul!

I instantly wrote two letters to Linton, announcing

the fact and urging him to come to see me as soon as he could. I gave them to Geary to be mailed. I then thought of writing to President Johnson, thanking him for the order. A doubt arose. Was it proper to return thanks for what I considered my due by rights? I did not deliberate long. How others might consider it I do not know, but the rule I have adopted for myself in all such cases is to do what I think right, what my own impulses dictate, without regard to the opinion of others. Because he has done me a wrong is no reason why I should not do right. The Scriptural rule is to bless those that despitefully use you. I addressed him a short note of sincere and grateful acknowledgments.

I wrote two letters to Linton because I wished to send by different routes — one by Augusta and one by Atlanta through Gip Grier, hoping one or the other might reach him in the shortest possible time. Lieut. Newton then brought me two letters from home; from William G. Stephens, 17th July, and Mr. Bristow, 18th July. So this has been a day of good things. By both I learned that all were well and that the corn crop was promising; the wheat had been thrashed, measuring 126 bushels. There were good rains at the time, which will, I trust, secure the corn crop. In great thankfulness to God, the giver of all good, was my heart uplifted.

Dinner. I had more appetite than yesterday, and ate more freely. I took a drink of Harry's whisky. This was in remembrance of him. Spent the evening walking in and out the shady passes; and reading Cicero on "Friendship." It was a great relief to me to walk out and in as I pleased and to feel once more that I am in some measure a free man.

At 5 went to Dr. Seaverns's office. He was gone to

Hull. Conversed with Harrington. I saw his thermometer and hydrometer. Met Lieut. Newton. Nearly the first thing he said was, "I told you it would be windy to-day." Sure enough, it has been. I went into the library and made the acquaintance of the Librarian, Mr. Barnham, as I understood his name to be. I then, alone, walked slowly, resting at times, all around the fort on the terreplein, looking out upon the sea which was now a true emblem of my soul in full tide. But as that tide shall subside, so must it be with this tide in my feelings.

On my return met Major Allen, just back from Boston. He shook me by the hand and congratulated me. Stated that he leaves Monday. Major Appleton was present and seemed kind and agreeable; Mrs. Appleton came up, and he introduced me. She gave me some pretty and fragrant flowers, for which I thanked her. She is quite a young-looking lady, and very agreeable in manners. At sundown I returned to my quarters.

Geary brought a glass of milk and some blueberries. He also kindled a small wood fire. I had had no fire in my room since morning. This is my first day here without constant fire, which is necessary, hot as the atmosphere may be, to keep the room dry, and clear it of smoke and other impurities. To-day, I smoked outside of my room.

Sunday — Slept better than for a week. Rose refreshed. Walked out at my own pleasure, without let or hindrance. I no longer live in my room. Wrote to Mr. Bristow and to Wm. G. Stephens and directed letters to care of Gip Grier, Atlanta; delivered them in person to Major Allen to be mailed. I called on him, not only to deliver the letters but to see about the parole I am to give under the new order. He was very friendly and affable, and told me the Adjutant would attend to the parole; he expects to take his final leave of the fort to-morrow. Returned to my quarters. Lieut. Wm. Ray brought me a copy of the new order which is in these words:

HEAD QUARTERS OF THE EAST,
NEW YORK CITY, July 27, 1865.

Telegram received:

"WASHINGTON, July 27, 1865.

"*Major General Hooker:* By directions of the Secretary of War, the Commandant at Fort Warren is authorized to extend to Mr. Stephens any indulgence and freedom from close confinement that may be beneficial to his health and to allow him to have enjoyment of books, papers, and society, with exercise in the open air, and furnish him such indulgence in fruits, food, and beverages as may be agreeable to him and beneficial to his health, using proper precautions for his safe detention, or taking his parole to remain in custody and make no effort to escape. He may receive the visits of his family and personal friends under such restrictions as the proper police of the Fort may require.

Acknowledge receipt.

(Signed) E. D. TOWNSEND, A. A. G."

Official copy respectfully furnished for the information of the commanding officer Fort Warren.

(Signed) D. T. VAN BUREN,
Br. Brig. Gen. A. A. G.

Also brought in duplicate my parole under the above order, which I signed. It is:

I, Alexander H. Stephens, of Georgia, hereby give my parole of honour that I will not make any effort to escape or communicate with any soldier (other than the officers of this Fort), prisoner, or citizen, without permission. That I will remain in my quarters during the hours from retreat to reveille and from half-past three to half-past four p. m., also during the time the steamboat is at the wharf, and that I will not knowingly violate any rule or regulation of the Post (which in duplicate I sign).

Fort Warren, B. H.

ALEXANDER H. STEPHENS.

In looking at the date of order, I was struck with the fact that it is 27th July, a notable anniversary of two important events in my life.

Reviewed Matthew. No one, it seems to me, can study the teachings of Jesus without being deeply impressed with their extraordinary purity and sublimity, viewed simply in the light of human teachings. The more one is versed in the lore of ancients or moderns on morals and wisdom, and in all that philosophers have declared on ethics and casuistry, the more deeply is one impressed with the preëminence of the code of Jesus. The standard raised by Jesus is the image of divinity itself. Some things in this gospel strike me as strange. Why did Jesus tell those on whom he performed miraculous cures to say nothing about it? Why enjoin his disciples not to make known that he was the Christ?

3.30 — Lieut. Newton called and brought me a small paper-box filled with fruit, and a note, from A. W. Salter, Boston, presenting the fruit, and couched in sympathetic terms. These are the first ripe peaches I have seen this year. Who this kind friend is, I cannot imagine. I must find out if possible. The handwriting is like a lady's, very much like Mrs. Craig's* used to be. When

* Daughter of Dr. Church, President of the State University (of Ga.); by her second marriage, Mrs. Robbe lived North and befriended Confederate prisoners.

I saw the address on the note, I thought it must be from her.

I am not as solitary as I thought. Coming in just now from a stroll in the long passage, I saw a mouse darting across the room and seeking shelter in an opposite hole. He had been feeding on crumbs that fell from my dinner when the plates were removed to the window sill. The poor creature seemed terribly frightened and made escape with the greatest dispatch; but he need not; I would not have hurt him; I would have petted him. I must tame this mouse if I can.

6 P. M.—Went to library. Librarian not in. Went to see Dr. Seaverns. He had gone to Hull. Sat with Mrs. Seaverns in the parlour. Looked over the doctor's books. Walked out and wound my winding way on and around the terreplein. Met Majors Allen and Appleton and Mrs. Appleton, they coming one course and I going the other. She descended from the parapet (they were on that) and gave me a bunch of sweet-scented flowers. After thanks, etc., and a few words more, I pursued my way and they theirs. Before I got half round, I came to them again. It was at the western bastion, where there is a bench; they were seated. They invited me up. Major Appleton came to assist me. This kind act I could not repel by refusing, so, with his aid, I ascended the parapet, and sat with them about fifteen minutes in agreeable conversation. It was getting late and cool, so I returned to my quarters. Geary had a good coal fire, as I had directed. He brought me for supper milk and bread. I took some of my sugar and one of my peaches and made a good dish of milk and peaches. On receipt of these peaches, I got Lieut. Newton to take six to Judge Reagan. At least, I asked him to do it

if not against orders; told him he need not inform Judge Reagan where they came from, but simply say a friend sent them. I have not seen him since to know what passed between him and Reagan on the delivery. I hope Reagan relished them.

July 31. — Twelve months ago this morning, then Sunday, Linton and I left Sparta for my home in Crawfordville. On that night was what he called our "Hegira to the Homestead." Never can I forget that night and its incidents.

The bugle sounds the hour of noon. I have just returned from a stroll. The air was pleasant and bracing, the walk was one of the most agreeable I have taken. I met Mrs. Appleton and passed the morning salutations with her.

5 P. M.—Went out on the terreplein. Walked all around twice, resting now and then. Encountered many persons, ladies and gentlemen, who seemed visiting at the fort. Some gazed at me intently. One man with two little boys went down to the library evidently with the sole purpose of getting a view of me; for he, with the boys, got there just as I was leaving and turned back as I came up. The library is on the same level with my quarters, that is, partly underground. On the walk I wore a new hat I got from Boston to-day through the sutler. The old one was looking shabby. Returned about sundown to my quarters. Met Dr. Seaverns; he had been to see me.

The evening paper gives an account of General Grant's reception at Faneuil Hall. Sunday's *Herald* and this morning's *Post* describe his arrival in Boston on Saturday. General Grant is a remarkable man and, if he lives and continues in good health, will figure largely in the future history of this country. I consider him one of the most remarkable men I ever saw. He is modest, unassuming, and possesses a wonderful degree of common sense, a thing uncommon in his day amongst men of position and station. I was never more surprised in any person than in General Grant when I saw him at City Point last February. Very soon after being in his company, I was deeply impressed with his genius and character. What is to be his future, time will determine. But the measure of his deeds and fame, whether for good or evil, is very far from being felt yet. The impression he made on me was favourable in every respect. In manners he is simple, natural, and unaffected; in intercourse, frank and explicit; in thought, perception, and action, quick; in purpose, fixed, decided, and resolute. His ambition, if such may be termed his aspirations, is high, honourable, and noble. Such is the opinion I formed of General Grant in my first acquaintance with him. Such is my present opinion.

Had Mr. Lincoln lived, under his administration with General Grant's counsels, the condition of the Southern States at this time, I think, would have been far different from what it is and will be. I look with more interest to Grant's future than to that of any man living. Every man is more or less the creature of circumstances. He is no exception to this rule. How far he may hereafter be controlled by circumstances which he cannot control, is a problem in the solution of which the destinies of this country are deeply involved. He is the Great Man of the Continent; great, not in learning, acquirements, or accomplishments, but in conception, thought, and action; one of those master spirits which seldom fail, if life and vigour of faculties continue to impress themselves upon the age in which they live and to mark grand epochs in their country's history.

Saw nothing of my mouse to-day. If he is about, he kept close, though I noticed that a piece of potato which I placed on the floor for him, should he seek food while I was asleep, was gone when I got up. Whether Geary or the mouse removed it, I do not know. I will bait my mouse again.

August 1. — Went up and witnessed the drill. Was unusually weak in the knees; could not stand long. Sometimes I fear I shall lose the use of my legs. Finished St. Mark. He is clear, as is Matthew, on Jesus's injunctions that His disciples should not reveal that He was the Christ. Yet Jesus told the High Priest that He was the Christ. A strange thing is Matthew's tracing Jesus's genealogy to David through Joseph, Mary's betrothed. How could this connect Jesus with David or Abraham in the line of regular descent? This reflection is directed into a new channel by what Jesus said in the Temple: "How say the scribes that Christ is the son of David? For David himself said by the Holy Ghost, The Lord said to my Lord, Sit thou on my right hand. David, therefore, himself calleth him Lord; and whence is he then his son?" It occurs to me that Jesus was impressing upon the people the truth that Christ was not, by prophecy, to be David's seed of the flesh; the idea that he was to be such being an error. Deep-rooted errors in the Jewish mind regarding the Messiah were hard to eradicate; even the disciples did not at once understand the incarnation; the error may have lingered in Matthew's mind when he was tracing the genealogy. It is plain that Jesus endeavoured to make the people understand that Christ was to be of the seed of Abraham and David not according to the flesh but the spirit.

The papers say that Captain Wirz,* of Andersonville, is the only military prisoner now in custody. The *Great Eastern* was to sail on the 21st or 22d ult. with the Atlantic Cable. Before many days, we shall hear something of deep interest from this effort to bridge the ocean with telegraph wires.

Lieut. Woodman returned to-day. He came in to see me. I was truly glad to see him. He feels to me more like an acquaintance and friend than any one I have met here. He made me a second call, bringing me a letter from Mrs. Raymond Burch. Lieut. Newton called and delivered to me a most beautiful bouquet, made of various most fragrant flowers, from Mrs. Captain Livermore. I installed it in a tumbler of water on my table.

12.30 — Just returned from a round on the terreplein. The men were all at their dinners, workmen and soldiers. Saw nobody but the guards. Never before has the fort presented such an appearance of quiet. I was never out at this hour before. Except for weakness in my two knees, I have felt pretty well to-day. If I had Linton here, I could spend the time pleasantly even in these bonds. Glancing over Cicero on "Friendship" occupied me until dinner. This book is an almost faultless production. Still, I believe Bacon's essay says more. But Bacon by no means supersedes Cicero. Bacon tears up the foundations of the philosophy, blasts the works from the quarries; Cicero polishes these rough materials

* Captain Henry Wirz was held responsible for brutal treatment of prisoners at Andersonville, where he commanded. He was included in Johnston's surrender and entitled to benefit of its terms, but he was arrested, tried by military commission, and hanged Nov. 10, 1865.

for use and ornament. Every young man should study Bacon on this subject: then he should study Cicero. I must postpone the notations I intended to make. My pen is in bad condition and my fingers are stiff and pain me.

Walked out, first to the library: door closed, librarian out. Went to Harrington's hospital rooms. Noticed his thermometers — the wet and dry bulbs; at 69 and 74, indicating great dryness in the atmosphere. Harrington told me the other day that he never knew the difference at this place greater than five degrees. It is therefore to-day at the maximum. Stopped at Dr. Seaverns's. He and Mrs. Seaverns were gone to Hull, the servant-girl said. She set a chair for me in front of the door, the doctor's easy-chair. I rested, and then ascended the ramparts to see the *Dictator* go out to sea; she was to go at high tide, about 6.30. How I got the information is rather an important fact in my prison life. While I was looking over the papers, Major Appleton paid me a visit. His object was to inquire about my diet, to ask how meals are served, and to make suggestions on that point if they are not served to suit me. It was all very kind of him. His visit seemed prompted by general motives of kindness rather than one particular object. During his visit he told me the *Dictator* was expected to go out. So I went on the ramparts to get a view of her.

On coming to the western bastion, saw Major Appleton on a bench, the only one on the parapet, with some gentleman whom I did not know. I passed on to where the musicians were performing, and took a seat on one of the circular stones on which the gun-carriages run around. Listened to the music. The band consists of 12 performers. After a while, Major Appleton joined me, taking a seat by my side. We conversed on the subject of grasshoppers, which, with locusts, and other like plagues, are a nuisance here just now. Mrs. Appleton joined us. Lieut. Woodman also. Nothing being seen of the *Dictator*, I proposed a walk to Lieut. W. He said good humouredly, "Well, it seems quite natural": and we started, I taking his arm as I was quite weak in the knees. We went around the terreplein, keeping outlook from the parapet for the *Dictator*. He showed me a large 200-lb. Parrot gun on the northern bastion, We met, and he introduced me to, Captain Livermore, whose wife has been so kind to me. Saw nothing of the monster monitor.

Night once more upon the earth; and I am alone in these quarters which constitute my present home. Unless the little mouse is eyeing me from his hole, I have no other companion. I think he is about somewhere; he may not be alone, may have plenty of company of his kind for aught I know. The bread I put out for him last night was all gone this morning. In speaking of companions, however, I ought not to omit the flies. I should do them as great injustice by such omission as they do me by their annoyance. I have much more of their company than I like. Perhaps I ought not to omit companions of another sort; whose nature is to stick to you closer than a brother and to keep you awake all night. Since my row with them the other day, I have not seen or heard anything more from them. If they have made any attack, it has been a sly one in small force. I have little doubt that some are about, for the fort is well stocked with them. Of course, I mean bedbugs.

Alone! Did I say? Oh, I am far from ever being alone. Right by my window the sentry or guard is ever walking; by night and day, in rain or shine, his step sounds on the hard stone. Like the ticking of a clock at all hours of the night that step is heard if I chance to be awake. Now, is this not company? The truth is, this is company, and I feel it to be. It is not exactly such as I like best, but prisoners cannot choose their company.

CHAPTER XIX

AUGUST 2.—Read St. Luke. Breakfast: salmon, steak, coffee, potatoes; and cornbread made according to my directions and better than ever before. Cook improving. Lieut. W. brought me copy of the *Republic*, of Richmond, July 11, which, he said, some of the generals had sent him. It publishes a list of persons whose property had been proceeded against for confiscation; some few are known to me.

A little girl, five or six years old, came into my room with a small bunch of sweet flowers, and gave them to me. Whose daughter she is, I know not. I thanked her kindly. Spoke soft words to her. She seemed pleased, and as she went out I heard her child's voice say to the guard, "He doesn't keep his door locked now."

I see in the *Post* that the President has had a relapse; the telegram says he is again too much indisposed to receive visits. General Dick Taylor, it is said, has returned to Washington from Fortress Monroe, having been permitted an interview with Mr. Davis. Am very uneasy about not hearing from Linton, Dr. Willis, or Mr. Knapp. There is something strange in this. Linton must have written. Why haven't I received the letters?

11.45—Walked out again. The sky is most blue and clear except where large fleecy clouds float lazily. Clouds and sky bring to my mind many a scene—scenes at home — at the old homestead — days in the field in my boyhood, and of late years too. Grass, clover, and vegetation here generally begin to wither and dry up, suffering for rain. Great numbers of grasshoppers are everywhere; never saw anything of this sort before. From the eastern bastion saw a large steamer going to sea. The noon signal was given. All hands, workmen and soldiers, except the sentries or guards, seem to knock off and take leisure at that hour. I remained on the terreplein, resting under the shade of the music-stand, thinking of scenes far away; of home, of Sparta, of Linton, and of where he and I were this time last year! We were at old man Robertson the woodwright's in South Carolina. We rested in the shade until our buggy was fixed; then we had a plain but good dinner in company with this strange philosopher of the wood-bench. I can now fancy ourselves there, lounging on the ground, waiting for the cool of the evening and thinking and talking of matters at home. Oh, that he were with me now! Why does he not write? Sorely was my heart fretted with these thoughts as I sat under the music-shed this day.

Lieut. Ray has furnished me with the following statement of my account with him up to 31st July:

Gold deposited	$560.
Premium on acc't sold $160.	53.20
	613.20
Bills paid	128.12
	485.08

Remaining on deposit in Gold . . .	$400.00
" " " " Currency .	85.08

Paid newspaper bill for July. Aggregate for all papers $6.27 — a rather frightful monthly expense. Ought I not to lessen it? I must consider this. Lieut. W. called and handed me *Harper's Weekly* of the 5th. This paper is always issued ahead of date. Its editorial in this, as in most issues I have seen here, is exceedingly bitter in feeling against the Southern people. Lamentable indeed will be the state of things in the South if such sentiment becomes predominant at the North. Should this be the case, what will become of the whole country I cannot imagine.

Had another row with bedbugs. I searched the coats I use as pillows, and the corners and edges of the shuck mattress; discovered a good many, though small. To none did I give quarter. Notwithstanding all my sadness of heart and lowness of spirits, the humorous did so lay hold of me while I was thus occupied, that I could hardly repress the inclination to laugh, especially when I suspected from suspension of footsteps that the guard was looking in on me engaged in this rather ungenteel work. My suspicion was but too well founded; turning toward the window, I saw him gazing upon me with intense curiosity. This did not cause me to desist. I was determined to make thorough work and rid myself of these pests if I could. It may be a low calling and a rather mean business in the eyes of one of my guards — this of a man pursuing and slaying bedbugs — but no one knows what he will come to. I hold nothing low or mean for a man to do which is necessary to health and comfort, when he has no one else to do it for him. It might be more becoming and more in accordance with the fitness of things were I to give my attention to a different sort of work which would enable me to procure from others this sort for myself. But when I am not permitted, I am bound by the laws of nature to do this service for myself. It may not always be so, or it may, and it may even be worse. Prison life is a horrible misfortune.

Evening *Journal.* Nothing of importance in it. I was anxiously looking for letters, especially from Linton or Dr. Willis; but none came from anybody. A man in prison is soon forgot, or little thought about, by the majority of those whom he considers friends. I know I am not forgotten by Linton: and the fact that I get no letter from him renders me very unhappy. Lieut. W. came to take me for a walk round the fort on the outside of the walls. We went out at the sally-port through which I entered here ten weeks ago to-morrow. The walk was pleasant, the scene new. I saw to our right, as we were going on the north side from west to east, some monuments indicating graves. Upon my inquiry, Lieut. W. told me there were a few graves there; one, that of a Georgian. I approached this; it is by itself, under a marble slab supported by granite pillars and inscribed to the memory of Johnston, Engineer of the *Atlanta.* He died 16th Oct., 1863. The monument was erected, as the inscription shows, by his brother officers, prisoners here at the time. Lieut. W. told me he died of a kidney disease. With a sigh to his memory, I passed on. I rested once on the circuit around the fort. We came in at the sally-port. I have not felt so well as yesterday. Pain in the left side; am weak and low-spirited. Now, while the shadows of evening gather, a corresponding twilight rests upon my soul.

Thursday, August 3.—Twelve weeks ago I was arrested and taken from my dear home. Ten weeks I have been an inmate of these walls. How long, Oh how long?

How many more weeks, months, or years, before I shall be permitted to visit that home — if that day is ever to come?

Lieut. W. called to let me know that the *Dictator* and the *Vanderbilt* were passing out. We went on the ramparts. The *Vanderbilt* came alongside the fort and we got a good view of her. The *Asia*, from Halifax, passed her just below the fort, firing two guns in salute; the *Vanderbilt* saluted by her flag alone. As the *Asia* passed the fort, she dipped the British flag; she had both United States and British flags flying, the former at the forward, the latter in the rear. Lieut. W. and another of the officers dipped the fort's flag in return. We were on the bastion by the flagstaff. Lieut. W. then carried me through one of the casemated bastions.

The heart yearned for letters, for something from Linton. It is nearly a month since the date, 6th July, of his last letter received. How long shall I be in suspense! Could I but get news that he is well! How it would revive my sinking spirits! When, Oh when shall I hear from him! Wrote to Gip Grier and to Harry. Lieut. Woodman brought me the "Life of John Wilson," which Mrs. Salter, of Boston, sent; he mentioned that she had addressed me a letter and he had informed her that all correspondence with me must be through the Commanding General of the Department of the East. We had a long and friendly talk.

While I was smoking after dinner, and promenading the passage, occasionally resting in the door at the end, a gentleman, a stranger here, saw me as I leaned against the door-facing. I perceived, in an instant, that he was agreeably surprised at something. He quickly went forward, and soon returned with several ladies, who stood and gazed down on me with marked curiosity. I stood, and gave them a fair opportunity to gaze to their hearts' content, puffing away at my pipe all the time. Who they were, I do not know. I don't think they evinced much sympathy for me; still, they may have felt kindly. One's feelings cannot always be judged by looks. It is enough, perhaps, that they evinced no unkindness.

Took up my book, stretched myself on my bunk; did not read far before I dropped asleep. Woke up when I heard the cry outside, "Boat! boat!" It was just 5; the evening boat had reached the wharf.

On the terreplein, I met little Annie Seaverns coming with a bunch of flowers for me. It was a beautiful little bouquet and quite fragrant. A thunder cloud lay over to the northwest. The thunder was not disagreeable music; it awakened long trains of recollections. There has been but little thunder here this summer. The clouds shut out the sun; it was very pleasant to walk. Oh, if I had Linton with me, how pleasantly we could spend the time here, even in my imprisonment! When I reached the western bastion, I found Lieutenants Woodman and Hibbell sitting on the bench. Lieut. W. assisted me up, and I took a seat with them. He handed me a letter, received for me this evening, from Mr. Baskerville, dated 31st July, replying to mine about the tobacco, and saying it had been sent by express. Mr. B. said my letter to Travis had not been received; Travis was there and well. This letter did me a great deal of good. On my way to my quarters, I passed Major Appleton sitting in front of his door. Stopped and talked with him. He mentioned an article on Headly [Washington's biographer?], that his father had spoken to him about; promised to get it and show it to me, if he could. I find that he is related to my old friend, Wm. Appleton, of Boston, and also to Appleton, of Maine, well known in our history. Samuel Appleton and his brother Nathan, he told me, are both dead. I am very much pleased with Major Appleton. Mrs. Appleton joined us before I left.

August 4. — Lieut. W. brought me a letter from Sheppard Knapp, 2d inst., which says Dr. Willis reached New York the evening before and had received my letter. The Lieutenant informed me that a Georgian, who had come to see me on permit from the War Department, was in his room; he believed the name was Abbot. He asked me to go up and see my caller. As we went out, he told the guard to let me pass up and down from my room to his during the day. He said that he was going out and would leave me with my friend. The visitor proved to be Mr. J. R. Parrott of Cartersville. I did not recognize him at first. I knew him well by name and reputation, but never met him to know him but once or twice before. This is the first old acquaintance who has called to see me since I have been here; at least, the first I have been permitted to see. I was truly glad to see him. It did me a great deal of good. We talked for some time. I wanted to light my pipe and thought we could enjoy ourselves better in my own room, so invited him down; but before we were seated, the guard came in and said it was against orders for Mr. Parrott to enter my room. I had understood that we might pass up and down at pleasure. But in this it seems I was mistaken, the permission applying to myself. I told the guard I regretted the mistake, and we returned to Lieut. Woodman's room, where we remained until Mr.

Parrott took the boat back to Boston. I had Geary bring dinner for both of us there.

Our conversation was long and agreeable. He had been in Washington for some time; came here because of desire to see me and to do anything for me he can. He told me that Senator B. H. Hill has been released. Expressed great desire that I should be; said it was through his offices that Governor Brown had had an interview with the President; or, as I do not recollect his exact words, that he had served Governor Brown all he could in getting a release. He knows the President personally. He expects to be in the Georgia Convention; said he was very desirous that I should be out of prison and in the Convention. I told him I was most anxious to be out either on parole or bail; I believed if I had not been released from close custody I should have died; I could not have stood it much longer; nor did I now think that I could stand long confinement here even on present terms. I had no desire to take part in public matters, yet, if permitted, should very cheerfully and willingly give my views upon some matters connected with suffrage. A wise settlement of Negro franchise I considered a matter of great importance for the future well-being of both races, especially if the blacks are to remain where they are. I gave him my plan. I said I should like very much to see the President and explain to him the system. If he approved, I should willingly make it known; if not, I should be silent. I was utterly opposed to throwing any obstacle in the way of the speediest mode that could be adopted for restoration of peace and harmony. The first great object of all the country's well-wishers should be the establishment of quiet, order, and civil government. As long as the policy of the

Administration was directed to this end, it ought to be supported by the people, though everything in it might not be best in individual opinions. I was anxious to see the Administration move back on the old track. Under present conditions, there could be nothing but confusion, lawlessness, and anarchy; military rule is, of all rules, the worst for any people.

I was highly gratified at this friendly visit. I feel greatly obliged to Mr. Parrott. He said he would do what he could for my release. I hope he may be able to do something effective. What effect the presentation of my views may have upon the President, if he makes such presentation, I have no idea. I am inclined to think the impression would not be favourable. For, somehow, I have an idea that the President is against allowing suffrage to the blacks in any form.

I bade him good-bye with a sad heart. Told him to see Judge Erskine, of Georgia, now in New York. and Judge Wayne and J. W. Forney in Washington; they might each and all do something for me, perhaps. If he would mention the subject to them, and they were willing, I should be greatly obliged. I cannot state one thing in a hundred that we talked about. Oh, how much we talked about Linton! His kind feeling as expressed toward Linton was the first thing that unlocked my heart for a free and full talk with him.

At Major Appleton's quarters, Mrs. Appleton handed me the publication on heraldry, of which the Major spoke yesterday. I was introduced to Miss Appleton, the Major's sister, I suppose. The Major soon joined us. We had a pleasant conversation. I think him an exceedingly clever gentleman. Mrs. Appleton is a charming woman. In the Heraldry *Journal* is a letter from me,

Feb. 11, 1854, to one Wm. H. Stephens of Copenhagen, N. Y. In the *Journal* I saw the Appleton coat-of-arms. The family dates back to 1300 and something. Returned at drumbeat to my quarters. For supper, milk and blueberries. Lieut. W. called and sat with me after drumbeat. Had a long and agreeable talk.

CHAPTER XX

AUGUST 5. — Read in John. Went up to see Lieut. W. He was out. Saw Captain Baldwin. He invited me into his parlour. Met two young ladies — Miss Ripley and another whose name I did not catch. Talked with the Captain until Lieut. W. came up. His room adjoins Captain Baldwin's quarters. Went in and saw him.

It is now ten, the hour this day last week that I was released from close confinement. One week since the last clank in locking and unlocking of my door fell upon my ears! The absence of that harsh, grating sound has, of itself, done me great good. But strange to say, the week since last Saturday seems the longest of my imprisonment. I have more incidents to measure time by. The days have certainly passed more pleasantly, but in retrospect the period seems much longer than for any other week. This, perhaps, is also due to my great anxiety to hear from home, and especially from Linton. Since my deliverance, to the extent that it has been granted, my whole soul has been yearning to commune with some congenial spirit in my better fortunes. May I get letters to-day!

No letter, but another visitor. H. G. Cole, of Marietta, called soon after the above entry. He was announced by Lieut. Woodman, who said he would bring the caller into my room if I preferred. I told him I should, and he soon returned with Mr. Cole. I received him gladly. We took our prison dinner together, just such a dinner as

Parrott and I had yesterday. We talked a great deal. The talk did me much good. This is the man for whose discharge from Charleston jail I made such exertions, without effect, last year. He was arrested in Marietta, 11th May, 1864, carried to Charleston, and kept in confinement until January with no charge preferred. I did all I could to get his release, but no heed was paid to my letters; I hear from him that those to himself were not received. This shows the carelessness of officials to have been worse than I knew. I alluded to his case in my speech before the Confederate Senate, when referring to abuses of military power and suspension of habeas corpus. Strange are the vicissitudes of life. He told me that Governor Brown was carried as prisoner through Marietta on the 11th May, 1865 — twelve months to the day from Cole's arrest, and on the same day that I was arrested. May Cole's efforts to serve me be more effectual than mine were for him! His will cannot be stronger than mine was. I bade him farewell with a sad heart. I have known him since 1840. What changes and scenes have we passed through since then! He left with me $100 in gold from Mrs. Judge Erskine, of Georgia, and $100 in greenbacks from himself. I took these amounts at his earnest request. I may need them, but I hope not. Lieut. W., who went to Boston to-day, has just come in and handed me some beautiful flowers, a paper box of peaches, and a bundle of papers, the London *Times*, from Mrs. Salter, of Boston. Oh that Linton would now come! When shall I see or hear from him? This has certainly been a day of good things to me, but one letter from Linton would have given my heart more relief than all these, much as I prize them. I handed Lieut. W. the money left by Mr. Cole.

5:30. — Walked out. A strange phenomenon struck my attention. A thundercloud had passed, and there seemed to be smoke coming over the walls on the eastern side of the fort as if a fire were outside. I ascended the parapet from the terreplein by the nearest flight of steps to see what it was, and found it fog. The whole sea was covered with dense fog, and as it would rise to the top of the walls it would sail over like smoke. On going round, I found it growing denser, and before I completed the circuit the whole was so filled with it that I could hardly see any person below. I was truly in a cloud. It swept by me like mist. The sun was for a while dimly visible through the mist, but became obscured. The fog came from the east. Thunder was heard in the distance. A steamer seemed to be stopped near by, befogged; she blew off steam for some time near the same place. It got so dark and thick above, I thought it might pour down rain, and descended to seek shelter. But I found very little fog below. I could see over the drill ground without difficulty. Dr. Seaverns was sitting in front of his door, and I went to see him and Harrington's hydrometer.

I sat and talked with Dr. Seaverns for a few minutes, when Major Appleton joined us. He handed me some extracts from a Georgia paper giving account of the meeting at Augusta, over which Judge Jenkins presided. Judge Jenkins's speech is most admirable. The Major said these extracts had come in a letter to General DuBose; he thought they might interest me; so, as General DuBose was gone, he handed them to me. He also handed me a pamphlet by Wm. H. Whitmore, entitled "The Cavalier Dismounted," requesting that I read it and give him my opinion, stating that he had not read it. Somebody had handed it to him in Boston. On the back is printed:

"We are the gentlemen of this country. *Robert Toombs in* 1860." I remarked that I thought Mr. Toombs had never uttered or written such a sentiment.

August 6.—I read "The Cavalier Dismounted." If the Major asks what I think of it, I shall refer him to Artemus Ward's interview with Brigham Young. Artemus remarked to the Prophet: "I believe you are a married man," to which the Prophet replied: "Pretty much." If Mr. Whitmore has made truthful exhibit of facts, I think the Cavalier is "pretty much" dismounted. But I am not inclined to yield the first point. I do not think his first text true; I have no idea Mr. Toombs ever said, or seriously said, what is ascribed to him. The writer puts up a man of straw and then claims credit for its demolition.

I regard any attempt by people of this republic to trace ancestry to the nobility of England or any other country as inconsistent with the spirit which should animate the breasts of descendants of the sires of '76, North and South. On the real issue in this pamphlet, that is, whether more "gentle blood" as it may be termed, of old England settled in New England or in the South, my opinion has always been that more settled in Virginia than in any other colony. Nothing more distinctly marks the character of a people than their religion. I believe Virginia was the only colony adopting the Church of England as its established system of worship. This shows the structure of her society, which in various respects followed more closely the English type than did that of any other colony.

To assume that the South was peopled by Cavaliers and the North by Puritans, making distinction thereby in the castes of the sections, is absurd. I know of but few persons who have ever attempted to impress such an idea upon the public. In some editorials in Richmond papers I noticed during the war some expressions inculcating this notion of caste difference and opposition, but I looked on these only as a device to inflame popular passions, and written perhaps by a New Englander domiciled in the South, as an evidence of his loyalty to the Confederacy. A few descendants of Cavaliers scattered through the South may also have employed such boast. Thus may have been influenced the Committee reporting on the Confederate Seal [a cavalier mounted].

A large majority of the colonists of the South were from other countries than England. Georgia, it is true, was planted by the English; yet little "gentle blood" was amongst her early immigrants excepting the trustees and superintendents. At the time of the Revolution her purely English element was comparatively small. The same may be said of North and South Carolina. Society in Virginia and South Carolina had more of the English tone than in the other colonies, and more in Virginia than South Carolina. In the former colony only, I think, did the tone impress itself upon the general ideas of the people. Notwithstanding the great influx of heterogeneous materials, there was still enough of this English element to hold the ascendancy and to move all other elements into its mode of thought, action, and development. The Episcopal Church was established, English ideas of aristocracy as to rights of primogeniture and as to other things were retained in a sort of apish fashion, nothing more; but even this seeming semblance of British aristocracy, so pleasing to the fancy of the F. F. V.'s [First Families of Virginia], did not obtain, I think, in any other colony. Nor did they find favour with the great majority in even that commonwealth at the date of the

Revolution, much less since. Every vestige of it, so far as external forms were concerned, was swept away under Mr. Jefferson.

That subordination of the black race which was called slavery gave rise to a certain development of society, not at all English, however, bearing some features of an aristocracy. But this was by no means so general as might be inferred from much lately seen in print about the subject of the "slave oligarchy" of the South. It was by no means the controlling force. In South Carolina alone, by her peculiar Constitution, could it be correctly said that the slaveholders as a class held the political power. The anti-slave element was always strong in Virginia; but for external agitation, I have little doubt slavery would have been abolished there long ago, or have been greatly modified. The same is true of North Carolina. Throughout the South no feeling was more general, none stronger with the voting majority, than a deep-seated detestation of the very name "Aristocracy." Eight-tenths of the people of Georgia, I believe, were thorough Jeffersonian Republicans and would have been as thorough abolitionists as Jefferson if they could have seen what better they could do with the coloured people than they were doing. They had a hard problem to solve, and the external agitation kept down internal inquiry and discussion as to whether there was any proper and safe solution. I do not think there was a county in Georgia where a man could have been elected to the State Legislature, or to any other office, upon the principles of an aristocracy, or if he were even known to favour any such doctrine.

As for Mr. Toombs, it was a matter of pride with him, a thing of which he boasted on the stump and the hustings, that Georgia had sprung from paupers and "tack-landers," that she had made herself what she was by her own exertions; as she was dependent upon none save herself for her achievements in the past and present, so he wished her to be in the future. Few men of his real genius and intellect, whom I have ever met, placed lower estimate than he on descent and heraldry. Deeds and worth, with him, constituted manhood. In writing to me from Europe in 1855, he stated that he had not been presented to a crowned head or a lord in the old world; his intercourse had been with the masses, with the people.

This morning, I finished John, in many respects most remarkable of the Gospels. John represents Jesus, on all occasions, as making known that he was the Christ. He makes no allusion to the injunctions, given by Christ, according to the other writers, that it should not be made known that He was the Christ. He makes no allusion to the Lord's Supper; this seems strange. He is the only one who mentions the washing of the feet.

12:45. — An editorial in the London *Times* states that Vice-President Stephens had written a very ingenuous letter, to say the least of it, about the Hampton Roads Conference. I suppose this alludes to the *Chronicle and Sentinel* publication. Thus it is with a man's character. A lie gets out: it is never headed off. Thus men form their opinions of other men through the medium of falsehoods. Not one in the thousands who will form a false opinion of me from that editorial will ever know the truth in the case, nor how harassed I have been by that misstatement.

In my walks saw a little boy reading. I stopped, took a seat by him, and rested while I talked to him. I asked what he was reading. A novel, he replied: it was a little primer-looking sort of a child's book. I asked him to let me see it. He handed it to me. It was a dime novel, "The Black Ship." I asked his name. He said he was Charles Nutler, son of the laundress here. On my further inquiry, he told me he was ten years old; had been to school in Boston from the time he was six until he was nine, which was last year, when his mother came to the fort. He has been here ever since, and has not been to school anywhere, but likes very much to read. He went to Sunday-school in Boston, but there is none here. He has studied reading, writing, and arithmetic; he is a promising boy. I told him he ought to read history. He said he would if he had any. "Call," said I, "at my room and I will lend you Prescott's 'Conquest of Mexico,' which is very interesting." "They won't let me go to your room," said he. "They won't?" said I. "Then, I will send it to you." "Who waits on you?" asked he. "Isn't it Corporal Geary?" "Yes," said I. "Well," he replied, "I will get him to bring it to me." "Very well. There are three volumes. I will send the first; when you finish that, I will send the second, and so on." "There are three volumes, are there?" said little Charles with a surprise indicating that he was assuming a bigger job than he had had any idea of. "Yes," said I, rising to go on with my walk, "there are three volumes, but they are not large ones. You can soon read them." With this I bade him good evening, and resumed my walk while he resumed his reading.

I came up with Major Appleton, Dr. Seaverns, and Lieut. Woodman standing in front of the Major's quarters. I told the Major I had read the pamphlet he lent me yesterday, and would bring it up to-morrow. He said I need not return it, and went on to ask what I thought of it. I told him I was interested in it, and commented on it "pretty much" as I have in these pages.

For supper, milk and bread. I feel very well to-night, though much weaker than yesterday. All things considered, I have passed this Sunday as well in mental feeling, if not better, than any since I have been here. I have been more quietly resigned somehow. I have great cause to be thankful to God for this condition of mind.

August 7.—Ante-breakfast reading in Acts. Peter, after the ascension, seems, according to Luke, to have remained in the belief that Christ was to come from the House of David after the flesh. This is strange. It shows how dimly even the disciples perceived at first the great truths of Christ's mediation.

To what I said yesterday about Mr. Toombs, it is proper to add that he was by no means disregardful of the good name of his ancestry; he simply never seemed to me to claim merit to himself barely on account of their good name. I have often heard him speak of them and their virtues. His father came to Georgia from Culpeper, Virginia. His grandfather, or great-grandfather, I forget which, came from England. During his sojourn in Europe in 1855, he visited the place from which his progenitor had come, and found branches of the family. Of a kinsman he met, he spoke in high terms as a man of great respectability and private worth of character; the Christian name I forget, as well as the name of the locality so sacred to himself in the "fatherland."

Toombs had great reverence for his parents; for their virtue, propriety, and uprightness, he revered their memory. His mother I knew. She was a most excellent

Christian woman. She died in 1848. He was devotedly attached to her, and was deeply affected by her death. His father died when he was only a few years old. He always spoke of his father with tenderest regard, but never boastfully. His father's energy, enterprise, and honesty were the attributes that seemed to claim his strongest veneration. Toombs was born, July, 1810, about twelve miles from my birthplace. I have often heard the old neighbours speak of his father as a man of strong and vigorous mind, a good neighbour and citizen, thrifty in business as a planter, and a most excellent, worthy man. Toombs himself has great fondness for agriculture. He is one of the most successful planters from the Potomac to the Rio Grande. His plantation discipline and his treatment of his slaves was on a perfect system of reason, justice, and humanity, looking as much to the welfare of his dependents as to his own pecuniary interests. Notwithstanding his engagements in law and politics, and the fact that his plantation was two hundred miles from his domicile, he held its management under complete control; planned all the crops, and by correspondence kept informed just how matters were going on, and gave directions. His system and its success was wonderful. He would have as overseers only men of sobriety, good sense, and humanity.

Toombs is one of the most extraordinary men I have ever known. As a talker, I have never known his equal. As a lawyer, I have never seen his superior before judge or jury. As a legislator in debate, few in House or Senate ever wished to encounter him; none ever did to win any laurels by it. His mind is very quick and active. Contrary to general opinion, he has always been a close and hard student; but his power of analysis and generalization are so great that he can acquire more in less time than any one I ever saw. In reading the report of a case, or an author on any subject, he at once seizes upon the real ideas, gleaning the vital part from the general verbiage by a process rapid as intuition. As public speaker or "stump orator," no one in any age or country ever had more power than he in the days of his prime. He was thoroughly read in local law, in United States history, and in national law. His true greatness did not consist in statesmanship; he was governed too much by passion and impulse. As lawyer, debater, popular orator, planter, political economist, it would be difficult to find his equal. His superior could not be found in his day.

As husband, father, and friend, his virtues show most conspicuously. He is generous, liberal, and noble. There is nothing sordid in him; nothing mean about him. He is open, bold, and frank to a fault. He has been, as he often says, his own greatest enemy in his freedom and extravagance of speech. His remarks are often pointed, cutting, and sarcastic, but there is no malice in his nature, not the slightest. Under impulse, he has often denounced in severest terms persons whom, when the excitement was passed, he would take cordially by the hand. There is not the least guile or hypocrisy in him; he speaks and acts just as he feels at the moment. Self-control and mental discipline he lacks more than anything else, to have made him one of the most influential men on the continent. He has brain enough, if its energy had been properly directed, to govern an empire. As there is enough waste of water at Niagara to turn the machinery of the world if it were controlled and applied, so with Toombs, there is and has been waste enough of mental power for want of system and discipline to control the destinies not only of this continent, but of all the nations intimately connected therewith.

Such are my opinions of the natural ability and genius of Robert Toombs. Of his defects, for he has them, as who has not, I will say nothing here. They were such as put upon him the stamp of human nature and the frailties incident to the fall of man. There is nothing in them, however, mean, low, or vile; nothing that impairs the lustre of his private and domestic virtues; nothing that touches the relations of husband, father, master, friend, or neighbour. Some spring from an undisciplined ambition, and some from nothing but an exuberance of good nature and conviviality. I have often thought of Toombs in reading of Alcibiades, although he is free from many vices that darkened the character of the Athenian. He is eminently a man of principle, and governed by the most scrupulous sense of right and justice in all matters except in those pertaining strictly to himself and the objects of his ambition. In this exception, lie some of the defects alluded to, but they are only small spots upon the sun as compared with the crimes of Alcibiades. In genius, he and the Greek have many points in common; and while in nothing is Toombs the Greek's inferior, in moral tone he is vastly the superior.

Dr. Seaverns called to see me, and to inform me that he is about to leave for New York, expecting to be gone two weeks, should so long leave of absence be granted. He expressed the opinion that perhaps he might not find me here on his return. I inquired if he had any reason for it. He said "No"; but that he does not think it the intention to keep me here long. This opinion would have been more cheering if grounded on anything authoritative. I received it as an evidence of the surgeon's personal kind feelings.

Went into the adjoining room, and offered to pay Mr. Devine, the tailor — he that gave me a pipe — for sewing a button on my pants Saturday before I got up; he would receive nothing. I thanked him sincerely and by way of making him some return that he could not object to, gave him some of my peaches. For this, the good lady who sent them would excuse me, I feel assured. Morning papers, but no letter. Oh how long, how long shall I remain in such suspense? My head aches. I see nothing in the papers I care a fig about. A letter from home, from Linton, is what I want. Sorely depressed do I feel to-day.

11.30 — Went to Lieutenant Woodman's room. Returned *Harper's Weekly.* Went to sutler's. Saw both the brothers Hall; had long and pleasant talk with them in their office or store. They told me that the things ordered had come — a button, Scotch Ale, and tin bath-tub. They gave me the button, and Geary came for the ale while I was there. I left at the noon or drum signal. Went on the terreplein. Walked round it twice. counted the steps and made it 1050; so, twice round is a little over a mile. Descended, somewhat fatigued but feeling better. Opened a bottle of ale and took a glass full with ice. Have been reading the "Life of John Wilson" [Christopher North]. Was much struck with this sketch of Miss Edgeworth in one of Lockhart's letters to Wilson: "Miss Edgeworth is at Abbotsford and has been for some time, a little, dark, bearded, sharp, withered, active, laughing, talking, impudent, fearless, outspoken, honest, Whiggish, unchristian, good-tempered, kindly, ultra-Irish body. I like her one day and damn her to perdition the next. She is a very queer character. Particulars some other time." This is rather racy word portraiture. Book laid aside. Musing, I have a presentiment that I shall hear good news. I don't think I am superstitious in the proper sense of that term, but I do believe in a Divine Providence and in His manifestations to me in spiritual communication. O Father, strengthen my belief! Whether this presentiment be true or not, O Father who knowest all things — things unknown to us — if this be but a vain fancy on my part, forgive its expression. Give me faith, patience, and fortitude.

Lieut. Woodman brought me *Harper's Weekly*. He remained some time and we talked about the Atlantic Cable. This was suggested by the *Tribune* on my table which compares the new cable with the old. The whole news-reading world will be agog and on tiptoe for a few days to know the result of the second great experiment to unite the Western and Eastern Hemispheres by telegraph. The *Great Eastern* is daily and hourly expected. A few days must end suspense on this big question. With earnest hopes for the success of the enterprise, I wait.

I read *Harper's Weekly*. My eyes are failing. Perhaps I use them too much. I cannot now, in this room at least, eat without the aid of glasses. I was surprised Friday when I went into Lieut. Woodman's room, and saw in his large mirror how white my head is getting. But the decline of my eyesight is far more serious than the whitening of my hair. For three or four days, the eyes have seemed weak and sore, apart from their dimness of vision.

A heavy cloud darkens the room so I can hardly see. A tempest of rain or wind, or both, is threatening. Not much lightning or thunder. The boat has come and gone. No letters for me — no news — nothing from home or any quarter. Oh, if those at home knew how I long for a letter from some of them, they would find some way to communicate with me or to get letters to me! Why do I not hear from Linton? My heart is sorely oppressed. It is now over a month since the date of his last letter. What is the cause of the delay? The rain pours, the floods come. Here I am, solitary and alone, in this darkened cell.

While the storm lasted, I went up to Lieut. W.'s room where I could look out, have more light; see the rain fall on the ground, always a pleasant sight to me, but which I had not witnessed since the shower that fell when we were on the *Clyde* in Hampton Roads. The Lieutenant showed me General Wade Hampton's letter to the people of South Carolina. From this it appears that Hampton has not left the State and does not intend to leave it, at least for the present. The letter is good in tone and spirit, but, in some respects, I question the policy advised. When the storm was over, I came down to my room, got my thick shoes and strolled forth. The sun was breaking through the clouds in the west; a rainbow was in the east. The ground was wet, but the air delightful. I had not walked long before Major Appleton joined me. We had a pleasant talk on rather abstruse subjects: nature, creation, the cosmos, life, the intellect, the soul, the Trinity, etc. I find that he is a Swedenborgian. He promised to let me have some of Swedenborg's writings. I have been waiting to learn something of this great theologian's doctrines. The walk and talk were very agreeable. The more I see of Major Appleton the more I like him.

CHAPTER XXI

AUGUST 8. — Rose at seven. Took a bath in my new tin bath-tub, the best I have had since I have been here. It was a perfect luxury. Strolled about. Took up "Life of Wilson" and stretched myself on my bunk. Had not read many pages before Major Appleton called with two pamphlets containing extracts from Swedenborg. Lieut. Woodman called; took my thermometer to see what it would stand at in his room.

10.30. — Lieut. W. again returned, bringing me a letter. The writing in the address I did not recognize. On opening it, how my heart leaped for joy when I saw from the hand, as well as the old blank-book paper, that it was from Linton. And only one who has gone through something similar can imagine how greatly rejoiced I was, when assured by its perusal that he and all were well; and especially, when by a second and third perusal, noting every word closely, I felt assured that he was in as good state of mind as I could expect or hope for. This letter was dated 20th July. There is some mystery about its detention. It was approved by General Hooker in New York on 1st August, eight days ago. It has been longer coming from New York than in reaching that point from Sparta. Whose is the negligence or fault? I cannot believe that the officers here are to blame; I am fully persuaded that they have promptly discharged their duty. This letter has done me a vast deal of good.

To the great Ruler of the universe, my heart goes up in gratitude. Oh, that He may have my brother and all that are his in His holy keeping! Though we are separated, may that brother's heart and mine beat in unison! He speaks of having written me four letters. Two besides this have come to hand. Of mine, he had received those of 3d and 8th of June and 4th of July; none of the rest. I do hope he has by this received mine of 29th July, and that he is on his way here or soon will be. May God bless, save, protect, and bring him to me speedily!

The papers say Mr. Seward has returned to Washington from Cape May. The *Herald* has a long article on the Atlantic Cable with maps, etc. Finished Swedenborg's "Doctrine Concerning the Lord." It is a master production, the clearest exposition I have ever seen of the doctrine of the Trinity. It embodies some ideas I have long entertained. But what seems to be his idea of the resurrection is not one of these. The Scriptural view, I think, is that our material bodies will rise with our spirits or souls.

A Real Prison Sketch, No Fancy About It

[*Prisoner* reading. Enter little girl, about four or five years old, standing at the door with some flowers.]

Prisoner. Oh what pretty flowers! Let me see them.

Child. [Handing them.] They are for you.

Prisoner. Ah! [Takes and smells them.] Thank you. They are so beautiful and so sweet. Where did you get them?

Child. My mamma gave 'em to me.

Prisoner. Ah! What is your name?

Child. Mabel Appleton.

Prisoner. Oh! It was you who brought me the flowers the other day! Those in the window—wasn't it you? See them in the window. Was it you that brought me those?

Mabel. Yes; and they are not faded yet.

Prisoner. No, I put them in water. [Rising and taking them down and showing them to her.] You see I have kept them fresh. They are almost as beautiful as when you brought them. Now, I am going to put these with them. [Puts them in the same glass.] See them, how beautiful they are! and smell, how sweet they are! [She takes the glass and smells.]

Mabel. My mamma says perhaps you will go away soon.

Prisoner. Ah, I hope I may. That would be good news to me.

Mabel. Why, what do you want to leave here for?

Prisoner. Oh, I want to go to my home and see all the folks there. I have some little girls, some little nieces, I want to see. One is just a little larger than you. She is a pretty, sweet little girl, very much like you. She wants to see me so bad and I want to see her and her little sisters. That is what I want to go home for. That is one reason I want to leave.

Mabel. What is her name?

Prisoner. Her name is little Emm Stephens.

[*Mabel*, looking on the floor, as if in profound thought about something, walks out.]

Prisoner lays down his book for some time. Thinks of home, little Emm, Becky, Claude, and their papa.

6.15. — Sallied forth on a walk. While I was on the bastion, six o'clock signal was given. From the ocean and the white-sail ships and dark-smoking steamers, my attention was drawn to a scene within the fort. The signal was of the day's end to all the workmen. Instantly, all noise of the stone-cutters ceased. Hammers, chisels, all tools, were dropped. The ground seemed alive with men moving about, as a schoolroom is alive with boys when recess is announced. Some go one way, and some another, for this article or that where it had been laid down during the day. All soon fall into a line to that part of the fort in which this class of inmates are quartered, some moving faster and some slower, some erect and some stooping. It is to me not an unpleasant spectacle, that of a weary labourer, coat on arm, trudging homeward from his daily toil at evening tide. It awakens many reminiscences of my youth. The associations are hallowed.

Lieut. W. joined me. We saw a propeller going to sea, a trading-vessel heavily laden. He told me that he leaves here soon. He has made arrangements to go into the hotel business at Hilton Head, S. C. He intends to leave by September. I was sorry to hear of his going. I should feel very sad at being left here by him. He asked me if I knew a man named Dawson, of Georgia. I told him I knew several of that name. He said he had been informed by the War Department that a man of that name had been granted permission to visit me. I told him I expected it was Andrew H. H. Dawson. He said that was the name. I shall be truly glad to see Mr. Dawson. On return from walk (at sundown, for we had sat on the bench on the parapet and talked until the sun was nearly set) I found on my table a plate of large fine apples and a card, "Mrs. E. E. Harrington's Compliments." Geary came in and told me Mrs. H. had sent them. In colour they are like my early May apples, but they are as large as our largest horse-apples. They fill the room with rich aromatic odour. Lieut. W. came and brought me a speech by Mr. Everett, Roxbury, May, 8, 1861, in which I am mentioned.

August 9. — Suffered a good deal of pain. About six Geary came in. I got him to bring me a cup of hot coffee. This did me some good. Resumed reading in Acts. Still quiet but weak. Daily papers. No news of the *Great Eastern* or cable. A statement that Mr. Davis is not to be tried by a commission and is to be sent out of the country.

Called on Major Appleton to return his books. Found him and Mrs. Appleton in. Sat and talked some time. Found both quite agreeable. He showed me several relics of the war; the most interesting were the keys to the jail at Darien, Ga. He invited me to call in at any time. Resumed my stroll. Saw a sailboat pass with a jolly party aboard; music and dancing on deck. The crowd seemed a gay one, enjoying themselves to heart's content. There was much waving of handkerchiefs toward the fort as the yacht, or whatever the craft may be called, passed the landing on the west side. I was on the western bastion. With wind and tide in her favour, the craft shot by like a thing of life.

Evening *Journal*. A break in the cable. No news from the *Great Eastern*, communication cut off. No signals at farther end of the line after 700 miles of cable was laid. General Mercer, of Savannah, has been sent to Fort Pulaski. What for, I don't know.

Sallied forth for evening walk. Met a number of strangers, coming from the other way, they on the parapet, I on the terreplein. A pleasure party had just come down in a boat, which was at the landing, as I saw on passing round. Never while memory lasts can I forget an incident that occurred upon my meeting with the *avant courier* of this party. This is enough to enter here. I went on round to the music-stand, where I sat down and wept; wept bitter tears of anguish for my beloved State in this, her hour of desolation, with worse prospects before her unless God in his mercy shall give wisdom from on high to those under whose control her destinies are soon to fall. Was of heavy and oppressed heart all evening. Saw a prisoner under guard carrying a bucket of water. Thought it must be Dr. Bickley. Found a small paper box containing peaches and tomatoes from Mrs. Salter on my table, for which she has my sincere thanks though I can express them only in this way.

Thursday, August 10. — Some incidents occurred last night that made an impression on my mind. Some one kept up an occasional whispering with the guard on duty between 6.30 and 8.30. The guard would keep his pace three or four rounds, then stop and whisper with this person. Their intercourse was in the lowest whisper, not a word could be heard by me. It was not a low talk, but a whisper in the strictest sense. Still, it could be heard just to the left of my window. It was repeated until this guard was relieved at 8.30. It was strange and mysterious. If it had been but once or twice, I should have thought nothing of it; if it had been low talk, I should have thought nothing of it, but the manner satisfied me that the intent was that I should not hear. This, too, was not all; for later, I woke — was it providential? I cannot tell, but again I heard the whisper in the same voices, the same stride of the same guard going a round or two and then stopping for the conference. I raised my head and caught two words, "Corporal Geary." I know, from the same man being on duty, that it was somewhere between 12.30 and 2, for the guard is relieved for four hours; each serves two hours and returns in four. From the name of him who waits on me, my curiosity was the more excited, especially as I could catch nothing else. Were they plotting in reference to me?

I lay awake until the relief guard came: then another strange incident occurred. The newcomer walked just long enough for the departing officer to be beyond sound of his tread, when he came inside and went into a room not far distant from mine; or, at least, the sound of his walking seemed to indicate this. There, he remained, how long I do not know, but he did not return to his beat while I was awake. I fell into another sleep. These unusual incidents impressed me deeply. What they mean, I cannot imagine. That there is something in the wind between those two whisperers which they were desirous I should not know, seems pretty clear. Whether the relief guard after 2.30 was in the secret, or whether his strange course had anything to do with it all, I do not know. This last man's time was not out when I awoke. He remained until 4.30. When I awoke, I saw him peeping in at my window. I got up and went to the window and gave him a scrutinizing look in return. His countenance and general bearing, I shall not soon forget. Geary made his appearance at six; I had a fire and was reading in Acts. He soon brought me a cup of hot coffee.

9 A. M. — Lieut. Woodman has just called to tell me he has been relieved of all duty and leaves on the 20th. He goes to Boston to-day, but will be down again and see me before his final departure. This announcement affected me a good deal. I feel more attached to him than to any other man in the fort. He has ever been kind and attentive. Have just sent for him. He returned and I presented him with Prescott's "History of Ferdinand and Isabella" as a slight token of my high regard, and in appreciation of his many acts of kindness. He accepted with thanks, etc. As he left my room, I could not suppress a flow of tears. This, however, was with myself, in my room alone. He nor any mortal, God alone saw it.

I see by the Washington telegrams that Hon. H. V. Johnson has applied for pardon. His application was presented by Mrs. Stephen A. Douglas.

Heard heavy firing at a distance. Went up on the terreplein. They were trying guns in South Boston gun-works, a man on the parapet told me. On the way round, one of the labourers putting down the circular stones on the east side of the fort for the circular gun-carriages to move on, rose, as I approached, wiping the sweat from his forehead with the fingers of his right hand, and said in Irish brogue: "Good day, Mr. Stephens." I knew from his tone that he felt kindly toward me. I stopped and talked with him some minutes. He used to work in Washington on the North Capitol. While I was talking with him about his work and hearing the explanations which he took interest in making, the noon signal sounded. Again I witnessed the spectacle of the labourers knocking off from toil, and winding divers ways to their quarters for dinner and rest. Some gathered up shoes, some jackets, and some coats, and bore these along. All seemed more or less jaded, but cheerful, and not one who passed me did so without a respectful and, in most instances, a kind recognition. Most were Irishmen.

I went to the library and got Richardson's new book, "The Secret Service, The Field, The Dungeon and The Escape." I doubt the author's accuracy. I doubt if he saw Negro women in raw hide shoes ploughing in Kentucky in February, which is too early for ploughing. Rawhide shoes I never saw anywhere. I heard that they were used by our soldiers to some extent, being made and fitted to the foot when the hide was fresh and green, with the hairside next the foot. How a man could see the kind of leather shoes were made of, worn by workers ploughing in a field which he was passing on a railroad train, I cannot understand. Then again, he speaks of seeing Negroes ploughing and hoeing in fields near Memphis. Now, what were they *hoeing? Hoeing* is a business not done in cotton-fields, and of such he is speaking in February. Overseers were there, armed with guns. This I never saw in all my life and in all my travels through the South. I have sometimes seen a man, superintending plantations, carry his gun with the view of bagging game, but never for any purpose in connection with his business as overseer. These are all small matters. But my rule with a record is to judge its accuracy as a whole by accuracy on those points within my knowledge.

Some one knocked at my door. "Come in," said I. Whereupon, a man in uniform, with sword, etc., whom I had never seen before, entered. He said nothing, but handed me a note and retired. The note was from Mrs. Appleton, requesting my autograph, and stating that she expects to leave to-morrow. This was disagreeable news; Mrs. Appleton has shown me great kindness, not only by acts but in manners. Her note I laid away amongst my letters. I wrote a reply. After thinking a while, I wrote another which I liked better and sent it by Geary.

My dear Mrs. Appleton: Allow me to express to you my deep regret and pain at hearing of your expected departure so soon from this place. Perhaps I may never see you again. In that case, accept this return of my sincere thanks for the many acts of kindness and sympathy you have shown toward me in my present suffering and affliction. Whatever fortunes await me in the future, these deeds of benevolence on your part, be assured, can never be forgotten while memory remains. May the smiles and blessing of Heaven rest upon you and all yours, wherever you may go, now and forever, is the earnest prayer of Yours most respectfully,

ALEXANDER H. STEPHENS.

MRS. MARY R. APPLETON.

Walked out. On starting I took the Major's "Ritual of the New Church" that he lent me yesterday; it was a present from his wife to him and I thought maybe he was going, too, and I wanted the book returned. I found no one in their rooms. Carpets were all up, furniture all, or nearly all, removed. I laid the book on the Major's table and went on. After I passed Harrington's office, Mrs. Appleton came running after me; I turned and met her. She invited me back to the Doctor's quarters, from which she had come. I talked with her and Mrs. Seaverns for some time. She leaves to-morrow, and the Major the next day. He quits the service and takes charge of business for a coal company in the Kanawha Valley. So, one by one, my friends leave me. No sooner do I begin to form attachments than they are broken. Into whose hands I shall now fall, I do not know. With a sad heart I bade Mrs. Appleton good-bye.

The western sky was obscured by a thick black cloud. A small monitor was lying out in the harbour. I looked upon that, musing; and at the thickening darkness of the west, fit emblem of the prospect before me. Soon, I shall be left here with no one with whom I have an intimacy except Geary, the corporal, and the Irish tailor who works in Geary's, room, Mr. Devine, who is very friendly with me.

When I turned, with heavy heart, I saw Major Appleton approaching, another gentleman with him. This gentleman I found to be Mr. Burlingame, an old Congress acquaintance. We met cordially. I was right glad to see him, and he seemed equally glad to see me. His sister is Captain Livermore's wife — no, Captain Livermore is Mrs. Burlingame's brother, that is the way of it, I believe. The Burlingames are on a visit to the Captain. The Major, Mr. Burlingame, and I walked on to the eastern bastion, and there sat down and had a long pleasant talk on public affairs. Mr. B. told me that he met the Hon. John E. Ward,* of Georgia, in China; Mr. Ward came over with him; he left Ward in Paris: had just now got a passport for Ward and Mr. Seward's permission for Ward to return home. I am in hopes he may exert his influence in getting me released on parole. I told him frankly that I was very desirous

* U. S. Minister to China, 1858–61; succeeded by Burlingame.

of release, and thought that, as so many others receiving it had been far more responsible for the war than I, I ought to be released on the same terms. We came down at the signal for retreat, he going in to take tea with the Major, and I returning to my quarters. I hope to see him in the morning. I made these entries by candlelight. Lieut. Newton called about eight and sat until after nine. We spent an agreeable hour. I feel obliged to him for his visit.

August 11. — Had another long talk with Mr. Burlingame. Met him on the sidewalk. Lieut. Newton had called, and told me he was out on the walk, giving me notice, I suppose, because of hearing me remark last night that I should like to see him again. Mr. B. invited me into Captain Livermore's quarters. We sat and talked for more than an hour, mainly on public affairs. It would be unjust to him to state here from memory anything he said. I will barely enter the substance of what I said on leading points. I expressed my desire for release on parole, and that the Administration be informed of my strong reasons for it. I said I did not think I could stand the winter here; though I can get along perhaps while warm weather lasts: especially if allowed communication with Reagan, thus diverting my mind. My trust business at home as lawyer, guardian, executor, etc., required my attention. I wished to look after my deceased brother's family and to provide for the education of his minor children, now at the age when this is most important. I wished to provide for those who had heretofore been my slaves. Also, release ought to be granted on public considerations, as similar paroles had been granted to others who were much more active in bringing on the war and in its management. In public affairs I had no wish to take part. My views were that a cordial coöperation with the Administration in all proper efforts to restore order and harmony, by bringing the seceded States back into practical relations with the General Government, ought to be given by all patriots, North and South. With regard to the new order of things, as affecting the Negroes, I earnestly desired that every effort be made to give the experiment a fair trial. A great social problem was presented for solution. I saw many difficulties and great dangers ahead, more perhaps than most people apprehended. I had devoted much thought to the subject, and while I was not sanguine, I was anxious that every possible effort be made to solve the problem in a way that would end in the advancement of civilization and humanity.

Regarding treatment of prisoners at Andersonville and other places, which was brought up, I said that the matter had caused me deep mortification and pain. From all I had heard, the sufferings of prisoners were terrible. I had no idea, however, that these sufferings were by design or system on the part of Mr. Davis and other authorities at Richmond. Something akin to what might be styled indifference or neglect toward our own soldiers on the wounded and sick lists I have witnessed with distress. I had thought there was sometimes great neglect even of these by those having them in charge. To this subject I had given a great deal of attention. I had never seen in Mr. Davis any disposition to be vindictive toward prisoners of war. I had seen what I thought evidence of his inattention: especially in one case that had given rise to some personal explanation between ourselves, in which he had relieved my mind of some very unpleasant impressions previously resting upon it. It seemed that he had done what I had not known before the explanation on his part that he had. I had no idea that there was any settled policy of cruelty on his part to prisoners.

In all my conversations with him, on the subject of prisoners, he put the blame of non-exchange on the authorities at Washington: he always expressed earnest desire to send home all we held upon getting in exchange our men equally suffering in Northern prisons; our prisoners, it was said, were treated as well as they could be under the circumstances: those at Andersonville were crowded into such a miserable pen because we had no other place in which to secure them: they had the same rations as our soldiers: ours suffered greatly to my own knowledge, not only in the hospitals, but in the field for food. The advice I had given was to release all prisoners on parole of honour, whether the authorities at Washington exchanged or not. I had advised such course as one of humanity and good policy. Against it was urged that if we were to release all our prisoners, our men would be held and treated not as prisoners of war but as traitors, and would be tried and executed as such; our authorities must hold Federals as hostages for Confederates. On the whole, therefore, while great and unavoidable suffering was endured by our prisoners, and some, perhaps, occasioned by subordinates, which could have been avoided, yet I had no idea that there was any settled design or system adopted by Mr. Davis or the heads of departments to aggravate hardships. And I could not, after looking over the whole matter, come to any other conclusion than that some blame rested on the authorities at Washington. War at best is a savage business;

it never had been and never would, perhaps, be waged without atrocities on all sides. Hence, my earnest desire during the late conflict to bring about pacification by peaceful negotiations at the earliest practical moment. I explained to Mr. B. and gave him the full history of my proposed visit to Washington in July, 1863. Our conversation lasted upward of an hour.

Went to Lieut. Newton's room. Sat some time with him, looking over his books. He showed me around in the quartermaster and commissary's rooms. Saw the great bakery and cook-rooms. Went into the hall where Company A. was at dinner. Everything was neat and clean. The room was filled with the savoury smell of good viands. Got on a pair of scales and Lieut. Newton pronounced my weight 94½ pounds. I learned that there are here now five prisoners instead of four. A new one came in the last few days. Lieut. Newton does not know who he is or why imprisoned; he is kept in close quarters and not allowed to go out at all. I feel anxious to know more about this unfortunate: "A fellow-feeling makes us wondrous kind." Besides, I never yet saw or heard of one confined in the walls of a dungeon, that I did not feel interest in his behalf. Misfortune ever excited my sympathy. At school, when a small boy, I read, with great appreciation of the sentiment:

> Teach me to feel another's woe, To hide the fault I see;
> That mercy I to others show, That mercy show to me.

All of Pope's "Universal Prayer," I committed to memory of my own accord when but a small boy, soon after I learned to read. I learned it in a borrowed book and committed it to my own memory to have it always with me.

3.30. — Just saw Reagan pass my window. I had got through with the biggest row I have yet had with bedbugs.

5.30. — Geary gone to Boston. Baily brought evening paper. The pardon of H. V. Johnson has passed. I am glad to hear it. Reading Richardson's book. As further evidence of inexactness, he speaks of Gen. "Daniel" E. Twiggs. General Twiggs's name was David. This, it is true, is another small matter, and the error may have been the printer's. As to the mistake about myself — my once being a "mail carrier" — that, as it stands, is not his. He reports a "*Colonel*" as relating that he knew me when I was an orphan boy, and that I was "mail carrier." I was an orphan boy; and at one time, if I could have got such a situation as mail-carrier, I would have gladly accepted it; that was when I sought the position of clerk in Thompson's store, in Crawfordville, say in the winter of 1826–27. But no such good luck, as I should have thought the opening, struck my path. That "Colonel" never knew me as a "mail-carrier." I doubt if he ever knew me at all.

Sallied out for a walk. Lieut. Newton overtook and handed me two letters. One from Dr. Willis states that he will call to see me about the 18th. The other from S. J. Anderson. What he says about "complete pecuniary arrangements" I do not understand. I trust he means no such thing as compensating any person for exertions in my behalf. I should be mortified at any such arrangement made by any friend of mine. I do not know exactly whether I would accept enlargement so procured. Met Annie Seaverns; she gave me some flowers.

Lieut. Newton called and brought a box of peaches

and canteloupes sent me from Boston, by Mrs. Salter perhaps. Also, my tobacco from Mr. Baskerville. It is excellent. He took me for a tramp round the fort outside. I was stronger than for a month. We stopped at Johnston's grave. The stone says, Edward J. J. Johnston, died 16th Oct. 1863, aged 36 years and nine months. The Lieutenant showed me where two men shot for desertion had been buried. He pointed out where they stood when shot. Their bodies were removed by friends. What a history might the life of each of these unfortunates present, if correctly portrayed! Who knows what trials, temptations, wrongs, griefs, and sufferings were theirs? We went to where the men practise target-shooting daily; from the ramparts above, I have often looked on them at practice.

Suddenly one of those sea-fogs bobbed up. The whole fort was enveloped as in cloud. We could hardly see anything. The reason I never noticed this phenomenon till recently is that I was always in my cell, and when I looked out and saw it that was foggy, I did not know but that it was fog such as we have in our country. The walk did me good. I gave Baily an apple, and Mr. Devine two fine peaches.

August 12. — PRISON SCENE. LIFE SKETCH. 6.30 A. M. —*Prisoner* wakes and sees the rays of the sun against the wall. Rises and looks at the thermometer, sees it is at 74, places it on the outside of his window and takes his bunk again. The guard cautiously approaches the thermometer, very much as quadrupeds of all species, from a cow to a puppy, draw near and reconnoitre whatever is set within their view which they do not exactly comprehend — advancing step by step, and endeavouring with nose and eyes to ascertain what it is, whether something of danger or something to eat, now approaching a little nearer, and now squatting back a little. Thus, the guard shyly approached the thermometer, evidently not knowing what it was and dubiously anxious to make an examination; *Prisoner* on bunk watching his motions. The guard is too low of stature to see *Prisoner* over the window-sill, though his head is visible to *Prisoner*. At lasts he gets near enough, and by rising on tiptoes, is high enough to gain a view, as *Prisoner* supposes, of the shining quicksilver bulb on the lower end of the tube: instantly there is a squat and retreat as if he was looking for the thing to go off. *Prisoner* rises, in his silk shirt and drawers, and goes to the window, takes the thermometer in full view of the guard and examines it, sees that it has fallen to 71, then hangs it on the wall at its usual place: all of which guard witnesses with curiosity manifest in countenance. *Prisoner* resumes bunk, which is too low for guard to see occupant. Here he lies for some time, when there is a tap at the door.

Prisoner. Come in. [Enter *Baily*.] Good morning, Mr. Baily.

Baily Good morning. Shall I make a fire?

Prisoner. You may put on a little wood, no coal. [*Prisoner* had a coal fire last night.] But first, I wish you would have a button sewed on my pants. The button is on the table. Take it and the pants to Mr. Devine.

[*Baily* retires with the pants and button. Quickly returns with the button sewed on.]

Prisoner. Ah! that is right. [Dresses while *Baily* makes the wood fire.]

Baily. When will you have your breakfast?

Prisoner. As soon as it is ready. [Exit *Baily* and returns.]

Baily. Breakfast will be ready in about ten minutes.

Prisoner. [Dressed] All right. [Takes up his Bible. Enter *Baily* with breakfast in thirty minutes. *Prisoner* lays down book and sits up to the table.]

Prisoner. What time does Mr. Reagan breakfast?

Baily. At half-past eight.

Prisoner. Does he board with Mr. Hall, as I do?

Baily. No, he gets his rations from the Post. Sometimes he buys vegetables.

Prisoner. Are his rations cooked and sent to him?

Baily. Yes, sir; his vegetables are also cooked for him.

Prisoner. Are you a corporal?

Baily. No, sir. I was clerk in the office for the prisoners under Lieut. Woodman.

Prisoner. And you still hold that position? You are just a private on that and other duties that may be assigned you in connection with it?

Baily. Yes, sir.

Prisoner. Do your parents live in Boston? [*Baily* is young, in appearance not more than 18.]

Baily. No, sir. They reside about thirty miles from Boston.

Prisoner. What church were you brought up in?

Baily. The Congregationalist. [*Baily* retires. *Prisoner* finishes breakfast, and walks his room, musing, and longing for somebody to talk to.]

[This sketch gives the incidents of the morning and some glimpse of my prison life.]

10 A. M. — Baily has just brought me a nice piece of watermelon, red meat and black seed. It is his own present. Thanks to him. It is excellent. First I have

seen this year. But it is not so sweet and delicious as Georgia melons!

Went out to take my leave of Major Appleton. He is not going until night; will call and see me first. Sat and talked with him until the morning boat was announced; then came to my quarters where I must remain while it is at the landing. In a few minutes after the last line was penned, I heard hasty footsteps approaching. A rap. "Come in." Enter Lieut. Newton accompanied by General Pratt, an old Congress acquaintance from Connecticut, and by a friend of his, introduced as Mr. Bacon. General Pratt I knew well in Congress: had high regard for him, and appreciated him as a gentleman of intelligence, integrity, and virtue: a true patriot of the old school. He had called to see me, bringing his friend. I was well pleased with Mr. Bacon.

We talked rapidly for about fifteen minutes, when Lieut. Newton, who had left us, returned. Lieut. Woodman came to inform the visitors that the boat was about to leave. I insisted that they should stay and dine with me and go up in the evening boat, but the General said he was obliged to go now. I was very much gratified at the visit. It did me good. I believe I am feeling better to-day than any day since I have been in this prison. General Pratt urged me to visit him, when I should be released. I told him I would if I could; I did not know when my release would be. He spoke as if he thought it would be before winter. I hope his opinion may prove well founded. In the papers, I see denial that H. V. Johnson has been pardoned.

12.30. — Called on Mrs. Livermore. Sat and talked with her a half-hour. Find her very agreeable and well educated. She lent me a book, "An Historical Research," anti-slavery in character, by George Livermore, of Boston, uncle to Captain Livermore. The Captain, I understand, will command here when Major Appleton leaves; his Christian name is Charles Frederick, for in the book is this: "Lieut. Chas. Fred. Livermore, with the kind regards of his uncle, G. L." It is now two weeks since my release from close confinement. I have improved wonderfully in strength and health.

4.20.—Major Appleton called to bid me good-bye. He sat and we talked until now; he has just left me. His name is J. M. Appleton. He has treated me with a great deal of kindness, and I deeply regret his leaving. My best wishes attend him. He has done all for my comfort and well-being since I have been under his charge that he could consistently with orders. Nothing more. For this, I am truly grateful.

5 P. M.—A tap was heard at my door. "Come in," I said. I turned, and saw Mrs. Appleton entering with beaming smiles and bearing in her hands a bundle of books; she was followed by two men bringing for my window a box of flowers that heretofore had been in the Major's. She remained but a moment, had to return on the boat. A last good-bye was given. I am alone again. The books are Swedenborg on "Heaven and Hell," "The Last Judgment," and others, all works I have been desirous of getting for some time and I am truly obliged to her on that account; besides, I deeply appreciate her spirit of kindness. Surely I have much more to console me than many other prisoners have had. Walked out. Met Lieut. Woodman and went to his room. Sat and talked with him until his tea time. Learned from him that the new prisoner is from the

North and charged with frauds in the military service. Walked on the rampart. Saw two propellers going in to Boston. Went to Harrington's office. Sat and talked with Captain Baldwin in front of his quarters. His rooms are over mine.

9. P. M. — Lieut. Newton called and sat for upward of an hour. Time spent in pleasant conversation about General Grant and others.

CHAPTER XXII

SUNDAY, August 13. — When I awoke the drum was beating, I thought for six, but on inquiring of Baily, who came, I learned that it was for eight. Breakfast was on my table almost as soon as I was ready. Finished Acts. Every time I read of Paul's arrest, imprisonment, and noble defense, the more I am impressed with his character. He was a man of great learning, ability, and eloquence; in tact in oratory not inferior to Cicero; in purity, uprightness, and genuine earnestness of soul, without a parallel amongst the ancients even as an orator. Eloquence, after all, depends more upon real zeal, unaffected earnestness, deep and strong convictions, than on any of the arts and graces taught in the schools.

Geary returned by morning boat. Bright, and with a smile, he announced himself, bringing the Sunday Boston *Herald*. I was glad to see him. He went to bring me a pitcher of water while I looked over the papers. Lieut. Newton had called to say that he was going up to Boston to-day and that Lieut. Woodman is in command of the fort. Captain Livermore is on detail service, on a court martial in a neighbouring island. Lieut. Woodman soon called, handing me a letter from Miss Nichols, of Washington City. She writes that she has seen Governor Corwin in my behalf and is hopeful that I shall be released before long. Hope is a good thing to rely on when we can get nothing more substantial. Can she refer to the Hon. Thomas Corwin, of Ohio?* I am in doubt. I thought he was in Mexico. She says he expressed sentiments favourable to me. How I longed for letters from home, from Linton!

Cut my canteloupe. Took out three slices, handed Geary the remainder and told him to divide with Baily and Mr. Devine. It was very fine, but fearing bad results, I took a drink of gin, the last of Lieut. Woodman's present. I have on hand some of Harry's whisky. That bottle is not empty yet.

Noon. Finished Richardson's book. Some little errors I have mentioned. His prison sketches are appalling; I had no idea there was such a state of things in Salisbury, N. C. He puts part of the responsibility rightfully upon Mr. Stanton.

1 P. M. — Returned from the terreplein. The sky is cerulean. All nature, the air, the ocean, everything is serene. Few sails of any kind are seen; the few visible seem to be at anchor, at rest. In the fort, all is still; no one stirring, no one to be seen except the guards on duty, and they seem conscious that it is Sunday: the surroundings for the first time since I have been here, reflect the fact that it is the Holy Sabbath. My mind wandered far away, dwelling on distant scenes.

How are all at home? How do the yard, the grove, the lot, and all things about Liberty Hall, appear to those who are there to-day? How would it appear, whom should I see and what would they be doing, could I but look upon my home? Is there preaching in the church? Is the road blocked up with horses and carriages, and crowds of persons walking round about and

* Former Governor of Ohio, U. S. Senator, Secretary of the Treasury, Chairman of House Committee of conciliation in 1860; Minister to Mexico, 1861–64. One of Mr. Stephens's Congress friends; Mr. Stephens's speech on the Galphin Claim, 1853, defends him.

passing in and out of the gate — while Tim, Dora, and Fanny * stand on the fence gazing at strange faces and things stranger than faces to their young, curious, inquisitive minds? Or, is it one of those quiet, still Sabbaths when nobody is astir but old Aunt Matt † and Eliza, ‡ such Sabbaths as I have often witnessed? These, and similar reflections flitted through my mind as I made my usual circuit. I even thought how pleasantly I could pass my days of confinement here if I but had Linton with me; and were a few changes made.

If, for instance, I could be taken out of this low, underground, damp room. If I could be allowed a better and more comfortable bed, one not filled with vermin. Could I be permitted to occupy one of the rooms above, removed from the scent of the foul air from the sink which reaches me here. With such furniture and comforts as I might then bring about me, could I but have Linton with me, I really do not know I could anywhere else enjoy more pleasure than in this Fort. Contemplation of the sad condition, desolation, and ruin of my country must of necessity force sorrow upon me, let me be where I may. Were I at home, I might see many things to oppress the heart from which I am relieved at this distance. We poor mortals show our short-sightedness in nothing more than in choosing what we suppose to be best for us. It may be best for to me remain here — without Linton — in this damp low room, on this hard stone floor with all the other discomforts.

Went all round the Island with Lieut. Woodman. It must be much more than a mile in circuit. I became fatigued. Saw soldiers bathing in the sea.

I have a presentiment that in this pending fourteenth

* Little Negroes; Harry's children. † An Aged Negress. ‡ Harry's wife, the cook.

week of my confinement I will see the last of its worst features. I record this impression reverently. It may be but a phantom of the imagination, yet it gives hope while it lasts.

August 14. — Violently ill again. Sent for Harrington. Lieutenants Newton and Woodman came to see me. Senator Henry Wilson called, and sat some time; Captain Baldwin was with him. I am now up, very weak. These paroxysms exhaust me. After my usual bath this morning, the extremities became cold; legs and thighs grew quite cold; I wrapped up in bed, but did not get reaction until Harrington administered brandy. At 1.30, Lieut. Newton called to tell me that permission has been granted by telegram from Washington for me to see Mr. Reagan one hour daily. This is a great privilege. He left to call again at two. He brought me Burns's works, as I requested, from Boston; price $2.50.

3.15. — Lieut. Newton has not come yet. Geary brought me a good bowl of soup.

Sutler has just sent his bill, $42.15. Paid it.

While I was writing the last line, Lieut. Newton called for me, and I went to see Reagan. It was all I could do to repress the flood that welled to my eyes as I entered his room and saw him approaching. His voice choked as he bade me "Howdy" — or what it was, I do not recollect. I know he spoke, and choked, and smiled. Nor do I recollect what I said. I was careful to say little until the mood upon me should pass. He had but one chair. Geary soon brought my cane-bottomed chair. Lieut. N. left us. Reagan was sewing on a button when we entered. He had on the same suit as when we entered this prison. Coat is pretty well worn. The pants, I think he bought at Hilton Head. We spent nearly an hour pleasantly indeed. I staid until Lieut. N. came to take him on his evening walk. I felt much better than in the morning. I was able to remain and enjoy myself the whole time. I soon learned that solitary confinement has been horrible to him; no less than to me, I think. He has not known that he could board, as I do, with the sutler.

"Well, what did you talk about?" somebody, if any such body ever reads this, will be ready to ask. If so, I have to say that we talked a little about almost everything and said nothing in particular. We spent the time pretty much as people in the country do when some one comes home unexpectedly after a long absence, all shivering in the cold, after nightfall, during the short interval between "howdy" and getting supper ready. We had no special talk on anything. He spoke in general terms of his application, of a document he had sent to Texas, advising the people to accept the condition of things. He showed me some flowers Mrs. Appleton had sent him, and spoke in the kindliest terms of her attentions. He showed me the little mauls he uses as dumb-bells for exercising his arms and the muscles of his chest. He told me how he had been living. We flew from one subject to another just as an elastic ball bounds from one point to another under any force that drives it along. So passed our brief first interview. I returned to my quarters, greatly rejoiced at this new arrangement, thinking that my presentiment of a change for the better was not altogether illusory, and with a grateful heart to the Giver of all good.

5.45. — Another paroxysm; was much weakened.

Mr. Harrington called; he talks sensibly upon diseases; his knowledge is practical; he has been in the hospital many years; and being kind-hearted and sympathetic, he could not fail to learn a great deal. He told me he should try to have me moved to another room, one on the upper floor, drier and healthier than this. I hope he may succeed.

6.30. — Walked up to Captain Baldwin's room; then took a few rounds on the pavement in front of the officers' quarters. This is the least walk of any day since I have been here, but I am glad I was able to take it, short as it was. The band played the most plaintive tune; one they often play.

There are two messes. One for the Major's (when he was here), the captains' and the officers' families, with the sutler. I get my meals from this. The other is that of the lieutenants over the way at Mrs. Nutler's. Mrs. Nutler is the laundress. The hours of meals differ, the lieutenants' being an hour earlier.

August 15. — Did not sleep much. There was much noise in rooms not far off, noise of revelry and dissipation without music or song. I guessed it to be a jollification that Lieut. Woodman was having with his brother officers before his departure. In this I was right, as Geary told me this morning. This in Zachariah impresses me: "Turn you to your stronghold, ye prisoners of hope: even to-day do I declare that I will render double unto thee." I am a prisoner of hope. But what is the double to be rendered unto me? Double chastisement or double deliverance? or is not the promise to me at all?

Sent Geary to sutler's for a pack of cards, so that

when I go to see Reagan to-day, we may entertain ourselves with a game of euchre or piquet; price $1.00.

Examined Colton's "New Atlas" of 1863. The other evening, while I was conversing with Captain Baldwin about the currents in the ocean, particularly the Gulf Stream, he asked if I had seen this Atlas, wherein the currents are marked out. I said I had not, but should like to see it; he sent it to my room. I find the currents, in the main, as I had supposed. Some egregious errors are in this Atlas. On my principle of testing general accuracy by accuracy in matters with which I am familiar, I examined Colton on such matters. He gives the census of my county,. Taliaferro, in 1860 thus: whites 1,693, free blacks 41, and slaves 2,849. I do not know exactly what the relative population was then, but am certain that there were not 1,200 more blacks than whites in it. He gives Atlanta's population thus: 1840, 1,000; 1850, 2,572; 1860, 4,416. Now, in 1840, I do know that there was not a soul in Atlanta. The place was not settled. I stood on its present site of Atlanta on the 21st July, 1843, and there was not a habited house there. It was a perfect forest. Some excavations for the railroad had been made, a store or gin-house put up, and a frame for a dwelling was in process of erection; but not a family was living there. Dr. Glenworth, of Sandtown, and myself, going from Decatur to Campbellton, stopped on that day at the present site and took lunch. I have not time now to point out the many small errors about Georgia in this Atlas. The error as to Atlanta's population for 1840 is no more striking than for 1860; instead of 4,416, it was not much under 12,000.

Last night, I examined Mr. Livermore's "Historical

Research or Opinion of the Founders of the Republic on Negroes as Slaves, Citizens, and Soldiers." The work shows much research. The general conclusions are correct. The criticism upon Chief Justice Taney's decision, I do not think exactly fair; the argument does not meet the points squarely. I doubt if Judge Taney would have denied a single position as to the facts assumed or set forth here. The legal consequences of these facts are entirely a different matter. Still in that Dred Scott case, I think Justice Curtis had the better of the argument. But Mr. Livermore does not seem fully to understand the extent to which Judge Curtis differed from the Chief Justice.

Lieut. Woodman called. Left me *Harper's Weekly*. The same bitterness continues in this paper against the South. The sketches illustrating the flight of "Jeff Davis," pretendedly by an English artist and made on the spot, are all gammon. There is no truth in them. Washington, Ga., where this parting scene between Mr. Davis and his cabinet is represented to have taken place, is well known to me. There are no such buildings in that town as this cut purports to picture from life.

10.30. — The surgeon from Gallops Island, who attends Dr. Seaverns's patients in his absence, called. I did not learn his name. He seems to be a pleasant and intelligent gentleman. I went round to see Reagan. Geary went with me to open the door to Reagan's quarters, carrying my chair. Reagan read me his letter to the people of Texas.* Lieut. Newton had told him that there was no objection to his showing it to me. He ad-

* Reagan says in his "Memoirs" (226-227) that this letter was approved by Senator Henry Wilson, of Massachusetts, Charles O'Conor, of New York, President Johnson, Secretary Seward, and others who urged him to get Texas "to lead off in that line of policy [qualified Negro suffrage] as the only means of avoiding military government. On my return home I found that the people were not in condition to reason on the subject, and I had to abandon the idea of trying to induce them to make such concessions as . . . would have saved them from military governments and universal Negro suffrage."

vises extension of the franchise, with some restrictions, to the black race, but with no discrimination against Negroes as a race in future extensions.

Without depriving any now possessing the franchise, he advises that, for the future, restrictions, applying to all alike, be thrown around it. I greatly prefer my plan; still, I see no insuperable objection to his. After talking over these matters, we entertained ourselves at euchre; then I taught him piquet. After leaving his room, I visited Captain and Mrs. Livermore. I learned from her that Mr. Hall, the sutler, no longer serves the mess from which I get my meals. He has given it up. It is now under her management. I did not inquire into particulars; I was just leaving when the change was announced to me by her in asking about my meals, if the times of serving and the character of food suited me, etc. I must make further inquiries. Perhaps I may have to contribute more as my share. I pursued my walk. The sea was calm; little air was stirring, and few sails to be seen. Away off to the right of Boston, in Chelsea perhaps, is a spot from which a vast column of smoke is forever ascending. At this spot, Lieut. Woodman told me soon after I came here, are copper works. The smoke from the furnaces, like the smoke from perdition, seems to ascend forever. Day and night, Sunday, and all other times it is ever rising.

ANOTHER FANCY SKETCH, YET NOT ALTOGETHER FANCY:

[*R. M. Johnston* entering by the window of imagination.]

Johnston. Well, sir, how are you?

Prisoner. [Rising quickly.] Why, Dick, how are you? I am so glad to see you. Another verification of the old adage, "Think of ——," you know. I was thinking of you, and here you are. How have you been? The last time you were here, you cut so abruptly upon the coming in of Lieut. Newton, that I feared you were scared off for good, had deserted me; were so afraid of being locked up here with me that you made up your mind to keep away from these not very interesting quarters. But be seated. Tell me why you came through that window. Why didn't you get permission to visit me, and come in at the door? I am permitted now to receive my friends. I am looking every day for Linton. I wrote him two weeks ago to come and bring you if you could come. I have various privileges extended to me now. I hope the midnight of my individual misfortunes is passed, and the dawn is at hand.

Johnston. What makes you think so?

Prisoner. I could not tell were I to try. You know my opinion about our triune nature—the material, the intellectual, and the spiritual. This feeling springs from the spiritual. Its operations are beyond all principle of bare intellectual ratiocination. But this is apart from what I intended to talk to you about. How are you getting on in Georgia?

Johnston. Bad enough, worse than I expected. This Negro problem is presenting new aspects. Far more difficult questions than even emancipation rise to view. What are we to do with these questions? The present and future are darker than any period in the past.

Prisoner. Quiet and repose is what the people need. They are not in condition to grasp and settle these questions. In *delirium tremens*, the first object is to get the patient asleep. There is no hope unless he can rest for at least a short time. The patient in this case, the body politic, is in excitement, has been bordering on *delirium tremens*, if not actually in that horrible state. The first essential is repose. This end should be attained by the earliest possible restoration of law and order, the bringing of the States back into practical relations with the Central Government. Whenever this is done upon almost any rational basis, normal functioning will begin throughout the organism, new life will manifest itself, and returning health.

Johnston. And are you hopeful of the future?

Prisoner. Yes, as much as for several years past. I have great confidence in the capacity of man for self-government. I believe in the vigour of the young manhood of the American people. I know the public is suffering extremely from late dissipations; the whole body is sick nigh unto death, North and South. This young Hercules of a Republic is bordering on *delirium tremens*, but I feel assured that if he can but get quiet, if sleep can be induced and his nervous balance restored, all will yet be well with him. With the normal action of the American system once restored, those great principles of civil and religious liberty which underlie all our institutions, and which are now overridden, will again arise in their original power and strength. But there are great difficulties ahead; the prospect is gloomy enough.

Johnston. I am glad to see you hopeful. I was beginning for the first time to despair. Heretofore, you have always presented a darker side than I had seen — since 1860 until now.

Prisoner. Do not suppose me more sanguine than I am. Things are no worse than I have expected, and not yet so bad as I am prepared to see them before they mend. The difficulties ahead are appalling. They may, however, be surmounted. This is the hope that calls every patriot to lend a hand to speedy restoration of peace, law, and order upon any practical basis. Let this be the first great object. If this fails, there is no fathoming the abyss into which we may be plunged.

Johnston. I am glad to find you more cheerful than you were. I suppose you are not entirely without something to amuse you even here? But I confess I see nothing that could stir a vein of humour in my nature.

Prisoner. [Laughing.] Why, sir, humour is a strange thing. I have sometimes been almost offended with myself for a disposition to laugh. I have fondness for humour in my saddest moments. I see a great deal in prison life to laugh at; if I had you and Linton with me, I think we could amuse ourselves as much here as men ought to when their country is passing through such an ordeal as is ours.

[Enter *Lieut. Woodman* bringing *Governor Alfred Cumming*. Exit *Johnston* through the window aforesaid.]

Governor Cumming spent only a few moments; returned to Boston by the boat. He promised to spend to-morrow with me. The *Great Eastern* has been heard from. The cable was [illegible word] 2d August.

Mr. Harrington tells me that the doctor who called this morning is named Monroe, and that he has recommended a change of quarters for me, removal from the stone floor to a room above. If this be granted, I shall be greatly relieved. Cole writes that it was at his instance I am allowed to visit Reagan daily. I begin to see the dawn. Unto Thee, O Father, be my thanks reverently poured forth!

On the ramparts, Lieut. Woodman joined me. We walked round twice, then rested on the bench. We went on the parapet, I taking his arm. I was a little afraid to walk on it without support; being weak, was afraid I should fall or pitch over. For supper, bread and milk. Days are shortening, nights lengthening. Longer time 'twixt candle-light and bed-going than in June. After supper, I read the Georgia papers that Governor Cumming left, and got all the information I could from the good, beloved, but down-trodden old State. My heart and my soul are with her. I read even the advertisements to see if I could find any familiar names. In one issue, I saw editorial notice of the order to take possession of Toombs's house and Steadman's order countermanding it.* I do hope DuBose got home in time. I am afraid my house will be confiscated in a similar way by the Freedman's Bureau. Lieut. W. came down and talked with me. I gave him a short sketch of myself and also of Linton. He inquired about Linton. He really seems to take an interest in my affairs.

August 16. — Was perplexed last night in regard to writing to the President for a personal interview. If he were to grant it, I do think I could show him that I am justly entitled to release on parole. If he should reject the application, it would be mortifying. I did not sleep much. I was feverish and restless. Rose early.

I have drawn up a letter of which this is a copy:

Mr. President: With profound acknowledgments for the relaxation of the order for my close confinement, I am induced to make another appeal to you. I am anxious to have a personal interview and conference with you. I am not without strong convictions that if

* The Freedman's Bureau ordered Mrs. Toombs to vacate it to their use. General Steadman restored it to her.

I could have such an interview I could easily satisfy you that my request for release on parole or bail should be granted no less on public than private considerations. Will you please grant such interview? If you should, and I should be released so far as to go to Washington, I need not assure you, I trust, that in case the further release on parole to go to my home should not be granted after the interview, I should return to this place. My conduct and well-known position before my arrest and since, I feel assured, is sufficient guarantee that in no possible contingency would I attempt to escape. My petition is earnestly though briefly submitted. Act upon it as you think best. Yours most respectfully,

ALEXANDER H. STEPHENS.

Went to see Reagan. Expect Governor Cumming by the morning boat. Geary came in while we were playing piquet, and told me that the gentleman, my friend, had come. I came back to my room, and much to my surprise, found Dr. Willis; but we had hardly concluded salutations when Governor Cumming was shown in. They spent the day. We took dinner in the mess-room — the first time I have eaten out of my cell since the 25th of May — no, the dinner with Parrott must be excepted. I was truly glad to see both. I felt sad, however, all day from a letter that Lieut. Woodman handed me soon after their arrival. It was from Linton. The tone affected me deeply. My friends left me at five. I read and reread Linton's letter. I shall now look for him daily. For supper had milk and some of my peaches that Mrs. Salter sent yesterday; she sent me some pears, too. I took Reagan some of both this morning. At 8.30, Lieut. W. called. I read to him Burns's "Soldier's Return." He sat and we talked until ten.

CHAPTER XXIII

THURSDAY, August 17. — This ever-memorable day has again returned. It is fourteen weeks since my arrest, since I was deprived of my liberty, and that without warrant, without charge, without judicial process; this in a land boasting of its freedom. I am impressed with an idea that with this week will end in some measure the darkness of my trials, and that the dawn will begin. It may be hallucination. O Lord, in very mercy grant my hopes be not illusions! I am strong in hopes that Linton will be here before long. Oh, that my hopes may be realized! It would do me so much good to see and have him here with me.

Papers came. Nothing of interest except announcement from Washington that Mr. Davis is to be tried, and at an early day, for treason before a proper court, and that the suspension of the habeas corpus writ is soon to be itself suspended. Lieut. Newton brought me a letter from Mollie Greer, 31st July, and one from Prof. R. M. Johnston, 25th. Mollie's greatly relieved me. All her brothers are at home and well. It is the first news I have had from them touching their safety in the late war. I am impressed with the fact that on the very day when I was recording my dream of being at Dick Johnston's home, Linton was with him. He was sick. Was not my spirit also with him?

Reagan read me his application for amnesty and all the papers appertaining to it, including his letters to

Mr. Seward and Attorney-General Speed. While we were engaged with these papers, we were gazed upon through the windows by a crowd of strangers visiting the fort. They had a band of music and were dressed in uniform as if belonging to some military force. After dinner I called at Captain Livermore's and sat and talked with Mrs. Livermore. Miss Livermore, Major Livermore's cousin, I suppose, was with her; quite good-looking, intelligent and agreeable. Mrs. Livermore was out in the squall last night; was in a yacht and became somewhat frightened.

August 18. — Was ill last night; sent for Mr. Harrington. He called again this morning before I got up. He is a very kind-hearted man. Lieut. Newton called soon after I was up. We had some conversation about the orders relating to privileges extended me. I have not seen that allowing me to see Judge Reagan an hour daily. I said I thought it would modify my parole to keep my room during Reagan's walk; and that I might even walk with him if I so choose to use the hour. He promised to look up that order and let me see it.

Lieut. W. called about the order releasing me from close confinement. Says it cannot be found amongst the papers here. I showed him the certified copy Adjutant Ray gave me. Lieut. Newton brought me letters from Sister Elizabeth and John A. Stephens. Nothing from Linton; and no news from Washington. Dr. Monroe called. Said no news from application for change of my quarters. The prospect looks dark, but somehow I feel hopeful that a change will take place before long. May God grant it!

Went to see Reagan. He requested me to bring away

and read a memoir he has prepared for his children. I do not know but that, in bringing it away, I might be violating my parole. I haven't been able yet to see the order allowing my conference with Judge Reagan, and do not know the conditions or restrictions, or if there are any. I told him that I had better get the sanction of the officer in command. Reagan has applied for release from close confinement and for privilege to mess with me. Called on Lieut. Newton, and asked to see the order. He told me it was lost. For dinner had a meat pie; I sent it to Reagan. Mr. Harrington gave me a bottle of bitters which he thought would be good for me. Called on Captain Livermore, now in command, and sought information about Reagan's memoir. He said there was no objection to my taking it to my room and reading it. I sat in the parlour and talked a while. Mrs. and Miss Livermore were there.

Finished Swedenborg on "Heaven and Hell"; "The World of Spirits," etc. Many things in this book are obscure to me. If I understand Swedenborg, salvation is not the result of immediate mercy and grace but the result of these combined with the acts and will of the recipient. These views accord nearly with my own. Divine vengeance, as taught by many, I could never comprehend. The Divine Being I was always inclined to regard as the very embodiment of love and mercy; punishments as the inevitable consequences of violation of law, moral or physical; Scriptural commandments and injunctions as admonitory, given to man to enable him to see the law and to avoid violation with the consequences, as he has power to do through Divine aid and faith in the Redeemer. I believe, too, in the cultivation of the higher attributes and qualities of man, his third part, which I call the soul, just as I believe in the cultivation of his second part, which I call mind or intellect. Soul-culture is as distinct, in my opinion, from mental-culture, as mental from physical; it has a sphere of its own and is governed by laws as different from those of bare mental culture, as the laws of the latter differ from the laws of bare physical culture. In religious or spiritual matters, as they are called for lack of a better term for things relating to the culture of the soul, reason, technically speaking, has nothing to do. The whole lies in a sphere beyond human reason.

6. P. M. — In the evening paper is an account of "Fort Warren." I think some items about me were got from Governor Cumming. Not that about the little girl; for none such was mentioned to him; the statement that I gave her a gold dollar is fiction. I had not one to give, nor should I have made such return for her kindness if I had one. I should have thought it might be offensive to her. But I did thank her kindly, tenderly, sincerely, and I felt disposed to kiss her, and would have done so but from the apprehension that that might not be kindly received. She was a beautiful, innocent little girl, four or five years old; Mabel Landon Appleton, as I understood her to give her name. Went on the ramparts. Lieut. Woodman joined me. I took his arm and we made two circuits. He told me his resignation had been accepted, and the acceptance would be here to-morrow. So, with to-morrow, his official connection with this Post and the army will cease. He said he should be down next week, but I suppose I shall never again have such a conversation or walk with him. This evening's stroll I suspect is the last we shall ever take together. I may see him when he returns and may

have the opportunity of speaking with him, but I do not expect ever to have with him again such free and easy talks as we have had on our evening strolls. He told me it was Judge Reagan who gave the little girl the gold dollar. He expressed regret that he should not be here when Linton arrives — "when your brother comes." This interest to see Linton made him feel more like a friend to me than before.

August 19. — Read in Zachariah: "Turn you to the strong hold, ye prisoners of hope: even to-day do I declare that I will render double unto thee." I was struck with the agreement between that verse and this in Nahum: "The Lord is good, a strong hold in the day of trouble; and he knoweth them that trust him." Strange feelings seized upon me. That the Lord is a strong hold in the day of trouble I know. But for His sustaining grace, I should have been crushed in body and soul long ere this. Yet do I fully trust Him?

Lieut. Newton called to see how I am. He said a box of fruit had come for me. He would send it down. Geary brought it and a lot of papers, all from Mrs. Salter, my kind and attentive lady friend in Boston.

It is now three weeks since the locks were taken from my door. Went to the library. Met Captain Baldwin at the door of his quarters. He invited me in; insisted that I should feel at home in his parlour; should come up there and sit during the day as it is more comfortable than in my room. Mrs. Baldwin is gone. No person there but the Captain and he is gone during the day to attend a court martial.

Last night, read Swedenborg's "Last Judgment." Like his other works, a wonderful production. The first chapters I can understand: further reading suggests that he had poured over abstruse subjects, endeavouring to reconcile spiritual mysteries with the laws of human understanding, until reason lost its balance. Still, there is nothing in his explanation of sacred text more mysterious than the text itself. Whether he was under Divine illumination or labouring under hallucination, I do not know, but that he was sincere, I believe.

Since my last big row with bedbugs, I have made it a business every day or two to search for and break them up. I have just been at this work of self-preservation.

As for my mouse, I have never, since the instance given, got a sight of it. But I have kept up my dropping of crumbs; they disappear when I am out or when my eyes are off the spot; I suppose the little creature is about but keeps close, not knowing that I would not hurt it. It may see from its hiding-place, what I do with the chinches, and draw conclusions which prompt it to keep out of my power. I have often felt sorry for what I have to do to these blood-suckers. Most willingly would I turn them loose and let them go away if they would go and stay, but this they will not do. Between them and me, therefore, there is "an irrepressible conflict." Either I or they must be extinguished. This seems to be fixed in the laws of our nature. I am sorry it is so, but so it is. Toward the mouse I feel very much as Burns expressed himself to one in his day:

> I doubtna, whyles, but thou may thieve;
> What then? Poor beastie, thou maun live;
> A daimen icker in a thrave
> 'S a sma' request:
> I'll get a blessin' wi' the lave,
> And never miss 't.

Not so with these vermin that feed on my blood. Of that I have not a drop to spare without missing it, to say nothing of the torture at having it sucked out as they do it. I would willingly let them alone if they would let me alone, and I would even contribute something to their support and sustenance. But to live and let live is not in accordance with the laws of their existence. Hence, they justly bring their death upon themselves.

10.30. — Boat brought papers, but no letters, no news from Linton. Gloom again creeps over my soul. I am disappointed and grieved at heart. O Lord, sustain me! The papers are largely taken up with the failure of the cable, or rather the accident that has befallen it. Whether it be failure or not, is not settled. I see that Mrs. Davis and family with Mrs. Howell, her mother, have arrived in New York. The *Times* has a leading article against the Southern people. I took Reagan a pile of English papers that Mrs. Salter sent down to me and him. He has sent me his memoirs. Met Captain Baldwin at his door, went in and sat with him until dinner was announced. He went to his dinner and I returned to my room.

My heart is filled with gratitude to the Father of all mercies. Lieut. Woodman has just entered my soom, bringing a telegram from President Johnson to the Commandant of the Post directing him to give me as comfortable quarters here as he can, and to say to me that he (the President) has received my letter and will reply. Oh, if I had Linton with me now, how full would be my joy notwithstanding I am a prisoner! How light is my burden compared with what it has been! The full dawn of day is certainly upon me! May the sun of my deliverance soon arise! Oh, may Linton soon come!

When Lieut. W. entered, I was reading Reagan's memoir. I have become interested in it, but can pursue it no more this evening. My feelings are too much excited. I pour out my heart in the last Psalm. "Let everything that hath breath praise the Lord."

Walked out. Sat at the door of Dr. Seaverns's quarters, talking with Mrs. Seaverns, a Mrs. Davis, and other ladies. Then went on the ramparts. Saw many sail-vessels west of the fort, all seemingly at anchor. I counted fifteen and one large brig, apparently a steam-propeller. What it all means I cannot imagine. My walk was lonely. I thought many things. Why has Linton not come? Why has DuBose not written to me? What is the prospect of President Johnson's replying to my letter? Suppose he should release me on parole, sending me home by sea from this place to Savannah. May I expect anything as good? and yet, that, now, before Linton comes, would be painful. Maybe Linton will reach here in a few days.

CHAPTER XXIV

SUNDAY, August 20. — I am in my new quarters. I am out of the hole. I am on deck. I am in a comfortable room, with fair and beautiful prospect out toward the South and rejoicing in a brilliant sunlight. I have just taken my dinner, and read letter from my old and true friend, J. A. Stewart, Rome, Ga. It was handed me in my new quarters. My heart is full; I will not attempt to give utterance to my emotions. If I did but have Linton with me, I should feel better.

This morning, I finished Reagan's manuscript and took it round to him with a few notes I had made. We conversed until one. I read him my first two letters to the President. On returning to my old quarters, I found Geary, who told me, "We have moved." He conducted me to our new quarters. I say "our," as he said "we," for he comes with me. The apartments consist of three rooms, a sort of parlour, in which I now am, fronting south, a room in the rear in which my bed is placed, a neat and comfortable bedroom; and one in the rear of that for Geary. By opening doors and windows, we have a draft through all the rooms. The new arrangement suits me admirably. I doubt if I could, as to rooms, be more comfortable in any hotel in Boston or New York. In furnishings I am rather deficient, but my situation is infinitely better than it has been. The removal is from a cell to a palace so far as comfort is concerned. If Linton now would but, or could but, come. Oh, what detains him? This question weighs heavily upon me. It is now 21 days since I wrote him to come.

7.15 P. M. — Took Reagan's manuscript to Mrs. Livermore, as she had expressed a wish to read it; she was present when I asked the Captain about my reading it, and evinced this desire. Captain Livermore was taking an evening nap. I sat with Mrs. Livermore a half-hour or more. She gave me a book of sermons by F. W. Robertson, of Brighton, England. After leaving the Captain's quarters, I visited Lieut. Woodman.

August 21. — Morning bright and beautiful, the first in my new quarters. Felt much better than for months. Last night, after nine, Captain Livermore and Lieut. Woodman called, and we spent some time in conversation. Captain L. showed me, in the Boston *Advertiser*, a piece about my confinement, health, etc. I spent last night, when not engaged with this company, in reading Robertson's Sermons. Robertson belonged to the Church of England, but his doctrines on the Trinity are those of Swedenborg. The sermon indicating this was preached 26th May, 1850, from I Thess. v, 23. It considers man in his *three-fold* nature of matter, and two other distinct principles, soul, and spirit, as I have been believing for a long time.

Lieut. Woodman called to take final leave of me. He said he might come on a visit to the fort again before leaving Boston for Hilton Head; if so, he would see me; it was not certain he would be here again. I gave him a letter as a testimonial of my regard for him and my recognition of his official courtesy, civility, urbanity, and kindness to me, hoping it might be of service to him should he meet with any of my personal friends in his new home, as they may thereby be induced to render him all aid in their power in extending his acquaintance in a strange land. We parted perhaps never to meet again, but I hope otherwise. I hope yet to have the pleasure of entertaining him with such hospitality as I can command at Liberty Hall. It would afford me great pleasure to meet him there, and make some return in kind for his many acts of generous sympathy toward me.

Old sayings about the dreams one may have the first night in a new room filled my mind when I retired. I lay awake for a long time. It is strange that while Linton has occupied more of my thoughts since I have been here than all other people and all other subjects combined, yet I have never once had a dream in which he figured prominently. I have dreamed of being at his house and of his being there and well, but in another room. In no instance have I dreamed of conversing with him.

1.30. — Found Reagan suffering with pain in the back. He did not get much sleep last night for the mosquitoes; his face was very much bitten. He was less cheerful than I have yet seen him. We took to piquet and euchre. I generally beat at the first, and he at the latter. In comes dinner. It is to-day set on another table in my bedroom. A very good dinner, and I had a pretty good appetite. Went to sutler's and got some shoe-strings, a pocket-knife, and a piece of red cord. Made me a window-curtain by pasting newspapers together.

Little Charles Nutler called on me, as I was coming

from Hall's, for the book I promised him. I told him to come along with me and get it. He said, "They won't let me in your room." "Oh yes," I replied, "they will let you in now. Anybody can go in my room now. Come along." Rather doubtfully he came, but when he saw where I was going, he brightened up hopefully. "Ah, they have moved you, have they?" "Yes," said I. On entering, the little fellow again exclaimed, "Oh, you have a good room now." "Yes," said I. "They don't lock you up now, do they?" "No," said I. "Didn't you feel bad when they kept you locked up?" "Oh yes, horribly bad." "But you got sort of used to it, didn't you, after you had been there awhile?" "A little used to it, but I believe I felt worse the longer I stayed there, locked up all the time." "How long are they going to keep you, I wonder?" "I don't know; not much longer, I hope." "Why, you don't mind staying here now, do you? Don't you like this place?" "Oh, I like the place very well, but I want to get home to see the people there." "I like it very well," said he, "but I am going to leave before long to start to school again." This is a sample of our conversation. I gave him Vol. I., "Conquest of Mexico." When he reads that he is to bring it back and get another. He is too little to be intrusted with all at once.

August 22. — I dreamed of Linton. It was a strange dream. I was travelling, was starting somewhere on a sort of omnibus. The vehicle was crowded. I was on the front seat, outside with the driver. I was expecting and looking for Linton. The consciousness of being a prisoner was in me, but what was the object of my movements or where I was going, did not seem to be in my mind. I had no idea about it. As we were getting under way and had taken the last passenger, filling every inside seat, I saw Linton standing some thirty yards in advance of us and to our right, apparently waiting. He was in the act of starting to meet us when my eyes first caught sight of him. He was greatly changed but I knew him. He looked tall and thin, taller and thinner, I thought, than I had ever seen him, and quite sunburnt, rather sallow than ruddy. He had on a colonel's uniform. I was delighted to see him; felt a little disposed, as he came up, to chide him for his delay; but when he approached near enough to speak, nature gave way in smiles and tears as I bade him howdy. This was done as he mounted the steps of the vehicle, while it kept in motion, and took part of my narrow seat in front. At this point, before a word was spoken by him that I can recollect, I awoke and the vision was gone. For a long time I lay awake. This strange vision made upon my mind a deep and vivid impression which continues.

Lieut. Newton called while I was writing the above. I asked if any letters came for me yesterday. He said one came but had to be returned to General Hooker for approval. He could not tell me who it was from. It occurs to me that Harry's son, Tim, also appeared to me in my mental rovings during sleep last night. He was not the Tim, the little boy, I left at home; was about half-grown; was not docile and obedient as always heretofore but self-willed and obstinate.

In my walk yesterday, a little incident occurred as I was ascending the stone steps to the ramparts. I cannot go into detail, and only mention the fact, that I may hereafter, if opportunity permits, enlarge upon it. It made a deep impression upon me. Reagan is better, but is still suffering greatly, in body and mind, from close confinement. This is a cloudy cool day. Somehow I am strongly impressed with the idea that I shall hear from Linton this evening. I am fondly indulging this hope. It keeps up the spirits. Corporal Geary brought a letter from Gip Grier, dated the 12th; acknowledges "all" my letters. I suppose he means those of 30th July, when I wrote through him to Linton, John A. Stephens, and George F. Bristow. He said he had sent my "letters" on, does not specify that he got the one for Linton, and had sent that on, but I hope this is the case. If so, he must have sent it as early as the 12th; and Bristow, if at home, got it by the 13th, and then, if my plan succeeded in carrying out, Linton, if in Sparta, must have got it by the 14th, a week ago yesterday. So, I feel almost certain that if he were at home then and well, he is now on his way here; and if he meets with no accident, will be here in a day or two. I answered Gip before making these entries. I see in the Boston *Post* that H. V. Johnson, of Georgia, is in Washington. He might be of some service to me if so inclined. I have no idea that he is *disinclined*, and yet he may not be inclined. He may be indifferent; that is, he may be completely occupied with his own affairs.

7. P. M. — Evening mail. No letters for me, so Lieut. Newton told me himself. He is the officer in special charge of prisoners since Lieut. Woodman left. I went to him in person, so anxious was I.

August 23. — Finished Robertson's "Sermons." Two, I place in the first rank of all sermons I have heard or read; that already mentioned and one on "Christian Aim and Motive." I may copy these in this Journal, making comments.

9.30. — It rained heavily last night. Lieut. Newton called to see me. He has been up all night on duty.

11.30. — Went to the sutler's and bought some pens and writing paper; and some tacks for putting up my curtain. Went on ramparts to see the boat come in from Boston, hoping it might have Linton on board and that I might get a glimpse of him. The boat came. I left the rampart before she landed. Saw no person on deck like him. Morning papers. Cut out several articles, such as the *Herald's* Fortress Monroe letter stating that preparations are being made there for the trial of Mr. Davis, an account from Washington of the postponement of the Wirz trial, and Governor Perry's second Greenville [S. C.] speech. My heart is sick at no news from Linton. Went to see Reagan. Found him better. We played piquet and euchre. I beat him for the first time at euchre. Lieut. Newton came in to tell me that he had left a letter on my table; said he did not notice it closely; it was a short letter from New York. This satisfied me that it was not from Linton or home, and I stayed my allotted time with Reagan. The letter is from S. J. Anderson. He promises to come to see me if he can get permission; he thinks he can on General Hooker's return to New York.

Thursday, August 24. — Another cycle of seven days; fifteen weeks since I have been a prisoner; thirteen since I have been in this fort, this little kingdom within a kingdom, this little despotism within a despotism. It is true I am much better conditioned than I have been, have more comforts and privileges, and feel more like a free man; yet these comforts and privileges come at the pleasure of him in whose temporal power I am. Despotic power still holds me in its clutches. How long, O Lord, how long shall this continue? Shall I ever again enjoy the rights of a freeman? Began Daniel.

Dreamed last night of Toombs. How changed from the Toombs of other days! My mind reverts to the dream of Linton. The more I think of it, the more I am impressed with the fact that he did not speak, nor was there any manifestation of joy on his side at seeing or joining me. He simply mounted the vehicle and took a part of the very narrow seat beside me. It rained that night. To dream of the dead is said to be a sign of rain.

Last night I read Coleridge. The Corporal brought me Matthew Arnold's "Essays in Criticism" presented by Mrs. Salter. She referred to this book in her note of the 20th; there has been, I suppose, neglect in delivery. There is not the same prompt attention in delivering letters or anything else to prisoners, or at least to myself, as when Lieut. Woodman was in charge. He used to deliver my letters in ten minutes after the mail arrived; often, at least, he did this. Now, I never get them short of two or three hours after; sometimes I think not until the next day.

12 M. — Called to see Captain Livermore's family. Mr. and Mrs. Leonard are visiting them. Mrs. Leonard is Mrs. Livermore's sister. She is a well-educated and highly intelligent lady. We conversed on many topics. Mr. Leonard is a partner, he informed me, of my old Congress friend, George Ashmun,* of Massachusetts. Mr. Leonard lives in Springfield.

* Ashmun offered in Congress, 1848, Stephens's amendment to the resolutions thanking General Twiggs for gallantry in the Mexican War; and reported in the Whig Convention of 1852, the Whig platform, which Webster amended at Stephens's suggestion.

Lieut. Newton has removed the restriction that I should remain in my room during Reagan's hour abroad. This evening, as Reagan returned from his walk, he stopped at the pump near my door. I went out and joined him in taking some fresh water; that, Lieut. Newton permitted.

While we were there, Mrs. Livermore came out and spoke to the Judge, apologizing for keeping his manuscript so long. Her winning and agreeable manner and her kind language seemed to do him good. Asked Harrington about the range of the thermometer here during the winter. He brought me the registry for last winter; the average for December at 7 A. M. was 30, the lowest 0, and the highest 43.

August 25. — I got a first view last evening of the new moon, three days old, in a perfectly clear sky and without the least intervening obstruction. She was also seen over the right shoulder. But she was so young, and blushing so, or rather paling so in the rays of the sun not yet down, that she was not brilliant. I only saw clearly her form and outline. What matters it how we see a new moon for the first time? Nothing, according to reason, and yet something in our nature prompts a desire for signs, auguries, and supernatural manifestations. It is born with us. It possesses us, and asserts its power before even reason. Reason may bid it down, yet it is there by a law of our nature, a law not of the reasoning faculty but of another part, which I call soul. And may not reason well pause in its own conclusions and consider whether a law so general in the nature of man is without effect, even though the operations are beyond its comprehension? I do not think I am at all superstitious.

Mr. Leonard called to take leave of me. Before he left, Lieut. Woodman came with a friend (whose name I did not distinctly hear), to take his final leave. After sitting some time, which was passed in agreeable conversation, all three gentlemen left me with final farewells. The whistle of the boat is now heard. Oh, that it may bring me good news! It is now three calendar months almost to the minute since I entered the walls of this fort, between 10 and 11 o'clock of the 25th of May.

In last night's Washington telegrams in the Boston *Post* this morning, I see that Linton reached Washington yesterday. This caused my heart to bound with joy! My prayer is thus far answered. He is, I hope, well and coming to me. He is on the way! I shall look for him to-morrow, and next day, and every day, until he comes. Governor [Joe] Brown is with him. I wish he, too, would come, but I hardly think so. I clipped an editorial from the *Tribune*, Greeley's second reply to Thurlow Weed. If Greeley is not an honest and truthful man, I have never met one. I do not agree with him in many things, but I have a high regard for his directness of purpose and integrity of motive. He is, on his line, a true and earnest man. He is withal an able man. The Corporal, while I was reading the papers, brought me a letter from Mr. Bell, a New York publisher, proposing to publish anything I may wish issued in book form. This is the letter, I suppose, that Lieut. Newton told me reached here some days ago and was returned to New York for General Hooker's approval.

The Corporal returned and brought me two boxes from Mrs. Salter, one of flowers and one of sweet cakes.

Called on Mrs. Livermore. The Captain came in

with two gentlemen, captains of engineers, I understood, of the name of Amesby. He told me he had received an order to-day to release Judge Reagan from close confinement. I was about to start on my daily visit to Reagan when the Captain told me this. The news did not retard my motions at all! When I reached his room, I discovered from the glow on his countenance that some other person, or a bird of the air, had anticipated me in communicating it. The joy and gladness it imparted showed itself not only in his looks but in the very motions of the body and the tones of the voice. We played piquet and euchre as usual. During this time, Lieut. Newton came and took the lock off his door. I could conjecture what his feelings were when the last clanking of that lock was heard. I doubt if anybody can who was never in a like situation.

Reagan called and sat with me until retreat was beat; except for about an hour before the evening boat, when we went on the terreplein, confining ourselves to the southern part. Orders came to allow Dr. Bickley and Vernon the northern ramparts for their walk. We are not to speak to them; or more correctly, in conformity with instructions to allow them more liberty, we cannot walk round the parapet. Reagan seemed weak and wearied, and I felt no disposition to walk; so we sat on the western bastion until the boat came; then stayed in my room until retreat sounded. Dr. Seaverns came in. I was surprised at his returning before his leave is out, which would not be until Monday. He sat and talked more than an hour with us. He has been to Chicago on a visit to his brother. After supper, Mr. Devine, the soldier tailor, who was my neighbour in my old quarters, called, and I was glad to give him a welcome. He seems like an old friend. He tells me he has been a soldier in the United States Army since 1837; is now on a sort of detail for his company to do their sewing, mending, and tailoring. He is an Irishman. The Irish somehow take to me by constitution or affinity. I told my good friend, for so I regard him, that I had another button off and must get him to sew it on. He seemed glad to do something for me.

August 26. — A telegram from Washington in the N. Y. *World* says Linton and Governor Brown are there, endeavouring to have me released on parole. I did expect a letter from Linton to-day; but I am not so deeply anxious since I see that he is in Washington. That news gives me great relief. But I fear he will be disappointed in his efforts. This will cause him pain and that will distress me more than my confinement. Intense as is my wish to be at home, yet I greatly prefer to stay here for years, if I should be spared so long, than that he should feel unhappy on account of my desire. With the privileges I now enjoy, I can bear imprisonment, can bear being cut off from all the dear ones at home if I can but be assured that they do not suffer mentally or physically on my account. I am anxious to see Linton and talk over all these matters with him. I want to talk to him as I have never yet done, of my reliance upon Divine power.

10 P. M. — After supper, Dr. Seaverns called and sat for an hour. Conversation turned on Southern society, enterprise, etc. I gave him a description of the Midway Community, the Midway congregation in Liberty County, as it presented itself to me in 1833, as one of the best examples of human society on the face of the earth.

I spoke of Louis Le Conte as the most learned man I ever saw, the most fully informed on all subjects to which I had seen his attention called.

Sunday, August 27. — Last night, before I got fairly to sleep and just as I began to doze, Linton seemed to be approaching my door hastily. I rose in great joy to meet him. As I seemed to rise, I awoke. It was a vision. He did not speak, nor did I. What to make of this, I do not know. I have not dreamed of talking with Linton since we parted at my gate. The whistle of the boat announces its arrival with the mail. May it bring me news of Linton if not Linton himself!

Boston *Herald* brought in by Geary. See that Linton and Governor Brown were trying to get an interview with President Johnson yesterday. If they succeeded, Linton may possibly reach here to-morrow. But I fear they failed; am in great suspense. Lieut. Newton brought me a letter from Joe Myers, dated New York, 25th inst. Myers says he and Linton left home Thursday, the 17th. He left Linton in Louisville, Ky., with Governor Brown and Judge Lochrane.* Myers is to remain in New York until Linton reaches there, then he is to come with Linton to see me. He says Linton was to stop in Washington; says all were well when he left home.

Lieut. Newton also brought two copies of the Augusta [Ga.] *Transcript* sent by Governor Cumming, I suppose. In pencil on one is this: "The New York *Commercial* correspondent says Alexander H. Stephens will soon be released." I saw yesterday a publication from the State Department which I think foreshadows a great

* Chief Justice of the Supreme Court of Georgia in 1871–72.

deal. It is to the effect that pardoned rebels can get passports, just as other citizens, to leave the country; and that application of rebels not pardoned will be acted on, etc. The policy indicated is, therefore, to grant leave to quit the country to those entitled to this pardon.

Noon. — Reagan and I walked on the parapet. The day was beautiful. Everything was still and quiet in the fort, reminding us of Sundays on a plantation where stillness reigns, and when all who are to be seen are lolling or lounging about at rest. The drill and constant sounds of music which were kept up on Sunday as on other days when first I came, have been discontinued. The morning beat of the drum and the reveille are yet heard, and some other hours are signalled by tap of drum or blast of bugle; but the regular everyday rounds of music are not continued; still, there is no preaching, no public religious exercise, on Sundays.

It is now a week since I have been in my new quarters. I have improved wonderfully in physical condition. In mind, I am greatly relieved from the oppression that bore me down so sorely while in the old.

Reagan and I again strolled on the parapet; saw a large steamer pass the fort to Boston. Some said she was an emigrant ship; some, that she was a U. S. transport bringing home Massachusetts troops.

August 28. — Geary brought me the New York *Day Book* of 26th, which came to Lieut. Woodman yesterday, marked for me. Samuel Anderson sent it, I suppose. In it I see an article headed, "Alexander H. Stephens." If he wrote it, I have no doubt his intentions were good, but it abounds in mistakes as is usual with such articles. Had some conversation with Corporal

Geary last night. Advised him, when discharged from the service, to go South, study law, and make a man of himself. I think from what I have seen of him that he would succeed at the bar. He is young, has energy, perseverance, integrity, a fondness for books and for information. A telegram from Washington in the Boston *Post*, says nothing has been done by the Georgians there on the subject of my release.

Saturday night. When Dr. Seaverns was here, I showed him how to make magic squares upon the principle which Dr. Le Conte taught me. He told me yesterday that he had tried and could not make one. I went round to-day and showed him again. Walked out with Reagan. Saw the transport arrive at Gallops Island with the 54th Mass. Regiment of Coloured Troops. They have come to be mustered out of service.

CHAPTER XXV

AUGUST 29. — Examined the original Greek on Robertson's text on the triune nature of man. Yesterday, Mr. Barnham brought me from Boston a Greek Testament, Greek Lexicon, Latin Grammar, and Robertson's "Sermons." I ordered some second-hand books. Last night after candle-light, I read Arnold on Joubert, and became interested in extracts from Joubert's writings.

The morning boat came. Last night's telegram to the *Post* says Linton had an interview with the President yesterday. I shall now soon know the result. Patience, patience! On the boat came C. T. Bruen, Journal Clerk in the late Confederate Senate, to spend the day with me.

The evening boat has come and gone. Mr. Bruen and I had a pleasant time. We took dinner in the mess-room. I must go round and see Reagan. Bruen's being here has kept me from him.

Met Reagan near my door. We went on the parapet. He told me of a telegram in evening paper stating that an officer who had been to see Mr. Davis reported that Mr. Davis spoke in denunciatory terms of Hunter and myself, saying if we had remained firm the Confederacy would have triumphed, etc. Reagan and I concurred in the opinion that Mr. Davis had not indulged in such expressions. At the same time, as I told Reagan, I have but little doubt Mr. Davis conscientiously believes as this telegram reports him to have expressed himself, so little does he realize what was the real cause of the collapse of the Confederacy. Supper under a new arrangement. Reagan and I hereafter mess together. We took our tea together in the mess-room this evening. He asked the blessing.

At night, alone. It was, in passing, a pleasant day. The visit of Bruen was interesting. What disturbs me is self-examination. At the table I, in a pretty full flow of spirits, illustrated several matters with humorous anecdotes, one of which it would have been improper to relate in the presence of ladies. It had nothing improper to the ordinary taste when told in a company of gentlemen. It was Martin J. Crawford's celebrated "cat story." Bruen and I laughed over its aptness; but as we passed out of the room, it occurred to me that Mrs. Livermore might possibly have heard it. Now, this disturbs me greatly; and it has caused me gravely to consider whether I should ever again in any conversation indulge in any vein of humour unfit for the ears of a lady. Ought men, even by themselves, ever to indulge in anecdotes from which, by sense of propriety, they would refrain in the presence of ladies the most refined? Is not the thing in itself degrading more or less to man's nature? It is useless to argue: "Oh, it makes no difference even if Mrs. Livermore did hear it; she knows you were not aware that she was within hearing." That is not the point. Ought we not at all times to act and speak, not only as we would in the presence of the best and purest on earth, but as we would speak in the presence of the best and purest in Heaven? Is not this the proper discipline of our minds, thoughts, affections, and actions? Ought not humour to be chaste? Is any humour chaste to which ladies cannot listen?

August 30. — Ill. I took a drink of Harry's whisky; this seemed to do me good, but a sad thought passed through my mind as I put down the bottle; and that was that Harry's whisky was most out. There is but about one more drink left. Bruen promised to send me a bottle of brandy. I cannot well do without spirits of some kind as a medicine. Breakfast with Reagan. The grace was said by me this morning at the Judge's request.

Last night I read Arnold on Spinoza and Marcus Aurelius. I have not yet been able to satisfy myself as to this critic's general object. It seems to me that it is not good, that his spirit is evil, that he conceals himself as well as he can and attempts to inculcate his own views through the teachings of others.

Will Linton come to-day? This thought absorbs my mind. He has not written to me. This is a mystery. Would he not have done so if he had not been under some deep affliction in body or mind, himself? It seems to me he would. This disquiets me. My earnest wish and prayer is that all may be well with him and that I shall yet see him. Oh, that this earnest desire of my heart may be fulfilled! but if this shall never be, teach me, O Lord, to bow to thy will.

Last night, I proposed to Geary to teach him Latin if he would take it up. Asked him what he thought about it. He said he thought it was useless to begin because he thought I would be released soon. I told him I thought my release quite uncertain; while I hoped it might be, and soon, yet we should not act on that supposition; and if he would begin, I would take pleasure in assisting him so long as I remain, let that be a long or short time. I handed him my Adam's Latin Grammar, and told him to look over the first page down to Penna, and see what he thought of it, and of the undertaking. Maybe after that, he would be able to come to a more definite conclusion. He took the grammar. I heard him reading aloud in his room some time afterward, as I have often heard him before, but whether it was Adam's Grammar or something else, I did not know. He is very fond of reading books as well as papers.

Mess board-bill brought in; to date from 18th August, at $1 a day less 19 cts. commutation, $11.34. Gave check. Reagan called and we played euchre. We quit even at four games apiece. When we first began playing, he usually beat me at euchre. To-day I told him the "dog and wolf" story to illustrate our turns of fortune, and it amused him. A man who had a dog which he bragged on as a wolf-killer, went to a neighbouring district to catch a noted wolf that had mastered all the dogs in the vicinity. He felt certain *his* dog would make an end of the wolf. A crowd joined in the chase. The wolf was started, the dog was on trail, the cry was up, pursuit was hot, the dog was soon out of hearing of the horsemen. Riding full speed in the direction of the last yelp, the man of the wolf-dog foremost, they came upon a traveller of whom the dog-owner asked, had he seen anything of the dog and wolf? "Oh yes," said he, "they went by here just now." "How were they going?" eagerly asked the dog-owner. "Oh," said he inquired of, "nip and tuck, hip and thigh, *but the dog was a little ahead.*"

Walked around to see Mrs. Livermore. She is an exceedingly pleasant and agreeable woman, well informed, intelligent, and of most winning manners, winning mainly by reason of perfect naturalness and simplicity.

A pleasant time Reagan and I had at table, talking of old Congress acquaintances, particularly of McConnell and Bowdon, his successor. I told the Judge of a remark McConnell made to me in the House about his condition in the next world, as he feared it would be. He was an extraordinary man, one of the most eccentric geniuses I ever knew. He was intemperate, profane, and yet very religiously inclined. He had a high regard for worship and always seemed to join devoutly with the chaplain in morning prayers. One day (he sat by me) while we were talking together, conversation turned on religion. He seemed deeply affected. He spoke of his wife with the most tender devotion; said she was a pure Christian, that she had prayed earnestly for him. "I know she will, when she dies, go right to heaven, while I fear," he added with tears in his eyes, "that I shall go as straight to hell. But I tell you, Stephens, if God does send me to hell, he will send one of the best friends there he ever had in this world." All this was said with the most perfect sincerity and the deepest emotion.

John Pettit, of Indiana, was well known to be a sort of freethinker; some said he was a disbeliever in the Christian religion. One day during the debate on the Oregon question — about terminating the joint occupancy of Oregon — a number of members were permitted by general consent to offer and have laid on the table propositions on this exciting subject. Pettit asked that the same leave be granted him. McConnell, who had a strong aversion to Pettit because he had opposed the election of a chaplain and because of his supposed irreligious sentiments, sprang to his feet and said, "Mr.

Speaker, I object." A decision was asked. McConnell, with great earnestness of manner, called on the members to vote down Pettit, not to grant Pettit the leave asked, because, he said, "Pettit does not believe in the Saviour who died for him." This coming from a man of his habits seemed queer, but in it he was thoroughly honest and in earnest.

Soon after the boat came, Lieut. Newton sent me in a letter from Linton. This was most welcome. It was written on Sunday. It ought to have been here yesterday. He makes no mention of my letter telling him of my release from close confinement, or of any letters received from me since his last. This is strange. I do wish he would come along here and not be spending his time and money in Washington. I am, however, greatly relieved.

General Denver, from Washington, came to see me, Judge Reagan with him. They sat and talked until tea time. Captain Livermore called and took General D. with him to tea. Reagan and I went to our room to tea, and then I learned from him to my surprise that General Denver is on a visit here to him and me from the authorities at Washington; Denver left Washington Saturday; he had not seen Linton. There is some mystery about this to me. After tea, Captain Livermore with General Denver returned to my room where Judge Reagan was. The General sat until 9. We talked over many matters, but he said nothing implying that he was an agent from Washington; he gave us the opinion that Reagan and I would be held here for some time and then released. He remarked that he thought there would he changes in the Cabinet before long; Stanton would certainly go out at an early day; and changes would then be made here. He thought Mr. Davis would be tried, and at Richmond. To-day, I got a letter from Messrs. O. D. Case & Co., of Hartford, Conn., proposing to publish anything I may be preparing for the press; they enclosed this letter from the Hon. Horace Greeley:

Office of the *Tribune*, N. Y., Aug. 28, '65.

Dear Sir: Messrs. O. D. Case & Co., of Hartford, Conn., publishers of my history of our great struggle, presuming that you may be prompted to give your view of this contest in some permanent form, would be glad to arrange with you for publishing your book, and would be willing to grant liberal terms. I assure you that they are abundantly able and have every facility for giving your work a large sale, and I venture to request that you do not arrange with any other house before conferring with them. Yours,

HORACE GREELEY.

The HON. A. H. STEPHENS.

Thursday, August 31. — Sixteen weeks are now complete since the bright morn when I rose for the last time at my quiet and beloved home to greet the bracing air. Four lunar months have rolled around, and I am still far from those scenes to me so dear. Breakfast at 8, Reagan and I together in our new mess-room. He told me that General Denver sat with him last night until 10; he and Denver left my room at 9. He thinks the main object of Denver's visit here is to see him about certain treasury drafts of the Confederate Government; to get information by which the funds as covered by these drafts, amounting to a few thousand pounds sterling, may be got possession of by the authorities at Washington. Reagan told all he knew about them, but that was not certain or definite. To me, the visit, without this explanation, seemed very mysterious. This may be the sole object. Answered Linton's letter of the 27th, addressing him at Willard's Hotel, Washington, but I have very little idea that my letter will reach him.

General Denver called to take leave. Sat a few minutes and then left with friendly parting expression of sympathy and the statement that he would do what he could for me. One thing he said gave me the impression that he thinks Mr. Seward rather vindictive toward me for some cause which he cannot understand.

Ten-o'clock boat came. I see from the Boston *Post* that Linton left Washington yesterday for this place, and that I shall probably be paroled. I am greatly encouraged. From this letter I do not think he left until he got the parole or learned that it was definitely decided that there would be no action soon. In the latter case, it would hardly have been published that there was a probability of parole, but rather that he had not succeeded. This is my intrepretation. I am hopeful, but shall not permit myself to be carried away with hope. Corporal Geary brought me a joint letter from Thomas Chafin, Jr., and his son, James, of Columbus, Ga.

I shall look for Linton this evening or certainly to-morrow morning. Oh, that no accident may befall him in coming! May our Father in Heaven watch over, guard, and protect him, and bring him safely here! Answered letters.

At 3.30, went to the ramparts and staid there until the boat arrived. I thought Linton might come. Boat came. No letters and no news from Linton. I shall wait patiently until to-morrow. I shall now look for him certainly by the morning boat. The Judge and I went again upon the ramparts. We saw Bickley and

Vernon walking on their part. We also saw the poor soldiers on a beat with burdens on their backs, evidently suffering punishment for some offense. The punishment seems to be to walk on a line or beat on the drill-ground back and forth, with heavy packs on their backs. They seemed very tired, and I pitied them. We returned to my room; then went to our mess-room for tea; then came back to my room where we sat and talked for some time; the subject was Mr. Davis. I gave the Judge an outline of the correspondence between myself and Mr. Davis last winter. While we were out, Mr. Harrington brought his hydrometric registry and left it on my table.

CHAPTER XXVI

FRIDAY, Sept. 1.—The summer has gone. September is here. How much longer shall I remain? Linton, I expect, will be here to-day. The news he will bring will settle the question whether I am to be paroled or remain.

7 P. M.—Alone in the twilight. What emotions have I experienced since my last entry! Linton came by the morning boat. I was certain, on my first view of his countenance, that he had not with him any order for my release, or any news to that effect. He soon told me by words what I had read in his face. I was not much disappointed; was not depressed; I was prepared. Governor H. V. Johnson came with him; did not enter my room with Linton, but followed soon after. Reagan and I were playing piquet when Linton appeared. Reagan quickly left, as he is not permitted to hold conversations with my visitors. Governor Johnson was unwell; rested on my bed a good portion of the day. Linton and I talked a great deal. We spent a pleasant day; he did not bring his baggage from Boston and went back this evening for it. Johnson went by same boat; is going back to Washington and to Georgia; said he would have another interview with the President on my account if he could get it. I indulge but slight hopes of early release; am prepared in mind to remain here for some time to come. I am not oppressed at the outlook. I am schooled to patience. I feel sad at Linton's

having to leave me, but am sustained by the prospect of having him back to-morrow to spend some weeks with me. This will be a great comfort.

Letters from John A. Stephens, Frank Bristow, Harry, the Hon. Peterson Thweatt [former Comptroller-General of Ga.], Mr. Baskerville, C. A. Beasley, and R. M. Johnston added to the good things received this day. But pleasures, like other excitements, leave the spirit in a state of ebb-tide. The news Linton brought from home was not all pleasant. Some was very sad; two of my county friends are dead, D. L. Peek and Esau Ellington. Things at home, too, are not going on as well as I could wish. I need not state particulars here. After dinner, Linton and I called on Captain and Mrs. Livermore; met Mrs. and Captain Perry, their guests. The boat left at 5; I bade Johnson good-bye with a full heart; also, Linton for the night. I felt very sad when I turned away from them. Oh, may Linton return in the morning safely!

Governor Johnson brought good news for Judge Reagan; he had seen in Washington Robert McMatthew, who was intrusted with the care of conducting Reagan's children to Texas. Reagan had not heard from his children since February. McMatthew told Johnson he had placed them safely with their grandmother in Texas. Reagan and I took supper by ourselves. Linton, Johnson, and I dined together.

Sept. 2.—Was taken ill last night. Linton returned by morning boat. Reagan spent the morning with me until he came. Dr. Seaverns called early. Corporal went for him. Linton has moved my bed into the front room. Mr. Harrington brought me some arrowroot nicely prepared.

Sunday Sept. 3.—After midnight, the fever I had had all day passed off. Read in Ezra. Linton read me portions of this journal. He read the first pages yesterday. To-day, he read on from where he left off yesterday. When he got to the second day's imprisonment here, I told him to stop. It made me sad. For some cause, his emotions overpowered him and he wept aloud. I, too, wept, but told him not to grieve. It was all over I hoped. I had suffered greatly, but did not now. The doctor called soon; called again before noon, and again this evening. Linton and I spent the day in talking. How pleasant a day it was to me! Linton dined in the mess-room. Our breakfast was served here. After dinner, Linton lay down for a nap. I walked round to see Reagan. We walked out on the ramparts. Then Linton and I walked on the ramparts.

Tuesday, Sept. 5.—Sundown. Retreat is beating. I have been crowded with company. Dr. and Mrs. James T. Paterson of Georgia, William D. Crocket and wife from Boston, and Malcolm Mosely (Dick Johnston's nephew), Sergeant in U. S. Infantry at Fort Independence, called. Had quite a dinner party. Seven of us sat down at the table. Geary waited upon us very well. All went by the boat at 5. Early in the day, I wrote to Harry, John A. Stephens, Mr. Baskerville and others. No news in the papers except a telegram from Washington saying it is now fixed to have Mr. Davis tried before the Chief Justice at Norfolk in October. Letter from John A. Stephens. All my people well. All well at the homestead. Senator Henry Wilson sent me a copy of his book, "Anti-Slavery Measures in Congress."

Sept. 6. — Linton and I walked out twice. In the evening, I joined Reagan in a walk. Dr. Seaverns called and sat with us an hour after night. Linton and I had called to see him but he was not in. We called on Mrs. Livermore; sat some time in conversation; the Captain was with us part of the time. Mrs. Livermore has sent us some of the best pears I ever ate. This entry is not made on the 6th but on the 7th, such has become my negligence of my journal since Linton came. Wrote several letters.

Linton got a letter from S. J. Anderson which gives the opinion that no demonstrations in my behalf by the Republicans in New York would avail anything, but that I will be pardoned and released "before long." This he learned, through Sheriff Kelley, from Republicans. Linton and I met Mrs. Appleton on the parapet. She was on a visit here, spending the day with Mrs. Seaverns. Mrs. Seaverns and little family of children were walking with her. I called to see her in the evening. Linton was reading my journal. After my visit, Reagan and I took a long walk on the parapet.

I wrote a number of letters of introduction for Mr. Micajah O. Hall who is going to Atlanta to open a bookstore. He has been a clerk in the sutler's office. Linton wrote to the Hon. B. H. Bigham, Washington, D. C. Dr. Seaverns called at 9 p. m. I was in bed; Linton was reading. He came to tell me that the ladies, Mrs. Livermore and Mrs. Seaverns, had wormed out a different answer to the charade from the one I got. Their answer was "wormwood" [see p. 306, 308].

Sept. 9. — The Corporal tells me that Mrs. Nutler, who has moved, will do no more washing here. What

I am to do, I do not know. She was the only person here who took in washing. The Corporal thinks I will have to send washing to Boston. Got two copies of the *Constitutionalist* of Augusta, Ga. In one, saw two letters from Judge Starnes to Colonel M. C. Fulton, of Snow Hill. The Atlanta *Intelligencer* comes regularly.

6 P. M.—Mr. Myers came. I was very glad to see him. He brought me a bottle of brandy and a box of cigars. We spent a pleasant day. He told me all the news about home, and of some things that have happened since he left. Amongst other things, he brought me the pen with which I am writing. It is a good pen; cost $4.50 in New York. I was sad when he left. Linton went out on the ramparts to see him depart; I sent by him to Mr. John Phillips, of Boston to supply me with a bedstead, bed, and bedclothes. Myers said he would send me an overcoat and five pounds of candles. I sent by him two peach seeds for Harry to plant, and also some sweet cakes for Ellen, Tim, Dora, Fanny and Quin [young Negroes, Harry's children].

Sept. 11.—Made no entry yesterday. It was Sunday. Passed the day pleasantly with Linton. He read to me most of the time, when we were not walking out. We spent a very pleasant time after candle-light, talking of old matters, scenes of his early childhood, his recollections of events at the old homestead before he was three years old, of Aunt Nimmie Gordon; and of many things which awakened pleasant but melancholy reminiscences. My old Aunt Betsy, Uncle Aaron, and many other persons once dear to us both, were talked of.

Sept. 12. — Linton went to Boston. Phillips brought my bed and other things down; $73.13. Reagan and I spent the day together and watched for the approach of the boat from Boston. Linton returned. Brought me various articles needed. Wm. Prescott Smith, of Baltimore, called. Promised to call again; was passing by to Portland, Maine.

Sept. 13. — Did not sleep well on my new bed. I thought from smell the feathers were old. Wrote to Senator Henry Wilson. Linton received a letter from S. J. Anderson which seems to settle the question of my release; all prospects buried for the present. Hon. Anson B. Burlingame came down to the fort at 4, with a party of friends. In this were Sir Frederick Bruce, the British Minister. Also Mrs. Van Lew and daughter, from Richmond; they came to see me. A Mrs. Revere also called, as did Mr. Livermore, father of the Captain, who, by the by, has been promoted and is now Major. General Schouler, Adj.-General of the State, called. He seems to be a warm friend to me. Mr. Burlingame seems quite kind-hearted. These gentlemen told me that Governor Andrew (of Mass.) has written to Washington in my behalf.

Sept. 15. — I told Linton I had a presentiment that I should be released before long. I was reluctant to tell him this, for I thought he might consider it superstitious, and so it may be, but O my God, in Thy mercy make it true! I dreamed of being at home, of seeing Bob and giving Charlton a coat. Judge Erskine, who now resides in New York, called to see me. By the evening boat, Major Jones, Quartermaster for New York State, who resides in Albany, called. He is my relative. He showed me a letter from Colonel Babcock, of General Grant's staff, stating that the General is in favour of my release. He presented me with a light walking-cane. I met him at City Point last February; he was kind and attentive to me there; sent me a dozen Scotch ale. Rev. Dr. Stebbins, of Cambridge, Major Livermore's uncle, called this evening; the Major brought him. Dr. Stebbins expressed strong sympathy for me and an earnest desire for my early discharge.

Sept. 16. — Linton was to have gone to Boston to-day to see after some matters for me; but, as I was taken ill and as Lieut. Newton was going up, he remained. I wrote to the President and to General Grant. I reminded the President of his promise by telegram to reply to my request for a personal interview, and again urged it as it is important for me to be released — if I am to be released — by the middle of October. To General Grant, I gave the facts of my case and asked him, if consistent with his sense of duty, to lend the great weight of his name and influence for my release on parole; this is a copy:

LIEUT. GEN. U. S. GRANT, WASHINGTON, D. C.

Dear Sir: All the apology I have to offer for this letter, as well as its explanation, is to be found in the facts herein presented. I am now in confinement in this place, as you are probably aware. I have been here since the 25th of May last. I am exceedingly anxious to be paroled as a great many others have been, who were arrested as I was. I think I am as justly entitled to discharge on parole as many of those to whom I allude. No man in the Southern States, I think, exerted his powers to a greater extent than I did to avert the late lamentable troubles of our country, no man strove harder to bring about peace, and no man can be more anxious to see peace, order, harmony, and prosperity restored than myself. You knew my feelings on this subject when we met at Hampton Roads. They were correctly set forth in your telegram to the Secretary of War; upon that, the Hampton Roads Conference was granted. When I parted with you, I assured you that while nothing definite had been accomplished, I was hopeful that good would result. In that hope I was disappointed. No one could have been more pained, mortified, and chagrined than I was at the result. I refer to this because you were then fully informed of my views. And I now drop you this line simply to ask you, if you feel at liberty to do so, to lend the great weight of your name and influence with the President, and the Secretaries of War and State, for my release on parole. I have applied to the President for amnesty, but if the President for any reason feels disposed to postpone decision of that matter, I am perfectly content. What I desire mainly is a release from imprisonment on parole, as others, or on bail, if it should be required. In no event would I attempt to avoid a prosecution or trial, if it should be thought best for any reason to adopt such a course toward me. I wish release both in consequence of my health and private affairs. My case and request are briefly submitted to you. Act in the premises as your sense of duty shall direct.

Yours most respectfully,

ALEXANDER H. STEPHENS.

Sunday — I feel better, but am not well. Read in Psalms. I talked with Reagan for some time. He is low-spirited. I advised him to write again to the President.

Sept. 18. — William W. Simpson, of Sparta, Ga., called, a most agreeable surprise. His news from home generally was interesting. He spent the day with us.

Reagan sent for me and submitted a letter he had written to the President. I liked it very well. He said he would send it this evening. Last night Linton and I read his memoirs.

Sept. 19. — Linton went to Boston. General W. Raymond Lee had written at Miss Van Lew's instance, asking Linton to meet him at his office this morning. Before he left, we had a long talk on revolutions and resort to violence as a means of advancing human rights or progress. He agreed, as heretofore, that these great ends are better attained in the forum of reason than in the arena of arms. By the boat, some friend sent a copy of the National *Intelligencer* in which appears in my behalf, an article signed "Justice." Who wrote it, I cannot imagine. The fact that none of the leading papers have republished it, convinces me that there is not that general sympathy in my behalf at the North which I supposed might exist. My views are changed on that point, and I am nerved with new fortitude and patience to bear my lot. I am now satisfied that I am nothing but a sort of political hostage, held without any regard to personal merits or demerits and simply to answer the purpose of designing men in accomplishing their own selfish ends. I am merely a victim to be sacrificed to propitiate others.

I see R. M. T. Hunter is in Washington, and in conference with Seward. Here I am held in this prison while leading fire-eaters, Mr. Davis and a few others excepted, are at large.

By evening boat I got a letter from the Hon. B. H. Bigham replying to mine; and one from Joseph Myers, New York; Myers says he has sent me a pair of blankets and a bottle of cologne; and that an overcoat has been sent to me as a present by some one. Bigham writes that Seward assigned as a reason for my detention, the fact that I was Vice-President of the Confederacy, and in the case of Mr. Davis's death, the presidency would devolve on me; it would be hazardous to set me at large until all the seceded States are back in the Union with Secession Ordinances abrogated, etc. This reason has not enough speciousness, even as a pretext, to commend it to my charitable consideration. Linton did not return. Reagan and I walked out. Waited two hours looking for the boat and Linton. We talked over our misfortunes pretty freely and fully. Dr. Seaverns called after supper and played piquet until 10.30.

Sept. 20. — I wrote this letter to the Hon. Wm. H. Seward:

Dear Sir: You will, I trust, excuse me for addressing you upon a subject of very great interest to me personally: I mean, my release on parole. I am induced to do this from a letter just received from a distinguished friend in Washington. That friend writes to me that the reason you assigned to him for my continued imprisonment was the fact that I was the Vice-President under the Confederate States organization and in case of the death of Mr. Davis the duties of that office would devolve on me, etc.: hence, the danger of permitting me to go at large until all the States of that organization should be restored to their proper relations to the Federal Government. . . . In my letter to the President making special application for amnesty, etc., I expressly stated that all further contest was abandoned; that it was not abandoned as soon as I wished it to be, but its abandonment, when it was, had my cordial approval;

and I accepted the results of the war [illegible words] and I was willing to abide by the results in good faith, and to take the prescribed oath of fidelity to the Constitution of the United States. Can you or the authorities at Washington desire to have stronger evidence than this that no such danger as suggested by you need be entertained from my enlargement? Indeed, I stated to the President that I would, if released, use my utmost exertions and influence in bringing about a restoration of peace and harmony in the country on the basis of the Executive policy. I present these facts for your consideration as a full answer to the objection raised by you to my release in that view. Again, if released on parole or bond, I should still be in custody of the authorities on such terms as they might think proper to prescribe. Allow me to add in explanation of my importunity on this subject, that it is a matter of the utmost importance to my present welfare and that of others, to say nothing of my health, that if I am to be released at all, it should be done at an early day — at least by the middle or latter part of October. By that time my business at home, the nature of which you are apprised of, now in suspense, must be attended to, or great confusion, if not ruin to me, must ensue. My presence is almost absolutely necessary for any proper settlement of estates and trust property in my hands. These matters have been postponed in expectation that I would be released, to give them my personal attention. They cannot be postponed beyond the close of this year. If I am not released before cold weather sets in, I could not, without great hazard and risk undertake the travel home before next summer. It is, moreover, essential to the well-being of the freedmen with their families on my place at home that I should perfect my arrangements with them at least by the first of November. They are anxiously and earnestly looking for me now daily. I must confess that I cannot see any reason of State policy that should keep me in prison — especially as so many others infinitely more responsible than myself for all these troubles have been fully pardoned. Of this I do not complain. I think the President has acted patriotically and wisely in the clemency exercised by him in this particular. I only mean to say that I cannot see any reason of State policy that applies to me that does not apply with equal force to many I could name of these.

Yours most respectfully,

ALEXANDER H. STEPHENS.

Linton came. Says the opinion prevails in Boston, with those he met, that I will be released soon. Hope their opinion may prove true. Got a letter from Frank Bristow; Tim had lost one of his calves; it died. I am sorry for the calf as well as for Tim.

Thursday — Nineteen weeks since my arrest; seventeen, I have been in this fort. I did not sleep well. Pain in the chest. A pair of superb bed-blankets came by the boat, where from I do not know.

P. M.—Linton got a letter from Gen. W. Raymond Lee, of Boston, or West Roxbury, stating that he thought he might safely say the day of my release is at hand. He invited us, when I shall be released, to spend an evening with him and meet Governor Andrew, etc. This was cheering news to me. Telegram from Joe Myers, informing me of his safe arrival home, and that all were well at my home and at Sparta. Lieut. Newton called, with board and appendages, to teach me the Garrison Game. I took the men and beat him the first time. Linton then took the officers and beat him with the men. It is on the "Fox and Geese" order, but much more complicated. Dr. Seaverns also called, and he and I played piquet until Newton left; then Linton and he played piquet.

Sept. 22.—Dr. Paterson came by boat. He brought a copy of the Boston *Traveller* containing a communication about my release on parole. We spent a pleasant day. He left by evening boat. No news in in the evening Boston *Journal*. I am now in suspense about my case. No reply from General Raymond Lee to Linton's note of this morning. Linton got a long and interesting letter from Mrs. Salter. Mr. Harrington brought me in his registry of the meteorological changes, etc.

A cat has taken up in my room. He belongs to the boat's mess, and has remained all day, quite domesticated. I patted him on the head this morning down in the mess-room of the boat's crew, and he took up with me immediately. Dr. Seaverns called after supper. Sat a while and told us of a ride in the horse-car to-day in Boston with Dr. Paterson and Mr. Crocket. Linton read to me Schlegel on Literature.

Sept. 23.—The cat staid all night with me. By the boat I got a basket of fruit from Mrs. Paterson: peaches, pears, and plums. Linton and I took a long walk. The evening boat did not come. We staid on the rampart until retreat beat. After I went to bed, the boat came. The Corporal brought me the *Journal*. No news. Nothing about my release. Did not go to sleep for hours, thinking of my imprisonment, and brooding over my suspense.

Sunday—Had bad dreams; dreamed of seeing several people hanged. After breakfast, Linton and I walked on the ramparts. He gave me this conundrum: "Why is your old overcoat (I had put it on for the walk) like a good Christian?" After searching my mind for some word that would express similarity in the line of tribulation or adversity, I gave it up. Whereupon, he said, "Because it has received Devine assistance." Mr. Devine had mended it. We whiled away an hour, waiting for the boat.

The cat, which we have named Tom, answers to his name and seems quite at home with us.

The mail came without the boat, or in advance of it. Somebody sent me the Boston *Express*, which has two articles advocating my release. Got my two Georgia papers; I see Judge Jenkins's acceptance of nomination to the State Convention. Linton got a note from General Lee, of Boston. It states that Governor Andrew has not returned, and that the opinion he expressed about my early release was based on opinions expressed to him by some who are in communication with the powers at Washington and who ought to know.

The boat came at noon, and with it the Boston *Herald* containing last night's Washington telegram. I was disappointed and mystified at seeing no allusion to my release. I feel heartsick. "Soon" and "before long," as applied to my release by those who use such terms, may mean weeks or months; even years, compared with life or eternity, may be styled, "soon," or "before long." I feel worse than for weeks.

Sept. 25.—The papers contained nothing about my release. Mr. Mallory at Fort Lafayette, the *Times* says, had an interview with Secretary Stanton. Linton had a letter from Miss Van Lew, at Yonkers, saying I would soon be released. She had seen General Hooker; said Governor Andrew would call to see me as soon as he could. This does not look much like my release at an early day. Governor Andrew was then with Secretary Stanton in New York. She requested Linton to write again, giving her the names of prominent and active secessionists who had been pardoned; also, those who had been paroled. Linton answered her; wrote her a good letter. The boat came. No letters. The Savannah *News* came, sent me from Hilton Head, I suppose, by Lieut. Woodman. No allusion in evening paper to my release. I feel more chagrined and humiliated than since my arrest; I feel that I have been treated with indignity and insult. I am enraged at myself for ever having made to President Johnson or Mr. Seward anything other than a simple statement of my case and a demand for my constitutional and legal right. I should feel better if I had borne in silence whatever they saw fit to inflict, even if it had been death.

Sept. 26. — I got a basket of fruit from Mrs. Salter, and Linton received a long letter from her. The label on the basket bore her name. Directly under was this in pencil, "How are you, Alex?" Who added this is a mystery to me. It is perhaps a taunt by some enemy. This brings to my mind a tract sent me a few days ago through the mails. It is a campaign tract for 1864, and is made up of what purports to be extracts from my speeches; all forgeries; I made no such speeches. Yesterday, in conversation with Major Livermore, I told him of these forgeries. I showed him my "Union speech," of November 1860, and as it appears in the "Rebellion Record." He showed me a letter he had received from the Hon. Mr. Upham, of Salem, expressing a wish to come to see me again. I thanked him and told him I should like much to see Mr. Upham.

I see in the New York *Times* an abstract of a sermon by Henry Ward Beecher, which is rather remarkable. He freely admits all I ever maintained about the inferiority of the Negro race to the white. The only real difference in our views concerns the system by which the influence of the superior race can be best exerted upon the inferior for the latter's advantage. Subordination of the inferior, I thought necessary. Hence, the "Cornerstone" idea in my Savannah speech.

Linton wrote to General Lee, inquiring if he could give any opinion from his sources of information as to whether I should be released in the course of a week. He also wrote to Dr. Paterson for me, asking him to send me the *Harper's Monthly* for October, containing Jordan's article on Mr. Davis and as many of the recent numbers of *Harper's Weekly* as he could get. He wrote Mrs. Salter for both of us. I paid Mrs. Livermore a visit, and had a long talk with her on the President's policy and the state of the country. I told her that I thought the President was committing a great error in bringing into prominence the secession element at the South instead of the original Union element. This, in my opinion, is but sowing dragons'-teeth, though I hope my opinion is not correct. It is acting over the old policy of the General Government after 1850: the Union men of that day were ignored; the secessionists were brought immediately into power; and the secession movements of 1860 were the fruits.

Sept. 27. — Wrote a letter to General James S. Pratt, of East Glastonbury, Ct., in answer to one from him.

Boat came. A letter from the Hon. H. V. Johnson, Washington, says nothing more encouraging than that I should with patience and fortitude bear what is upon me in hopes of deliverance after a while. He had not been able to get an interview with the President. The Hon. Mr. Upham, of Salem, Mass., spent the day with us. He was in Congress with me; he is an intelligent and agreeable gentleman. The time passed pleasantly. We walked on the ramparts. Mr. Upham is a friend of mine. Major Livermore delivered me a message from Lieut. Woodman, and a card bearing his "kind remembrances." He is at the Sea Island Hotel, Hilton Head, S. C. Evening boat brought two letters for Linton. One from Mrs. Salter in which she says that Colonel Ives, who married Miss Cora Semmes, is her brother. The other, from General Raymond Lee, in answer to Linton's note, advises Linton to remain until next week to see if I shall not be released by then. Governor Andrew, he says, has not returned, but is expected by Monday night. Dr. Seaverns called after supper and sat until late. We had a long talk on public affairs, the policy of the administration, my confinement, etc.

Thursday — Thursday is said to have been an unlucky day for the house of Henry VIII., of England. On a Thursday, he died; so did his son Edward, his daughter Mary, and the great Elizabeth. It has certainly been an unlucky day for me. This completes the twentieth week since my arrest. If I had known, when I entered these walls, that I should be here eighteen weeks, could I have stood it? I might; no one knows what he can stand. But I feel certain such knowledge would have greatly increased my tortures of mind. For though I did think I might be imprisoned for years, yet there was a latent hope that confinement would be short. This sustained me even in the darkest hour. Wrote to Lieut. Woodman. Linton is reading the first volume of this journal. I am low-spirited. O Father, let not my presentiment of two weeks ago be unfulfilled! I know Thou dost move the hearts of men; in Thee, and not in them, do I put my trust.

A despatch to the *World* says "it is believed that General Howell Cobb has been arrested on charge of complicity in the atrocities at Andersonville." I think this can hardly be true. Dr. Paterson writes Linton to come up to Boston to consult upon some plans which he has on foot in my behalf; says it is understood that the President has left the case to Seward. I answered the Hon. H. V. Johnson's letter; expressed the hope that he might be in our State Convention and that all things would then be done rightly; said I thought the suffrage, under proper restrictions, ought to be extended to the freedmen, that they should be permitted to testify in the courts, and that provision should be made for the education of their children. Linton left me to go up to Boston.

Sept. 29. — Last night, Reagan took supper with me and sat until 9.30. We played piquet. He beat some of the games, but I beat most. Dr. Seaverns called. He was amused at a story I told Reagan, illustrating our game. I had seven cards, hearts, all but the king, three aces and a six sequence; I stood at 98 and he at 10. I thought I was safely out, I announced my hand. Reagan called, "Not good," to my astonishment. He had seven spades and seven sequence on the king, four kings and three jacks, and four other sequence, which gave him ninety; this, with the ten scored, put him out. The story was this: "When Colonel Alfred Cumming, a very popular man, was running for Mayor of Augusta, the contest was thought to be very close. About three on election day, a friend, in great excitement, came to him in his office and found him very quiet. He was strong with the people, and master of all electioneering arts. The friend, surprised to find him so composed, said, "Colonel, they are giving us the devil down at A ward. They have polled at least twenty-five illegal votes there; the day is lost, I fear." "Never mind," said the Colonel coolly, "if they are giving us the devil at A ward, we are giving them hell in the same way at B ward. Don't be uneasy about the result." And so it turned out; he had beat his opponents on their own line of attack. "So," said I to Reagan, "while I thought I was giving you Jesse on hearts, you were giving me fits on spades." Reagan last night turned over the spittoon again. He is terrible on spittoons. This is twice he has turned one over in my room. He seemed quite concerned about it.

Tomcat has deserted my room for several days. What has become of him, I do not know.

Wrote another letter to Mr. Seward, simply to say that Linton would remain here until next Tuesday; if I am to be released by the middle of October, a few days earlier would make no difference to him (the Secretary), I supposed: and it would add greatly to my gratification and Linton's if I should be permitted to accompany him home; I did not wish to annoy the Secretary with importunities, but merely to let him know in case a release was contemplated at all, how I would be affected by a month's, a week's, or even a day's delay. I was without authenic information, but wrote because divers rumours that I was to be released before long had reached me. I thought it was proper he should know how a few days earlier or later might affect me as to my private business at home and my personal accommodation in getting there.

Walked out. In our walk on the rampart, Reagan called my attention to some sort of sea-monster out in the harbour just south-east of the south-eastern bastion. What it was we could not make out. It moved about in the water exactly like a serpent, holding its head above the surface. From currents produced by its movements, it appeared to be not less than fifteen feet long; it might have been twenty. We got sight of no part but the head and breast. It moved up to a rock, and put its head and breast on it, much as a water-moccasin does. We were about 400 yards away, and could see only its general outline. The head looked at that distance fully as large as a man's. In our second walk on the rampart, we staid until the boat came to the wharf, saw Linton get off, and then returned to our respective quarters. Linton brought no special news. Dr. Paterson had conversed with him on his plan, which was a petition from Boston men, etc.

Sept. 30. — I got a passport for Dr. Salter and family to visit me. Linton sent it by mail. Linton met the Hon. John E. Ward in Boston. Just returned to this country. He sent me kind messages, and the *British Quarterly Review* for July, which has an article on the American War. Mrs. Salter sent me "Silvio Pellico." A Washington telegram in the *Herald* states that certain State prisoners at Fort Warren, Fortress Monroe, etc., who are expecting unconditional release are soon to be ordered to Washington for trial; that the provost-marshals are getting evidence against them. This, I am disposed to regard as a settler of the question of my early release. Be it so. All I desire on this line is an early hearing. Suspense is what hurts me most. This intimation of a trial, however, I regard as merely a mean trick; to divert efforts made in my behalf, it is pretended that the Government has strong evidence against me. I consider it as a semi-official answer to my letters about my early release.

Yesterday, notice came to the garrison to get ready to be mustered out at an early date. There was a general shout by the men when the news reached them; all seemed greatly elated. This morning, preparations are being made for their early return home. Linton and I walked on the rampart. Showed him where Reagan and I saw the sea-monster yesterday, the rock on which he put his head and breast. Linton thought it at least 400 yards from the bastion. Went round to see Reagan. He had seen the telegram in the *Herald*. It had affected him, I think.

Lieut. Newton has brought me a letter from Mr. Seward. It is in these words:

Department of State, WASHINGTON, Sept. 26, 1865.
ALEXANDER H. STEPHENS, Esquire,
FORT WARREN, Boston Harbour, Mass.
Sir: Your letter of the 18th instant has been received and submitted to the examination of the Attorney-General.
I am, Sir, your obedient servant,
WILLIAM H. SEWARD.

Comments are unnecessary.

Sunday — October is here and I am here too, in Fort Warren. Linton wrote Mrs. Salter to come down to-morrow. In the evening he wrote to Becky [his little daughter]. We walked out three times this beautiful day. I went to see Reagan. Had a good long talk with him. He was transcribing his biography in a blank-book. Seemed oppressed, but not wholly uncheerful. Geary went to town to-day. Baily waits on us in his stead. I finished "Silvio Pellico" * last night. Read aloud to Linton.

Oct. 2. — I am looking for Mrs. Salter. Dr. Seaverns called with a message from Mrs. Appleton, and two photographs of herself out of which I was to select one for my keeping. I made my choice. I must write to her. [Copy found among his papers]:

Dear Mrs. Appleton: A thousand thanks to you for your kind remembrance and the photograph through Dr. Seaverns. Verbal acknowledgements are all the requital I can make now for favours bestowed. These utterances of the heart, however, you will, I trust, accept at the greatest value that sincerity can give them. Please present my highest regards to the Major when you write to him. Give little Mabel a kiss for me. The whole group — father, mother, and the little darling — will ever hold a cherished place in my memory.

Yours truly and sincerely,

ALEXANDER H. STEPHENS.

Linton told me this morning that he will go not before Thursday. This is gratifying to me, yet I fear he ought to go. The boat whistles at Gallops Island. I am

* Silvio Pellico's book is a record of his prison life.

anxious to see Mrs. Salter and her daughters. Oh, if the boat should also bring good news for me from Washington! How my heart would beat with joy, and in gratitude to God! The boat whistles at the landing. Soon our friends will be here.

Mrs. Salter did not come. No news in papers except that the Hon. L. P. Walker has been pardoned. So it goes. I am glad at another's good fortune. But I do complain of being kept here to the hazard of my health and the ruin of my private affairs while leading men who forced the South into secession against my efforts are not only permitted to go at large but are pardoned. The course of the Administration toward me seems personal and vindictive. Dr. Seaverns told me this morning that an old lady died here yesterday, the mother of Mrs. Nutler, the late laundress.

Reagan came round after the boat left, and brought the joyous news that the indulgence is extended him to meet his friends generally, and to mess with Linton and me; and that he is to be removed from his damp underground cell to a room on a level with mine. This was good news indeed, and I felt exceedingly glad. He, Linton, and I immediately took a walk together on the rampart. The day was beautiful. On our return, Reagan and I played piquet. We all dined together; this was very pleasant.

Boat brought Mrs. Salter and her two daughters, Miss Mary and Miss Edith. I was much pleased with the mother as well as with the daughters. The youngest, Edith, is about eleven years old; Miss Mary is grown, and has an intellectual, as well as a modest appearance. Miss Edith gave Mr. Reagan a basket of delicious grapes. Mrs. Salter brought me a picture, which she presented, requesting me to hang it at the head of my bed while there, and to take it home with me. It is the portrait of a man devoutly holding the cross. She also left with me a work by a French author on Protestantism and Catholicism. They all went back by the boat. Linton accompanied them to the wharf. I got the Corporal to take the basket of books packed this morning — books Mrs. Salter had lent me. The Judge and I staid in my room.

I feel deeply mortified with myself for the irritation of spirit I permitted myself to-day over my imprisonment. It is wrong to grow impatient under conscious wrong. O Father, forgive me the trespass as I forgive all who trespass against me! "Father, forgive them; for they know not what they do." Reagan, Linton, and I supped together. I felt badly thinking of my passion. May the Lord forgive it! Lieut. Newton brought the board-bill for Linton, me, and our visitors, up to 23d September. I gave a check for it, $54.18.

Oct. 3. — Mr. Phillips came down. Said he would have another bed, of good feathers, sent. Linton wrote a note to Mrs. Salter, and by the boat got one from her reporting arrival home last night. I rather looked for Governor Andrew, as General Lee said in his note to Linton yesterday that the Governor would come yesterday or to-day. Major Livermore called, and showed me a letter from the Hon. Charles W. Upham, desiring a copy of Harry's letter which I read to him the day he was here. While the Major was talking, the whistle of a boat was heard. He thought it might be from a boat bringing Governor Andrew, and left. Linton, Reagan and I walked on the rampart, and saw a small boat at the wharf; supposing that Governor Andrew might have come in it, we returned. But we have seen nothing of him.

I read Harry's letter to Major Livermore. He asked if Harry wrote it himself. I told him I did not think so, but I had not the least doubt about its being his own dictation and, in most instances, his own words. We had a long talk on reconstruction. I told him frankly that I thought, with all due deference to the wisdom of the authorities at Washington, President Johnson had committed a great error in his reconstruction policy in building up the old secession element in the South. None should have been proscribed, yet the basis of reconstruction should have been on the old Union element, the men who believed that the Union was not a curse to either section but that it was, when properly administered, for the best interest of the people of all the States, etc.

The boat arrived out of regular time. Brought General Ripley. At night, Linton and I played *François Fou*. He beat me badly as he generally does. I went to bed and he read me to sleep with Disraeli's "Curiosities of Literature."

Oct. 4. — I could enjoy myself very well here if it were not for agitation of the question of my release. I am most anxious to go home; but this would cease to disturb me so much were I once satisfied that it is impossible, and were I not kept excited by hope and expectation. Evening paper copies from Georgia paper the news that it had been telegraphed to Atlanta that I am paroled. This was doubtless to affect the elections that took place in Georgia yesterday.

Linton wrote this evening to Mrs. Salter. By the boat he got two notes from her, or rather letters; I received a box of grapes and pears; also got a box of fruit from Mrs. Erskine and "Pepys' Diary" from Judge Erskine. Tomcat has come back again and is domesticated. Linton and I played *François Fou* for several hours; after supper, we resumed the game. He then wrote a long letter to Mrs. Salter.

Oct. 6. — Last night Linton got a letter from Mrs. Salter, stating that she, Miss Mary, and little Edith would come down to-morrow. After I went to bed last night, Linton answered her note. I answered Gip Grier's letters. Got another letter from Secretary Seward.* I cut from the papers several notices of my imprisonment, advocating my release. Amongst others Judge Bigham's letter to G. W. Adair, Atlanta, Ga.

Oct. 7. — Mrs. Salter, Miss Mary, and little Edith came by the boat. Linton went to the wharf to meet them. A most pleasant day we had of it, indoors and out. Mrs. Salter brought me a beautiful floor-cloth, thick and warm, and rich in colours, just such as I have in my library at home. Miss Mary read to us "Enoch Arden," and other pieces from Tennyson. I never before saw any beauty in Tennyson. Her reading gave his productions a charm I had never perceived before. Little Edith amused herself with the marble

* He undoubtedly preserved it, but it is not among his papers.

and board with which the Garrison Game is played. She also went out and found two beautiful puppies which she brought in, nestled up to her breast. We walked out on the parapet, Judge Reagan with us. The sky was beautiful; on the whole, it was one of the most charming and agreeable days I have spent at this Post. Geary had gone to town, so Baily waited on us at dinner. Mrs. Salter carried away the measure that Mr. Devine took for a sackcoat, vest, and pants for me. She also took with her some of my clothes to mend. I have a letter from Robert A. Matthews, Washington, and one from Mr. Force, of Greensboro, Ga., who is in Boston and wishes to see me.

Sunday — Rested well last night. Dreamed of Bob at home. Linton said this morning he did not think he slept an hour all night. Wet, gloomy, day. Judge Reagan got a letter from his mother-in-law, the first directly from her in several months. The wood has given out. I sit with my overcoat on. Dr. Seaverns called. We had a full conversation on the subject of the collapse of the Confederacy It began by his asking me if I had seen General Jordan's article in *Harper's Monthly.* I told him that Jordan's article was superficial. The errors and blunders of Mr. Davis noticed by Jordan were small matters compared with errors not noticed. The first great error was in favouring secession; the second was the end he aimed at by it, the establishing of a close Southern Confederacy; the third was the policy adopted to secure that result; all, I thought, serious errors in statesmanship. I enlarged upon all these views, differing widely with Jordan on conscription, etc.

Oct. 9. — I got this letter from General Grant, or rather, from his aide:

WASHINGTON, D. C., Oct., 1865.

A. H. STEPHENS, Esq.,
FORT WARREN, Boston, Mass.

Lieut.-Gen. Grant desires me to say in reply to your note of Sept. 16, that he has already spoken once or twice to the President in reference to your case, and will do so again. Respectfully yours,

C. B. COMSTOCK, BRET. BRIG.-GEN., A. D. C.

Linton got a letter from Miss Van Lew, in which she alludes to me. Whereupon I wrote her as follows:

My dear Miss Van Lew: I am truly obliged to you for your message through my brother. You will please accept my sincere thanks for your kind remembrance, and especially for the interest you manifest in having me released from this place. I was elated some weeks ago with the hopes of an "early" release, but I say to you frankly that I am now free from such illusory anticipations. I have settled down into a quiet state of mental composure, prepared patiently to wait the course of events. Whether the objection to my release, which you mention as having heard, has anything to do with my prolonged imprisonment, or has effected a change of purpose once formed in my favour on the part of authorities at Washington, I do not know. My continued imprisonment has, at times, seemed to me so unaccountable that I have been forced to attribute it to some malign influence, springing from motives of vindictiveness to me personally for some cause or other to me entirely unknown.

There is not the slightest foundation in fact for the "objection" which you have heard mentioned, to wit, that my "Union speech at Milledgeville, in 1860, was a prearranged thing for Secession service, to win influence, and that at the time it was made, the other speech, so contrary and opposite, was already written," etc.

My speech for the Union, in November, 1860, was an earnest and honest outpouring if ever such emanated from human heart and head. And never before or since have I uttered a sentiment inconsistent with it. Since I have been here, I have been taunted by anonymous communications calling my attention to certain *extracts* from *speeches* made by me, which were published at the North in pamphlet form under the heading of "Campaign Tract for 1864." These are forgeries outright. None such, either in words or sentiments, were ever made by me. One other remark on the statement of facts on which this objection rests. I never *wrote* a speech to be delivered in my life, except college essays or addresses. The Union speech was extemporaneous. The only report ever made was that by Mr. Marshall. Upon that speech and its sentiments, even down to abiding by and sharing the fortunes and fate of my State if she should go against my counsels, I now stand. This much I feel it is my duty to you and myself to state.

My course, whether right or wrong, has been at least uniform, conscientious, and consistent with my principles. I opposed the movement that led to the war with my utmost power in the most perfect good faith. I opposed it on grounds of policy alone, not on grounds of abstract right. I am in no way responsible before God or man for the origin of the war (at least intentionally), nor for its continuance, much less its atrocities. I did all I could to avert the monster evil in the beginning, and after it was upon us, I did all I could to mitigate its horrors and to end them as speedily as possible. After the war was commenced, all my energies were directed to getting the questions involved taken from the arena of arms and submitted to the forum of reason and justice for peaceful solution and adjustment, not upon a sectional but upon a broad and continental basis. My offending has this extent. No more.

Please excuse so much about myself. Your message seemed to make it not only proper but almost necessary for your own correct understanding of my true position in these matters. With sentiments of the highest esteem toward you and kindest regards toward your mother,

I remain, Yours Truly,

ALEXANDER H. STEPHENS.

Oct. 10. — Dreamed of the Hon. Solomon G. Haven. He was in Congress with me. He died since the war. Dreamed of the Hon. Francis H. Cone who has been dead some time. Last night Captain Allen, of the fort, called and sat with us. He is from Buffalo. We talked of Haven, who was once Mayor of Buffalo.

Linton made a communication to me to-day which deeply impresses me. What it was I will not state here further than that it was in relation to his future life.

The evening boat now leaves Boston at 3 and gets here at 4. Tomcat has become quite domesticated again. Yesterday Linton tried an experiment in seeing how much Tom could eat. He ate all we left from dinner, and still looked for more.

Oct. 11. — Letter from John A. Stephens stating that all are well. The freedmen, from his account, were doing well. He and Major Henly Smith were candidates for the Convention.* The letter was dated 30th September; the election was to take place on the 4th October; so I suppose John is elected, of which, if so, I shall be truly glad. Linton sent his letter to Mrs.

* Called under President Johnson's proclamation providing for restoration of the State "to its constitutional relations with the Federal Government."

Salter to-day. By boat we got the papers, nothing in them except the *Journal* which states that Dr. Seaverns, of this post, and several other surgeons, are to be mustered out of service. The *Tribune* expresses the hope of Reagan's and my early release. The New York *Day Book* sends an extract that I wished to see, a published letter by Lieut. Newton, of this fort, about me. It makes out a very good case of treatment toward me. I am "furnished meals from the officers' mess." I am furnished at my own expense. This is very kind, indeed. My room is comfortably supplied. This, too, and all else I get here, except soldiers' fare and soldiers' rations, is at my own expense. I do not consider it very humane to imprison a man and impoverish him by allowing him to spend what he has while depriving him of all power to make more, or even to save what he has made.

Received a suit of clothes, presented by Pierce and Bacon, of Boston; vest and pants came to-day; the coat, cap, and shawl yesterday. Also by express an overcoat from New York, sent by Mr. L. W. Harris, of Carter, Kirkland & Co., and presented, he says, by Thos. F. Hooker, formerly of Rome, Ga., and now of Aberdeen, Miss.

CHAPTER XXVII

THURSDAY, Oct. 12.—This never-to-be-forgotten day of the week is again upon me. It is a blustering morning. Linton went up by the boat.

Soon, Dr. Seaverns appeared and stated that orders had come for my release. Major Livermore soon followed with the telegram. It embraced Judge Reagan and myself. So, I am again free as far as personal locomotion is concerned. It is just twenty-two weeks to the day since the first keys were turned upon me as a prisoner. What events come to me on Thursday! Major Livermore said he would give me a copy of the order. Meantime I see in the Boston *Post* the General Order embracing Judge Campbell, General Clark, Judge Reagan, myself, and Trenholm. I wish Linton were here. Wrote letters to John A. Stephens, C. T. Bruen, S. J. Anderson, Lieut. W. H. Woodman.

Linton returned by the evening boat. He, Reagan, and I took a last evening walk on the rampart. Dr. Seaverns called after supper and sat some time.

Oct. 13.—I rose early and now make this last entry. I expect to start by this evening's boat for my dear home. It is a long and hazardous trip for me, beset with many dangers, and I am beset in the outset with many anxieties concerning many things. But, O God, in whom I put my trust, deliver me from all evil!

CRAWFORDVILLE, GA., Oct. 27, 1865—Thanks be to the Giver of all good, the Father of all mercies, and the Bestower of all blessings, I am once more at home! I am sitting in the same room and at the same table from which I arose to suffer arrest on the 11th of May. As a sequel to this Journal, I record briefly some of the incidents intervening between my departure from Fort Warren and my reaching home, yesterday, *Thursday:*

On the 13th of October, Linton, Judge Reagan, and I left Fort Warren at 4, on the *William Shand*, the regular evening boat. I gave Corporal Geary my bedding and room furniture and nearly all the things that I had had brought there for my use and comfort, except books and wearing apparel. The amount paid by me for these articles was about $100. Linton gave him $10 in currency. I gave Major Livermore my copy of Greeley's "American Conflict"; Lieut. Newton my Prescott's "Conquest of Mexico"; Dr. Seaverns my Robertson's "Sermons," Greek Testament, lexicon, etc. To Corporal Geary I gave my copy of Burns's "Poems" and wrote him a friendly farewell letter. All the officers of the fort and all the men seemed kind in feeling toward me, and all who met with me took a friendly leave. Mrs. Livermore was sick, I did not see her, but addressed her a note. I saw Mrs. Seaverns, the doctor, Mrs. Harrington, Captain Baldwin and Mrs. Baldwin. Lieuts. Niebuhr and Newton accompanied us to Boston. Linton was quite unwell and hardly able to attend to anything. I packed all his clothes and felt very badly on his account. We slept at the Revere House, where rooms had been ordered for us by friends in Boston.

It was about 6, and a little after dark when we reached Boston. Great numbers of persons called to see us at the Revere House, amongst them Mrs. Salter and Dr. Salter. Linton and I had a room to ourselves, and Reagan one to himself. Mrs. Salter brought me an invitation from Mr. Thos. W. Pierce to spend Saturday and Sunday at his country place. Saturday morning I bought two trunks and packed all our things, carpet-bags and all, in them.

Sunday — Went out to Mr. Pierce's Saturday night, Judge Reagan with me. Linton remained at the Revere House; was better when we left him than on the previous evening. We went by train some 25 miles, starting at 5 p. m., and reaching Pierce's about 7.30. Mr. Pierce is a relation of ex-President Pierce, and a gentleman of wealth and great generosity. He has a beautiful place at Topsfield; is a merchant and was worth about four million before the war. He had large interests at the South and may lose a good deal there. Saturday night there was a heavy fall of rain. It was greatly needed; there had been an unusual drought throughout New England. I told our host that our welcome had brought the long-prayed for rain. Several gentlemen were invited to meet us at dinner, but in the storm which has continued all day, no one came except Mr. Edward Pierce, our host's brother, and the Hon. Mr. Hillard,* who drove out from Boston in spite of the weather; no trains run on Sunday.

We spent a pleasant day at Topsfield. It is a famous spot. Here is where the witches lived; and where two old women, whose names I forget, were arrested for witchcraft. The stone-pile on the road where, it was charged,

* Reference probably to G. S. Hillard, lawyer, legislator, author and journalist. U. S. District Attorney for Mass., 1866-70; or Francis Hilliard, jurist, legislator, and author may be meant.

they held their nightly orgies, is still pointed out. Mr. Pierce has a variety of fruit trees — especially pears — Massachusetts is noted for pears. By far the best pears I ever saw grew in this State.

Oct. 16. — We left Topsfield at 8; drove over four miles to depot. Mr. Pierce has a splendid team; said he could get $6,000 for the pair. Reagan drove to Boston with Mr. Edward Pierce; Mr. Hillard travelled with Mr. F. W. Pierce and me on the cars. All the persons I saw or met on this trip, common people and all, seemed delighted to see me out of prison. Reached Boston at 10; found Linton better. Many persons called to see me.

Oct. 17. — Last night great numbers called. It was late before I got to bed. I wish I could mention all my visitors; their names are on the cards which I have kept and laid away. Mr. Hillard was the last to leave. He sent by me a message to President Johnson, that if he, the President, will pursue the course he has mapped out, he will get the support of everybody in New England whose support is worth having. In this, I did not fully agree with Mr. Hillard, but received the message as he gave it. He went with me to take leave of Mrs. Salter's family. It was past midnight before we got to sleep. Linton was better but not well. We rose early and took the cars by Springfield and New Haven to New York, Reagan, Linton, and myself. I forgot to state that Lieuts. Newton and Niebuhr called Saturday and took leave of us. Also, Sergeant Malcolm Mosely, who had come up with us from Fort Independence.

Oct. 18.—In New York; at Astor House. Great numbers of people called, amongst them the Robbe family (Elizabeth Church Craig) and S. J. Anderson. Quite unwell, which prevented my calling on Mr. and Mrs. Robbe.

Thursday — Left for Washington at 7; that is, Linton and I left. Mr. Reagan remained in New York. I have parted with him perhaps forever. We had been with or near each other since the 14th of May. At Fort Warren, we spent some pleasant days together. Prisoners or common sufferers in any cause are apt to become attached to each other. I became much attached to Reagan. I think him a clever, upright, honest man. He had but few opportunities for education or culture in his youth. He is, in the common acceptation of the term, "self-made." The real foundations of his character are truth, integrity, and energy. He wrote, while in close confinement, a biographical sketch of his early life for the information of his children. This he let me read. Its perusal was exceedingly interesting to me.

Oct. 20. — In Washington. Reached here last night at seven. A great many old acquaintances and other persons called to see me. Saw Joseph H. Echols and Judge O. A. Lochrane of Georgia. Called to see President Johnson early in the morning; went about 7.30, Lochrane with me. Met at the White House door an Irishman who knew me. Said he had known me ever since I brought Mr. Smith O'Brien there to introduce him to Mr. Buchanan; he gave me his name, but I didn't hear it distinctly. I asked him if he could deliver my card to the President. He was very glad to see me and seemed disposed to favour me in any way he could; said he could not deliver it, but would hand it to Slade* who would. I told him to bring Slade to me; this he did. I asked Slade if he would deliver my card to the President personally. He said he could. I think my Irish friend had given him a private talk in my behalf. I gave my card to Slade. It was a blank piece of square-cut paper with these words written on it:

"Alexander H. Stephens would like to present his respects in person to the President, if agreeable and convenient to him."

I was immediately invited by Slade up into the sitting-room, where I waited a while. The President came in. We held an interview of about an hour and a half. I delivered Mr. Hillard's message. He directed his secretary to leave us, and we had the interview to ourselves.

The conversation took a wide range. It was upon public affairs generally. I gave him my own views very fully and freely upon the subject of Negro suffrage. I told him the adjustment of that question belonged exclusively to the States separately, but in my judgment the States ought not to exclude the blacks entirely from the polls. I outlined the plan of a classification I had thought of, but said I believed it too late now to consider such a change in our system. As things are, I thought the principle should be established of allowing the franchise to such members of the black race as could come up to some proper standard of mental and moral culture with the possession of a specified amount of property. Such

* Answering inquiry, Col. W. H. Crook, of the official staff of the White House from Lincoln's time till now, wrote me: "William Slade was President Johnson's steward, a man of whom he was very fond." *Editor.*

an arrangement would be right in duty. It would have a good effect at the South in breaking the strength of the violent radical element, and it would have a beneficent effect upon the black population in holding out a strong inducement for improvement. I thought the blacks should be allowed to testify in the courts; arrangements for schools should be made, and some system adopted to require them to educate their children.

Our talk was civil and agreeable. I can only give in brief its outlines. My inference from the conversation was that his policy was to have the Negroes, as soon as possible, removed from the country as the Indians were. He was very evidently desirous to have the proposed Amendment * to the Constitution of the U. S. adopted by the South. I could see no purpose for this but the ultimate removal under this Amendment of the Negroes by Congress.

Oct. 21. — Linton better. Last evening we called to see John C. Burch, the Misses Nichol, and Judge Wayne, also my old landlord and cook, Crotchett. John was glad to see us, drove out to his brother Raymond's, and brought Raymond, Raymond's little daughter, Maggie, and her brother, Alexander, in to see me. Margaret is named for my mother, and Alexander for me. They sat with me till past midnight.

This morning we started for Lynchburg. The Burches were at the depot to see us off. We passed through Alexandria, by Manassas, Gordonsville, Charlottesville, and reached Lynchburg at 5 p. m. The desolation of the country from Alexandria to near Charlottesville was horrible to behold.

* The Thirteenth, abolishing slavery.

Oct. 22. — We — Linton, Judge Lochrane, and myself rested at Lynchburg. Professor Holcombe, a Mr. Mosely, and a Mr. Britton called to see me. They expressed the opinion that I would run some hazard of personal violence in passing through East Tennessee on the route we were following. The account given of the state of things there was very bad. I was fixed, however, in my determination to pursue that route.

Oct. 23. — Left Lynchburg for Bristol at 7. Took our leave of the hotel and of Ralph, one of the best coloured servants or waiters I ever saw. Passed the mountains, the tunnel. Met on the cars a daughter of William Ballard Preston; she lunched with us. We took dinner at no place, took supper at Wytheville. I had a good sleep on two seats in the cars fixed for the purpose. We reached Bristol about 5 a. m., took breakfast and changed cars.

Oct. 24. — Passed through East Tennessee. From all we heard, a terrible state of things is there; no law; all men who sympathized with the Southern Cause, it is said, have to leave the country or be killed. Just before we reached Knoxville, an elderly man came in to see if he could get a seat for his mother. The seat was procured; an old woman, seemingly eighty, or upward, maybe a hundred, was brought in. She was very infirm and decrepit. The son, an old man, said his mother had never been on the cars before. She seemed alarmed when we started. He stood by her and told her there was no danger. He went no farther than the next station; there he bade her farewell; he said: "Well, mother, I must leave you here; there is no danger.

Good-bye." He took her hand, she choked in her utterance of good-bye, and the big drops trickled down her cheeks. She seemed to be quitting the country. From Knoxville to Dalton I paid fare — not being able to find the U. S. quartermaster on whom I had an order for transportation from that place to Crawfordville. Got to Dalton at 2; staid until 10.

Oct. 25. — War has left a terrible impression on the whole country to Atlanta. The desolation is heart-sickening. Fences gone, fields all a-waste, houses burnt. Reached Atlanta after 7.

Thursday — Linton and I left Atlanta at 6, parting from Lochrane there. We took dinner at Union Point and reached home at 3 p. m., 24 weeks to a day from my arrest.

Oh, how changed are all things here! Change, change, indelibly stamped upon everything I meet, even upon the faces of the people! I learned at the depot that all were well at the lot and at the homestead. But poor Binks was dead. The cars had run over him some weeks ago, when he was going with Harry to the mill at Union Point. This news filled me with sadness. Among the other and great pleasures I had promised myself was this small — no, not *small* — one of meeting Binks. Harry was at the depot and told me the sorrowful news. As we came from the depot to the house, the children, Ellen, Tim, Dora, Fanny, and Quin, all met us out by the Academy. The children all cried for joy. Dora blubbered right out; the eyes of all, except Fanny and Quin, were tearful; Eliza met us at the gate; her eyes, too, were full.

The house and lot looked natural and yet withal sadly changed in some respects. I seemed to myself to be in a dream. But my heart went up in fervent thanksgiving to Almighty God for preserving and guiding me back once more to this spot so dear to me.

And with this entry this Journal closes forever: Linton this day left me for his home. He went to meet again his dear little ones. He has been constantly with me since the 1st of September. He has a severe cold, and I fear he got wet to-day for it commenced raining soon after he left. I am to look after my affairs here and at the homestead, to see my dear ones there. Next week I am to go over to see Linton and his children. May God bless him!

CONCLUSION

CONCLUSION

DURING Mr. Stephens's stay in New York, his room at the Astor House was thronged with callers, among these Senator Wilson, George T. Curtis, and a number of other prominent men. His appearance, as described by the press, was that of a "skeleton with eyes more piercing in their gaze by reason of the straggling white locks that fell over his temples in silken threads." Until his imprisonment, his hair had kept its glossy chestnut. He "walked with the feebleness of age"; his "conversation, manner, and handgrasp indicated his natural goodness of heart."

The Georgia Legislature, convening under the Johnson reconstruction measures, elected him, over his protest, to the United States Senate. In a letter, Feb. 5, 1866, to President Johnson, explaining "the motives of the Legislature," Mr. Stephens said:

> It was thought that as the Hon. H. V. Johnson [elected for the short term] and myself had been the most prominent exponents of the Union sentiment of the large body throughout the South who had gone with their States against their judgment, our utterances would be received as most expositive of their views now — to say nothing of secessionists, who, I assure you, as I did at Fort Warren, are more ready to listen to me now. I have no desire for office. Still I could not refuse the call of the people to serve them if I be permitted to do so. I can of course do nothing unless my parole shall be enlarged, and I be at least permitted to go to Washington

and confer with you. I do not wish to embarrass you in your policy for the restoration of the Union. If you think my presence in Washington would not only do no good in this respect but would in the least degree embarrass you, I do not ask enlargement of parole. But if, on the contrary, you may be of opinion that it would do no harm and might possibly do some good, then I respectfully ask it. Individually, I think that a personal conference with you and others at Washington might do some good. Still, I may be mistaken.

The parole was granted Feb. 26. On Washington's birthday, he addressed the Legislature, advising cheerful acceptance of the issues of war, charity, patience, a fair trial of the new system as affecting the Negro, with qualified suffrage for the race. "The whole United States is our country to be cherished and defended as such by all our hearts and arms," he said. The address was widely published and applauded. His evidence before the Reconstruction Committee of Congress was of similar temper on like points, though a brave and candid exposition of the Southern attitude on all matters about which he was questioned. The New York *Times* pronounced it "statesmanlike" and "the ablest analysis of Southern political action" yet given. Of the Washington atmosphere toward him socially and of his impression of it politically, we are informed by Mr. Stephens in this letter in April 8, 1866, to his brother:

The President received me with frankness and, I may say, cordially. The Cabinet received me as cordially as any Cabinet ever did. All sides — Democrats and Republicans, Conservatives and Radicals — seemed glad to see me. General Grant seems to be very marked in his regards for me. The invitation given me to spend the evening with him, to which I alluded in my other letter, was for one of his receptions. There was a very large company. President Johnson was there — the first instance of a President of the United States ever going out into society, as it may be termed, or accepting an invitation to join a party of friends on such an occasion. I was impressed with one thing; that is, that General Grant and the President seemed a little awkward, or not at ease, in the characters they were acting; both seemed to be out of their element. This, in Grant, I was pleased at; but somehow, I would have preferred to see the President more graceful and elegant — or rather, more at ease. Everything passed off agreeably. There was a perfect jam, and a great array of fashion and court style. I was more *looked at* than any man present, and more talked to, though I endeavoured to keep in the background. Sir Frederick Bruce sought an introduction to me. He is a gentleman of fine appearance and talks well. I declined to see him on his visit to Fort Warren; Mr. Burlingame told me, at the time, that Sir Frederick wished to see me, and Major Livermore said if I would request to see Sir Frederick, he would, under his orders, allow it; but I told Mr. B. that it might not be approved at Washington, as I was a State prisoner and Sir Frederick a foreign minister, etc. Sir Frederick alluded to his visit, etc.

I called to see Senator Wilson yesterday. This was in discharge of an act of duty for his personal kindness to me at Fort Warren. He introduced me to Mrs. Wilson at General Grant's party; I therefore called to see them both. We had a long pleasant talk, differing widely on many points, but agreeably.

Nothing will be done toward the admission of Southern members this session. This question will most probably be decided by the fall elections. The most radical men in Congress — the most rabid — talk with me heartily, freely, and fully; and, I think I may say, almost unanimously would prefer to see me in the Senate to any other man from the South — or at least, they say so. So my election has certainly done the State no harm. The point on which they are going to rally is a proposition to amend the Constitution on the suffrage question — to allow admission to those States which will agree to an amendment allowing representation on the ratio of votes. I need not say that I think it will be a dangerous platform for us before the Northern people. How easily this might have been avoided by the Southern people in allowing a wisely-restricted suffrage to the black race in their new constitutions! This platform emanates from no real philanthropic sentiment for the Negro; it is founded upon a desire for power. It is not believed that the South will grant suffrage to the black race. The object is to deprive the South of political power, and to leave the poor unfortunate sons of Africa, as our fellow citizens, to their fate.

Mr. Stephens was never allowed to take his seat in the Senate. The friendlier feeling, which was beginning to obtain between the sections at the time of his release, was soon turned to exceeding bitterness by the action of a Radical Congress in overthrowing Johnson's reconstruction measures and inaugurating the period which has become infamous in our history as that of carpet-bag, scalawag, and Negro rule in the South. Mr. Stephens was a delegate in August, 1866, to the National Union Convention in Philadephia from which so much good was hoped and so little came. Replying March 29, 1867, to a letter from Dr. E. M. Chapin, Washington, D. C. he gives his views of the times:

My judgment was that it [the Convention] would prove a failure. . . . The Congress plan of Reconstruction will be carried out, whether the whites who are not disfranchised join in forming the new organizations or not. . . . I think they should be governed by the public interest only. They should not be controlled by sympathy for the disfranchised class. As for myself, I would not only cheerfully submit to proscription forever, but I would offer up my life if thereby a restoration of the Union under the Constitution could be effected. By taking part, they may secure control, and thus save themselves from the dominion of the black race. Thus might they erect a temporary shield against impending danger. All depends upon the ethnological problem: Whether self-government can be successfully maintained by the Caucassian and African races, when they exist in the proportion that they do in this section, upon the basis of perfect political equality in all respects. I do not think the problem can ever be solved so. My earnest desire is that the experiment may succeed. Had the existence of the Union been recognized by Congress, as it was by the President, and had I not been disfranchised, my purpose was to devote all my energies to giving the experiment of the civil equality of the black race before the law the fairest possible trial. I was not opposed to a qualified suffrage with the door open for enlargement. "Blood is thicker than water." No man-made law can prevent antagonism between races — between Scotch and English, Irish and English, German and French, when interests or prejudices clash; much less between the white and black races. . . . We cannot remain long under military rule without the North's sharing our fate. . . . The only hope is for reaction at the North in time to save the Republic.

To the Hon. Montgomery Blair he wrote Feb. 3, 1867:

For your letter and the pamphlets I return my thanks. I have carefully read General Blair's speech. . . . If both races would act rightly, all might move on smoothly. No labour is so well suited to the South, and nothing is more essential to the direction of that labour than the superior skill and provident care of the white man. All possible effort should be made to bring about harmonious action. This can only be done in conformity with nature. The natural inequality must be recognized. With this should follow ample legal protection for the weak against the strong. . . . After the most intense study, I have come to the conclusion that one of three results will be the issue of our race question: (1) The races will be brought to harmonious action on the line indicated. (2) A war of races ending in the destruction of one or the other. (3) Exodus of the black race. A few of my many reasons for preferring the first to General Blair's colonization idea are: (1) I believe it to be the interest of both races to live together on the basis outlined, if it can be worked. (2) The expense of removing three and a half million people would be enormous — probably more than the Government could meet. (3) The sufferings and loss of life attending the migration of such a vast multitude would be enough to shock human nature. (4) The Negro race can not maintain civilization except when in contact with a higher type of humanity.

He devoted his time of political inaction to writing his "Constitutional View of the War Between the States," and his "School History of the United States." In 1881, he wrote a "History of the United States." The first is his masterpiece. The London *Saturday Review* said of it, "No contribution to the history of the Civil War of equal value has yet been made, or is likely to be made, unless some one of General Lee's few surviving lieutenants should do for the military history of the struggle what Mr. Stephens has done for its political aspect." He taught "for recreation" a law class of young men who "agree to reimburse me hereafter for their board."

His "War Between the States" brought him $35,000

in royalties on a sale of 70,000 copies. A newspaper venture absorbed most of the profits from his books, and his bounties and hospitalities kept him in straits. He bought, in 1871, the Atlanta *Sun*, that he might have columns of his own in which to fight the proposed coalition of the Liberal-Republicans and Democratic parties; which coalition came about, however, with Greeley for Presidential standard-bearer in 1872. His course in opposing Greeley was unpopular. Before an Atlanta audience, Dec. 20, 1872, he said:

Three weeks ago I was requested for my views on the public situation. I appointed the second day after the election. When the time arrived, I was not here. Mr. Greeley's obsequies were being performed. I knew him well. Between us personally never a harsh word or feeling passed. He was as truly an honest man as any I ever met. That is true, notwithstanding our great political differences. He belonged to that party which advocated centralized government; that doctrine and party I could not favour. It was inappropriate for me to speak of matters which had necessary reference to him, in the hour of his funeral. I have canvassed Georgia for twenty years. I have been diseased and infirm all that time. I have made more than a thousand appointments, perhaps, and never failed to fill more than two till now: these by an occurrence which laid me aside for two months [the Cone encounter], and that some of you may remember. These matters I state in reply to a fling at me in the papers.

The charge had been made that I was not in accord with the people of Georgia, that I do not move with her Democracy. What are the principles of her Democracy? Were they not the principles adopted in this hall in August, 1870? Who brought them here? That brother of mine to whom such touching allusion has been made. That brother came from my house. They brought you into power. . . . Am I thus accused because I did not go with the Convention of 1872 in its nomination of Greeley — when the majority adopted the candidate but utterly refused the platform? I did not think that good policy. You all know now its results. . . . The liberties of this country depend on these principles taught by the Revolutionary fathers: that this is a great confederated republic and not a consolidated empire. With a hundred and fifty thousand earnest men, there will be no difficulty that cannot be overcome in recovering our liberties. There are true men at the North, men true to Democratic principles in New Hampshire, Maine, Massachusetts. It is a great mistake to suppose that there are not true men there, as true, liberty-loving men as you are.

"The principles that brought you into power" is a reference to the Georgia Platform in 1870, framed by Mr. Stephens and his brother. On this platform the State wrested her government from carpet-bag rule. In the fall of 1872, the people sent Mr. Stephens to represent his old Eighth District in Congress. He was again in the seat which he had occupied for sixteen years, and perhaps he was more at home in it than he had ever been when presiding over the Confederate Senate. He had an influence there that had never been his in the Confederate Senate. He addressed himself to his old task of reconciling sections, preserving peace, and, as always, of proclaiming the sacredness of the Constitution. A newspaper described his appearance:

An immense cloak, a high hat, and peering somewhere out of the middle a thin, pale, sad face. How anything so small and sick and sorrowful could get here all the way from Georgia is a wonder. If he were laid out in his coffin, he needn't look any different, only then the fires would have gone out in the burning eyes. Set as they are in the wax-white face, they seem to burn and blaze. That he is here at all to offer the counsels of moderation and patriotism proves how invincible is the soul that dwells in this sunken frame. He took the modified oath in his chair, and his friends picked him up in it and carried him off as if he were a feather.

"Whatever he wants done is done, and every measure he advocates passes," a Northern paper said kindly but not quite correctly. He tried to adapt himself to conditions, doing the best he could "with circumstances as they arise," according to the rule he cites so often in his Journal. For instance, believing Tilden to be the legally elected president, he advised acceptance of the finding for Hayes because resistance might have plunged the country into another war. He was criticized for this and for several other stands that he took, but events or a maturer consideration justified him in each case. His speech on the unveiling of Carpenter's picture of Lincoln, "The signing of the Emancipation Proclamation," was the dramatic event of his term of 1878 in the House. It is no mean proof of his wisdom and tact that he discharged his office of representing the South on this occasion in a manner approving itself to both sections. Yet he simply told the truth as he saw it. The larger part of his tribute to Mr. Lincoln personally is printed in the earlier pages of this book; taking up its concluding sentences, we produce his tatement of Lincoln's purpose and of the South's part in emancipation.

Every fountain of his heart was ever overflowing with the "milk of human kindness." From my attachment to him, so much the deeper was the pang in my breast at the horrible manner of his taking off. . . . Emancipation was not the chief object of Mr. Lincoln in issuing the Proclamation. His chief object, to which his whole soul was devoted, was the preservation of the Union. The Proclamation itself did not declare free all the coloured people of the Southern States; it applied only to those parts of the country then in resistance to the Federal authorities. If the emancipation of the coloured race be a boon or a curse to them, then, representing the Southern States here, I must claim in their behalf, that the freedom of that race was never consummated and could not be until the Southern States sanctioned the Thirteenth Amendment, which they did, every one of them, by their own former constituencies.

"During the conflict of arms," he said, "I frequently despaired of the liberties of our country both North and South." He pleaded for friendship between the sections, for conscientious discharge of duty to the Negro, and for faithful adherence to the Constitution. This was the spirit of his every argument as long as he was in the House.

In 1882, he retired from Congress, after a service, all told, of twenty-six years, to become Governor of Georgia, accepting the position in spite of great age and feebleness, because her people assured him that he alone could unite her jarring factions and heal her political wounds. Transference of his domestic life from his familiar quarters at the National Hotel, Washington, and his beloved Liberty Hall to the Executive Mansion in Atlanta was a trial for him at his years, but he was deeply touched at the mark of public confidence which placed him there. During his brief period of office he was very busy and not unhappy. The one criticism recorded of his administration is that he made excessive use of the pardoning power.

Again we will take up the thread of his family life. A romance grew out of his brother's visit to him at Fort Warren, where Mrs. Salter and her daughters were his good angels. Judge Stephens and Mary Salter had met before, when she was very young and when they were both visitors in Washington City, where her uncle, Joseph C. Ives, and his wife, the sister of Senator Semmes, were living and were as great social favourites as they afterward found themselves in Richmond. During the war, Colonel Ives, though a New Yorker, was on Mr. Davis's personal staff, his sympathies following those of his wife. The development of an attachment, which ended in marriage in 1867, was the natural sequence of the meeting between Linton and Mary at Fort Warren, a sequence that gave much happiness to Mr. Stephens as well as to themselves. A great sorrow befell Mr. Stephens in 1875 when Linton died, and the "light of his life" went out. But he found relief from grief in renewed public activities and in fresh interests in friends and associates and in the young nieces and nephews that clustered around him. Upon "Billy," as William Grier Stephens was affectionately called, Linton's mantle most nearly fell. Billy died, and then John A. Stephens became the staff of the statesman's declining years. From Mr. Stephens's numerous letters to John, space must be claimed here for a few characteristics extracts; as for this, written at Liberty Hall to John in Atlanta just before the Convention of 1870 to which Judge Stephens and Herschel V. Johnson were delegates:

I wish you would go to the Post Office and get me 500 stamped envelopes. Linton tells me he will be in the Convention. I have written Governor Johnson asking him to come and see me on his way to Atlanta.

Shall I take the liberty of inviting him to your house? Or, will you write to me and ask me to extend an invitation to him for you? I know the Governor's means are limited, and it may be that it would be very acceptable to him to be invited to stop with a friend. I know that in my life such an invitation would on many occasions have been very acceptable. If he accepts, I want you to consider the extra expense as chargeable to me. I will willingly foot the bills for all the good eating — and he likes good eating — that you may furnish him. If you will write me a letter telling him and Linton to go to your house, I will myself deliver it.

Of course John wrote the invitation, and dutifully fell in with his uncle's plan to establish for himself an Atlanta centre of hospitality. As John was vicarious entertainer, so was he minister of mercy. After Harry's death in 1881, Mr. Stephens wrote from Washington:

Be sure and attend Harry's sale. I want you to buy all the shucks, corn, etc., unless the bids go above the town price. I do have sympathy for the poor old horses and will give more for them than they are worth. I should buy them simply to feed them. If my feelings are thus for dumb brutes which have served me faithfully, how much stronger are they to human beings! I wish Eliza and her children to have all the aid in my power to render them comfortable. I shall write her of my views of what she shall do and what I will do to aid her. I wish you to attend to having her dower properly assigned. My deed to Harry is of record.

Rarely is there a letter to John that does not charge him with some commission for an old servant or some other beneficiary. One knows not whether to smile or sigh at Mr. Stephens's quaint interest in the family babies, as displayed in thoughtful epistles to "Sister

Mary" and "Cousin Emma" (John's wife) about the trials of these infant prodigies in croup and measles. His care for business and domestic affairs of his nephews was unfailing. "I was exceedingly anxious to know how you were fixed up for the reception of Cousin Emma; whether you had got your furniture moved in time to occupy your house that night," he writes, on John's moving to Atlanta in 1869, a young lawyer making up as well as he could for time lost in the war. "How are you getting on in your practice?" "I have no objection to association of my name with yours in bringing the case. It is just such a case as I like to plead. From the facts stated, your client has been greatly wronged." The following, written eight days after John reached Atlanta, repeats advice given to Linton years before:

I am glad to hear you have got a case. This is your first in your new location, and I can not do better than to repeat that a young man's first cases at the law are the most important to him he will ever have. His reputation is at stake. It should be a leading object with him to succeed in them beyond expectation. He ought to take no case except such as he believes on investigation to be right.

This to John, in 1870, is a blow at graft:

What Mr. —— meant by what he said to you about the State Road, I cannot conjecture. I do not wish you to have anything to do with him. Lobbying before a corrupt legislature is one of the lowest and meanest businesses anybody can engage in. A legal opinion, professionally given, has no sort of impropriety in it. I have given such in more cases than one. In such, I represent a client's interest before the Legislature as I would before a court. But this is a very different thing from becoming interested in procuring legislation not as a matter of legal right and duty but of policy, and that, too, without any consideration of the public interests. Were I a member of the Legislature, I should advocate a sale or lease of the State Road if I could get it effected upon proper terms, but nothing could induce me as an attorney to accept a fee or reward from outside parties to procure such legislation. If a question of law should arise as to how such a lease or sale was to be perfected, I should not hesitate to charge a proper professional fee for giving an opinion. But I could never be induced to offer an opinion to influence the Legislature to sell or lease the road. That, in my judgment, would be exceedingly reprehensible. I hope you will even have nothing to do with parties who can make such propositions to you.

It happened that the road was leased later in the year, and Mr. Stephens took an interest to the "extent of his property." The next year, there was a cry of "swindle." When information seeming to show that the State had been cheated in the lease was received by Mr. Stephens, he promptly deeded his holdings back to the Commonwealth.

He named one condition to his candidacy for governor that the public did not know; it was that John and "Cousin Emma" should enter the Mansion with him: "I shall die there, and I want you to close my eyes," he said. They did not care to give up their cozy home for that temporary abode, but they went with him; and it was a great pleasure to him to have them there and to hear the children pattering about the place. He proudly made John Adjutant-General of Georgia, a position which the gallant ex-Confederate held with credit to himself and to his State, under successive governors until failing health compelled him to resign the year before his death in 1887. Never in the history of the Mansion before or since have so many needy people and so many tramps been fed there in the same period of time — or perhaps any period — as during Mr. Stephens's residence. "Cousin Emma" dutifully endeavoured to keep the gubernatorial nose from the grindstone. One morning she entered his room, where he was dictating to his secretary, and proudly displayed her accounts, showing a good saving in housekeeping expenses for the month. "Uncle Alex" praised her thrift, and turning to his secretary, said: "Seidell, add $25 to the check in that last letter for the woman who asked me to help her."

From the Sesqui-Centennial in Savannah, where the people greeted him lovingly, Mr. Stephens came back to the Mansion to die. Sunday at dawn, March 4, 1883, after a brief illness, he breathed his last. Thursday, he was laid to rest in a vault in Oakland Cemetery pending removal of his remains to Crawfordville, where he now sleeps in the grounds at Liberty Hall.*

While he lay in state in the Capitol in Atlanta, many of the poorest class of whites came from a distance to pay their respects. Many Negroes came. Never before in the history of Atlanta was there such a funeral procession as the long line of military and civic bodies and mourning populace which followed him to the tomb. Not only in Georgia, not only in the South, was pub-

* The ownership of Liberty Hall is now vested in the Stephens Monumental Association, which is seeking to establish at Crawfordville, as a memorial to Mr. Stephens, a school for poor boys and girls. The Daughters of the Confederacy have some oversight of the dwelling and will doubtless have final charge of it and arrange for its preservation as a National shrine.

lic tribute paid to his memory. In far-off Vermont, State offices were closed on the day of his funeral and the National flag was displayed at half-mast over the Capitol. When the news of his death reached Washington City, the House of Representatives unanimously adopted a resolution expressing "hearthfelt sympathy with the people, not only of Georgia, but of the whole country, in the loss of a statesman and a patriot."

THE END

INDEX